LEGACY OF FLIGHT

LEGACY OF FLIGHT

The Guggenheim Contribution
to American Aviation

RICHARD P. HALLION

UNIVERSITY OF WASHINGTON PRESS
Seattle and London

This book was published with the assistance of a grant from
The Daniel and Florence Guggenheim Foundation.

Library of Congress Cataloging in Publication Data
Hallion, Richard.
  Legacy of flight.
  Bibliography: p.
  Includes index.
  1. Daniel Guggenheim Fund for the Promotion of
Aeronautics, inc. 2. Aeronautics—United States—
History. I. Title.
TL521.H34   629.13'007'2073   76–49161
ISBN 0–295–95542–2

"Aviation will always owe a debt of gratitude to Daniel Guggenheim."

CHARLES A. LINDBERGH

Acknowledgments

THE role of the private foundation in affecting any area of endeavor is a complex issue to analyze and interpret. As Waldemar A. Nielsen has stated, private foundations are "aggregations of private wealth which, contrary to the proclaimed instincts of Economic Man, have been conveyed to public purposes."[1] As such, their activities are especially intriguing. Modern foundations can trace their ancestry back to ancient societies in Europe and Asia. They have taken many forms, and have endured the criticisms of sometimes hostile skeptics. Some have greatly influenced society and its institutions; others have come and gone virtually without notice. This is a study of one such philanthropic effort: the Guggenheim grants supporting American aeronautics during aviation's formative era. At a time when most foundations engaged in strictly charitable works, Guggenheim funding subsidized a wide range of scientific, educational, and social programs relating to aeronautics, programs from which Guggenheim interests stood not to benefit in any way, and which had a profound and lasting impact upon subsequent aerospace developments.

A subject as rich and broad as Guggenheim support of aeronautics requires the encouragement, assistance, and help of a number of individuals. It is this assistance that eases the historian's task, and makes his craft the more pleasurable. I wish to thank Oscar S. Straus III of The Daniel and Florence Guggenheim Foundation for facilitating my research in the Papers of The Daniel Guggenheim Fund for the Promotion of Aeronautics at the Library of Congress, and the foundation for supporting publication of this work, which is in no sense an "official" history. As the author, I alone bear full responsibility for the product. My research was not subject to any restrictions, and the foundation has not influenced in any way the content or subject matter covered, the analysis made, conclusions drawn, and judgments reached. I owe a special debt to Dr. G. Edward Pendray, who strongly supported this work.

The personnel of the National Air and Space Museum, Smithsonian Institution, have always offered their complete support of my research, both on the Guggenheims and on other topics. I especially want to acknowledge my appreciation to Michael Collins and Melvin B. Zisfein, the Director and Deputy Director, respectively. Dr. Howard S. Wolko, Assistant Director for Science and Technology, offered many suggestions and insights on aviation technology, particularly on the development of flight structures. Frederick C. Durant III, Assistant Director for Astronautics, provided comments on Robert Goddard and Guggenheim support of rocketry. Donald S. Lopez, Assistant Director for Aeronautics, offered advice and encouragement. Walter J. Boyne and Robert C. Mikesh provided information on early experimental air routes and Guggenheim blind flying research. Alexis Doster III furnished material on Guggenheim assistance to the California Institute of Technology and Leland Stanford University. As always, Paul Garber provided a wealth of anecdotes and personal recollections. Dr. Tom D. Crouch and Frank H. Winter read portions of the manuscript and offered helpful suggestions on early American rocket research. Catherine Scott, Dominick Pisano, and Mimi Scharf greatly assisted in the location of many little-known reports and publications. Lucius E. Lomax prepared the figures for Chapters 7 and 8.

Dr. Monte D. Wright and Dr. Frank W. Anderson, Director and Deputy Director of the Historical Office, National Aeronautics and Space Administration, extended their full cooperation, and Lee Saegesser, NASA Archivist, assisted in locating source materials. Dr. Eugene M. Emme, NASA Historian, provided helpful suggestions on sources. Dr. Ronald Wilkinson and the staff of the Manuscript Division, Library of Congress, unhesitatingly handled numerous requests for records during my research in various manuscript collections. At the National Archives, James Paulauskas and L. Lane Moore of the Industrial and Social Records Branch guided me to pertinent record groups. John E. Taylor of the Modern Military Records Branch and Elaine Everly of the Old Military Records Branch located U.S. Army and Navy records concerning aeronautics. Thomas Thalken and Robert Wood, the Director and Assistant Director of the Herbert Hoover Presidential Library, West Branch, Iowa, arranged for examination of various collections dealing with aviation, and made a subsequent trip to West Branch most enjoyable. John E. Wickman, Director of the Dwight D. Eisenhower Library, Abilene, Kansas, and Phil Lagerquist, Chief Archivist, Harry S Truman Library, Independence, Missouri, provided access to materials relating to the Cornell-Guggenheim Aviation Safety Center. Arthur Renstrom, Head, Aeronautics Section, Library of Congress, furnished information on the Guggenheim Chair at the Library of Congress and the early years of its existence.

I owe a debt of gratitude to the late Brig. Gen. Charles A. Lindbergh, to Judith Schiff, Chief Research Archivist, Sterling Memorial Library, Yale University, and to Raymond H. Fredette. Shortly before his death on August 26, 1974, General Lindbergh arranged for the author to have access to relevant documents in the Charles A. Lindbergh Papers at Yale. During a lengthy telephone conversation, he graciously furnished information and personal insights into the history of Guggenheim aviation activities. I will always recall his assistance with deep appreciation.

Various other individuals also contributed to my understanding of Guggenheim activities. Lt. Gen. James H. Doolittle, who performed the Guggenheim fund's blind flying trials, and Brig. Gen. Benjamin S. Kelsey, who flew as safety pilot on those trials, furnished information on blind flying research and also suggested useful documentary sources. Dr. R. Cargill Hall, Historian at the Jet Propulsion Laboratory, Pasadena, California, offered comments and suggestions on the early history of the Jet Propulsion Laboratory. Dr. Frank J. Malina of the International Academy of Astronautics, one of the earliest American rocket pioneers and a founder of the Jet Propulsion Laboratory, provided insights and material relating to the origins of the laboratory. During brief visits, Fred E. Weick offered his recollections on developing the NACA cowling and "safe" aircraft design, and Charles Dollfus, eminent French aeronautical historian and balloonist, contributed to my understanding of the Guggenheim fund's foreign activities. Harold D. Hoekstra provided valuable source materials on the Guggenheim school at the University of Michigan. Dr. Otto C. Koppen, Professor Emeritus of Aerospace Engineering, Massachusetts Institute of Technology, a pioneer in short-takeoff-and-landing (STOL) aircraft development, discussed the Koppen-Bollinger Helioplane and the earlier Guggenheim safe aircraft competition. Jerome Lederer, founder of the Flight Safety Foundation and Director of the Cornell-Guggenheim Aviation Safety Center, added to my knowledge of Guggenheim aviation safety efforts and Harry Guggenheim's concern for flight safety. My research efforts have been encouraged and supported by my colleagues of the Technical Committee on History, American Institute of Aeronautics and Astronautics, especially Dr. Richard K. Smith, Dr. David W. H. Godfrey, G. Edward Rice, Charles Eyres, Johannes Ruys, and the late Ralph B. Oakley. Dr. Charles H. Hildreth, Office of Air Force History, and Dr. Irving B. Holley, Jr., Department of History, Duke University, read the manuscript. Dr. William M. Leary, Department of History, University of Georgia, provided valuable comments and suggestions on the manuscript. Dr. John D. Anderson and Dr. Jewel B. Barlow of the Department of Aerospace Engineering, University of Maryland, offered advice and insights.

In Great Britain, Peter Mann and staff members of the Science Museum, South Kensington, London, furnished information on the Handley Page Gugnunc. Philip Jarrett, Companion, Royal Aeronautical Society, and Assistant Editor, Aeroplane Monthly, provided little-known facts about this unique British STOL aircraft which flew in the Guggenheim safe aircraft competition. Stephen Piercey, photo archivist of Flight International, also dug deep for photographic documentation on the Gugnunc. W. C. J. Van Westerop, Conservator, Aviodome, Schipol-Centrum, The Netherlands, discussed the safe aircraft competition and early Fokker transport design.

I am grateful for the assistance of numerous archivists and librarians who located books and documents relevant to this study. In particular, I wish to thank Dr. Judith Goodstein, Archivist, and Jackie Kuhl, Archives Assistant, at the Robert A. Millikan Library, California Institute of Technology, Pasadena, California; Brooke Whiting, Curator of Rare Books, University of California at Los Angeles; and Nancy Dean, Library Assistant, Department of Manuscripts and University Archives, John M. Olin Library, Cornell University, Ithaca, New York. Also, William H. Rae, Jr., Associate Director, University of Washington Aeronautical Laboratory, Seattle, Washington, furnished recollections and valuable data on the Guggenheim grant to the university and the F. K. Kirsten Memorial Wind Tunnel.

Finally, I am indebted to the faculty of the Department of History, University of Maryland. Their advice, encouragement, and support have always been readily available and gratefully received. I especially appreciate the counsel of Dr. Walter Rundell, chairman of the department; Dr. Keith Olson; Dr. Gordon Prange; Dr. Donald Gordon; Dr. Horace S. Merrill, and Dr. James Flack. Dr. Wayne Cole often took time to discuss instrument flying techniques and the Guggenheims, drawing on his experience as an instrument flight instructor and his extensive knowledge of Charles A. Lindbergh. The graduate students and teaching assistants of the department have furnished many hours of friendly and thoughtful discussion. One could not research and work in a more congenial atmosphere.

RICHARD P. HALLION

Washington, D.C.
November 1976

Contents

Illustrations

xv

Tanager clambers aloft steeply

Tanager in level flight

Gugnunc in flight, flaps down and slats extended

Ryan YO-51 Dragonfly

Arctic explorer Richard Byrd's airplane, the *Josephine Ford*

Charles Lindbergh's airplane, the *Spirit of St. Louis*

Team that helped make Lindbergh's national tour a success

Robert Goddard with first liquid-fuel rocket

Guggenheim and Lindbergh visit Goddard at rocket test site

A Goddard rocket climbing upwards from launch site

Harry F. Guggenheim in 1948

Figures

LEGACY OF FLIGHT

CHAPTER I

American Aviation in the Mid-1920s

THE armistice came to Europe's battlefields on the eleventh hour of the eleventh day of the eleventh month of 1918, greeted with disbelief at first, and then with incredulous enthusiasm. Soldiers who had been hostile enemies minutes before edged out of their trenches and poured across no-man's-land, Allied khaki mixing with German *feldgrau*. Starshells, rockets, and flares erupted in the sky. The armies celebrated life, as soldiers for centuries had greeted peace. Aloft, airmen pirouetted their frail craft in a frenzy of maneuvers. They, too, had reason to greet the peace with joy. In time, the warriors, both victors and vanquished, returned to their homelands, and an uncertain tranquility set upon Europe. Former soldiers took up long-neglected trades. The sputtering of fragile warplanes was replaced by the sputtering of primitive commercial air transports.

At the end of the First World War, aviation had achieved a sort of rambunctious adolescence. Pilots and engineers who had accomplished rudimentary technical improvements in the airplane to meet the needs of war now turned their attention to the broader uses of aviation in a peacetime world. A few promotors were attempting to win public confidence in air transport by operating limited airfreight and passenger services over short distances. In the United States, the federal government supported regular transcontinental airmail service, and various government agencies were busily undertaking basic aeronautical research and development.

Through 1918, the principal use of the airplane had been as a weapon of war, despite some prewar attempts to create regularly scheduled Zeppelin passenger services. The military pilot, usually an aerial sportsman transformed by events, first saw action in a passive role as an observer of enemy troop movements. Gradually, after aerial reconnaissance had proven its worth, pilots began arming their planes to shoot down enemy observation aircraft. Each measure brought a rapid countermeasure; large groups of opposing aircraft clashed in deadly "dogfights." Pilots started dropping hand grenades and makeshift bombs from their planes. Germany introduced the long-range Zeppelin as a strategic bomber. When it proved vulnerable to fighters and antiaircraft fire, the Germans switched to large multi-engine biplane bombers. The British then made plans to bomb German industrial centers from bases inside France, and Italian and Russian bombers raided Austrian targets. In short, each nation had developed specialized aircraft for a variety of military roles: aerial dogfighting, bombing, trench strafing, reconnaissance, antisubmarine warfare, and training. With the signing of the armistice, they suddenly had a huge surplus of airplanes at their disposal, as well as thousands of trained pilots.

Postwar military aviation advocates soon discovered that general staffs around the world had, by and large, little interest and faith in the airplane. Four long years of stalemate on the western front, for example, had done little to convince the traditionalist military heirarchy in Europe that military aviation should receive continued governmental support. Thus, in both Europe and America, numerous pilots and maintenance men drifted away from the military services, trying to make a living in the civilian world.

Quite naturally, many attempted to focus public attention on aviation. The aviator's prewar exploits had thrilled thousands, and during a war as grim and anonymous as the First World War, the deeds of the military pilot seemed to stand out before any others in their reaffirmation of heroism and the glory of individual combat. In 1918, the American people added the names of "Captain Eddie" Rickenbacker and "Balloon Buster" Frank Luke to their list of combat heroes. Their admiration was tinged with amazement that reasonably intelligent men would entrust their lives to frail wood and fabric biplanes. The popular image pictured pilots as a fatalistic lot who scorned death, partied until dawn, and then took off bleary-eyed, disappearing into a sunrise, never to return.

Though overdrawn, this image accurately reflected existing conditions. The airplanes of World War I were frail—many pilots died simply because their airplanes broke up in flight. They burned when hit, and pilots did not have parachutes. The journalists who waxed poetic about youth locked in Homeric combat in the skies over Europe could not have understood the frustration of the British scout pilot who blurted out after one particularly frightful mission: "Some people say Sopwith two-seaters are bloody fine machines. I think they're more bloody than fine!"[1] One lesson emerged from the aerial carnage in Europe: pilots needed assurances that their aircraft were well-built, reliable machines that would not fail them during operations. Unfortunately such assurances were missing during the First World War, and indeed through the early 1920s as well. Responsible military service chiefs often lacked the necessary technical and practical background to spot slipshod or impractical designs, and the lack of any well-organized aircraft procurement and testing system played into the hands of the huckster and unethical promoter. Lack of federal air regulation in the United States allowed literally anybody to build or fly a plane even for commercial use.[2]

There is, for example, the singular story of the Christmas Bullet, a single-engine fighter prototype built by William Christmas, M.D., for the U.S. Army Air Services. Dr. Christmas believed that airplane wings, like bird wings, should be flexible and of cantilever design—i.e., without external bracing of any kind. Consequently, when completed, the single-engine Bullet had a robust-looking fuselage, joined to two thin and obviously understrength wings. In January 1919, Christmas hired a newly returned pilot to test-fly the weird plane. Predictably, on its first flight, the Bullet shed its wings and crashed, killing the pilot. Such misfortune did not deter Dr. Christmas, who promptly built a second prototype and convinced a Royal Air Force pilot to fly it. He, too, perished, when the Bullet plowed into a barn. Christmas still considered the plane a sound design, and so stated to a House committee in August 1919, neglecting to mention the two accidents.[3] As Dean C. Smith, an out-of-work ex-Army pilot stated, "If you were really desperate, I learned . . . you could get on as test pilot for Doctor Christmas, flying the Christmas Bullet."[4]

While some aircraft were unsafe from the outset, others became untrustworthy after years of neglect. The absence of airplane inspection enabled pilots to fly dilapidated and worn aircraft with patchwork engines, rotting wooden frames, and missing components. "The lack of control of Civil Aeronautics is increasingly evidenced with the record of each week's fatalities," wrote S. S. Bradley of the Aeronautical Chamber of Commerce of America in a letter to Secretary of Commerce Herbert Hoover in 1922. "Such control is necessary, not only to protect the pilots, their passengers and goods in flight, but equally important for the safety of the non-flying public," he added.[5] Within four days, eight persons in New York and Vermont had died through negligence. Two planes disintegrated in flight; two others crashed because of pilot irresponsibility. In another more tragic example a reckless pilot buzzed an automobile off a road, resulting in the death of the driver.[6]

Many unemployed airmen purchased war-surplus Curtiss JN-4 "Jenny" trainers, and joined the barnstorming circuit. War-surplus trainers rarely cost more than a few hundred dollars. Flying around the country, offering rides at county fairs for five or ten dollars the barnstormers introduced thousands to flying. They were continuing a tradition of exhibition and sport flying that had existed before the First World War, and the beneficial effect that this had on making Americans "air-minded" cannot be overemphasized. Further, many of these pilots began rudimentary local passenger-carrying services, operating what persons later called air taxi or charter airlines. Most of these operations continued sporadically until the depression brought a sudden end to small-time airline ventures. The barnstorming circuit attracted all kinds of pilots, from the reckless to the highly skilled. At any one time, about six hundred of these "gypsy pilots" were winging their way about the country. Yet, despite the good that barnstorming sometimes accomplished, it also hurt the growth of aviation in America by reenforcing the popular image of the impulsive and "daredevil" pilot who crashed his plane at least as often as he returned it safely to earth. Statistics reflected the appalling condition of American aviation. In 1923, the Aeronautical Chamber of Commerce estimated that reckless barnstormers caused 179 crashes, killing a total of 85 people and injuring another 162. By 1924, barnstorming pilots caused two out of every three fatal accidents.[7]

Despite the woeful state of affairs, Congress did not act for another two years, when the passage of the Air Commerce Act of 1926 marked a long-awaited victory for the forces of air commerce regulation. The act created an Aeronautics Branch within the Department of Commerce and, under the able leadership of William P. MacCracken, Jr., and Clarence M. Young, this new unit cracked down on irresponsible designers and reckless pilots, insisting on rigid qualification standards for both pilots and planes.[8] After the Department of Commerce initiated licensing of pilots and planes, reckless barnstorming disappeared, replaced by new professionalism that emphasized safe, careful flying and a respectable public image. In 1926, for example, Dale A. Seitz, one of the most successful of the midwestern barnstormers, advertised his aerial troupe as the Seitz "Safe and Sane Flyers," with "United States Government Licensed Planes and Pilots," and warned, "No Stunt Flying With Passengers."[9]

Sometimes, however, the public was in as much danger from reckless passengers as from careless pilots. Charles A. Lindbergh and H. J. Lynch, two no-nonsense, responsible airmen, went barnstorming in a Lincoln Standard J-1 biplane trainer through Montana. Stopping near the town of Red Lodge, the two men landed on the prairie and waited for customers. Soon a large touring car raced from a nearby road over to the plane, and a prosperous-appearing rancher asked Lindbergh and Lynch to fly him over the town. While Lindbergh waited, Lynch and the rancher took off and disappeared. Fifteen minutes later the plane reappeared and landed. The rancher hopped out, smiling broadly, paid his ten dollars and left. "Slim," Lynch said, "in all the years I been flying, I never had a ride like that." Once aloft, the rancher had directed Lynch to fly low over Red Lodge. Then he pulled two large revolvers from his jacket and blazed away at the town, oblivious to the danger of harming the plane or the citizens of Red Lodge. Grinning, the rancher than looked back at the horrified Lynch and shouted over the roar of the engine, "I shot this town up a'foot, an' I shot this town up a'hossback, an' now I shot this town up from a airplane!"[10] Clearly, any attempt to promote the growth of commercial aviation required regulation to prevent such aberrant behavior. Some airmen in Europe and America had already started limited commercial airfreight and passenger services, and successful air transport operations sorely needed disciplinary regulation to prevent unsafe pilots and passengers from creating air tragedies.

Historians have called 1919 the "First Year of Air Transport."[11] That year marked the advent of the postwar passenger-carrying airplane, born amidst the glut of surplus wartime airplanes. Within two months of the armistice, on January 8, 1919, Germany authorized airline development. The first German airline was the Deutsche Luft Reederei (D.L.R.), which in February 1919 opened passenger service between Berlin and Weimar, via Leipzig, with war-surplus A.E.G. and D.F.W. biplanes. On August 24 the Zeppelin transport company, *DELAG* (Deutsche Luftschiffahrt Aktien Gesellschaft), reestablished passenger service between Berlin and Friedrichshafen with the Zeppelin *Bodensee*.[12] In France, the Farman brothers, well-known aircraft designers, began scheduled passenger service between Paris and Brussels using Farman F.60 Goliath twin-engine biplanes in March 1919, naming their airline the Lignes Aeriennes Farman. Later they extended service to London.[13] Great Britain delayed its entrance into international civil aviation until April 1919, when the government finally approved civil air transport operations. R. E. G. Davies has attributed Britain's procrastination to "a quite innocent lack of vision," rather than "international gamesmanship."[14] On August 25, 1919, a De Havilland D.H. 4A of Aircraft Transport and Travel flew from London to Paris with one passenger and some cargo, initiating the world's first international daily civil airline service.[15] In one respect, Great Britain was far ahead of equally early American efforts: Air Ministry regulations required licensing of pilots and airworthiness certification of all commercial aircraft.[16]

In the United States, the development of commercial aviation was tied closely to the growth of airmail. In comparison with the commercial passenger services established in Germany, France, and Great Britain, Americans could point in 1919 to only two small lines, West Indies Airways and Aero Limited, which operated Aeromarine Model 50 and Curtiss HS2L flying boats on passenger trips between Miami and Nassau, and Key West and Havana, largely to furnish thirsty Americans fair haven from the barrenness of Prohibition.[17] As in Europe, operators used surplus military aircraft, some good, some bad. One American attempt to develop specialized air transport aircraft, however, deserves special mention.

The man behind this attempt was Alfred W. Lawson, a pioneer aircraft journal editor and manufacturer, and one of the more interesting figures in early American aviation history. Lawson, who emigrated with his parents from England, was largely self-taught; he played professional baseball with various regional teams. For some unknown reason, his interest turned to aviation, and in 1908 he published the magazine *Fly* in Philadelphia.[18] His journal, the first popular aviation magazine in America, folded in two years, and he moved to New York, where he launched a more successful magazine, *Aircraft*. Dedicated to aviation education, Lawson proved to be an accurate and thoughtful observer of the aeronautical scene. Recognizing the harm that accidents did to aviation's image, Lawson acidly commented on prewar barnstormer Lincoln Beachey by writing that the public should not look upon flying as dangerous "merely because a few exhibition flyers undertake extremely hazardous performances in the air to please a crowd of morbid spectators."[19] During the First World War, Lawson established the Lawson Aircraft Company of Green Bay, Wisconsin, and built a small number of single-engine two-seat biplane trainers, known as M.T. 2's.[20]

Lawson was not an outstanding pilot or designer, and his real talent lay in his organizational ability. He was able to attract competent individuals to work for him, such as Vincent J. Burnelli, Andrew Surini, and Carl Shorey. After the armistice, he turned toward civil aviation. Lawson rejected outright the use of existing surplus military planes. He realized that commercial aviation required specialized aircraft for airmail and passenger duties, and not simply ex-military bombing, training, or observation planes hastily modified to carry one or two passengers. Lawson's company engineers, Vincent Burnelli, John Carisi, Frank Schober, Russell Shaw, Carl Shorey, Andrew Surini, and Lee Wallace, designed a twin-engine biplane with a completely enclosed passenger cabin and cockpit, the Lawson C-2. It spanned ninety-one feet, with a length of forty-eight feet, could carry a maximum of twenty-six passengers, and had a range of four hundred miles. This was the first multiengine passenger airplane ever designed in the United States, and it was a historic milestone on the road to the commercial airliner.[21]

Lawson and pilot Charles Wilcox with members of the design team as passengers, flew the C-2 from Milwaukee to Washington, D.C., in late August and early September 1919, via Chicago, Toledo, Cleveland, Buffalo, and New York City. While in Washington, Lawson gave demonstration flights in the plane to numerous senators and congressmen, as well as to Secretary of War Newton D. Baker and his wife. The C-2 received glowing newspaper reviews during its entire flight.[22] Returning to Milwaukee, the plane suffered minor damage during a hard landing, but after repairs at Dayton, it continued on to Milwaukee without further incident. The last sad chapter of the Lawson airliner now began.

Despite its promise, no potential airline operators were willing to invest in a new, expensive aircraft with so many surplus warplanes cluttering airfields across the country. Lawson sunk what money remained into an even larger trimotor biplane, the Lawson L-4. This giant plane spanned 111 feet 5 inches, with a length of 54 feet 2 inches. It could carry twenty-four passengers and three crew members at 110 mph for 850 miles.[23] Lawson scavenged parts from his earlier C-2 for the new plane, named the "Midnight Liner." It had sleeping berths and a shower bath, and cost $50,000. Lawson hoped to begin Chicago to New York passenger and mail service in August 1920. Development of the plane, however, lingered until 1921. During the recession of 1920, Lawson's stockholders demanded a return on their investment. Lawson stalled, promising to fly the plane in February 1921. This date passed, and finally, on May 8, 1921, Lawson and pilot Charles Wilcox attempted to take off. The field was entirely unsatisfactory; a farmer had even plowed right across it. Nevertheless, Lawson was so desperate that he took the risk. Wilcox advanced the throttles, and the L–4 rolled ponderously along. The ploughed area slowed the plane down, but the pilot finally got off the ground, mushing along nose-high, heading for a house. Wilcox banked away, the left wings snagged an elm tree, and the L–4 plunged to earth, tearing itself to bits before coming to rest, its passengers miraculously unhurt.[24] Financially ruined, Lawson left the aircraft industry entirely, his dreams of Lawson-built airliners plying the air shattered.* Lawson's efforts certainly foreshadowed the development of large multiengine specialized air transports with sleeping accommodations; his C–2 and L–4 were simply born at the wrong time, for air transportation in America had not advanced far enough to take full advantage of the capabilities of these two extremely promising aircraft.[25] American air transport remained in its infancy until after passage of the Kelly Act in 1925. Prior to that time, the closest that the United States came to commercial air operations was the Post Office Department's airmail service.

To many Americans in the early 1920s aviation meant the U.S. Air Mail. Pilots had conducted experimental airmail flying in the United States as early as 1911.[26] On May 15, 1918, the U.S. Army established an experimental airmail route between Washington, D.C., and New York, as an adjunct to training. On August 12, the Post Office Department took over the army operation, using civilian pilots flying a mixture of aircraft, but relying chiefly on 90 mph De Havilland D.H. 4B single-engine biplanes. At the request of the Post Office Department, Congress in 1919 appropriated funds to establish a transcontinental airmail service between New York, Chicago, and San Francisco. During 1920, the Post Office Department initiated trial service between New York and Cleveland, Cleveland and Chicago, Chicago and Omaha, and Omaha and San Francisco, using a combination of daylight mail flights and night express trains. On September 8, 1920, Post Office mail pilots completed the initial westbound "through flight,"

---

* Lawson died on Nov. 29, 1954, in San Antonio, Texas, at the age of eighty-five (*New York Times*, Dec. 14, 1954). His last years were filled with pathetic attempts to assert his place in aviation history. During the 1930s he championed a "direct credits" money scheme as the best method of ending the depression, attracting a large following. He founded a religion, "Lawsonomy," the "knowledge of life and everything that pertains thereto," and in 1943 bought the former Des Moines University changing it to the Des Moines University of Lawsonomy.

transferring sixteen thousand letters from New York to San Francisco twenty-two hours faster than by the quickest mail train.[27] Finally, in February 1921, the Post Office was ready to attempt an all-airplane transcontinental mail delivery. At 4:30 A.M. on February 22, 1921, a D.H. 4 left San Francisco with a cargo of mail. Thirty-three hours and twenty minutes later, it arrived in New York, having completed the journey in less than half the time required by using day flights in conjunction with night mail trains.[28]

The Post Office eliminated all rail transportation in connection with the air mail on July 1, 1924. Lighted beacons helped direct night mail pilots on their flights across the United States. In February 1925, Congress passed the Kelly Act, which led to federal subsidy of airmail service whereby the Post Office let out contracts for civilian firms to carry the mail. Elsbeth E. Freudenthal has stated that "the ownership of the air was transferred from the government to private companies."[29] This is not the great overstatement that it first appears. The Kelly Act was crucially important to the subsequent growth of American air transport, for it encouraged local aircraft operators to carry the mail and enter the air commerce field. When they began carrying passengers as well, America had the makings of its modern airline industry. The Post Office finally discontinued the government airmail service on September 1, 1927.[30] From this point onward, private contractors hauled the mail for a government subsidy, except for a brief and bloody interlude in 1934 when, as a result of political pressure, the army flew the mails.

The airmail pilot faced a series of dangers fully as deadly as any confronted by the military pilot in combat. The chief foe was weather—rapid weather changes could observe his route with fog or clouds that might be so high he could not climb over them, and so low that he would crash trying to get under them. Adverse headwinds could exhaust his plane's endurance. Sleet and ice could ruin a heavily loaded mailplane's performance, turning it sluggish and unresponsive, its wings and control surfaces coated white with ice and frost. Radio navigation beacons, despite research at the Bureau of Standards, were almost a decade in the future. Reliable "blind flying" instrumentation was as yet unknown. The pilot relied on his senses and flew, virtually, "by the seat of his pants." Though some of the airways had lighted beacon towers, so that on a clear night a pilot could see them stretching before his plane like an arrow pointing toward his destination, these were virtually useless in bad weather. The infamous "Hell stretch" of the Alleghenies between Ohio and New York claimed many a victim when bad weather closed in, or when engine failure doomed a pilot to a nighttime descent in the mountains. Thirty-one of the first forty airmail pilots died in crashes. If he lived, the American airmail pilot became the most skilled bad weather and night flyer in the world.

On October 1, 1925, mail pilot Charles H. Ames left Hadley Field, New Jersey, bound for Chicago via Bellefonte, Pennsylvania, and Cleveland. "Bellefonte" conjures memories among surviving airmail pilots that "Ploesti" does to World War Two bomber veterans. As with so many others, the weather was clear when Ames left. When he reached the Alleghenies, however, "he encountered that worst of all bad conditions for aviators, fog."[31] He tried to fly under the fog, failed, and crashed into Nittany Mountain, near Hecla Pass. Searchers did not discover the wreckage and body until October 11. Other pilots survived truly by miracles. One night, flying east from Omaha, Dean C. Smith cruised through rolling country between the ground and a low deck of clouds. Eventually, he climbed a small hill and entered the cloud deck, realizing that he could not descend lest he ram into the side of a hill. He climbed to eight thousand feet, still in cloud; without any useful instrumentation to guide him, he soon suffered disorientation and lost control of the plane. His D.H. 4 tumbled earthwards in a spin. He recovered from the spin, but when the plane pulled out from its resulting dive, it stalled, and began spinning again. This continued through five or six stalls, spins, dives, and recoveries. As he tried to pull the plane out from its last dive, tree tops flashed by below his wings; the D.H. 4 broke out from the clouds, in level flight over cleared land. Smith cut the engine, and landed, trembling violently.[32] Another time, on his first flight from Chicago to Omaha, Smith encountered another enemy of the airmail pilot—engine failure. The only field in sight was a crowded cow pasture. Smith lined up the rapidly sinking D.H. 4 to miss the cattle, but at the last second, a cow ambled in front of the plane. A wing tip struck the cow a mortal blow, cartwheeling the plane. Smith stood up from the splintered wreckage in time to see the cow give "one reproachful moo," then collapse. He turned over the mail to the railway in a nearby town, then sent the following legendary telegram to Washington: "On trip 4 westbound. Flying low. Engine quit. Only place to land on cow. Killed cow. Wrecked plane. Scared me. Smith."[33]

Airmail operations grew safer as pilots built up experience and as the Post Office and Department of Commerce installed more lighted beacon airways, the initiation of the federal airway system. The introduction of parachutes for mail pilots saved many lives that might otherwise have been lost. Charles A. Lindbergh, while a private airmail pilot for the Robertson Aircraft Corporation, jumped safely once near Chicago when fog closed in and his D.H. 4 exhausted its fuel supply.[34] Nevertheless, the saga of the airmail indicated the very great need for accurate pilot display instrumentation, ground radio aids and navigation aids, development of "blind flying" instrumentation, and continued research aimed at producing efficient, safe, and reliable aircraft.

———————

During the early 1920s, the federal government did not have the extensive research and development facilities that it later acquired. The army and the navy undertook limited experimental work on aircraft and airplane components, and the Commerce Department's Bureau of Standards performed some research on pilot instrumentation and radio navigation. The National Advisory Committee for Aeronautics (NACA), the nation's civilian aeronautical research agency, performed basic wind tunnel and aerodynamic research, but often its advisory function to other government agencies hampered its research efforts. Eventually, as a result of pressure from the public, the aircraft industry, and the President's Aircraft Board headed by Dwight Morrow, Congress passed three acts in 1926 that helped stimulate civilian and military aeronautical research and development, freed NACA of its advisory role and permitted it to concentrate on research, and helped provide civil aviation with the regulation it had lacked for so long. These three acts were the Army and Navy Five Year plans, and the Air Commerce Act of 1926.

By late 1925, the entire American military aviation situation was precarious. Both the Army Air Service and naval aviation forces relied on World War I vintage equipment. Senior officers who, for the most part, lacked knowledge of and appreciation for aeronautics directed the nation's military aviation programs. It was in this climate that Brig. Gen. William "Billy" Mitchell championed the bomber versus the battleship. While he did show, during trials off the Virginia Capes in July 1921, that an airplane could sink a capital warship, the "set piece" nature of the trials—the ship lying at anchor, with no anti-aircraft fire—did not apparently concern his enthusiastic admirers. He soon became a gadfly to the military hierarchy. Reduced to his permanent rank of colonel, and transferred from Washington, D.C., to Fort Sam Houston, Texas, Mitchell created an uproar when he charged that the crash of the navy dirigible *Shenandoah* on September 3, 1925, resulted from "incompetency, criminal negligence, and almost treasonable administration of the national defense by the War and Navy Departments."[35] Not unexpectedly, the army quickly moved to court-martial Mitchell. In mid-September 1925, at the suggestion of Commerce Secretary Herbert Hoover, President Calvin Coolidge convened a special nine-man President's Aircraft Board, chaired by financier Dwight Morrow. It was to investigate the entire American civil and military aeronautical establishment, in light of Mitchell's charges, and make recommendations for future air policy decisions.[36]

The Morrow Board's report, submitted in November 1925, led to the Air Commerce Act of May 20, 1926, the first federal attempt to regulate civil aeronautics, the Navy Five Year Aircraft Program, which Congress passed on June 24, 1926, and the Army Five Year Aircraft Program, approved July 2, 1926. During its investigation, the Morrow Board dismissed many of Mitchell's charges. It recommended setting up a position of assistant secretary for aeronautics in the Commerce, War, and Navy departments. Congress reestablished the Army Air Service as the Army Air Corps, with representation on the Army General Staff. This did much to solidify the precarious position of aeronautics within the service, but it still was far from the independent air arm Mitchell had championed.[37]

In civil aeronautics, the Morrow Board report reaffirmed conclusions reached earlier by the Joint Committee of Civil Aviation of the Department of Commerce and the American Engineering Council. This body, which Commerce Secretary Herbert Hoover formed in May 1925 to survey the civil aviation field, had recommended that Congress enact a civil aeronautics law establishing a Bureau of Civil Aeronautics in the Department of Commerce. This bureau could then regulate civil air navigation in America, license pilots and inspect aircraft, maintain air routes and air navigation facilities, regulate international civil aviation as it affected the United States, and encourage and promote the growth of civil air transport service. The Aeronautics Branch of the Department of Commerce, which the Air Commerce Act of 1926 created, undertook all of these responsibilities.[38]

Despite the weaknesses of military aviation, it had contributed several well-known "firsts" that drew the public eye to the possibilities of aircraft and commercial air transport. In May 1919, a navy Curtiss flying boat, the NC-4, completed the first transatlantic flight by flying from Long Island to Nova Scotia, to Newfoundland, to the Azores, to Portugal, and finally to Plymouth, England. The journey took over three weeks, from May 8 to May 31.[39] In May 1922, the army had established a 4,383-mile "model airway" serving Air Corps activities at thirty-five cities from coast to coast. The Air Corps used the route primarily for training and official transportation, though some civil pilots flew over it also. The route had twelve radio-meteorological reporting stations, a feature of subsequent commercial airways. A year later, in May 1923, two army pilots flew nonstop across the United States from Roosevelt Field, Long Island, to San Diego, California, in a single-engine Fokker T-2 monoplane. That flight took twenty-six hours and fifty minutes; during the 2,470-mile journey, the Fokker had averaged 92.05 mph. Airplane manufacturer Anthony Fokker congratulated the two pilots, stating prophetically, "Your flight is a milestone in the development of commercial aviation. In ten years the route you flew will be covered by aerial passengers and freight service just as Bleriot's route across the English channel is today."[40]

On April 6, 1924, four army Douglas World Cruiser single-engine two-place biplanes left Seattle, Washington; two returned to Seattle on September 28, having completed the world's first globe-circling flight, the first transpacific flight, and the first westbound Atlantic crossing. During the 175-day voyage, they covered 26,345 miles in a flying time of 363 hours. A broken oil line forced one plane down in the Atlantic, but a navy ship rescued the crew. Lack of blind flying instrumentation and adequate navigational aids caused the crash of another. All of these record flights demonstrated not only the growing potential of the airplane, but also the necessity for further research to provide the pilot with all the equipment and instrumentation necessary to enable him to complete his flight safely and in all types of weather conditions.[41]

The public eye, distracted by visions of daredevil barnstormers and numerous accidents, failed to observe the growing attempts to put flying on a scientific and practical basis. Such attempts required scientific research and development in such diverse fields as aerodynamics, flight propulsion, structures and materials, instrumentation design and display, and pilot training. The navy maintained research sections within its Bureau of Aeronautics, established on August 10, 1921. During the early 1920s, the navy concerned itself with building rigid airships, and conducting flight trials of airplanes from the service's first aircraft carrier, the U.S.S. *Langley*. The army's aeronautical research center at McCook Field, Dayton, Ohio, earned the nickname "the crucible of aviation technology." This was due, to great extent, to a remarkably farsighted officer, Col. Thurman H. Bane. Bane, a West Pointer (class of 1907), learned to fly in 1916, then transferred his interest to the scientific study of flight. He taught aerodynamics to flight cadets and, in 1919, assumed command of McCook Field. Until his resignation from the service in 1922, Bane directed a variety of research activities, including development of the first practical aircrew parachute by Maj. E. L. Hoffman, tests of aircraft engine superchargers, and high altitude flight research climaxed in a record altitude flight to 33,113 feet by Maj. Rudolph W. "Shorty" Schroeder on February 27, 1920.[42]

Aeronautical research and development was, however, not entirely left to the military. The federal government maintained one agency specifically charged with aeronautical research, the National Advisory Committee for Aeronautics (NACA). Congress had created NACA on March 3, 1915, to "supervise and direct the scientific study of the problems of flight, with a view to their practical solution."[43] Until the passage of the Air Commerce Act of 1926, NACA's work was largely advisory; other government agencies such as the Post Office called upon it for advice on air policy and planning. When the Air Commerce Act of 1926 placed the responsibility for civil aviation regulation in the hands of the Department of Commerce, NACA could turn its full attention to scientific research and development.[44] As an advisory agency, NACA had recommended setting up experimental airmail routes, federal regulation of air navigation, and cross-licensing of aircraft patents to facilitate aircraft design and production. In 1919, NACA had asked Dr. George W. Lewis, professor of mechanical engineering at Swarthmore College, to direct the committee's research. NACA created a research establishment, the Langley Memorial Aeronautical Laboratory, at Langley Field, Hampton, Virginia, placing its first wind tunnel in operation in 1920. Over the next four years, the committee staff engineers studied structural characteristics of aircraft wood and aluminum, behavior of propellers at high speeds, and even investigated jet propulsion for aircraft, concluding that the jet-propelled airplane could not yet compete with the propeller-driven aircraft.[45] NACA engineers, in conjunction with the Bureau of Standards and the Army Air Services, also examined airflow around airfoils (wing cross sections) at velocities near the speed of sound. Such research foreshadowed the intensive research in the 1940s to overcome the "sound barrier."[46]

While NACA concentrated on aircraft structures, propulsion, and aerodynamics, the Department of Commerce's Bureau of Standards devoted attention to the practical pilot-oriented side of aeronautical research, with emphasis on improving engine reliability and developing pilot instrumentation. Blind flying was the greatest enemy of the pilot, for it shut him off from his visual route references, turning many an ordinary flight into a potential tragedy. During the 1920s Bureau of Standards radio engineers became interested in using ground radio beacons to signal the pilot his course. In 1920, at the request of the War Department, the bureau developed an airborne radio direction finder which responded to two ground transmission antennae. The plane was on course when the pilot obtained equality of signal intensity from the two ground antennae. Flight trials at Washington, D.C., and McCook Field were successful, but bureau engineers unfortunately delayed beacon studies while conducting research on radio compasses, not emphasizing beacon research until 1926, when blind flying had assumed critical importance.[47]

By the mid-1920s, American aviation had asserted its promise. Airmail pilots carried the mails across the country routinely. To aid them in their task, the federal government had begun installation of beacon lights, radio voice communication, and weather reporting stations. Nevertheless, aviation still lacked broad public support. "Gypsy" pilots still killed themselves and hapless passengers at the rate of one fatality per 13,500 miles, eighty times as dangerous as the risk faced by the airmail pilot.[48] While the Air Commerce Act of 1926 virtually ended this aerial carnage, the harm done lingered on in the public mind, and mitigated against the development of airline passenger services. Something had to be done to instill public confidence in aviation.

Very real technical problems plagued aviation. The worst of these, from the viewpoint of pilot and passenger, was the problem of "blind" or "fog" flying. In 1927, Dr. Jerome Clarke Hunsaker, former chief of navy aircraft design and assistant vice-president of the Bell Telephone Laboratories, stated dismally that "safe landing in fog is not today possible and no means are in sight to make it so. Safety for the passengers can then depend only upon communicating by radio to the plane such information as will lead the pilot to find a clear field."[49] Another problem was low mechanical reliability. In the airmail service, over a seven-year period, mechanical trouble caused 1,618 emergency landings—42 percent of all forced landings. Rigid government inspection of mail planes, initiated in 1922, greatly contributed to growing air safety. Between 1921 and 1925 the number of mechanically caused forced landings steadily decreased, increasing the safe-mile-per-accident ratio from 2,180 miles in 1921 to 10,280 in 1923, and 14,390 in 1925. Just the same, mechanical failure occurred with distressing frequency and was a definite obstacle to safe passenger service.[50]

This reliability problem caused many airmen and airmail and passenger carriers to favor multiengine aircraft, especially three-engine "trimotor" airplanes.* They reasoned that if a single-engine airplane experienced engine trouble—the greatest single source of mechanically caused forced landings—the aircraft had to land immediately. A twin-engine aircraft, especially a large biplane, might have to do the same if one engine failed, since the other engine could not sustain the plane, with its inherent high drag characteristics, cargo, passengers, and the dead engine. Since it was highly unlikely that two engines would fail simultaneously, the trimotor offered twin-engine backup in the event that one engine failed.[51] In 1925, Dutch airplane manufacturer Anthony Fokker modified his F.VIIa single-engine high-wing monoplane to trimotor configuration by adding two Wright J-4 Whirlwind 200 hp piston engines under the wing, one on each side. A single J-4 replaced the F.VIIa's 400 hp Liberty engine in the nose. Fokker called the new plane the F.VII-3m. It was the first Fokker trimotor, and it completed its maiden flight on September 4, 1925. Fokker had designed the plane for the express purpose of winning the first Ford Airplane Reliability Tour. The Ford tour was the idea of Harvey Campbell, a member of the Detroit Board of Commerce, who hoped to promote air travel and the growth of Detroit as a center of aircraft manufacturing. Edsel Ford donated the tour trophy, worth $7,000. On September 28, 1925, seventeen airplanes left Henry Ford's Dearborn airfield for a six-day circuit of the Midwest. Just before dark, on October 4, 1925, Fokker's big trimotor swept across the finish line easily beating its competitors. The age of the trimotor transport had arrived.[52]

Subsequently, William B. Stout, the designer of the first American all-metal airplane and the man who had convinced Henry and Edsel Ford to enter the aircraft manufacturing business, turned to trimotors. Like Anthony Fokker, Stout modified his single-engine Model 2-AT monoplane into the trimotor 3-AT, an ugly and inefficient airplane that Harold Hicks, Thomas Towle, and other Ford enginers redesigned as the Ford 4-AT "Tri-motor," the famed all-metal "Tin Goose." It first flew on June 11, 1926.[53] Until the advent of the low-wing

---

* Hunsaker estimated the chances of engine failure in a single-engine plane as one per 100 flights of two hundred miles each. He concluded that the chances of a forced landing in a trimotor due to two engines failing were one per 1,666 flights of two hundred miles each, only one-sixteenth the risk of the single-engine plane.

Boeing 247 and Douglas DC-2 twin-engine monoplane transports, Fokker trimotors and Ford "Tri-motors" dominated the air transport scene.

Other problem areas worried designers and pilots. As aircraft weights went up, the stall speed—the velocity at which an airplane's wing stopped generating lift—also rose. This caused more pilot fatalities during takeoff and landing. Several technological improvements seemed to offer promise, especially the wing flap and the leading edge wing slat, but they were as yet unproven. A growing number of people within the flying community began to ask, in effect, why not develop a stall- and spin-proof airplane from the outset, a plane that would have exceptionally good low-speed flying characteristics down to speeds as low as 30 mph?[54] Some argued that the time of the dabbling inventor had passed and aviation now required large numbers of scientifically trained engineers. These individuals urged universities and colleges to graduate engineers specially trained in aeronautics. Others clamored for "model airways" where new aircraft, weather reporting stations, and radio communication facilities could work together on a regularly scheduled experimental passenger run, a sort of aerial proving ground. Still more wanted aeronautical education in elementary and secondary schools to make Americans "airminded," and a national town-marking campaign to paint town names on the largest buildings to facilitate air navigation.

Clearly, American civil aviation had reached a turning point. Its development could continue, or it could founder. Into this turbulent atmosphere stepped a sixty-nine-year-old wealthy New York entrepreneur, Daniel Guggenheim. He had never flown in an airplane, and a serious heart condition ensured that he never would.[55] A philanthropist who believed the wealthy had a special duty to use their wealth for the social betterment of mankind, he often quoted the Hebrew proverb, "Who gives in health gives gold; in sickness, silver; after death, lead."[56] Together with his son Harry, Daniel Guggenheim had decided to advance civil aviation through philanthropy. His assistance could not have come at a more crucial time.

CHAPTER 2

Daniel Guggenheim and the Beginning of Guggenheim Aeronautical Philanthropy

ONE morning in 1848, a crowded sailing ship docked at the port of Philadelphia, bearing a small group of immigrant Jews from the Swiss town of Lengnau. Among the passengers were fifty-six-year-old Simon Guggenheim, his wife, his twenty-year-old son Meyer, Meyer's four sisters, and seven stepchildren by Rachel Weil Meyer, the woman Simon married after his first wife died. The Guggenheims' three-month Atlantic crossing deposited them in America just as the initial revolutions of 1848 erupted in Europe. They had come to the United States to escape the civil war raging between the Catholic and Protestant cantons in Switzerland, as well as to avoid economic depression and find relief from Swiss anti-semitism. Simon had wanted to emigrate to America for years, but had to wait until his second marriage provided him with the necessary money to pay for passage of fourteen people from Lengnau to Koblenz, down the Rhine River to Hamburg, and thence to Philadelphia.[1]

Simon Guggenheim arrived in the United States like thousands more of "the Uprooted," penniless, with no job prospects and no language skills. After securing lodging in Philadelphia, Simon and his son Meyer started peddling household goods. Simon canvassed Philadelphia itself. Meyer, younger and stronger, sold his wares in the coal mining towns of Pennsylvania. He soon discovered that miners' wives wanted stove polish that would not cover them with grime. Intrigued, he took a sample to a chemist, had it analyzed, and had the chemist replace the offending ingredient with a substitute that worked as well without leaving the housewife's hands soiled. Simon retired from peddling to mix the polish at home, while Meyer sold it in the country. The polish made Simon and his son financially solvent, so much so that Meyer felt secure enough to marry one of his stepmother's four daughters, Barbara Meyer, in 1852. Between 1854 and 1873 she bore him eleven children, Isaac, Daniel, Murry, Solomon, Jeannette, Benjamin, twins Simon and Robert (who died, age nine), William, Rose, and Cora.[2]

Meyer Guggenheim's next big financial venture was selling an instant coffee mix to the Union Army during the Civil War. Valuing education for his children, he sent them to a Catholic day school in Philadelphia and then on to public high school. Broadminded, he supported both the Hebrew Education Society and Catholic Charities.[3] In the mid-1870s he decided to import lace and embroidery from Switzerland; he sent his second oldest son, Daniel, to Switzerland to learn the business. This started a tradition with Meyer of relying on his son Daniel as his chief counsel in all major business decisions. When Meyer's father Simon died in 1869, his son was already well on the way to financial success. About 1880, Meyer Guggenheim bought into two Colorado lead- and silver-mining ventures, the A.Y. Mine and the Minnie Mine, at California Gulch outside the boom town of Leadville, Colorado. He had paid between $5,000 and $25,000 (sources cannot agree on an accurate figure) in obtaining the one-third ownership rights from Charles H. Graham, a Quaker friend of Meyer who speculated in western lands. The purchase marked the beginning of vast Guggenheim mining and smelting interests.[4]

For weeks all Meyer Guggenheim received from his mine superintendent were telegrams requesting more money, especially to keep the mines from flooding. Then one afternoon he opened a telegram that read, "Rich strike fifteen ounces silver sixty percent lead." Meyer Guggenheim was a millionaire. From each ton of ore he could expect at least $19.35 worth of silver, plus a very valuable 1,200 pounds of lead. By 1882, the A.Y. Mine alone cleared $2,000 worth of silver per day. By 1889, Meyer had cleared $1,383,000; the next year mining experts valued the Minnie and A.Y. at $14,556,000.[5] In 1882, with four of his seven sons already engaged in the family business, Meyer Guggenheim formed the firm of M. Guggenheim's Sons. All seven, even the youngest, would receive the same percentage of interest, the young ones assuming business responsibilities as they matured.[6]

Meyer Guggenheim next moved from mining to ore smelting, to prevent profit losses from smelting fees. In 1888, Meyer Guggenheim and his sons left Philadelphia and headquartered their business at 2 Wall Street, New York City. They dropped the lace and embroidery import business, and shifted their interests to mining and smelting. In March 1888, the Guggenheims set up a smelting plant in Pueblo, Colorado, called in smelting expert August Raht, and soon drew in $50,000 per month from the plant. Daniel Guggenheim, acting for his father, negotiated smelting concessions with the Mexican government, and set up another smelting plant. A third followed in Perth Amboy, New Jersey, in 1895.[7]

Four years later, to further advance the family business, the Guggenheims established a corporation especially to seek out new mineral areas to mine. This firm was the Guggenheim Exploration Company, popularly called Guggenex with $6 million in capital. The Guggenheims hired John Hays Hammond, Cecil Rhodes' mining engineer, to serve as chief consultant.[8] In the meantime, Henry H. Rogers, who ran Standard Oil together with William Rockefeller, the younger brother of John D. Rockefeller, fixed his sights on the smelting industry, and determined to run the Guggenheims into the ground. He established the American Smelting and Refining Corporation, ASARCO, commonly called the "Smelters Trust." In December 1900, having won a series of small skirmishes with Rogers' ASARCO, Daniel Guggenheim and his brothers bought up a majority of stock in ASARCO, wresting control of the Smelters Trust from Rogers and Rockefeller, and boosting their wealth by $43 million.[9]

By 1900, Meyer had retired from active participation in Guggenheim affairs. Four years later he died after suffering complications from surgery. In effect, the control of M. Guggenheim's Sons, Guggenex, and the other family ventures passed into the hands of Daniel Guggenheim, the second eldest of Meyer's sons. A man short in stature, Daniel Guggenheim was long on business talent. Financier Bernard Baruch, who got Daniel Guggenheim and John D. Ryan, the two copper kings, to furnish the government with copper at half the prevailing market price during World War I, used to remark that Daniel Guggenheim, like Samuel Gompers, "sat taller than most men stand . . . he was no double dealer." While a driving competitor and formidable foe, Daniel Guggenheim never forgot the needs of the worker. He supported labor organization, and won the respect of Ida Tarbell, who said of him, "He was earnest in his sympathy for the laboring men and radical in his ideas of what should be done to improve their lot."[10]

Daniel Guggenheim married Florence Schloss of Philadelphia in

1884, and they had three children, Meyer Robert, Harry Frank, and Gladys Eleanor. After 1900, he directed the Guggenheims' growing presence in mining around the world. He pushed the brothers into the copper industry by developing Kennecott in Alaska, then opened the Chilean copper fields. In 1916, largely at Daniel's behest, the brothers replaced M. Guggenheim's Sons with a new firm: Guggenheim Brothers, in the Equitable Building at 120 Broadway, New York. They also shut down Guggenex, and it remained closed until Harry Frank Guggenheim reopened it in 1959. In January 1921, Daniel Guggenheim visited Herbert Hoover, then chairman of the European Relief Council in New York, and offered the famed mining engineer a guaranteed minimum income of $500,000 annually if he would become the senior partner in Guggenheim Brothers. The old entrepreneur explained that the brothers were advancing in years, and that they "wanted a new partner of wide experience." Hoover and his wife thought the offer over for a week; President-elect Harding had already offered him the cabinet position as secretary of commerce. Though the Guggenheim offer meant great wealth and greater freedom than public service, Hoover turned it down.[11] When copper prices dropped in the early 1920s, John D. Ryan of Anaconda offered Daniel Guggenheim $70 million for the Chile Copper Company, the Guggenheims' Chuquicamata holdings. Ryan needed a cheaper source of copper to produce a profit for Anaconda, and Daniel believed it a fair price. Accordingly, on March 1, 1923, Guggenheim Brothers sold Chuquicamata to Ryan, bringing the spectacular growth of the Guggenheim mineral industry to an end. Observers wondered what Daniel Guggenheim would do next.[12]

Prior to World War I, Daniel Guggenheim had considered several philanthropic ventures, including private aid to agricultural schools and establishing a committee of experts to examine the plight of the industrial worker. He rejected both these plans, the former because of existing federal grants to agricultural schools, and the latter because of various congressional committees formed for studying the problems of labor. In 1923, Daniel Guggenheim resigned the last directorship he held, in ASARCO, ending his formal participation in Guggenheim business affairs. He retired to Hempstead House, a magnificent forty-room mansion overlooking Long Island Sound on Sands Point; he had bought it in 1917 from Howard Gould, who had modeled the edifice—complete with a sixty-foot castle tower and turret—after Kilkenney Castle in Ireland. In the living room hung sixteenth-century tapestries, and the 350-acre grounds contained a nine-hole golf course, a tea house, and a casino. Here Daniel Guggenheim, with his wife, planned his philanthropic activities. In 1924 they founded The Daniel and Florence Guggenheim Foundation to advance the "well-being of mankind throughout the world."[13] Next he turned to aviation.

Daniel Guggenheim's interest in aeronautics was intrinsically bound to the relationship of New York University and Daniel's son Harry Frank Guggenheim. Born in West End, New Jersey, on August 23, 1890, Harry F. Guggenheim grew up while the Guggenheims, under his father's leadership, were at the height of their mining and smelting activity. An active youth, fond of sports and having fun, Harry Guggenheim enrolled in the Sheffield Scientific School at Yale in 1907 to study mining. He left in 1908, because of his own desire to get into business, and to marry Helen Rosenberg. He joined a family smelting team at Aquascalientes, Mexico. Two years later at the behest of his father he enrolled at Pembroke College, Cambridge, England. While at Pembroke, he majored in economics and political science, studying under economist John Maynard Keynes, and minored in chemistry. For relaxation he played tennis; his aggressive court style won him a Cambridge tennis Blue and the presidency of the Pembroke College Lawn Tennis Club.

He received his B.A. from Pembroke in 1913 and returned to the United States, taking his place at 120 Broadway alongside his uncles. Despite the family's own national origins and the international character of its business, Harry Guggenheim absorbed the Anglophile atmosphere of Yale and came away from his schooling at Pembroke with the deepest respect for English institutions and traditions. Before the United States entered World War I, Harry F. Guggenheim was thoroughly Anglo-American in outlook.[14]

While at Cambridge, the gregarious Guggenheim had made many friends among his fellow students. When war erupted in 1914, an entire generation of English youth rushed off to serve with a quiet and fatalistic dedication so aptly captured by the British poet and novelist, Robert Graves. One of these was H. C. "Carly" Webb, a close friend and former tennis partner of Harry Guggenheim. Webb soon perished on the fields of France, and his death deeply saddened the young Guggenheim, who determined to ready himself for the coming American involvement he saw as inevitable. For some reason, as yet unclear, he decided to learn to fly. In early 1917, while relaxing in Florida, he took ten days flight instruction at Palm Beach. When

he returned north in March 1917, he joined a small private unit training at Port Washington, at Manhasset Bay, Long Island. Guggenheim's training coincided with that of a militant Yale University student, Frederick Trubee Davison, son of Henry P. Davison, a partner
in J. P. Morgan & Company.[15]

Frederick Trubee Davison, known to his friends as Trubee, later
became one of Harry Guggenheim's closest associates. In 1915, he had
spent the summer as an ambulance driver in Paris; after his return
to Yale in the fall he determined to train a group of his fellow students as pilots, and lead them into combat, should the United States
enter the war. He contacted eleven other Yale men, and in 1916 they
began flight training at their own expense at Manhasset Bay. Henry
Woodhouse, the militant and interventionist editor of *Aerial Age
Weekly*, put Davison in contact with navy secretary Josephus Daniels.
While Daniels could not yet incorporate Davison's "Aerial Coast
Patrol" in the Naval Reserve, he did smooth the path to official cooperation between the navy and the Yalies. They flew joint maneuvers
with the sea-going reserve, acquiring experience in spotting mines
and otherwise acting as the eyes of the fleet. To expedite their activities, Davison's group organized the Yale Aero Club; it attracted
more members and drew support from the aeronautical community,
including Glenn Curtiss, the airplane manufacturer. They now called
themselves "The First Yale Unit." At the request of the navy, they
moved down to Palm Beach. Just after the United States entered the
war, the navy commissioned Trubee Davison as lieutenant (j.g.) and
the rest of his little band as ensigns. Henry Woodhouse, as a gift, sent
the unit a Lewis machine gun. In June, the unit returned to Hunting-
ton, Long Island. The next month, while taking final flight check for
his naval aviator rating, Davison crashed and broke his back. Though
he suffered no paralysis and later served on staff duty, Davison's days
as an active naval aviator were over.* The unit he had formed went
off to war without him.[16]

Among the men who soon went overseas was Harry Guggenheim.
After coming back from Florida and joining a training group at Manhasset Bay, he purchased a triplane flying boat; a friend borrowed it

* Davison graduated from Yale, *honoris causa*, in 1918, and received an LL.B.
from Columbia in 1922. He served as a member of the New York Assembly
from Nassau County from 1922 to 1926, and after passage of the Air Corps
Five Year Program, he received appointment as the first Assistant Secretary of
War for Aeronautics. He served in this position from 1926 to 1933. During
World War II, Davison rose to brigadier general in the U.S. Army Air Forces.
From 1933 to 1951 he was president of the American Museum of Natural His-
tory. Davison died on November 14, 1974, in his home on Peacock Point, Long
Island, age eighty-eight.

and crashed it at Lake George. Harry Guggenheim continued his training on Curtiss twin-engine pusher flying boats, aided by Glenn Curtiss himself. He completed flight training in June 1917, and the navy commissioned him a lieutenant (j.g.) on September 14, 1917. For his first month of service, Lieutenant Guggenheim, USNR, puttered about Long Island for the navy's Bureau of Navigation. Then, on October 20, he left for duty overseas. Guggenheim put in time in Paris, London, and Rome. He served on temporary duty with the navy's Northern Bombing Group in France, later with the Independent Air Forces on the western front, and at a training camp outside Bordeaux. While with the Northern Bombing Group, Guggenheim negotiated with the Italian government in Rome to get seventeen Caproni heavy bombers for navy use until the navy could acquire British-built Handley Page aircraft. During the negotiations Guggenheim outmaneuvered a U.S. Army major trying to get the bombers for the army, Fiorello La Guardia. The Capronis went to the navy, but many crashed during ferry flights from Italy to France across the Alps, mostly due to engine failure. Only eight arrived safely at Orly Field, outside Paris.[17] Harry Guggenheim thoroughly enjoyed his naval service. He made many close friends who later assumed major positions in the aircraft industry and federal government, among whom were Trubee Davison, Artemus L. Gates, David Ingalls (the navy's first fighter ace), and Rear Adm. Hutchinson I. Cone, commander of all naval aviation forces in Europe. Promoted to full lieutenant in March 1918, Harry Guggenheim advanced to lieutenant commander, USNR, in October 1918. The navy discharged him on September 13, 1921.[18]

Harry Guggenheim continued flying as a private pilot after the war, keeping alive the wartime contacts he had made. Daniel Guggenheim, always intensely interested in the activities of his children, now developed an interest in the possibilities of commercial aviation. He already had recognized its military potential, writing to his son in 1918, "I wonder whether you think as much of the aeroplane in bringing the war to a final end as I do?"[19]

It remained for Prof. Alexander Klemin of New York University to provide the catalyst that generated Daniel Guggenheim's generous donations to support aeronautics. Alexander Klemin was a short, stocky engineer from England who had come to the United States and enrolled in Jerome Hunsaker's pioneering aeroengineering course at the Massachusetts Institute of Technology (MIT). When Hunsaker left MIT in 1916 to head the navy's Aircraft Division in Washington, D.C., he recommended that Klemin succeed him as director of MIT's aeronautics department. Klemin stayed at MIT until the United States entered the war and he founded, together with Lester D. Gardner, the magazine *Aviation*. A brilliant engineer, Klemin failed to get a commission because of his brashness and unwillingness to correct gracefully those less capable than himself. Such were his talents, however, that Col. Virginius E. Clark, then the commanding officer at McCook Field and later the inventor of the famed Clark Y airfoil section and the Duramold plywood aircraft construction method, took Klemin on board as a sergeant. Klemin viewed the rank as a blessing. "I was in full charge of research," he recollected, "yet so low in rank that I made a poor target for reorganization or demotion."[20] While at McCook, Klemin instituted the first really scientific method of distributing sandbags to static test airplanes on the ground and prepared manuals to supervise flight-testing of aircraft. After the armistice, he entered the private aircraft industry as an engineer. Then, about 1922, he met Prof. Collins P. Bliss, instructor in mechanical engineering at New York University.

At that time, only five schools in the United States had programs in aeronautical engineering. These were the Massachusetts Institute of Technology (MIT), California Institute of Technology (Caltech), University of Michigan, University of Washington, and Stanford University. Only Michigan and MIT had degree programs. Aeroengineering courses generally grew out of mechanical engineering programs, inspired by a few interested students and pushed through by such farsighted faculty members as Jerome Hunsaker of MIT, A. A. Merrill and Harry Bateman of Caltech, Felix Pawlowski of the University of Michigan, and William F. Durand of Stanford.[21]

Klemin and Bliss decided to offer mechanical engineering seniors at New York University an elementary aerodynamics course as an option in place of a course in electrical engineering. First offered by Bliss in February 1923, the course was such a success that he offered it again the following year. In the meantime, Bliss and Klemin had designed a four-course program for seniors, consisting of a course in airplane design, one in propeller design, one on airship design, and one on aerodynamics. Dr. Charles H. Snow, dean of the College of Engineering, approved the program, and in September 1924, the University Council appointed Klemin as an associate professor of aeronautical engineering, to supervise the program. The university designated the program as an experimental one for three years, but insisted that financial support must come from outside individuals. Bliss and Klemin, by no means certain of success, began contacting persons prominent in aeronautics, business, and finance, in an attempt to acquire the necessary backing. Alexander Klemin and Collins Bliss got their first big support from airplane manufacturer Glenn Curtiss, who donated to the school a small wind tunnel with a four-square-foot test section. When all of the aeronautics graduates found jobs within the industry, New York University Chancellor Elmer Ellsworth Brown decided to place the aeronautical engineering program on a permanent footing. To do so, however, would require at a minimum $500,000.[22]

In March 1925, Chancellor Brown formed an organizing committee for seeking a permanent endowment. This committee consisted of chairman General John J. Carty, vice-chairman F. Trubee Davison, Artemus Gates, and Harry F. Guggenheim, with Collins Bliss and Alexander Klemin as university representatives. Guggenheim had joined the committee at the invitation of Klemin. Presumably these two men met through their participation in Long Island sport flying activities after the war. Chancellor Brown proposed a public campaign to secure funding for the creation of a chair and laboratory in memory of Quentin Roosevelt. The proposed laboratory drew support from Maj. Gen. Mason M. Patrick, chief of the Army Air Service; Rear Adm. William Moffet, chief of the Navy Bureau of Aeronautics; and from Paul Henderson, an assistant postmaster general.[23]

During a luncheon at the Princeton Club in New York City, some members of the organizing committee proposed a public campaign to raise the $500,000. Harry Guggenheim disagreed. He rightly gauged public opinion, realizing that the American people were not so interested in aviation as to contribute vast sums of money to a single school. He suggested that New York University seek out a single individual with enough money to support the school independently.[24] He requested Chancellor Brown to prepare a letter explaining the necessity of such a center, and offered to show it to his uncles.[25] In early May 1925, Collins Bliss contacted General of the Armies John J. Pershing as to his views on the proposed school at New York University. Pershing, in a letter to John Carty, a former army general in charge of the NYU organizing committee, responded, "To my mind, the encouragement of commercial aviation is necessary to the full development of military aviation. It need not be pointed out that aviation has come to be a most important, if not a vital, factor in national defense." As for Bliss's announcement that the committee planned to contact the Guggenheims, Pershing wrote, "I cannot think of a finer thing for a family of such standing, or for any individual member of it, to do than to create this endowment."[26]

On May 25, 1925, Chancellor Brown wrote a letter to Daniel Guggenheim, which Harry delivered to his father. The recent creation of The John Simon Guggenheim Foundation for education by Daniel Guggenheim's brother Simon, in memory of his son John Simon, had influenced Brown, together with the "public spirit" of the Guggenheim family.[27] In his letter, Brown mentioned that New York University had prepared the necessary promotional literature to conduct a public subscription campaign, but that before taking this step, the university had selected the names of "six or seven gentlemen" who might be willing to furnish the necessary capital themselves. The school had planned to establish the chair in memory of Quentin Roosevelt, but Brown now proposed that since Daniel Guggenheim's name was chief among the men being considered, "perhaps you and some other members of your family would . . . care to endow what might well be known as the Guggenheim School of Aeronautics."[28] Though various sources disagree on particular details, they all agree that Harry Guggenheim showed his father the letter while visiting his parents at Hempstead House. As Klemin recalls, Daniel Guggenheim read the letter from Chancellor Brown "with the rapidity and concentration which were habitual to him," and said immediately, "Don't show this letter to your uncles, Harry. I will do it myself. I have given all my life to work underground; now let me see what I can do to help above ground."[29]

On June 12, 1925, Daniel Guggenheim wrote Brown, signifying his intention to endow the Daniel Guggenheim School of Aeronautics at New York University for $500,000. In his letter, he spoke of the need for "placing aeronautics on the same educational plane that other branches of engineering enjoy. . . . aviation is capable of rendering such service to the nation's business and economic welfare as well as to its defense that our universities should concern themselves with the education of highly trained engineers capable of building better and safer commercial aircraft. . . ."[30]

Daniel Guggenheim publicly announced his gift of $500,000 to New York University on June 15. The money provided for a laboratory building with a wind tunnel, propeller laboratory, and research areas, at a cost of $225,000. The remaining $275,000 would endow three chairs in aeronautics, the hiring of laboratory assistants, and maintenance costs.[31] The university then turned to assembling an advisory committee to supervise the spending of the Guggenheim grant. Late in September 1925, Chancellor Brown asked aviation

pioneer Orville Wright to accept the chairmanship of the NYU
Guggenheim school advisory committee. Wright consented to head
the body; the other members chosen by Brown included vice-
chairmen Harry Guggenheim and Charles L. Lawrance, president
of the Wright Aeronautical Corporation, and various committee members including F. Trubee Davison, William P. MacCracken, Jr., a distinguished aviation lawyer, aircraft designer Sherman Fairchild, and
designer Grover Loening.[32]

On Thursday morning, October 23, 1925, four hundred faculty
members, students, and representatives of the aviation industry gathered while Daniel Guggenheim, with Chancellor Brown and student
members of NYU's army reserve officer training program watching,
broke the ground for the Daniel Guggenheim School of Aeronautics.
Speaking to the onlookers, Daniel Guggenheim said, "As I am an old
man whose active days of toil are passed, I shall dedicate the rest of
my life with the active aid of my son, Harry, to the study and promotion of aeronautics. I shall do this as a part of my duty to my
country whose ample opportunities have ever been at my hand and
whose bountiful blessings I have had the good fortune to enjoy. Were
I a young man seeking a career in either science or commerce, I should
unhesitatingly turn to aviation. I consider it the greatest road to opportunity which lies before the science and commerce of the civilized
countries of the earth today."[33] His audience clapped appreciatively,
but Daniel Guggenheim and his son Harry already had their sights
set on goals far more extensive than just one school of aeronautics at
one university.*

---

* The Daniel Guggenheim School of Aeronautics, New York University,
officially opened on Oct. 27, 1926, in dedication ceremonies attended by F.
Trubee Davison, then the Assistant Secretary of War for Aeronautics, Harry F.
Guggenheim, Gen. John J. Carty, and Chancellor Elmer Ellsworth Brown. At
that time, the student enrollment in the School of Aeronautics had reached
fifty-seven: twenty-one freshmen, thirteen sophomores, five juniors, four seniors,
four graduates, and ten special students. By the end of 1927, NYU had spent
approximately $186,000 of the Guggenheim endowment for a two-story build-
ing, a nine-foot wind tunnel, and other equipment. See "Opening of Guggenheim Aeronautics School," *Aviation* 21, no. 22 (Nov. 29, 1926): 920; Teichmann, *Report on the Daniel Guggenheim School of Aeronautics*, p. 9.

CHAPTER 3

The Creation of The Daniel Guggenheim Fund for the Promotion of Aeronautics

DANIEL Guggenheim considered the grant to New York University simply the beginning of a larger, undefined program of aeronautical philanthropy. Harry Guggenheim mentioned to his friend Ivy Lee, head of a New York public relations firm, that his father was very interested in funding more schools of aeronautical engineering, but that he himself thought that ways must be found to build the aircraft industry so that it could support the graduates of such schools. Ivy Lee, who later directed public relations for the Guggenheim programs, suggested to Harry that his father start a fund for the promotion of aeronautics.[1] Harry Guggenheim discussed plans for such a promotional scheme with various individuals within the aeronautical community. His plans won the support of pioneer Orville Wright, whom Harry had contacted in October 1925.[2] Daniel Guggenheim, prepared to put several million dollars in such a promotional venture, reasoned that the offer should be tendered to the government, to secure the added support that the federal government could furnish. Accordingly, late in December 1925, Harry Guggenheim left for Washington, D.C., to see Dwight Morrow, who had chaired Calvin Coolidge's air board. Harry outlined a plan whereby Daniel Guggenheim would make available $2,500,000 to sponsor education, research and development, and aviation promotion via publications, brochures, and publicity demonstrations of safe flying.

Morrow arranged for Harry Guggenheim to see President Coolidge later that morning. The president listened quietly as Guggenheim advanced his plan. Then he called Secretary of Commerce Herbert Hoover and invited him for lunch at the White House. Hoover arrived shortly, and Guggenheim, Hoover, Coolidge, his wife, and a

31

presidential aide discussed the plan over lunch. The president believed the plan a good one. The only part he questioned was a statement Guggenheim made to the effect that the airplane satisfied the need for greater speed in travel. "What's the use of getting there quicker," Harry Guggenheim recalled Coolidge saying, "if you haven't got something better to say when you arrive?"[3] That afternoon Guggenheim returned to New York, with the complete support of the president and the secretary of commerce.

In early January 1926, Harry Guggenheim began asking prominent American scientists, financiers, and aviation personalities if they would care to serve on the board of directors, later termed trustees, of the proposed fund. He realized that the fund, if it were to be successful, would require the services of expert consultants that he and his father could rely on for suggestions and recommendations. Harry Guggenheim displayed uncommon ability in his selection of suitable individuals, and they subsequently served the fund with distinction. He contacted Dwight W. Morrow, Dr. William F. Durand, Elihu Root, Jr., John D. Ryan, Rear Adm. Hutchinson I. Cone, and Orville Wright. His father Daniel suggested Maj. Gen. George W. Goethals, Dr. Albert A. Michelson, and F. Trubee Davison.[4] All of these men accepted Harry Guggenheim's invitation, and all of them were well qualified for their positions as trustees. Orville Wright, with his brother Wilbur, had invented the first man-carrying powered airplane and had successfully flown it at Kitty Hawk, North Carolina, on December 17, 1903. Since then, he had served as the doyen of American aeronautical engineers. Morrow had directed Coolidge's aircraft board, making recommendations that Congress would soon pass into law. Rear Adm. Hutchinson I. Cone had graduated from the U.S. Naval Academy in 1894, and served with Dewey at Manila Bay during the Spanish-American War. He was fleet engineer for the "Great White Fleet's" round-the-world voyage, then head of the navy's Bureau of Steam Engineering. During World War I he had commanded all U.S. naval aviation forces in Europe until wounded in October 1918 when a German U-boat sank the S.S. *Leinster*. F. Trubee Davison had been the founder of the First Yale Naval Aviation Unit.[5]

William F. Durand, a professor emeritus at Stanford University, had graduated from the Naval Academy with the class of 1880. After naval service he studied for and received a Ph.D. in mechanical engineering from Lafayette College. He taught at Cornell and Stanford, helped found the National Advisory Committee for Aeronautics in 1915, and had served on the Morrow Board in 1925. Maj. Gen. George

W. Goethals had directed the building of the Panama Canal. Elihu Root, Jr., a lawyer, was the son of the former secretary of war in William McKinley's cabinet, and secretary of state in Theodore Roosevelt's. Financier John D. Ryan, a "Copper King," had headed Woodrow Wilson's Aircraft Production Board during the latter part of World War I, helping to untangle snags and bottlenecks that previous mismanagement had created. As Second Assistant Secretary of War, Ryan directed the Army Air Service from August through November 1918. Albert A. Michelson was one of America's foremost scientists. A graduate from the U.S. Naval Academy in 1873, Michelson had taught physics at the academy, then went to the Case School of Applied Sciences at Cleveland as a professor of physics. Michelson had measured the speed of light, and also determined that the center of the earth was a solid. He developed the spectroscope, and in 1907, received the Nobel Prize in Physics, the first American scientist so honored.[6] These, then, were the individuals Harry and Daniel Guggenheim selected to supervise the administration of the proposed Guggenheim fund.

By early January 1926, Harry Guggenheim had secured the acceptance of Rear Admiral Cone to fill the position of vice-president of the fund. Harry Guggenheim knew that he himself would be the fund's president.[7] By January 14, all the proposed members of the board of directors had notified Guggenheim of their acceptance. The next day, Harry Guggenheim met with Herbert Hoover in Washington to inform the secretary of commerce about the progress of the fund, and to show Hoover a draft letter dated January 16, 1926, from his father to Hoover, by which the Guggenheims proposed to introduce the fund. The letter won Hoover's approval. In the letter released to the public on Monday, January 18, Daniel Guggenheim announced "a Fund which will co-operate with you and with all agencies of the Government and the public generally in advancing the art and science of aeronautics and aviation." The elder Guggenheim donated $2,500,000 to the fund. He would immediately place $500,000 at the disposal of the trustees for their use as they saw fit, and would hold in readiness a further $2 million for release "as and when the judgment of the trustees may indicate that the money can be used wisely." The fund would not be a money-making enterprise. Any profits the fund made would go back into the fund to carry on additional work. The fund would not be permanent; rather, "the whole art and science of aeronautics and aviation being now in its infancy, it will be possible with the sums thus contributed, to bring about such an advance in the art, that private enterprise will find it practicable and profitable to 'carry on,' and thus render a continuous and permanent endowment for this purpose unnecessary."[8]

The proposed Daniel Guggenheim Fund for the Promotion of Aeronautics had four major purposes. First among these was the promotion of aeronautical education in universities, colleges, and secondary schools and among the general public. Second, the fund assumed a research function by supporting "the extension of fundamental aeronautical science." Third, the fund intended to "assist in the development of commercial aircraft and aircraft equipment." Finally, the fund would "further the application of aircraft in business, industry and other economic and social activities of the nation." Daniel Guggenheim instructed the fund trustees to restrict their work to civil aviation activities, avoid duplication of existing work by other aeronautical organizations, avoid infringing on those areas that were best left to the control of the government, and to plan their research and study projects carefully and follow each one through to a conclusion. Finally, to prevent the fund from developing a costly bureaucratic structure, he urged that the trustees "maintain a simple, inexpensive directing organization, depending on outside established agencies, wherever possible, to carry out the aims of the Fund." He concluded his letter to Hoover by stating, "I have confidence that the Fund can serve an important purpose. . . . The time is ripe for action. There is urgent need in our country for immediate practical and substantial assistance to aviation in its commercial, industrial and scientific aspects. No less urgent is the need to awaken the American public, especially our business men, to the advantages and possibilities of commercial aircraft—in a word to make the American public in a very real sense 'air-wise.' "[9]

During the January 15 meeting with Harry Guggenheim, Herbert Hoover gave final approval to the fund's plans and, to assist Harry Guggenheim during a trip to Europe to study the European aviation scene, he prepared and sent letters to the State Department and the various American commercial attachés in Europe.[10] Harry Guggenheim planned the tour in conjunction with Rear Admiral Cone, but before leaving he still had to get the fund underway. On January 18, Guggenheim Brothers announced creation of The Daniel Guggenheim Fund for the Promotion of Aeronautics, reprinting the letter to Hoover in full. In a news release entitled "Status of Civil Aviation," the Guggenheims stated that with the exception of the airmail service, the United States lagged behind European nations in commercial air service. As of 1926, European nations flew five hundred commercial planes in regular service over 14,200 miles of air routes whereas in the United States aircraft manufacturers were "almost exclusively engaged" in producing military warplanes. To match the European investment proportionately, the United States would require five thousand airplanes, an investment of $100 million. Paradoxically, the Department of Commerce had found the conditions in the United States "the most favorable in the world for commercial aviation," because of the nation's political unification, geography, lack of customs and border restrictions, and generally better weather than over European air routes.[11] On January 19, 1926, The Daniel Guggenheim Fund for the Promotion of Aeronautics filed a certificate of incorporation with the New York secretary of state at Albany, stating its purpose as "the advancement of aeronautics within the United States of America." To attain its goals, the fund could acquire property, build aircraft, conduct lectures and issue publications, and extend financial aid or other assistance to any individuals, agencies, or associations working to advance aeronautics in the United States.[12]

A week later the board of directors of the fund held its first meeting. During the meeting board members elected Harry F. Guggenheim president of the fund, and Rear Adm. Hutchinson I. Cone as vice-president. At this meeting, Harry Guggenheim offered a plan which he had been working on with his father and Alexander Klemin since the early fall of 1925. This plan subsequently served as the guide for future fund activities. He divided the area the fund should investigate into education, scientific research, commercial development, and educational information. Under education he urged the popularization of aviation in the schools by loaning educational films, adding aeronautical construction to manual training classes, encouraging the building of display and flying model aircraft, and promoting gliding.* University instructors could lecture seniors in civil and mechanical engineering courses on aerodynamics and aircraft design, the design of airports, preparation of landing fields, and aerial surveying. The fund could endow chairs of aeronautics in other sections of the country, especially the West Coast, "inasmuch as there is practically no aeronautical instruction available west of Michigan."[13] Harry Gug-

---

* Guggenheim's advocacy of gliding as a method of encouraging airmindedness in youth is interesting insomuch as gliding in Weimar, Germany, served to provide aeronautical training to young men who later, under more favorable political conditions, spearheaded the growth of the Nazi *Luftwaffe*.

genheim estimated it would require at least seven years before the industry would feel the education impact of the fund, since at least a year would elapse before the fund could establish a chair, then four years before the school graduated its first students, and then roughly two years before the graduates located themselves firmly in positions of responsibility within the industry. Finally, the fund could encourage prize competitions for papers, donate special apparatus and equipment for aeronautical engineering training and education, assist in the trade school instruction of mechanics, publish bulletins and special texts, and offer fellowships for study at both domestic and foreign institutions and companies.[14]

Harry Guggenheim believed that the fund should not attempt to create its own scientific research organization, since such an organization naturally tends to build its bureaucratic structure at the expense of specific research activities. He suggested the fund investigate helicopter development, and also methods of enabling a plane to fly safely in fog, or fly "blind," by means of radio direction finders and "leader cables."[15] The fund could further support aeronautical research via research grants. To aid commercial development, Harry Guggenheim suggested that the fund hold design competitions with prizes for the best-designed and most efficient commercial aircraft. Further, the fund could draw up specifications for an ideal commercial air transport aircraft, and contract for its design with a company, or hold a design competition. Finally, in disseminating educational information, the fund could set up lectures, publish booklets, circulate a regularly issued bulletin to libraries, schools, colleges, newspapers, and magazines, and, in general, act as an aeronautical information clearing house.[16] Subsequently, the fund engaged, to a greater and lesser extent, in all of these activities and endeavors.

The aeronautical community warmly greeted creation of the fund. The authoritative journal *Aviation* declared that "the gift of $2,500,000 made by Daniel Guggenheim . . . is an act which can only be received with the warmest appreciation from the air fraternity as a whole."[17] Secretary of Commerce Hoover thanked Daniel Guggenheim for his "magnificent gift to the American people," and in a Commerce Department release stated that the Guggenheim fund "will, I am confident, produce great benefits to the whole art and to the country as a whole. Neither the Government nor private industry can more than enter the borderland of fundamental scientific research. . . . Mr. Guggenheim has made it possible for our scientists to explore many fields of physics which would otherwise remain unknown at least for many years."[18] Immediately, inventors, educators, aircraft designers, pilots, and often plain cranks, began writing to the fund and to the Department of Commerce requesting information, offering proposals, and, most frequently, asking for money.[19]

On February 2, 1926, the fund directors authorized Harry Guggenheim and Rear Adm. Hutchinson Cone to visit European aviation establishments.[20] Guggenheim left first, and Cone departed the United States a few days later; they did not return to the states until about April 28, 1926. Guggenheim and Cone, not always together, observed the aeronautical situation in England, France, Spain, Germany, and Holland. While in England, they arranged for Cmdr. Jerome C. Hunsaker, USN, then naval attaché at the American embassy in London, to tour Italy and report to the fund about aeronautical developments there. Cone and Guggenheim met with virtually all the major aircraft manufacturers, designers, and aviation administrators in Europe. Indeed, even a partial roster of the individuals interviewed by Cone and Guggenheim is a veritable "Who's Who" of European aviation in 1926. In England, for example, they met Frank Courtney, C. F. Fairey, Charles G. Grey, Sir Richard Glazebrook, Frederick Handley Page, Geoffrey de Havilland, Geoffrey T. R. Hill, Prof. Bennett Melvill Jones, R. H. Mayo, Sir Philip Sassoon, and Hugh O. Short. While in Holland they met with A. G. von Baumhauer and Frederick Koolhoven, and in Germany they saw Adolf Rohrbach, Ludwig Prandtl, Georg Madelung, and Dr. Claude Dornier. In France they interviewed among others, Henri Bouche, Charles Dollfus, and Louis Breguet. In Spain they conversed with Emilio Herrera and Juan de la Cierva, the brilliant designer of the Autogiro. These are simply the most outstanding of the more than one hundred people whom Guggenheim and Cone interviewed and questioned. After touring Europe individually, Cone and Guggenheim met in March to reexamine those facilities that particularly interested them.[21]

While sailing back to the United States in late April 1926, Harry Guggenheim sat in his cabin and prepared a report to present to the directors of the fund. Generally, the European universities had not impressed Guggenheim or Cone as being markedly superior to American schools in regard to aeronautical education. "The present infant state of the industry throughout the world has discouraged the training of aeronautical engineers," Guggenheim concluded.[22] Only Germany had more centers of aeronautical training than the

United States, but the training did not appear superior. In laboratories and research facilities, Europe seemed inferior to the United States, but in the numbers of trained scientists engaged in aeronautical research, Europe far outnumbered the United States. Guggenheim was particularly impressed by Prof. Ludwig Prandtl of Göttingen, Germany's—and Europe's—foremost aeronautical scientist, and a pioneer since 1901 in wind-tunnel research and theoretical aerodynamics. "He carries on a large part of the important fundamental aeronautical research work in Germany with the assistance of postgraduate students who come to study under his guidance," Guggenheim wrote. "In this manner he has developed and continues to develop highly trained research workers. The United States would seem to have need of such a center. This is difficult of attainment because its success would be dependent upon the scientist about whom such a center were created." [23]

Despite the large-scale commercial aircraft operations in Europe, Guggenheim found much at fault in the European air transport system. The principal failing, he believed, was the government subsidy, whereby all European airlines received government funding to make up for losses and lack of revenue. While acknowledging that the subsidies were responsible for keeping many of the air carriers in business, Guggenheim concluded that they stifled the incentive required for the development of new and specialized transport aircraft. Operators were content to operate older and even war-surplus equipment rather than design new aircraft with improved reliability and comfort. There were other failings as well. The short air routes could not compete with established road, rail, and water transport. National boundaries cut all the major European air routes. The poor winter weather curtailed flight operations during several months each year. As in America, Guggenheim found that the average European viewed the airplane with skepticism and distrust. Indeed, the lack of air transport revenue in the winter months was due not only to weather but also to the absence of American tourists in that season: Guggenheim surprisingly discovered that "Americans comprise a far greater percentage of the total passengers carried than do the people of any other nation." [24]

On the basis of his European trip, Harry Guggenheim listed thirty-five areas in which The Daniel Guggenheim Fund for the Promotion of Aeronautics could assist aviation development. The fund subsequently undertook most of the projects he had suggested. Among the more noteworthy suggestions made by Guggenheim were the promotion of international meetings and exchange programs of European and American scientists, locating a scientist "of ability bordering on genius" and inviting him to the United States to direct a research facility, encouraging research on fog and blind flying, and financing transatlantic seaplane passenger service. He also suggested that the fund bring an outstanding meteorological scientist to the United States to advise and develop a national meteorological service for aviation, publish a handbook of aeronautical science, establish an international library and scientific information exchange center at the Aero Club de France, in Paris, and assist other European aero societies such as the Royal Aeronautical Society in Great Britain.[25]

Current aeronautical research and development work in Europe deeply impressed Harry Guggenheim, particularly devices that promised to reduce aircraft landing speeds and increase airplane stability. The potential of these developments convinced him to propose that the fund organize a "safe plane" competition with prizes for aircraft having the lowest landing and stalling speeds, best control at low speeds, and the ability to take off and land in a confined space. This became one of the most important of the fund's activities, and served really as the first international competition for what future engineers termed STOL (short-takeoff-and-landing) aircraft. The impetus came about through meetings Harry Guggenheim and Rear Admiral Cone held with four leading European designers and aerodynamicists, Frederick Handley Page, Geoffrey T. R. Hill, Geoffrey de Havilland, and Juan de la Cierva. These men had all undertaken research to improve the low-speed stability and control characteristics of aircraft. They had arrived at three separate conclusions, however, as to what solutions or improvements seemed best. These were the wing slat and flap, the tailless airplane configuration, and the Autogiro.

The wing slat and flap, tailless configuration, and Autogiro subsequently exerted great influence on aircraft design and operation. Handley Page and de Havilland favored the wing slat placed on the leading edge of the wing. When a plane slowed and increased its nose-high angle of attack, the slat would automatically extend, forming a gap or slot between the slat and the wing. The slat, in effect a little wing itself, prevented the air moving over the top of the wing from breaking away from the wing surface in turbulence and causing an increase in drag, a decrease in lift, and possibly leading to a stalled condition, in which the plane would simply stop flying and start to drop. With the slat, this disagreeable sequence of events would not occur until the plane reached a much lower speed and/or a much steeper angle of attack. A 1926 biplane without a slat might stall at 50 mph. With a slat, its stall speed might be reduced to 35 mph. Another addition was the trailing edge flap, in its simplest form, simply a hinged portion of the trailing edge of the wing that pivoted downwards when activated. This served to increase the camber of the wing, and thus its lift, further lowering takeoff and landing speeds. These two methods of direct lift control, the slat and flap, appeared singly, but often together, on every subsequent STOL aircraft design.[26]

Geoffrey T. R. Hill and Juan de la Cierva came up with more radical solutions. G. T. R. Hill, an engineer who flew as a test pilot during the First World War, believed that the average airplane was inefficient, in that it had a weight-increasing and drag-producing collection of tail surfaces which ensured stability and control. Accordingly, he designed a tailless airplane, the Pterodactyl, in 1925, to demonstrate the aerodynamic efficiency that could be achieved by this type design. It featured a sharply swept wing to put the wing control surfaces behind the plane's center of gravity and to allow for the shifting of the plane's center of pressure during flight.* Like the pioneering tailless biplanes of John W. Dunne in 1914, Hill's Pterodactyl, which first flew in 1924, had the added advantage of being inherently stable during its flights. Realizing that the Royal Air Force lost, on an average, fifty pilots killed per year due to pilot error, Hill stated that "I set myself to try to design an aeroplane which would never, through an error on the part of the pilot, get out of control."[27] While in England at the Royal Aircraft Establishment at Farnborough, Cone and Guggenheim met Hill and saw his prototype Pterodactyl in flight. Concerned with the number of American fatalities occurring in crashes caused by stalling at low speeds, Cone and Guggenheim viewed the stall-free Pterodactyl with favor, and Harry Guggenheim recommended that the fund finance an American demonstration tour of Hill's tailless airplane.[28]

The wing slat and flap and the tailless airplane all attempted to alleviate the danger of the stall. If a plane stalled at high altitude, the pilot could recover with no difficulty. At low altitude, however, a stalled airplane could mush, dive, or spin into the ground before it picked up enough speed for its controls to regain aerodynamic effectiveness. Juan de la Cierva, however, set out to design an airplane that would never crash no matter how low its speed. The result was the

* Hill, at the behest of the Air Ministry, later joined the Westland Aircraft Works and produced a succession of advanced Pterodactyls, the Mk. IA, IB, IV, and V. The Mk. IV even had variable wing sweep, whereby the wing could sweep forwards or backwards to improve trim, and was fully aerobatic. Tailless aircraft, like Hill's and the later flying wing designs of John Northrop, never succeeded in overcoming the suspicions and lack of confidence generated by their freakish appearance.

Autogiro, a predecessor of the helicopter that showed much promise, but came to a disappointing end.

Cierva, the son of a wealthy Spanish family and a mathematician of exceptional talent, had designed a large trimotor biplane bomber for the Spanish Army in 1919. It completed several successful flights when its test pilot, with an exuberance born of overconfidence, entered a tight turn at low altitude. The plane stalled and crashed, without injury to the pilot. Cierva debated leaving aviation altogether and going back to civil engineering. What bothered him most was that such a little error should have such a bad effect. He decided to develop an airplane that could fly as slowly as possible yet still not be in danger of crashing from stalling, by utilizing a large free-wheeling rotor mounted on top of an airplane fuselage. The plane would have a conventional piston engine and propeller to drive it through the air. Even if the piston engine failed, and the Autogiro descended straight down, the air passing through the rotor would cause it to spin and produce lift, so that the Autogiro would descend gently to earth. Unlike a helicopter, in which the engine is connected to the rotor, the Autogiro had a free wheeling rotor. This prevented it from achieving true vertical ascents from the ground, though later techniques involving pre-spinning the rotor prior to lift-off via a clutch to the engine enabled the Autogiro to make "jump" starts. Likewise, it could not hover motionless in the air. Cierva also incorporated hinges at the roots of the rotor blades to compensate for differences in the lift generated by the advancing and retreating blades. This gave the machine automatic stability, and was the answer helicopter designers had awaited for years.[29]

Cierva's first successful Autogiro, piloted by Lt. Alejandro Spencer, completed its maiden flight at Getafe Aerodrome outside Madrid on January 9, 1923. It was the most significant flight since that of the Wright brothers, for it opened up the whole sphere of rotary-wing flight. Cierva introduced the Autogiro to England in 1925, and in October, British test pilot Frank Courtney demonstrated it before Air Ministry officials at Farnborough. The tests were successful, although during one vertical descent with the engine off, the Autogiro picked up sufficient vertical speed to smash its landing gear.[30] During Cone and Guggenheim's trip to Europe, both men saw Courtney demonstrate the Autogiro at Farnborough, and they had the opportunity to interview Cierva. As with Hill's tailless airplane, Guggenheim recommended that the fund sponsor an American tour of the Autogiro. As events turned out, the Pitcairn and Kellett concerns in the United States proceeded with Autogiro development, making the fund's participation unnecessary.* When The Daniel Guggenheim Fund for the Promotion of Aeronautics hosted its safe airplane competition in 1929, Harry Guggenheim and other organizers hoped to have at least one Autogiro entry; unfortunately, this did not come to pass.[31]

While in Europe, Cone and Guggenheim also sought out foreign consultants who could aid the fund in its various endeavors. They asked several individuals to serve as foreign representatives of the fund. The men chosen were Maj. R. H. Mayo of Great Britain, an engineer; Charles Dollfus of France, a noted aeronautical historian and balloonist; Georg Madelung of the Deutsche Versuchsanstalt für Luftfahrt; and A. G. von Baumhauer of Holland, an aeronautical engineer. The fund arranged for the Associazione Italiana di Aerotecnica, an Italian aviation society, to direct its Italian affairs. These representatives served to promote knowledge of the fund, collect information for the fund, and disseminate publications and information provided by the fund to interested Europeans. During the four-year life of the fund, some of these individuals died or resigned and were replaced. The most influential foreign representative was R. H. Mayo, who undertook numerous studies, research projects, and investigations for the fund. He played a leading role in subsequent Guggenheim safe aircraft discussions, and wrote an official history of the fund that served as the basis for Reginald Cleveland's *America Fledges Wings*.[32]

On the eve of his departure from England for the United States, Harry Guggenheim told R. H. Mayo that "safety was the vital necessity to civil aviation."[33] This became the dominant theme of future fund activities. Guggenheim circulated his report on the European tour to the fund directors when he and Rear Admiral Cone returned to New York. Guggenheim's call for "reasonable though strict govern-

---

* The Autogiro offered much promise, and the Cierva company in Great Britain, together with Pitcairn and Kellett companies in the United States, undertook much development work with them in the late 1920s. Herbert Hoover, while president, became very interested in the Autogiro, and once invited Assistant Secretary of the Navy for Aeronautics David Ingalls to fly one up to his retreat at Rapidan for the weekend. Ingalls flew up in a Pitcairn OP-1 and demonstrated it for the president making flights with the president's son Herbert Hoover, Jr., as a passenger. (Ingalls interview, Hoover oral history project, Hoover Library.) Yet the Autogiro, the potential solution to the stall accident, never developed enough support to be used widely. Ironically, Juan de la Cierva died in an airliner crash at Croyden airport, outside London, on Dec. 9, 1936, when an airplane in which he was a passenger took off, *stalled*, and crashed. With the principal champion of the Autogiro gone, its development languished. The next stage in the rotary revolution belonged to Igor Sikorsky and his helicopter.

mental control" was answered within a month by congressional passage of the Air Commerce Act of 1926, inspired by the Morrow Board and signed into law on May 20. It created an Aeronautics Branch within the Department of Commerce, and the new position of Assistant Secretary of Commerce for Aeronautics. It required the licensing by written and flight examinations of private and transport pilots, and the certification of all aircraft. Hoover appointed William P. MacCracken, Jr., a World War I aviator and a graduate of the University of Chicago Law School, as the Department of Commerce's Assistant Secretary for Aeronautics. He took office on August 11, 1926, and quickly earned a reputation as an administrator totally uncompromising on matters of air safety.[34]

While the passage of the Air Commerce Act of 1926 caused a de-emphasis in fund regulatory promotion, this was but one small part of the overall Guggenheim program. The European tour had given Cone and Guggenheim numerous ideas on improving American aeronautical education, promoting public confidence in air transport through reliability tours, and in sponsoring airway development, aeronautical research, and design competitions. On June 2, 1926, the fund directors gathered at 120 Broadway, in room 3454, for a special meeting. During the previous weeks, Cone, Davison, Durand, Wright, and Harry Guggenheim had met and discussed the European tour report. Some of the fund directors feared that too much emphasis on "safety" might reenforce public opinion that flying was indeed unsafe, thus damaging the cause of civil aviation. The majority believed that the American public was "extremely ignorant" about aviation, but that it had a strong predisposition to view flying as dangerous. Simply stating that flying was safe would not change public opinion, and thus it was necessary for the fund to educate the public to both the reasons for danger, as well as those for safety, in flying. One important part of this education could be the demonstration of devices such as the slat and flap, or aircraft such as the Autogiro, developed to minimize the danger of flying, and make commercial aviation safer.[35]

In a letter to board members issued the same day as the special meeting was held, Harry Guggenheim commented that the best way of securing safety in flying appeared to be the development of multi-engine aircraft that could fly safely with one engine not functioning, reducing stalling speeds, improving low-speed control and handling characteristics, perfecting inherently stable aircraft, perfecting navi-

gation and communication instruments, especially for fog and blind
flying, and reducing the fire hazard to aircraft. "The success of commercial aviation should be assured," Guggenheim wrote, "the day that
the public can be convinced not by statistics, but by actual demonstration that airplanes are inherently no more dangerous than steam-
ships or railroads."[36] "I recommend," Guggenheim stated, "that the
Fund adopt as its primary policy 'the Promotion of Safety in Aviation'
and that it concentrate its efforts towards every practicable means to
accomplish this purpose."[37] He than suggested that the fund open a
school of aeronautics on the West Coast, encourage research on fog
and blind flying, establish an international safe aircraft competition,
assist the British Royal Aeronautical Society in collecting and disseminating technical information, support other European aeronautical organizations, finance and publish a handbook on aeronautical
science, and publish a series of bulletins and pamphlets for public
aeronautical education.[38]

Board members had already generally approved these recommendations by Harry Guggenheim, which were really the most important
ideas presented earlier in his European tour report. At the special
meeting on June 2, 1926, then, the board of directors gave their unan-
imous approval to his proposal that the primary policy of the fund
be the promotion of safety in aviation. At that same meeting, the directors undertook a host of other projects, including endowing two
schools of aeronautical engineering on the West Coast, approving
plans for a safe aircraft competition, encouraging development of
blind flying instrumentation and navigational equipment, issuing
grants to the Royal Aeronautical Society and the Aero Club de France,
and establishing a fund to allow publication of bulletins and pamphlets.[39] The growth of The Daniel Guggenheim Fund for the Promotion of Aeronautics had reached the point where it could, and did,
branch out in numerous directions simultaneously. Subsequent activities of the fund would involve education, commercial development, research, and aeronautical promotion.

CHAPTER 4

The Beginning of National
Aeronautical Engineering Education:
The Seven Major
Guggenheim University Grants, 1926-30

BETWEEN 1926 and 1930, The Daniel Guggenheim Fund for the Promotion of Aeronautics established six schools of aeronautical engineering within the United States. The fund also sponsored creation of an aviation law institute, and a university-supported airship research institute. Further, the fund created a special aeronautical education committee for elementary and secondary schools, and awarded grants to graduate students and faculty members at various institutions enabling them to study abroad, conduct independent research, or teach special aviation-related courses. This was an elaboration on the earlier creation of the Daniel Guggenheim School of Aeronautics at New York University. By mid-century, almost all of America's senior aeronautical engineers were graduates of these Guggenheim-sponsored schools.

In his letter to Herbert Hoover announcing the creation of The Daniel Guggenheim Fund for the Promotion of Aeronautics, Daniel Guggenheim had written that the fund would undertake "to promote aeronautical education in both institutions of learning and among the general public."[1] Almost immediately, the fund received numerous letters from interested faculty members at colleges and universities across the country. A. A. Potter, the dean of engineering at Purdue University, for example, wrote to Harry F. Guggenheim asking that the fund consider Purdue when choosing the academic beneficiaries of Daniel Guggenheim's philanthropy.[2] But Purdue, like most schools that contacted the fund, had no background in aircraft engineering. Though the second largest engineering college in the United States, just behind the Massachusetts Institute of Technology, Purdue had no courses in aeronautical engineering, nor, apparently, anyone save

Dean Potter interested in the subject. Purdue's forte was locomotive engineering, and in this field it led the world.[3] Of necessity, then, The Daniel Guggenheim Fund for the Promotion of Aeronautics turned first to those institutions that had already expressed an interest in aeronautical education through faculty- or student-sponsored courses or research projects. For a start, the fund concentrated on three midwestern and western schools, the California Institute of Technology, Leland Stanford University, and the University of Michigan.

The geographical location of these schools played an important part in determining the fund's policy towards them. As of January 1926, only six schools offered much course work in aeronautical engineering: New York University, the Massachusetts Institute of Technology, Caltech, Stanford, the University of Washington, and the University of Michigan. Only NYU, MIT, and Michigan had degree programs. Michigan, located far away from aeronautical industry centers, had a surprisingly advanced program, and Caltech, Stanford, and the University of Washington each had interested faculty offering some courses and conducting research. Both Daniel and Harry Guggenheim quickly recognized that the Midwest and the West Coast were areas where the fund could assist interested students in finding an aeronautical education. Already some manufacturers were located on the West Coast, especially William Boeing at Seattle, Washington, and Donald W. Douglas at Santa Monica, California. Clearly, western aviation concerns would increase. Proper educational facilities would stimulate this increase, and furnish the growing industry with well-trained engineers.

Even before the creation of The Daniel Guggenheim Fund for the Promotion of Aeronautics, Dr. Robert A. Millikan, chairman of the Executive Council of the California Institute of Technology, had written to Harry F. Guggenheim suggesting that the Guggenheims endow a school of aeronautics at Caltech. Millikan, a distinguished physicist who had won the Nobel Prize for 1923 for isolating and measuring the charge on an electron, had come to the California Institute of Technology from the University of Chicago in 1921, determined to increase Caltech's national stature. During World War I he had served as vice-chairman of the National Research Council and as chief of the science and research division, U.S. Army Signal Corps. Millikan contacted Harry Guggenheim late in December 1925, after having discussed plans for an aeronautical laboratory at Caltech with

Gen. John J. Carty, who had worked with the Guggenheims in establishing the school of aeronautics at New York University.[4]

Millikan urged Harry Guggenheim to persuade his father to endow a school of aeronautics at Caltech because of the school's outstanding reputation in physics—under Millikan's direction, the Norman Bridge Laboratory of Caltech had already become one of the world centers of physical research—and because of a core of interested faculty and students pursuing aeronautical training, including Millikan's own son Clark. The school already had a small four-foot-square wind tunnel capable of generating 40 mph velocities used for preliminary research. Finally, the school was close to existing aircraft manufacturing companies, especially the Douglas Aircraft Company, and the good weather conditions prevailing in Southern California ensured that the aeronautical industry around Los Angeles and Pasadena would continue to expand.[5] In support, he submitted a letter from Donald W. Douglas, one of the nation's leading airplane manufacturers, who wrote, "We find innumerable cases where if facilities were handy for test and research work, we would avail ourselves of them. As it is now we do not do as much of such work as we should as it is cumbersome because of distance and other obstacles to have it done at existing Eastern laboratories."[6] Millikan proposed that the school investigate aircraft stability and control, autogiro development, aircraft drag characteristics, airplane stress analysis, and wing slot and slat behavior.[7]

Caltech already had a small core group of instructors interested in aeronautics. Harry Bateman and Richard Tolman were highly trained physicists, and Albert A. Merrill was largely a self-taught inventor. The three men represented the joining of an inventive Baconian tradition with a theoretical and Platonic pure-science approach; Millikan himself constantly stressed that the time of the practical inventor in aviation had largely ended, and that well-trained scientists and engineers must take his place.[8] Merrill had helped form the Boston Aeronautical Society in 1895, and served as its secretary-treasurer. In 1913 he had given a series of lectures on aviation at the Massachusetts Institute of Technology, the first aeronautical instruction ever offered at that school.[9] Four years later he joined the Throop College of Technology, the former name of Caltech, and built a small wind tunnel at the school. Merrill was one of the lesser known yet more intriguing of America's aeronautical pioneers. Theodore von Kármán, Caltech's later aeronautical director, alleged that Merrill and Bateman did not discuss aeronautics because of their different backgrounds, the one a practical inventor who did not care for mathematics, and the other a Cambridge-trained mathematician who specialized in fluid mechanics.[10] Merrill championed development of an inherently stable aircraft whereby the plane's center of gravity could be shifted for trimming purposes by increasing the angle of attack of the wings relative to the plane's fuselage via pivots at the wing roots. He built such an aircraft, a single-engine "stagger decalage" biplane, and test-flew it, but a fire at Caltech's aeronautics laboratory on July 24, 1927, destroyed the plane, and brought his research to an end. From 1918 to 1926, Merrill, Bateman, and Tolman offered limited aeronautical engineering courses to interested students, including Robert Millikan's son, Clark, a Yale Ph.D. in physics. Neither a department of aeronautical engineering nor an aeronautical engineering degree program existed.[11]

On January 6, 1926, ten days before the creation of the Guggenheim fund, Robert Millikan met with Harry and Daniel Guggenheim in New York. He proposed that the Guggenheims grant the California Institute of Technology $500,000 to develop and maintain a permanent aeronautical research center. The annual interest on the half-million dollars, $27,000 per year, would enable Caltech to hire two research professors, a wind-tunnel operator and wind-tunnel model maker, and four graduate students. Cautiously, both Guggenheims indicated their interest and general support of such a grant, without discussing specific financing.[12] Millikan kept in contact with Harry Guggenheim and fund vice-president Hutchinson Cone during their tour of Europe, and met with the two men in New York on April 30, 1926, after their return. At this meeting, he reiterated his contention that because of the outstanding caliber of Caltech's physics faculty, and because of its close proximity to growing centers of aircraft production, the Guggenheim fund should endow the school. He proposed, however, that instead of just hiring faculty, the fund also support equipment purchases including installation of a ten-foot diameter wind tunnel for research, a model shop, and a testing laboratory. Then the Guggenheim fund could endow an annual grant of $10,000 for ten years for hiring faculty and meeting expenses. Already Millikan's son Clark, together with Arthur L. Klein, had undertaken to design the tunnel.[13] After listening to the proposals Millikan offered, Harry Guggenheim suggested that Millikan put his ideas in a letter which Guggenheim could then submit to the fund trustees for official action. Millikan did so on May 14 in a letter which stated "very splendidly and fully the case of the California Institute of Technology."[14] Millikan then awaited official action by the Guggenheims.

Complicating the potential grant to Caltech were coincidental discussions between officials at Leland Stanford University and the Guggenheims over grants to that school. Like Caltech, Stanford had a respectable reputation in the field of engineering. Thirty-five years old in 1926, Stanford had a general endowment of $28 million. Its outstanding aeronautical engineering advocate was Dr. William F. Durand, a sixty-seven-year-old retired mechanical engineering professor who had conducted aeronautical research at Stanford since 1916. Durand had served on the Morrow Board and on the National Advisory Committee for Aeronautics. In 1916 he had persuaded officials at Stanford to build a special wind tunnel for propeller research as an adjunct to the mechanical engineering department. Together with Stanford professor E. P. Lesley, Durand had conducted numerous tests and research on aircraft propellers for a decade. The wind tunnel had a diameter of eight feet, was of open circuit design, and could produce a 90 mph air stream. Inside the tunnel throat was a long cast aluminum housing containing an electric motor that would rotate a test propeller mounted on an extension shaft at the end of the streamlined housing. It could record airspeed, air density, and propeller thrust, torque, and rotation speed. By 1926, Stanford had submitted twelve reports on aircraft propellers to NACA, and four more, covering research on more than sixty different designs, to the Army Air Service at McCook Field. Harry and Daniel Guggenheim well knew the reputation of William Durand, for he was a member of the Guggenheim fund trustees. They were most receptive, therefore, when Stanford president Dr. Ray Lyman Wilbur wrote to the fund in May 1926, requesting a grant of $330,000 to acquire research instrumentation, and to hire an aerodynamicist, a mathematical physicist, and a structural engineer.[15]

On June 2, 1926, during the fund's first meeting after Harry Guggenheim's trip to Europe, Harry Guggenheim brought before the board of directors the letters of Robert Millikan and Ray Lyman Wilbur requesting grants for Caltech and Stanford. During the discussion that followed, board members expressed general approval of the grants, stipulating only that the grants providing for faculty salaries be for a limited number of years rather than perpetual endowments. The board then unanimously approved in principle that The Daniel Guggenheim Fund for the Promotion of Aeronautics appropriate $500,000 for creation of a school of aeronautics at the California Institute of Technology and to assist in development of a school at Stanford.[16] Five days later Harry Guggenheim notified both Millikan and Wilbur of the board's action.[17]

Guggenheim's and Millikan's plans for endowing Caltech were

more advanced at this point than those providing for Stanford. Guggenheim had already notified Millikan that the fund had whittled down Millikan's request for $500,000 to $305,000, consisting of $180,000 for a laboratory building, wind tunnel, and equipment; $100,000 for a professorship paying $10,000 per year for ten years; and $25,000 for research funds of $5,000 per year for five years. Because Caltech would be virtually starting from scratch on its laboratory and school, it received a proportionately larger grant than Stanford, which already had a modest laboratory. The Guggenheims planned to grant Stanford $195,000, but this was still exceptionally generous. Stanford's candidate for directorship, Prof. E. P. Lesley, had assumed control of the university's aeronautical research after Durand's retirement. Caltech, however, was another matter. Here Harry Guggenheim saw the chance, expressed in his European report, of creating an aeronautical research center directed by some European scientist of outstanding reputation.

Robert Millikan already had in mind just the man for the Caltech school: he was Dr. Theodore von Kármán, professor at the Technische Hochschule at Aachen, Germany, and, next to Ludwig Prandtl himself, the most outstanding aeronautical scientist in Europe. Von Kármán, who, until his death in 1963, played a leading role in American aeronautical research, was a man with catholic interests. A stocky Hungarian Jew of medium height, von Kármán was multilingual, could converse knowledgeably on music, art, and literature, and possessed unusual mathematical ability. He contributed seminal papers in many fields, including aerodynamics, hydrodynamics, strength of materials, and jet propulsion. During the First World War, while serving in the Austrian air service, von Kármán had developed a tethered helicopter, one of the world's first. After the war, he helped start sport gliding in Germany and directed aerodynamic research at Aachen. Von Kármán had already met Robert Millikan once, when the physicist visited Europe shortly after joining Caltech. At that time, Paul Sophus Epstein, a close friend of von Kármán and one of many talented physicists whom Millikan had lured to Caltech, urged Millikan to bring the Hungarian scientist to Caltech.[18]

Millikan discussed with Harry and Daniel Guggenheim the idea of bringing von Kármán to the United States to examine American aeronautical research facilities. The father and son quickly assented. Accordingly, in mid-summer 1926, Millikan telegraphed von Kármán and asked him to meet with the Guggenheims in New York, and then visit Caltech. Von Kármán, who had already planned a trip to Japan for the same purpose, consented to visit the United States between

September and Christmas, 1926.[19] Millikan informed Harry Guggenheim by letter on July 7 that he had arranged for von Kármán to visit the United States and examine the aerodynamic research facilities at Caltech and Stanford, as well as those at New York University and the Massachusetts Institute of Technology.[20] On July 13, Millikan again wrote to Harry Guggenheim, announcing that the trustees of the California Institute of Technology had approved the aeronautical program submitted by the fund for the development of Caltech's aeronautics training.[21] Guggenheim responded that he would persuade von Kármán to deliver a series of lectures on aeronautics in the United States to serve "as a stimulus to investigators, teachers, and advanced students in this field."[22] At the same time, Harry Guggenheim telegraphed William Durand at Stanford, notifying Durand that Caltech's trustees had approved the proposed grant, and asking that Stanford's trustees expedite their negotiations so that, if all went well, the Guggenheim fund could announce simultaneously the grants to Caltech and Stanford. Durand agreed that it was "very desirable, in fact really essential that the publicity regarding the two schools should appear simultaneously."[23] Apparently Durand feared that release of the Caltech grant prior to the Stanford announcement might possibly lure potential students away from Stanford to Caltech. Simultaneous release, on the other hand, would emphasize the complementary nature of the aeronautic programs at the two schools.

From this point, events moved swiftly. Ray Lyman Wilbur asked Harry Guggenheim for a grant of $195,000, as Guggenheim had proposed, consisting of an annual grant for ten years of $15,000 per year, $30,000 for purchase of test equipment, and $15,000 for enlarging the existing aeronautical research building on campus.[24] Guggenheim took the matter up with the fund's executive committee at the beginning of August 1926, and by August 6, the executive committee of trustees had agreed to endow the two schools. Though fund president Harry Guggenheim telegraphed the news to Wilbur and Millikan, and the fund issued a special bulletin, official notification of the endowments did not come until after a special meeting of the fund trustees on August 24, 1926.[25] Then, Harry Guggenheim wrote letters of formal notification to Robert A. Millikan and Ray Lyman Wilbur, announcing creation of the Daniel Guggenheim Graduate School of Aeronautics at Caltech, and the Daniel Guggenheim Experimental Laboratory of Aerodynamics and Aeronautical Engineering at Stanford.[26] Public announcement followed on September 6, when the journal *Aviation* published the details of the two grants.[27] As with the earlier grant to New York University, the public announcement of the Caltech and Stanford endowments generated favorable comment from the aeronautical community.

By early September, the Guggenheim fund had already announced the impending arrival of Theodore von Kármán in the United States. The Hungarian aeronautical scientist arrived in New York aboard the S.S. *Mauretania* on September 24, together with his sister Josephine "Pipo" von Kármán. Rear Adm. Hutchinson Cone, the Guggenheim fund's vice-president, met them on the pier and took them to Daniel Guggenheim's estate at Port Washington. During a weekend stay on Long Island with Daniel Guggenheim, von Kármán casually remarked that America lacked a café tradition—American scientists did not meet informally at cafés to discuss problems and difficulties in their work, as did their European counterparts. This, he believed, hurt American scientific research. Daniel Guggenheim, who had previously endorsed several of von Kármán's ideas, including publication of a series of engineering handbooks, now replied with a smile, "I will not enter the café business, even for science's sake."[28]

After leaving Hempstead House, von Kármán journeyed to Pasadena. There Harry Bateman, A. A. Merrill, Richard Tolman, Paul Epstein, Clark Millikan, and Arthur Klein showed von Kármán their plans for the new aeronautics center. Von Kármán approved the plans, but with some modifications. He changed the proposed design of the ten-foot wind tunnel from an open tunnel to a closed-circuit return-type tunnel similar to the one in operation at the Technische Hochschule. This tunnel, when completed in 1930, had an energy ratio (the kinetic energy of the airstream divided by the power input to the fan) of 5.6 to 1, indicating that the electric motor driving the wind-tunnel fan needed only to produce a small amount of power to generate a strong airstream. Capable of 200 mph test speeds, the tunnel was so efficient that NACA Director of Research, George W. Lewis, sent NACA observers to examine the tunnel during its operation.[29]

Von Kármán departed from Caltech in mid-October 1926, and returned to the East Coast, investigating various schools on the way that the Guggenheims had supported or were considering for endowments. These schools included the University of Michigan, the Massachusetts Institute of Technology, and the Guggenheim school being readied for opening at New York University.[30] Finally, he arrived in Washington, D.C., where from December 3 to December 13, he presented a series of six lectures on advanced aerodynamics, including discussion of propeller theory, boundary layer formation, induced airframe drag, and air resistance, in a program chaired by Edward P. Warner, Assistant Secretary of the Navy for Aeronautics, and held at the New Museum Building (now the Museum of Natural History) of the Smithsonian Institution. The lectures drew large audiences composed of individuals within the federal government, private industry, and the academic world, and served to focus the attention of the whole aeronautical community on the importance of systematic research to advance the aviation sciences.[31] Von Kármán, his American reputation now considerably enhanced, left for Japan, to help that country establish its first major aeronautical research center.* By this time, however, the grants to Caltech and Stanford were old news; the Guggenheim fund had announced another education grant, this to the University of Michigan.

The University of Michigan was the first university in the country to offer a specialized four-year program leading to a bachelor of science degree in aeronautical engineering. It established an aeronautics department in 1916, and by 1926 had graduated over one hundred students, the majority of whom joined the aircraft industry.[32] The individuals who persuaded Dean Mortimer Cooley to create the department were Felix Pawlowski and Herbert Sadler. Pawlowski, known affectionately by his students as "Pavvy," had studied aeronautics under Prof. Lucien Marchis while doing graduate work in mechanical engineering at the University of Paris, and in 1910 he taught himself to fly in a Bleriot monoplane. In 1911 he came to the United States and attempted to secure a position as a professor of aeronautical engineering. Only the University of Michigan responded, and he moved to Ann Arbor—but as a teaching assistant in mechanical engineering with permission to give instruction in aeronautics. In 1916, Pawlowski, with Herbert Sadler, succeeded in persuading Dean Cooley to create a complete four-year B.S. program in aeronautics, taught in a reorganized Department of Naval Architecture, Marine Engineering, and Aeronautics. Pawlowski became assistant professor of mechanical engineering; together with Herbert Sadler and, later Ralph Upson and Edward Stalker, he taught courses in general aeronautics, theory and design of propellers, aeroplane design, theory of balloons and dirigibles, theory and design of kites,

* Von Kármán visited the United States briefly at the behest of Robert A. Millikan in 1928 to review the progress of the Guggenheim school at Caltech. In December 1929, he assumed the directorship of the Guggenheim Aeronautical Laboratory, California Institute of Technology, later world-famous as Caltech's GALCIT.

design of aerodromes and hangars, and advanced aeronautical research.[33]

Like Pawlowski, Herbert Sadler was a European, from England. His great-granduncle, James Sadler, was England's first balloonist, making an ascent on May 5, 1785, from Moulsey Hurst, accompanied by William Windham, M.P.[34] Sadler himself taught marine engineering at the University of Glasgow, where one of his fellow instructors was the British pioneer glider pilot Percy Pilcher, who, like his mentor Otto Lilienthal, died in a gliding accident. Sadler came to the United States shortly after the turn of the century, joined the faculty at Ann Arbor as a professor of naval architecture and marine engineering, and organized the University of Michigan Aero Club. When Felix Pawlowski arrived from France, Sadler joined forces with him to start a regular program of aeronautical instruction at Michigan. The university granted its first M.S.Ae.E., to William F. Gerhardt, in 1918; six years later he also received Michigan's first Sc.D. in aeronautical engineering. In the early 1920s, Edward A. Stalker and Ralph H. Upson joined Pawlowski and Sadler on the Michigan faculty. Stalker had received a B.S.Ae.E. from Michigan in 1919, and earned his master's in 1923. As an assistant professor, Stalker specialized in aircraft engine development, championing research on two-cycle engines. Ralph H. Upson, who held a mechanical engineering degree from Stevens Institute of Technology, joined the faculty as a lecturer in lighter-than-air vehicle design. He exerted much influence on subsequent American airship design, advocating the development of metal-clad external skin helium-filled airships, an idea that did not receive its deserved recognition at the time. By the mid-1920s, then, the University of Michigan had an advanced department of aeronautics taught by faculty members of unusual ability.[35]

Late in December 1925, Rear Adm. Hutchinson I. Cone wrote to Dean Mortimer E. Cooley of Michigan and to President Samuel W. Stratton of the Massachusetts Institute of Technology, asking that both men meet with him and explain the programs of aeronautical education at their schools so that Daniel Guggenheim could best decide how to utilize his proposed fund for the promotion of aeronautics. Though Cone did not mention the possibility of issuing grants to Michigan or MIT, the implication that the fund might make such endowments was clear.[36] Dean Cooley, an old friend of Cone—the two men had jointly established the Naval Postgraduate School in Engineering—invited Cone to visit Michigan, and the former naval officer did so after his return from Europe.

In mid-May, Harry Guggenheim, on Cone's advice, asked Herbert

Sadler to submit a report on aeronautical education at Michigan together with a proposal for future development and organization.[37] Sadler quickly responded, stating that the university needed to expand its interests to include research on aircraft design, air transportation, and aircraft operations. He submitted a detailed report in mid-July, suggesting that Michigan needed research professorships to permit faculty members to conduct their own research without the added burden of teaching; professorships in applied aeronautics, especially air transportation economics and airfield design; and research fellowships to provide graduate students as research assistants for the faculty. Beyond this Michigan required research instrumentation to complete its eight-foot 250-mph wind tunnel then being built, and a smaller high-speed tunnel for propeller research, and various machinery and tools for model fabrication.[38]

The Guggenheims, as they had done with Caltech and Stanford, now studied possibly endowing the University of Michigan and the Massachusetts Institute of Technology at the same time. MIT had also been in contact with the fund since late December 1925; whereas Michigan needed funds to complete its wind tunnel, MIT needed a laboratory building to house its existing wind tunnel and related research equipment. On October 26, 1926, during a special meeting of the board of directors of The Daniel Guggenheim Fund for the Promotion of Aeronautics, Harry F. Guggenheim asked the board members to approve grants to Michigan and MIT enabling those institutions to expand their facilities. The members gave their preliminary approval to granting Michigan an appropriation "not in excess" of $78,000, and granting MIT an appropriation "not in excess" of $200,000.[39] Harry Guggenheim notified Dean Mortimer Cooley and Michigan President Clarence C. Little the next day of the fund's action. The $78,000 provided $28,000 for the completion of the wind tunnel and new equipment, and $50,000 in installments of $5,000 per year for ten years to establish a Daniel Guggenheim Chair of Aeronautics.[40] The fund publicly announced the creation of the Daniel Guggenheim Professorship of Applied Aeronautics at the University of Michigan, together with the equipment grant, on December 2, 1926.[41]

By the end of 1926, then, the Guggenheim fund had already authorized grants totaling $578,000 to three universities. Since this exhausted the original $500,000 that Daniel Guggenheim had made available to the trustees in January 1926, fund president Harry Guggenheim requested another $600,000 from his father. Daniel, pleased with the fund's progress to date, lost no time in sending a check for that amount on December 16, 1926.[42] Earlier in the month, the fund trustees had elected Robert A. Millikan a fund trustee.[43] A month later, on January 16, 1927, the Guggenheim fund announced a grant of $230,000 to the Massachusetts Institute of Technology for an aeronautical engineering building.[44]

Like Michigan, the MIT grant came about through a letter from Rear Adm. Hutchinson Cone to MIT president Samuel W. Stratton on December 28, 1925. Late in January 1926, Stratton met with Cone and Harry Guggenheim at the fund headquarters in New York. During the meeting, he outlined the progress of aeronautics at MIT, stating the school's equipment and building deficiencies. Harry Guggenheim asked that Stratton submit a report to the fund on MIT's needs.[45] MIT's aeronautics department dated to the original lectures in aeronautics given by Albert A. Merrill in 1913. Even then, many faculty members at MIT recommended establishing an aeronautical laboratory at the school. MIT president Richard Maclaurin, a member of President William Howard Taft's National Aerodynamical Laboratory Commission formed in 1912, had recommended that the federal government establish a federal aeronautical laboratory near one of the nation's outstanding engineering schools; his implication that MIT should be the benefactor was clear.[46] The federal government, however, took no action on Maclaurin's suggestion.

During the same time, Frank Caldwell and Elisha Fales conducted propeller research at MIT under the direction of Gaetano Lanza, head of the department of mechanical engineering.[47] In 1913, Maclaurin arranged for Assistant Naval Constructor Jerome C. Hunsaker to teach courses on aerodynamics at the school. The next year, following a trip to European areonautical establishments, Hunsaker returned to MIT and directed construction of a four-foot wind tunnel based on one at the British National Physical Laboratory.[48] When Hunsaker left for active naval service in June 1916, Alexander Klemin replaced him; when Klemin left for army service, Edward P. Warner took his place. Warner later became one of the most important men in American aeronautics. A graduate from Harvard in 1916 and from MIT a year later, Warner was an outstanding mathematician. He joined NACA in 1919 and became its chief physicist and later director of flight research at Langley Memorial Aeronautical Laboratory, Hampton, Virginia. In 1920 he returned to MIT as an associate professor of aeronautical engineering, staying in Boston until mid-1926.

Students remembered him as a tall, friendly instructor, his suit pockets bulging with papers, who could perform intricate mathematics in his head far faster than the best pupils could with pencil and paper. In 1926, Coolidge appointed Warner as the first Assistant Secretary of the Navy for Aeronautics. Warner and Harry Guggenheim, through personal as well as business contacts, were close friends.[49]

In April 1926, Prof. Charles Fayette Taylor of MIT wrote to Harry Guggenheim. Taylor, a former chief engineer of the Wright Aeronautical Company who pioneered the development of stress coatings to indicate the forces and loads generated within the structure of an aircraft engine, wrote that the entire area of engine research was open for development. Taylor's letter deeply interested Guggenheim, who agreed with much of what Taylor said. Taylor advocated jet propulsion, writing, "It would seem that the present type of water-cooled powerplant is approaching the limit of its development, but that much remains to be done in the field of air-cooling and in the development of new types of powerplants such as the gas turbine. If the latter could be developed to the point of practical application it would seem to possess fundamental advantages in respect to mechanical simplicity and the ability to use fuel of low volatility."[50]

Taylor foresaw the potential of the jet engine, which revolutionized aircraft technology in the 1940s. In 1926, with aircraft flight speeds in the 150 mph range, the piston engine still seemed satisfactory, and the jet engine did not enter the thinking of any major aircraft engine manufacturers. Only a few diehard advocates, such as Taylor in the United States, Frank Whittle in Great Britain, Hans von Ohain in Germany, and Secundo Campini in Italy, pursued jet propulsion through the 1930s. Taylor was far more optimistic about the possibilities of jet flight than another early American jet investigator, Edgar Buckingham of the Bureau of Standards. It is counterfactual to argue what might have been, had Taylor pressed more vigorously for jet research, perhaps with a Guggenheim grant. The sad fact remains that by 1940 the United States was clearly in last place in turbojet research behind Great Britain, Germany, and Italy. A navy report as late as January 1941 stated that gas turbine propulsion was completely out of the question for aircraft, this despite the world's first turbojet flight in August 1939 by the German Heinkel He 178. When the United States did fly its first turbojet-powered aircraft, the Bell XP-59A Airacomet, in October 1942, it utilized two British-designed engines.[51]

The Massachusetts Institute of Technology during and after the First World War, had graduated a number of well-trained students who went on to occupy highly responsible positions within the government and aircraft industry. President Stratton, when he submitted his report on MIT's aeronautics program to the Guggenheim fund in late May 1926, alluded to this past record. Stratton wrote that MIT's chief need was a new building to house its wind tunnels. The tunnels were in deteriorating wooden sheds "good for but a year or two at best."[52] Further, the school needed more office space for classroom and staff use, the total cost for the new building and classroom and office space estimated at about $225,000. Stratton emphasized that MIT wished a balance between teaching and research. He believed that the school could best use its wind-tunnel facilities to solve general aerodynamic problems, such as reducing propeller-fuselage airflow interference and finding ways to predict the longitudinal and lateral control characteristics of an airplane, rather than devoting its facilities to any single research area, as Stanford was doing with propeller research.[53] "Our principal desire," he wrote, "in connection with aeronautics at the Institute, is to build up the best possible place for graduate work and research in the field of aeronautics."[54]

Harry Guggenheim and Hutchinson Cone were immediately receptive to Stratton's proposals, though they did not desire to undertake more than the financing of building construction. By July 1926, the Guggenheims already foresaw a grant to MIT, and estimated completion of the laboratory building by about October 1927.[55] In September 1926, Everett Morss, treasurer of the MIT Corporation, submitted an estimate for the laboratory building. For a four-story building 150 feet long and 60 feet wide, MIT architects estimated a total cost of $247,500. MIT could complete construction of the building by July 1, 1927.[56] This figure was higher than the Guggenheims were willing to grant; Harry F. Guggenheim had privately expressed to Samuel Stratton his opinion that, if the building were of plain construction without exterior trim, it should cost no more than $200,000. The Guggenheim fund trustees were of the same mind, and at a special meeting held on October 26, 1926, to consider possible grants to the University of Michigan and to MIT, the trustees approved "an appropriation not in excess of $200,000" for MIT's laboratory building, "the exact amount of this appropriation to be left to the discretion of the President of the Fund, after further study of this matter with Dr. Stratton."[57]

In December, Edward P. Warner warned Harry Guggenheim that the MIT project might well fall through if the fund limited its appropriation for construction to $200,000. Harry Guggenheim himself had misgivings about the amount of the fund, though he believed that the MIT Corporation could contribute matching funds to support building construction. Nevertheless, on January 13, 1927, Harry Guggenheim informed Stratton that the trustees had tentatively approved a total grant of $230,000 for building construction, of which $200,000 would be made available immediately, and the remaining $30,000 would not be formally authorized until after the spring 1927 trustees meeting. Three days later the fund publicly announced the $230,000 grant to MIT.[58] The new building, designed by the Boston architectural firm of Coolidge & Carlson, provided space for housing two wind tunnels, four laboratory rooms, storage and locker space, a library, a "working museum," and a drafting room.[59] MIT completed construction of the buff brick and Indiana limestone laboratory building in early 1928, and the school held the dedication on June 4, 1928, in a ceremony attended by Harry Guggenheim, Samuel Stratton, Harvard President A. Lawrence Lowell, Edward P. Warner, William P. MacCracken, Maj. Gen. James E. Fechet, and NACA Director of Research George W. Lewis.[60] MIT had spent $63,638 to equip the building, and in 1928 General Motors chief Alfred P. Sloan and Henry M. Crane donated an additional $85,000 to create an engine laboratory next to the Guggenheim building.[61]

Before the fund closed down in 1930, the Guggenheims made two more major university endowments for aeronautical education, one to the University of Washington in June 1928, and the other to the Georgia School of Technology in March 1930. Actually, after making the grants to Caltech, Stanford, Michigan, and MIT, the Guggenheims believed that the fund had done enough to sponsor aeronautical engineering research and training at American universities. What changed their minds was the realization that the Northwest and South lacked centers of aeronautical education comparable to those now located around the rest of the country.

In February 1926, Francis W. Brownell, a vice-president of the Guggenheim-owned American Smelting and Refining Corporation (ASARCO), received a telegram from Milnor Roberts, dean of the College of Mines, University of Washington, asking Brownell to sound the Guggenheims out on a grant for a school of aeronautics. Brownell and Roberts were close friends, and Brownell and Harry Guggenheim had worked together for years. Accordingly, Brownell contacted Guggenheim, who promised to give the matter his attention. Roberts and University of Washington president Henry Suz-zallo contacted Harry Guggenheim in May, emphasizing the school's connection with the Boeing company, faculty research for the navy, and propeller development. Guggenheim politely responded that the fund was considering the school; the matter lay dormant over the next year.[62]

During the intervening year, three events caused the Guggenheims to shift in their views. First, they had the opportunity to examine the background of the University of Washington's interest in aeronautics. In 1916, William E. Boeing, an adventuresome and modestly wealthy timber magnate, joined forces with naval engineer Conrad Westervelt to form the Boeing Airplane Company in Seattle. He recruited a number of his engineering staff members from University of Washington graduates, and both in appreciation to the school and in canny realization that the school could aid the future growth of his company, he donated a wind tunnel and established a chair in aeronautics. After the war, however, interest in aeronautics at Washington waned until Professor Frederick K. Kirsten, an electrical engineer, put the wind tunnel into operation once again, in 1921. Kirsten offered three aeronautics courses, one on aerodynamics, another on propeller design, and the last on airplane design. Additionally, the students journeyed to the Boeing plant for firsthand experience in aircraft manufacturing. By 1926, the school had forty-eight students enrolled in these courses. At the same time, Kirsten was experimenting with new "cycloidal" propeller designs that offered promise, and Boeing's engineering department, with but a single exception, consisted entirely of University of Washington graduates.[63]

Additionally, over the intervening year, changes took place at the university and in the commercial aviation scene. M. Lyle Spencer, a professor in the School of Journalism, became the new president of the University of Washington. Spencer, a dynamic, farseeing administrator, believed that the university could render a full measure of service to the state of Washington by emphasizing transportation studies, research on hydroelectric power, courses in forestry, conservation, and fishery management, and by creating a well-staffed and well-equipped school of aeronautics. M. Lyle Spencer and C. E. Magnusson, dean of the College of Engineering, approached Harry Guggenheim in September 1927, asking for a $425,000 grant—$290,000 for a laboratory and instruction building, and the rest for equipment, maintenance, and salaries. Guggenheim replied that the fund did not contemplate extending its financial aid program, and that, in any case, the proposed grant was excessively high. If the fund extended its school air program, Washington would receive full consideration.[64] Aircraft manufacturer William E. Boeing wrote Harry Guggenheim the following month, stating that a grant to Washington could greatly assist the research work of the Boeing company by providing the company with well-equipped research facilities. Further, the company could then assist in the education of the student engineers by giving the "full cooperation of the Boeing Airplane Company...."[65]

During the fall of 1927, the University of Washington became more attractive in the eyes of the Guggenheims because of the importance of the state of Washington as a link to air commerce north to Alaska, the growth of the airmail services in the Northwest, and because the navy, in November 1927, authorized the university to initiate aviation ground school courses for its naval ROTC attachment.[66] By early 1928, when the Guggenheims planned to extend their educational activities both at university and secondary school levels, the university in Washington headed their list of possible endowments. In early May, Harry Guggenheim wrote to M. Lyle Spencer, inviting him to apply for a construction grant. The Guggenheims were willing to finance construction of a building at the University of Washington if the university could get state aid to equip it. Spencer responded on May 11 with a request for $290,000 for a construction grant; this was identical to the construction grant estimate contained in his earlier proposal in September 1927. Guggenheim, disposed favorably towards the grant, took it up at the annual meeting on June 15, 1928, of the fund trustees, who approved the expenditure of $290,000 for an aeronautics building provided that the state legislature of Washington contribute funds to equip it. Spencer now turned to estimating expenses and getting support from the state legislature.[67]

The Board of Regents of the University of Washington approved the Guggenheim grant in late July 1928, and directed Spencer to find an individual to head the aeronautics department. By January 1929, the state legislature had passed an emergency grant of $48,000 for equipment for the new building, and the governor signed this special measure on February 20. Early in November 1928, Capt. Emory S. Land, USN, asked Capt. Holden C. Richardson, USN, the director of the navy's Bureau of Aeronautics, if he would be willing to assume direction of the Washington school upon his retirement from the navy. Land had replaced Hutchinson Cone as vice-president of the Guggenheim fund in August 1928, when Cone left to head the U.S. Shipping Board. Richardson declined Land's offer, however. Harry Guggenheim suggested several other possible candidates, including Virginius E. Clark, Maj. Leslie MacDill, and MIT professor

Shatswell Ober. Spencer, however, failed to persuade any of them
to come. By June 1929, when Harry Guggenheim sent the fund's
check for $290,000, Spencer still had not located a qualified candidate.
At this point, Boeing suggested that Prof. E. O. Eastwood, head of
the department of mechanical engineering at the University of Washington, at least start organizing an aeronautics department. Harry
Guggenheim agreed, stating "It would be far better to have a first-
rate mechanical engineer and executive at the head of your Department than an aeronautical engineer without the qualifications of
leadership." Eastwood outlined a program in aeronautical engineering leading to a Bachelor of Science degree, and appointed two instructors to join Frederick Kirsten and himself as faculty members.
On April 11, 1930, the university dedicated the Daniel Guggenheim
Hall of Aeronautics, as officials designated the Tudor-Gothic structure built with Guggenheim funding, in ceremonies attended by
William E. Boeing. The university implemented Eastwood's bachelor
program in aeronautics later that same year.[68]

With the grant to the University of Washington, the Guggenheim
fund had established or supported schools of aeronautics at major
universities in every geographical division of the United States except the South. Over the summer and fall of 1929, as the activities of
the fund reached a climax, especially the fund's blind flying research
and safe aircraft competition, fund president Harry F. Guggenheim
began tentative examination of aeronautical education in the South.
He believed that, to round out the fund's educational program, it
should make such a grant to a suitable southern institution. Harry
Guggenheim brought up the matter of a southern grant to the fund
trustees in a special meeting on October 1, 1929, and they authorized
him to make a survey of suitable recipient institutions, in preparation
for awarding one school an endowment of no more than $300,000.[69]
He appointed a committee consisting of William F. Durand, Robert
A. Millikan, Rear Adm. Hutchinson Cone (on leave from the U.S.
Shipping Board), and Capt. Emory S. Land, USN, the new vice-
president of the fund who had replaced Cone. Land served as committee chairman. On October 29, 1929, the fund announced its
intention to establish "the first aeronautical engineering school in the
South."[70]

Unlike the grants made to the other Guggenheim schools, the endowment of a southern school presented special difficulties. No pro-

gram or school of aeronautics existed anywhere in the South, from Virginia to Florida or the Carolinas to Texas. Hence the Guggenheims did not have any really "air-minded" schools to begin with. The fund's task became one of examining the leading engineering and scientific institutions in the South, with a view to building from scratch a complete aeronautics department. For this reason, the grant to the South was more complicated than any of the fund's other grants. Further, President Hoover had appointed Harry Guggenheim as ambassador to Cuba on September 15, 1929.[71] Guggenheim had a deep and abiding interest in Latin American affairs, particularly in increasing cooperation and commerce between the United States and its hemispheric neighbors, an interest that continued until his death.* He left for Cuba in November 1929, and though he frequently returned briefly to the United States, he became so embroiled in Cuban affairs, especially in trying to steer a neutral course between supporters and opponents of Cuban dictator Gen. Gerado Machado, that he had literally no time for fund activities. Vice-president Emory S. Land and the other fund trustees thus had complete responsibility for administering the southern grant.

* Guggenheim later wrote of his Cuban experience in *The United States and Cuba* (New York: Macmillan, 1934). While in Cuba, he championed repeal of the Platt Amendment. Such a stand, however, did little to allay suspicions in the minds of anti-Machado forces that Guggenheim was, in effect, the power behind the dictator. Guggenheim certainly did not support Machado's repressive regime, despite attempts by Machado to create such a public image. While in Cuba, Guggenheim hired advisers on foreign trade, the sugar industry, and Cuban finance to assist him, paying for their services with his own money. See O'Connor, *The Guggenheims*, pp. 440–47. For an anti-Machado, anti-Guggenheim tract, see Cuban Information Bureau, *Ambassador Guggenheim and the Cuban Revolt* (Washington, D.C., 1931). Guggenheim's emphasis on developing strong commercial ties and air transport links with Latin America is best exemplified in his speech "Aviation and the Americas" presented before the Institute of Politics, Williamstown, Mass., Aug. 5, 1929 (DGF Papers, box 2). See also DGF news release, Aug. 5, 1929, highlighting this speech (DGF Papers, box 2). After the Second World War, Harry Guggenheim became a critic of the Truman Doctrine and the policy of Containment, arguing that the vital interests of America lay in its own hemisphere, and not in Asia or Europe. He urged development of closer ties and strengthening of the Organization of American States as one method of achieving "hemispheric integration." See *Hemispheric Integration Now: An Address* (Gainesville: University of Florida Press, 1951). During the Eisenhower years, Harry Guggenheim visited frequently with Eisenhower and John Foster Dulles, recommending that overall responsibility for Latin American diplomacy be given to an individual senior to the assistant secretary of state for Latin American affairs. Dulles rejected such a plan on the grounds of administrative organization. In September 1957, Harry Guggenheim advised representatives of Cuban dictator Fulgencio Batista to instruct Batista to hold free elections and abandon his dictatorial ways, the same advice he had given—with the same lack of effect—to Machado, in the early 1930s. See Milton Lomask, *Seed Money*, pp. 70–71.

Land's committee began by examining twenty-seven southern schools. Land visited each of the schools and studied its engineering and scientific course programs, its finances, and how it was run. By January 1930, when the committee met to examine the final competitors, all but four had been rapidly eliminated. The four survivors were Vanderbilt University at Nashville, Tennessee; Rice Institute at Houston, Texas; the Georgia School of Technology; and the University of Alabama. The committee next sent notices to these schools asking for further details on their programs and plans in the event they would receive the Guggenheim grant. Almost from the outset, the Georgia School of Technology and the University of Alabama dominated the running, and of the two Georgia was in the stronger position.[72] It received funding from the state of Georgia, the city of Atlanta, Fulton County, tuition fees, and endowments, as well as federal support under the Smith-Hughes Act. Its annual state funding alone came to $302,000. Neither Vanderbilt nor Rice could match Georgia's financial picture. Further, Georgia's president, M. L. Brittain, did not let parochialism or politics influence the university. He recruited top-rate instructors from around the country, paid them well, and did not interfere in their instruction. He demanded rigorous instruction, and Georgia's strong engineering and mathematics departments, headed by D. M. Smith, were the equal of any in the country. Though Land personally favored the University of Alabama, he came to realize that Georgia offered the better technical instruction. By the beginning of March 1930, the committee members were unanimous in their support of the Georgia School of Technology.[73]

The Daniel Guggenheim Fund for the Promotion of Aeronautics had come to an end on February 1, 1930, after four years and fifteen days of existence. Its secretary, J. W. Miller, had arranged that $300,000 would go to establishing an aeronautical engineering school in the South despite the closing of the fund. On March 3, 1930 Emory S. Land informed Brittain that the fund, as its last act, had awarded an endowment of $300,000 to the Georgia School of Technology for establishment of a southern aeronautical research center and a Daniel Guggenheim School of Aeronautics.[74] Brittain immediately called a dinner meeting, attended by the state governor, the mayor of Atlanta, and various public officials to ensure that the aeronautics school would have continuous support from the state. All pledged their support. Brittain now turned to finding the best available man to head the new aeronautics department. He completed inspection trips to Caltech, MIT, and NYU, and visited Dr. George W. Lewis, director of research for the National Advisory Committee for Aeronautics.

Lewis suggested Montgomery Knight, working with NACA's Langley Memorial Aeronautical Laboratory at Hampton, Virginia, and a specialist in aerodynamics and aircraft safety. Brittain appointed Knight to head the school, then took $150,000 of the $300,000 grant and used it to construct the building and install a $50,000 nine-foot wind tunnel. The rest of the grant he placed in 5 percent bonds as a hedge against financial difficulties—a most wise move, as events turned out. Knight set up a course curriculum identical with the mechanical engineering program for the first two years. Students in their third and fourth years took courses in aerodynamics, theory of flight, structural analysis and airplane design, engine design and theory, and aeronautical research. Georgia Tech began construction of the aeronautical building in June 1930, and held the first classes in it in January 1931.[75]

During the mid-1920s, the rigid airship occupied the attention of many military and civilian aeronautical enthusiasts. Despite the loss of the *Shenandoah* in 1925, airship advocates predicted that the rigid airship would dominate America's aerial commerce, especially since the nation had a plentiful supply of helium, and thus did not have to rely on highly flammable hydrogen as a lifting gas. Concerned with the promotion of aviation, the Guggenheims could not afford to overlook any type of vehicle promising to assist the development of air commerce. The heart of American lighter-than-air (LTA) nonrigid and rigid airship research lay in Akron, Ohio. Here, during the First World War, Akron's Goodyear Tire and Rubber Company had built small nonrigid blimps for observation and antisubmarine duties, testing them at an airfield at Wingfoot Lake. After the war, the firm manufactured balloons and the rubberized gas cells used in the airship *Shenandoah*. In 1925, Goodyear developed the blimp *Pilgrim*, an advanced design which, in shape, was similar to the later Goodyear blimps made famous by their advertising flights around the country, halting effortlessly above Niagara Falls or the Rose Bowl. In October 1923, Goodyear president Paul W. Litchfield arranged with Luftschiffbau Zeppelin director Hugo Eckener for a transfer of patents from Zeppelin to Goodyear. The next year, Zeppelin's chief designer, Czechoslovakian-born Dr. Karl Arnstein, emigrated to the United States, together with twelve other Zeppelin engineers, to form the Goodyear-Zeppelin Corporation. Arnstein became Goodyear's vice-president for engineering.[76]

The Guggenheim interest in lighter-than-air vehicles received its major impetus from the long and tireless efforts of George F. Zook, president of the University of Akron. Zook first contacted the Guggenheim fund in March 1926, while Harry F. Guggenheim and Hutchinson I. Cone were away in Europe. The following October, he arranged for a meeting with Harry Guggenheim at the fund's New York headquarters. Zook met with Guggenheim on November 10, 1926, and broached a plan whereby the Guggenheim fund would endow the school with $250,000 for research on lighter-than-air flight.[77]

Harry Guggenheim avoided making any immediate commitments, though he indicated his interest in lighter-than-air craft to Zook. At the same time, Zook pointed out the advantages of rigid airships for military duties, especially naval reconnaissance, and their potential for passenger and commercial service. He further indicated that Akron was the nation's center of lighter-than-air research, and would most likely remain so for many years to come. While it did not possess a department of aeronautical engineering, the University of Akron did have a good science section emphasizing engineering and chemistry, and many of its graduates worked for Goodyear, or for either the Firestone Tire and Rubber Company or B. F. Goodrich Company, both of which had their plants in Akron and were also, to a lesser extent than Goodyear, interested in developing airships. Zook believed a research center at the University of Akron could study the materials used in airship design, such as duralumin alloys, fabric external coverings, and the "gold beaters" skin used to coat the internal gas cells. The center could also examine types of lifting and propulsion gases, different engines, and structural design. A grant of $250,000, at 5 percent interest, would provide $12,500 annually, enough for hiring one research professor, two research fellows, and providing equipment and supplies.[78]

After leaving Guggenheim, Zook continued his quest, visiting various airship enthusiasts around the country. He saw Rear Adm. William A. Moffett, the navy's senior champion of lighter-than-air vehicles, and Moffett offered Guggenheim any assistance he might be able to render the fund in promoting airship research.[79] Harry F. Guggenheim, while recognizing that Akron was in fact the nation's center of airship activities, feared that a grant to the University of Akron might be construed as an attempt to assist the Goodyear company to the disadvantage of its competitors. Zook hastened to reassure Guggenheim and H. I. Cone that, in his talks with airship advocates around the nation, they had assured him that "there would be no feeling of partiality, but, on the other hand, they were all very strongly for a research organization."[80] Meanwhile, the University of Akron, at Zook's direction, had appointed a board to study a lighter-than-air research laboratory. Zook succeeded in persuading Rear Admiral Moffett, Air Corps Major General Patrick, Assistant Secretary of Commerce for Aeronautics William P. MacCracken, Jr., Goodyear president Paul W. Litchfield, and airship designer Ralph H. Upson to serve as board members.[81] These men, together with Karl Arnstein and several others, met with Zook on May 29, 1927 and discussed proposals for an airship research center at Akron. "It was agreed," Zook later wrote, "that such a research institute devoted largely, though not necessarily exclusively, to lighter-than-air problems should by all means be established."[82]

For over a year, Zook's efforts lay fallow. Then, in February 1929, Jerome Hunsaker, a vice-president of the Goodyear-Zeppelin Corporation, recommended establishing an airship institute where "a few advanced thinkers might be put to work with benefit to the art. I see no place but Lakehurst or Akron for them to get contact with the problems of the art."[83] By this time, Harry Guggenheim and his father were all in favor of creating a lighter-than-air research center. Yet, they were still uncertain where to locate it. R. B. Moore, the dean of science at Purdue University, had heard of the proposed grant to Akron, and he quickly contacted the Guggenheim fund, stressing Purdue's good engineering department and his own background as a chemist and lighter-than-air advocate as grounds for establishing the airship institute at Purdue.[84] Fund vice-president Emory S. Land wrote to Harry Guggenheim, "When and if the L.T.A. crowd get together behind some suitable institution then the Fund will be in a position to take action. In the meantime we will have to await developments from (a) Hunsaker, (b) Akron university, (c) Purdue, (d) L.T.A. crowd."[85]

In an attempt to resolve the controversy, Harry F. Guggenheim in April 1929 sent out questionnaires on the desirability of creating an airship research institute to leading airship advocates, including among others naval officers Garland Fulton, Charles E. Rosendahl, and William Moffett, Air Corps officers J. A. Paegelow, and Mason M. Patrick, industrial engineers Carl Fritsche, Ralph Upson, and Paul Litchfield, and NACA officials George W. Lewis and Joseph S. Ames.[86] Their responses generally favored Akron from the practical, industrial side of airship development, and Purdue from the theoretical side because of its stronger science department. Some dissenters, such as Carl Fritsche and Ralph Upson, suggested MIT or the University of Michigan. The majority of army and naval officers, representing the services having the most airship experience, strongly backed Akron. By June 1929, Harry Guggenheim had made his mind up: the center would go to Akron.[87]

At the same time, Harry Guggenheim was not so certain that the institute should be solely under the direction of the University of Akron. He favored instead a cooperative center, managed by the University of Akron in conjunction with a school having a strong aeronautics department with an aeronautics director who could also assume control over the airship institute. The logical choice seemed Caltech. On June 12, 1929, Guggenheim met with Robert A. Millikan and Jerome C. Hunsaker at his home, Falaise, at Port Washington, Long Island. Together, the three men mapped out the future program of the airship institute's development. Harry Guggenheim forecast that Southern California would become a base for transpacific dirigible operations, and that Akron would certainly remain the center of lighter-than-air activities, because of the Goodyear works. Hunsaker agreed, and added that the center should be under the direction of the Guggenheim Aeronautical Laboratory of the California Institute of Technology, since Caltech had an outstanding science and engineering faculty, as well as a new Guggenheim-created school of aeronautics. Further, Hunsaker recommended that the fund appropriate $250,000 for the airship center at Akron, and arrange for Theodore von Kármán to become director of the airship institute. At this time, von Kármán was still at Aachen, and uncertain whether or not he would come to the United States at all.[88] During July and August 1929, Robert Millikan and Harry Guggenheim wrote to von Kármán in Aachen, urging him to come to the United States and direct Caltech's aeronautics department. They also asked him to direct the proposed airship institute, but von Kármán was reluctant to take charge, leading Harry Guggenheim to remark to Millikan, "Obviously our friend goes into the water inch by inch."[89]

By the late summer of 1929, University of Akron president George Zook had arranged for the Akron Airport Board to furnish space at the Akron airport for the proposed airship laboratory. During an interview with Jerome C. Hunsaker, he also agreed to match any Guggenheim grant with $95,000 raised by the Akron city council to help support building construction. Now, Harry F. Guggenheim believed, the fund had sufficient support to complete its plans. On October 1, 1929, during a special meeting of the Guggenheim fund board of directors, he announced that for the past several months, fund representatives had discussed with Caltech, the University of Akron, the Goodyear-Zeppelin Corporation, and the Akron Municipal Airport, "the desirability of establishing an institution to be known as 'The Daniel Guggenheim Airship Institute.'"[90] Further, during these meetings, the parties concerned had drawn up a tentative agreement whereby the Guggenheim fund would donate $250,000. Of this sum, $75,000 would go to Caltech to provide a $10,000 annual fellowship fund for five years, a $2,000 annual director's salary for five years, and a $3,000 annual miscellaneous expense fund for five years. Another $175,000 would go to the University of Akron, including $150,000 for building construction and equipment costs, and a $5,000 annual maintenance fund for five years. The fund directors unanimously adopted the proposal and the fund publicly announced creation of the institute on "Tragic Tuesday," October 29, 1929, the same day the bottom dropped out of the New York Stock Exchange, plunging the country into the Depression.[91] Three weeks later, Harry Guggenheim mailed off the fund's checks to George Zook and Robert Millikan.[92]

Under the terms of the agreement, the Daniel Guggenheim Airship Institute would be directed by Caltech for the first five years. If, at the end of the five-year period, Caltech withdrew from its position of leadership, a special advisory board consisting of representatives of the University of Akron, Caltech, the American Society of Mechanical Engineers, the Society of Automotive Engineers, and the National Advisory Committee for Aeronautics, would appoint a new director. The director of the airship institute would be an employee of the California Institute of Technology, residing in Pasadena and visiting Akron as necessary; the assistant director and manager would be a resident of Akron, and would have charge of all work at the airship institute, under the "general technical direction" of the director at Caltech.[93] As previously agreed, Theodore von Kármán became director of research at the Guggenheim Airship Institute in the fall of 1930. He sent to Aachen for Dr. Theodore Troller, and placed responsibility for the design and construction of the building and its research facilities in Troller's hands. In 1931, construction started on the airship institute building, a four-story structure housing a vertical wind tunnel, laboratories, offices, and shops.[94]

By March 1930, when the fund completed its last financial transactions, the Guggenheim family had granted $1,693,000 to establish schools and research centers at seven leading American universities, in addition to the prefund grant of $500,000 to New York University in 1925.[95] Hundreds of students, including graduates, undergraduates, and interested government and industry representatives, were enrolled in aeronautical science courses. This contrasted to the situation at the end of 1926, when the Guggenheims found that only ninety-six students were studying for degrees in aeronautics in the United States, most of whom were students at New York University, Caltech, Stanford, or the University of Michigan, all of which had already received Guggenheim grants.[96]

Without a doubt, the Guggenheim fund gave birth to widespread, well-organized, university-level aeronautical education and research in America. The fund created schools featuring programs balanced between education and research, while cautiously insuring that the industry would not be glutted with mass-produced, mediocre, and ill-trained engineers and scientists. The Guggenheim fund had a tremendous impact on American aerospace education, an impact reflected in the fact that by mid-century virtually all the senior aerospace engineers and scientists in the United States, and in many foreign countries as well, had graduated from Guggenheim-funded schools. Such a legacy would certainly have pleased Daniel Guggenheim, who died in Hempstead House on September 28, 1930, at the age of seventy-four.

CHAPTER 5

Extending the Guggenheim Aeronautical Education Program

BOTH Daniel and Harry Guggenheim realized that aeronautical education meant more than establishing a number of research centers and schools across the country. It also required educating youth and the general public in the increasingly important role aviation would play in American and world commerce. Further, it necessitated offering training in business and law, as they affected aeronautical and aviation commerce and development, and providing for the storing and acquisition of aeronautical literature. The Daniel Guggenheim Fund for the Promotion of Aeronautics arranged for all of these through a series of additional educational activities, including creation of its Committee on Elementary and Secondary Aeronautical Education, grants to the Harvard Graduate School of Business Administration and the Northwestern University School of Law, establishment of a course in aerial surveying at Syracuse University, creation of a summer program to train flight school instructors at New York University, a grant to the Library of Congress to acquire a permanent collection of aeronautical literature, and grants to various foreign aeronautical societies and flying clubs to preserve aeronautical documentation.

Charles A. Lindbergh's epochal flight across the Atlantic in May 1927 provided Americans with the postwar hero they so desperately sought in the 1920s. He was the authentic hero, a man who, by skill, careful planning, good organization, and courage, managed to complete a task many thought impossible: a solo, nonstop flight across the Atlantic from New York to Paris. After the Lindbergh flight, millions of Americans gained a new respect for the airplane. If a man could fly a small single-engine airplane across the Atlantic, surely the time would come in the future when larger and more advanced airplanes would traverse the oceans regularly, carrying passengers and freight—and maybe bombs as well.

Harry and Daniel Guggenheim, viewing the post-Lindbergh awakening interest in aviation among the American people, decided to undertake a program in aeronautical education aimed primarily at the youth of the United States. The fund would promote a general appreciation of aviation and its role in society through creation of a committee on elementary and secondary education. Such a program was easier said than done. As fund trustee William F. Durand noted, "One embarrassing feature of the situation is the present lack of any special preparation on the part of teachers. . . . Broadly speaking, the teachers, at the present time, are no better informed than are their pupils and in some cases presumably less so."[1] He recommended that any general aviation education program discuss and cover such topics as the history of aviation, the language and terminology of aviation, and general aeronautical information, such as the difference between an airship and an airplane, and meteorology.[2]

To implement their proposed educational program, the Guggenheims turned to New York University, specifically to Dr. John W. Withers, dean of the school of education, and Alexander Klemin, director of the Daniel Guggenheim School of Aeronautics. At a meeting of the fund's board of directors on November 28, 1927, the board granted an appropriation of $5,000 to investigate the possibilities of teaching "some phases of aeronautics" at the public school level. At Withers' suggestion, and upon the recommendation of Harry F. Guggenheim, the Guggenheim fund, on December 6, 1927, added an additional $15,000 to this original $5,000 grant.[3] By the middle of that month, Withers and Harry Guggenheim had drawn up the general plans for the committee. It would consist of about fifty individuals divided into two groups, a small executive group based in New York which would meet frequently and formulate plans, and a large advisory group composed of local representatives nationwide. Ultimately, the committee would have eighty members from all over the United States.[4] On January 27, 1928, the fund publicly announced creation of a Committee on Elementary and Secondary Education to make the next generation "air-minded." The chairman of the committee's executive body was Dean Withers, with Klemin as a member.[5]

By February 1, 1928, the committee's executive body had determined that the best course towards furthering an appreciation of aeronautics lay through developing well-written and authoritative texts for elementary (first through sixth grade), junior high school (seventh through ninth grade), and high school (tenth through twelfth grade) classes. The committee also decided, in mid-March 1928, to compile an annotated bibliography of the literature relating to aviation. Withers appointed Roland H. Spaulding of NYU's education faculty to compile it. With the assistance of Klemin, Spaulding prepared the bibliography, which the Guggenheim fund published as *Books on Aeronautics* in late 1928. By September 1929, the fund had distributed seven thousand copies to public schools nationwide. Later Spaulding also prepared a dictionary of aeronautical terms and phrases, which the fund published, after its demise, in 1931.[6]

In the spring of 1928, the Committee on Elementary and Secondary Education completed final arrangements for a summer school course at New York University to train teachers in aeronautics. The Guggenheim education committee hoped for a class of about twenty summer students, comprised of teachers from around the country. Instead, the actual enrollment numbered fifty-two, and consisted chiefly of school superintendents, vocational training instructors, and social studies teachers. The committee continued the course during the fall semester of 1928 at NYU, and twenty-five students, twenty-two of whom were teachers, signed up for it. These students then returned to their school districts, where they established similar courses, carrying out the purpose of the educational committee to make American youth air-minded.[7]

During 1928, the education committee undertook a nationwide survey of the American public school systems to determine the number of schools in the country that offered courses in aeronautics. The results were not encouraging. Of 2,970 schools polled, only 576 responded; 371 reported that they did not offer aeronautical training, though 45 of these responded that they would be interested in doing so. Another 205 did offer some form of aeronautical instruction; 29 offered it in specialized aeronautical courses, 114 subsumed the aeronautical material within other subjects, and 85 offered extracurricular aeronautical education programs. Twenty-one school systems offered aeronautics at the elementary school level. Another 93 taught it at the junior high school level, and 130 at the high school level.[8] The Guggenheim committee undertook publicizing its work in a series of addresses before the National Education Association at its national meetings in New York and Cleveland in 1928 and 1929. NEA response was favorable, and the public exposure resulted in numerous inquiries to the fund for further information by interested teachers and school system superintendents.[9]

Withers and other members of the Guggenheim education committee decided to embark on another program in early 1929: the training of ground-school instructors capable of educating student pilots. The Aeronautics Branch of the Department of Commerce had stipulated that prospective pilots complete not less than one hundred hours of ground-school instruction by qualified teachers, but the number of well-qualified teachers was low. Harry Guggenheim, after consultation, requested the fund trustees to appropriate $11,722 to finance such a course, and, on July 22, 1929, the trustees did so during a special meeting. Roland H. Spaulding directed the establishment of this ground-school instructor training program and NYU held a special eight-week course during the summer of 1929. The course material covered airplane engines and instrumentation, air commerce regulations, administration and supervision of ground-school instruction, air navigation, and meteorology. Forty-one students signed up for the program, and all but three later received the Department of Commerce rating as a ground-school instructor. Students specialized in one or more of the subjects, such as instrumentation or meteorology.[10] The ground-school instructor training course at NYU was the first of its kind in the nation. Spaulding later served as a consultant with the army and navy on aviation training, receiving the Brewer Trophy for his aviation education contributions.[11]

The Guggenheim Committee on Elementary and Secondary Education continued to function until the fund closed down in early 1930. By that time, the fund trustees had approved a $25,000 grant to the committee, raising its total appropriations for 1928–31 to $56,722, including the $11,722 for the aviation ground-school instructor's course held in the summer of 1929. After dissolution of the fund, Spaulding and Withers continued to direct teacher-training programs in aeronautics, placing NYU at the head of the public school aeronautical education movement. Oddly, most American educators seem to have rapidly forgotten this Guggenheim contribution to American aeronautical education. A seminal 1954 study by the American Council on Education in cooperation with the Civil Aeronautics Administration made no mention of the Guggenheim program and glossed over pre-World War II aeronautical education by inaccurately stating, "The content of aviation education prior to 1942 was defined generally in terms of aeronautical skills."[12] Yet, its own proposed program differed in few, if any, respects from what John Withers, Harry Guggenheim, and Roland Spaulding had attempted a quarter century before. It still followed William F. Durand's dictum that any aeronautical education program must treat the history of aviation, the vocabulary of aviation, and general aeronautical knowledge. The American Council on Education did add that modern youth must understand aviation in terms of its economic impact and social change, but Harry Guggenheim had already reached this conclusion in fund pronouncements, especially on the role of aviation and air commerce in building closer international links among different peoples.

In the spring of 1928, the Harvard University Graduate School of Business Administration asked the fund for a grant of $15,000 to establish a three-year research program "for the study of the economic and industrial effects and possibilities of commercial aviation." [13] Harry Guggenheim believed that a grant to the school could contribute to the development of aviation, and on June 15, 1928, the fund trustees voted Harvard an appropriation of $15,000; the first research fellow appointed by Harvard under the grant was Herbert Hoover, Jr. [14] A more lasting and important donation, however, was the Guggenheim fund's grant of $11,666.67 to Northwestern University Law School for the creation of the Air Law Institute, the first of its kind in the United States.

In contrast with the long and sometimes tedious negotiations involved in creating the other Guggenheim-funded schools, the creation of the Air Law Institute at Northwestern came with almost astonishing rapidity. The Air Law Institute was the idea of John H. Wigmore, dean of the law school at Northwestern University, and Fred D. Fagg, a doctor of law and a former World War I fighter pilot. Wigmore was an outstanding authority in criminal law, especially in the law of evidence. Fagg had just returned to Northwestern from the Institut für Luftrecht (Air Law Institute) at Königsberg, Germany, where he had spent a year as American exchange professor. The Institut für Luftrecht, created in 1926, was the first of its kind in the world, and when Fagg returned to Northwestern, Wigmore saw a chance to make Chicago a center for the study of aviation law. Chicago already had two aviation law specialists, Prof. George G. Bogert of the University of Chicago, who had drafted the state's Uniform State Aviation Law, and William P. MacCracken, Jr., then the Assistant Secretary of Commerce for Aeronautics, though he planned to return to private practice in Chicago in the fall of 1929. [15]

Wigmore completed his plan for an air law institute at Northwestern by early 1929. It called for an appropriation of $35,000 to fund the school for its first three years: $15,000 for the first year, and $10,000 per year for the next two years. On June 11, 1929, Robert R. McCormick, the publisher of the *Chicago Tribune,* offered to contribute one-third of the sum needed to create the air law institute.[16] Wigmore publicly announced plans for the institute the next day, and justified its need by stating, "The law, as it relates to aviation, is chock full of problems that must be worked out. . . . It took 200 years to work out the liability of common carriers. Similar laws must be worked out for air carriers."[17]

Wigmore approached the Guggenheim fund for assistance late in June 1929, emphasizing the need for the institution and the importance of having Fred D. Fagg on the faculty.[18] Over the next week, Guggenheim fund vice-president Emory S. Land checked on Wigmore's reputation; aircraft industry executive Reed G. Landis endorsed Wigmore's plan and suggested that the Guggenheim fund assist Northwestern University.[19] Henry Breckinridge, a prominent New York attorney who often acted for the fund on legal matters, stated that "Wigmore stands at the head of the profession," adding, "I think you are entirely safe in anything that would be headed up by Dean Wigmore."[20] As early as July 9, 1929, Harry Guggenheim and Emory S. Land were sufficiently interested in the project that Land, an old friend of Reed Landis, could write, "I trust that we may be able to work out something which will be of assistance in putting the project over."[21]

The only matter that now concerned Land and Guggenheim was the amount Wigmore wished the fund to grant. Land wrote Wigmore on July 6 asking whether it was Wigmore's wish to have the fund bear one-third of the total cost, as had McCormick of the *Tribune.*[22] In the meantime, William P. MacCracken offered his support to Wigmore and endorsed the project in a telegram to Harry Guggenheim. On July 10, 1929, Wigmore responded to Land's letter by formally requesting that the Guggenheim fund support the air law institute by providing one-third of the projected $35,000 costs for its first three years, the same terms McCormick had offered.[23] Nearly two weeks later, on July 22, 1929, Harry Guggenheim recommended that the Guggenheim fund executive committee bear one-third of the $35,000 needed to create the Air Law Institute, and the trustees unanimously approved the Wigmore request.[24] Harry Guggenheim notified Wigmore of the board's action the next day.[25]

Wigmore subsequently asked Harry Guggenheim if he would be

willing to serve as one of seven directors of the school; Guggenheim replied that he could not, as it would be outside the province of the fund, but he suggested Henry Breckinridge, a man "intensely interested in all phases of aviation."[26] Wigmore did choose Breckinridge, and also William P. MacCracken, to serve as directors. By early September 1929, Wigmore had succeeded in obtaining the remaining one-third needed from five prominent Chicago bankers, lawyers, and industrialists, Earle Reynolds, Edwin N. D'Ancona, Elias Mayer, Melvin L. Emrich, and Martin L. Straus. Guggenheim fund secretary J. W. Miller sent Wigmore a fund check for $11,667.67 on September 12.[27]

The Air Law Institute at Northwestern got underway in the fall of 1929, with the creation of an air law library. The next year, the institute began publication of the *Journal of Air Law*, under the editorship of Fred D. Fagg. This authoritative journal quickly gained preeminence in its field. The Air Law Institute also began issuing a newsletter that pointed to new ordinances, statutes, regulatory orders, and decisions, and contained an air law bibliography with supplements and, upon request, a reference list "to aid in the solution of any specific problem of air law."[28] Fred D. Fagg continued as director of the Air Law Institute until 1937, when he left to become director of the Department of Commerce's Bureau of Air Commerce. A year later, he returned to Northwestern as dean of the School of Commerce.[29]

The Daniel Guggenheim Fund for the Promotion of Aeronautics also undertook a limited program of graduate fellowships enabling two aeronautical engineers to study at leading European aeronautical institutions. The fund awarded these fellowships to Milton J. Thompson, an instructor at the University of Michigan, and to Paul E. Hemke, an instructor at the U.S. Naval Academy. Harry F. Guggenheim had conceived the fellowship for study abroad program in early 1928, to enable graduate engineers to "pursue in research centers abroad under guidance, studies which they cannot pursue in the United States with equal advantage."[30] He asked Felix Pawlowski of the University of Michigan if he could suggest a student. Pawlowski recommended Milton J. Thompson, who held an M.S. from Michigan and was a specialist in theoretical aerodynamics. Pawlowski suggested that the fund send Thompson to Warsaw, Poland, where he could study under Prof. C. Witoszynski at the Warsaw Aerodynamical Institute, a center for the study of aerodynamic theory.[31] Coincidentally,

Pawlowski's suggestion came at a time when Witoszynski had contacted Dr. George W. Lewis, NACA's director of research, asking if NACA could give him assistance on investigating longitudinal and lateral aircraft stability. Lewis asked Emory S. Land if the Guggenheim fund could help. Coming on the heels of Pawlowski's suggestion, the fund viewed Lewis's request with great favor, and Harry F. Guggenheim notified Pawlowski that the fund approved sending Thompson to Warsaw for one year, at a cost of $2,250.[32]

Thompson left for Europe on the steamer *Polonia* on September 8, arriving at Warsaw in the middle of the month. Soon Thompson was working with Witoszynski on the effect of hinged flaps upon an airplane's longitudinal stability characteristics, and the Warsaw Polytechnical School agreed to appoint him a candidate for the degree of Doctor Rerum Technicarum. Thompson sent copies of all his technical reports to the National Advisory Committee for Aeronautics, where NACA scientists quickly praised Thompson's own research and the apparent high quality of work at the Warsaw Institute.[33] In mid-1929, Pawlowski asked Harry Guggenheim for an additional one-year grant to permit Thompson to complete his doctorate. At first, Harry Guggenheim resisted, believing that the United States had urgent and immediate need of well-trained engineers like Thompson. Pawlowski, however, managed to convince Guggenheim that the country needed not only men capable of conducting research, but well-trained scientific administrators capable of directing it, and that Thompson showed good promise for the latter role. Accordingly, in May 1929, the Guggenheim fund granted Thompson $2,100 to complete his additional year of study.[34] He returned to Michigan after completing the degree, and became acting chairman of the school's aeronautics department in 1935.

The Guggenheim fund also sent another engineer to study abroad, Paul E. Hemke. Hemke held a Ph.D. from Johns Hopkins University; from 1924 to 1927 he served as a NACA physicist at NACA's Langley Memorial Aeronautical Laboratory. Then, in 1927, he joined the U.S. Naval Academy at Annapolis, as an instructor in mathematics and aeronautics for naval postgraduate students.[35] Hemke approached the Guggenheim fund about its fellowship program in early August 1928, at the suggestion of Rear Adm. S. S. Robinson, the superintendent of the Naval Academy. Hemke originally wished to go to Aachen or Göttingen, but fund vice-president Emory S. Land suggested England, since, with von Kármán and others, American schools already had a fair appreciation of aeronautical education and research as conducted in Germany. After discussions with George W. Lewis and Joseph S. Ames of Johns Hopkins, Hemke decided to go to England and work with Prof. Bennett Melvill Jones at Cambridge University. Jones, a distinguished aeronautical scientist, invited Hemke to spend several months at Cambridge, researching aircraft stability and control at low speeds using Air Ministry airplanes belonging to the Cambridge University Air Squadron.[36]

Originally, the Guggenheim fund hoped for Hemke to spend a full year in England, with perhaps a short side trip to Germany for comparative purposes. In fact, however, Hemke was unable to get additional leave from the Naval Academy, and his time in Europe was six months. Accordingly, the fund reduced the amount of the grant from $2,500 to $1,800. Hemke left for Europe on September 7, 1929, aboard the steamer S.S. *Minnesota*, arriving at Cambridge in October. Upon arrival, he set right to work with Jones, and also with William Farren. During the Christmas break he did manage to visit some aeronautical establishments on the Continent.[37] After Hemke returned from England, he resumed his teaching position at the Naval Academy. He left the academy in 1931 to establish an aeronautics department at the Case School of Applied Science in Cleveland, then in 1936 he established a department of aeronautical engineering at Rensselaer Polytechnic Institute, remaining at Rensselaer until his retirement as provost in 1964.[38]

The Guggenheim fund, already committed to establishing schools of aeronautical engineering and supporting graduate training abroad, also studied the possibility of supporting such related subjects as aerial photography. The Guggenheim fund granted Syracuse University $30,000 in May 1929 to create a program in aerial surveying and mapping. The fund had expressed an early interest in aerial photography. The fund's third bulletin, "Aerial Service," issued on January 7, 1927, revealed how an aerial survey of Middletown, Connecticut, had increased the local tax base from $20,500,000 to $31,500,000, largely through the discovery of 1,896 buildings previously not figured in tax assessment. The increased tax base enabled the city to obtain more appropriations for new schools, roads, and municipal buildings.[39]

Louis Mitchell, the dean of the College of Applied Science at Syracuse, had written Harry Guggenheim in March 1926, asking if the fund would issue a grant to the school for a program in aeronautical engineering or meteorology.[40] These early efforts came to naught, however, for the fund did not select Syracuse as one of the schools destined to receive major grants. Harry Guggenheim did leave open the possibility that the fund, in the future, might endow the school.[41]

Louis Marshall, a trustee of Syracuse University and a close friend of Harry Guggenheim, wrote to Guggenheim in October 1928 stating that an increasing number of students wanted courses in aeronautical photography and surveying. He wondered if the Guggenheim fund might be willing to subsidize a course program in photo and survey work at Syracuse. Guggenheim asked Louis Mitchell for further details, and in mid-December 1928, Mitchell reported to Harry Guggenheim that the school had formed a special faculty committee on aerial photography consisting of S. D. Sarason, L. B. Howe, and Earl F. Church, all experienced in aerial and photo surveying. Mitchell proposed a series of courses covering general photography, instrument use, economics of aerial mapping, mosaic and survey map construction, maps for air navigation, and flight training for pilots. Guggenheim approved the whole program, but informed Mitchell that the fund could not support pilot training, as this was outside the scope of the fund's activities.[42]

In February 1929, S. D. Sarason informed Louis Mitchell that the survey courses would require a total of $75,000, mostly for equipment purchases, including the purchase of Fairchild automatic aerial cameras costing $3,709 apiece. When Mitchell informed the Guggenheim fund of this estimated cost, fund vice-president Emory S. Land quickly replied that such an estimate was far beyond what the fund could offer, and he suggested that Mitchell submit a smaller figure. By mid-May, Harry Guggenheim had simplified the proposed grant to the point where he suggested that Mitchell submit a request for $30,000 to the fund. On May 27, 1929, Chancellor Charles W. Flint submitted the $30,000 request. Four days later, during a special meeting of the fund's executive committee, the trustees approved the grant, establishing an aerial photographic surveying and mapping center at Syracuse. Harry F. Guggenheim telegraphed Flint the same day, informing him of the fund's decision.[43] Four months later, when Harry F. Guggenheim began closing down the fund's activities, the trustees approved an additional grant of $30,000 to Syracuse to meet the future needs of the center. The photographic surveying center at Syracuse was the first of its kind in the nation, another example of how Guggenheim money broke new ground in aeronautics.[44]

The Guggenheim fund also supported various institutions preserving and collecting aeronautical documentation and literature. It assisted the Library of Congress with a $140,000 grant in October 1929, and also supported efforts by foreign aeronautical societies to preserve aeronautical documentation. In January 1929, fund vice-president Land wrote to Dr. Herbert Putnam, the librarian of the Library of Congress, asking that Putnam inform the fund as to the current holdings of the library with regards to aviation. Land added that the fund did not wish to create libraries, but that it might consider establishing an aeronautics section at the Library of Congress.[45] Putnam quickly replied that the Library of Congress possessed about twelve hundred titles on aeronautics, stating, "that resources for the study of aeronautics not merely as an art but as a science, and its historical development, should be available at the National Capital seems obvious. The collection at the Library of Congress is clearly inadequate."[46] Putnam added that the National Advisory Committee for Aeronautics, the Air Corps, the Department of Commerce, and the Smithsonian Institution possessed other collections of books and pamphlets, the most extensive of which was the Samuel P. Langley Aeronautical Library at the Smithsonian, containing about sixteen hundred volumes, seven hundred pamphlets, and newspaper clippings. Putnam assured Land that any grant would help build a collection of books and published works available to the public "as a matter of right and not as a concession of courtesy."[47]

By the end of January, Harry Guggenheim had already agreed in principle to a grant for the Library of Congress.[48] He then sought outside advice, having Emory Land ask George W. Lewis and other government officials for their views. All agreed that while each federal agency might require its own small working reference library, the nation required a center where researchers could examine a comprehensive body of aeronautical material and literature. "The logical place," Guggenheim wrote Herbert Putnam, "would seem to be the Congressional Library."[49] He then suggested that Putnam meet with representatives of the various agency reference librarians in Washington and work out some plan relative to the Library of Congress. Putnam held a meeting on February 27, 1929, with Lt. John D. Barker of the Army Air Corps, Dr. William L. Corbin of the Smithsonian Institution, Stafford Kernan of the Department of Commerce, and John F. Victory of the National Advisory Committee for Aeronautics. All agreed that an aeronautical research center at the Library of Congress was most desirable, and commended the Guggenheim fund for its suggestion. Corbin offered to transfer the entire Langley Aeronautical Library from the Smithsonian to the Library of Congress, an offer quickly approved by Smithsonian Secretary Charles G. Abbot. The men also agreed that the Guggenheim fund should not simply provide funds for the collection of material, but should also under-write the salary of an expert with a good technical and bibliographical background to direct the acquisition and organization of the material.[50]

The idea of a Guggenheim-endowed "chair" of aeronautics at the Library of Congress met with tentative approval from Harry F. Guggenheim and Emory S. Land, and during the ensuing months, Putnam, Guggenheim, and Land planned how to use any grant the library might receive. At the same time, Putnam mentioned to Harry Guggenheim that the library planned to acquire the Tissandier Collection of aeronautical literature from a British dealer, the Maggs Brothers. Harry Guggenheim advised Charles Dollfus, the fund's French representative, to assist the library's efforts in any way he could. On July 26, 1929, Herbert Putnam met with Land, Harry Guggenheim, and William F. Durand at the fund's New York headquarters. During this meeting, Guggenheim gave his approval to appointing a special aeronautics curator at the library using a grant from the fund, and he advised Putnam to choose a likely individual for the position. Putnam immediately asked Durand, but Durand declined, after giving the matter great thought, because of his other commitments to the fund and to Stanford. At a meeting of the fund's board of directors on October 1, 1929, the trustees approved a grant of $140,000 to the Library of Congress.[51]

The grant provided $75,000 for a Daniel Guggenheim Chair of Aeronautics, $9,200 for two years' salary for the aeronautics director, $4,800 for two years' salary for an "expert assistant," and $51,000 to permit the acquisition of a collection of historical documentation pertaining to aeronautics. After two years, the librarian of Congress and Congress would assume joint responsibility for annual appropriations, salaries, and upkeep.[52] The Guggenheim fund publicly announced the forthcoming grant to the Library of Congress on October 29, 1929, and six days later, the Trust Fund Board of the Library of Congress approved the grant, including the Guggenheim Chair of Aeronautics. Trust Fund Board chairman Andrew W. Mellon notified Harry F. Guggenheim of the action, adding the board's "very hearty appreciation of the action of the Trustees of the Fund."[53]

Putnam then turned to finding a suitable occupant for the Guggenheim Chair. After examining several candidates, and on the advice of Land, Putnam selected Dr. Albert F. Zahm, an aeronautical pioneer and director of the navy's aerodynamic laboratory at the Washington Navy Yard. Zahm, who held a Ph.D. from Johns Hopkins, had built a very early university wind-tunnel laboratory at Catholic University in 1901. He had been influential in creating the National Advisory Committee for Aeronautics, and had worked as an adviser for Glenn Curtiss.[54] Zahm joined the Library of Congress as holder of the Daniel Guggenheim Chair on January 2, 1930. He began his duties in time to supervise the acquisition of four outstanding collections of aeronautical literature. These were the Tissandier, Victor Silberer, Hermann Hoernes, and Maggs collections.

The collections arrived in the United States aboard the S.S. *Aquitania*, and consisted of thirty-three cases weighing a total of over three tons, purchased by Herbert Putnam from the Maggs Brothers, book dealers in London. Maggs wrote Putnam that "we think you will be delighted to have this magnificent collection, and we are delighted that we are the cause of your getting it, with one lingering tear in each eye that it will leave England forever."[55] The Tissandier collection consisted of eighteen hundred volumes and pamphlets, mostly of sixteenth and seventeenth century aeronautics, patiently collected by pioneer balloonists Gaston and Albert Tissandier, with additions by Gaston's son Paul. Bibliophiles considered the Tissandier collection the single most important grouping of eighteenth-century aeronautica.[56]

The Victor Silberer collection contained 895 items acquired by the nineteenth-century Austrian balloonist and aeronaut Victor Silberer, including many rare periodicals. The Hermann Hoernes collection, assembled by nineteenth-century Austrian military aeronaut Col. Hermann Hoernes, contained 783 items acquired during Hoernes' official assignments in Germany, France, and England. The Maggs Brothers collection numbered 621 items on random aeronautical topics. In addition, the Library of Congress now had the Langley collection, formerly at the Smithsonian, which contained 2,115 books and pamphlets. In January 1929, Librarian Herbert Putnam reported that the aeronautics collection at the Library of Congress numbered 1,200 items; by April 1930 this had jumped to 9,327, and in June 1933, Zahm reported that the collection contained 19,896 volumes and pamphlets, as well as some priceless manuscript collections, including the papers of Octave Chanute, virtually an insider's history of American aeronautics from 1890 through 1910. As Harry Guggenheim had hoped, the aeronautical collection of the Library of Congress was the finest in the world; it has remained so since.[57]

Harry Guggenheim and the Guggenheim fund did not neglect ensuring that relevant and significant foreign aeronautical documentation would exist for the future historian to examine. Between August 1926 and the closing of the fund, the Guggenheims granted a total

of $88,000 in several smaller installments to four European aeronauti-
cal societies. The fund sent $25,000 to Britain's Royal Aeronautical
Society, $28,000 to the Aero Club de France, $20,000 to the Associazione Italiana di Aerotecnica, and $15,000 to the Aero Club von
Deutschland. The grants to the French and German aeronautical
societies established special documentation centers. The French
center, the Centre de Documentation Aeronautique, consisted of a
technical library and research facility under the direction of Paul
Tissandier.[58] The German aeronautical club, with an initial $5,000
Guggenheim grant, created the Von Tschudi Archiv des Daniel
Guggenheim Fund under the direction of German military aviation
pioneer Wilhelm Siegert; after Siegert's death, the archives passed
into the hands of Erich Offermann. Between 1929 and 1932 a series of
bibliographical guides to historical and technical aviation literature
were published. The archives ground to a halt after 1933, when German political conditions dictated a breaking from foreign associations,
especially, one would imagine, from one founded by an American
Jew.[59]

   In August 1927, the Guggenheim fund issued a $5,000 grant to the
Royal Aeronautical Society for "supervising the collection and dissemination of important technical information not otherwise widely
disseminated."[60] The society, under the direction of president Air
Vice-Marshal Sir Sefton Brancker and secretary Captain J. Laurence
Pritchard, used the grant to double the size of its journal and to print
scientific abstracts from the world's technical aviation press, as well
as increase the number of annual lectures and widely disseminate
reprints of these lectures.[61] Pritchard remarked in a letter to the Guggenheim fund's British representative Maj. R. H. Mayo that "it is my
firm belief, and I know it is of all the leading designers and others to
whom I have spoken, that this Fund has done more good for the advancement of the cause of aviation throughout the world than anything else."[62] Before the Guggenheim fund closed in 1930, it issued
three more grants to the Royal Aeronautical Society to continue the
work begun under the earlier funding. In January 1928 the society
received $5,000 to cover its activities through 1928; in December 1928,
the fund augmented this with another $5,000 grant to fund its work
through 1929. Finally, in October 1929, with the Guggenheim fund
closing down, Harry Guggenheim sent the society another $10,000
to support a further two years' work.[63]

   As with the Royal Aeronautical Society, the Guggenheim fund supported Italy's Associazione Italiana di Aerotecnica (AIDA) in publicizing aeronautical information. The fund awarded a $5,000 grant

to AIDA in November 1927, and issued another $5,000 grant in January 1929, following this with a final $10,000 grant as the fund neared the end of its existence. AIDA used these grants to increase the aviation coverage in its monthly magazine, *Aerotecnica*, including publication of abstracts from foreign aviation journals and English-language translations of articles appearing in *Aerotecnica*.[64]

In four years, through their educational programs, the Guggenheims presented the United States with a comprehensive program of organized aeronautical education, running from small elementary school programs to university-level research courses. Aeronautical education often went hand in hand with aeronautical promotion, and, including his $500,000 grant to New York University, Daniel Guggenheim authorized $2,692,388.67 for educational activities.[65] This money provided the United States with research centers and educational institutions specializing in aeronautical engineering, air law, aviation education, the commercial and social impact of air transportation, and dissemination of aeronautical information. The Daniel Guggenheim Fund for the Promotion of Aeronautics also greatly influenced aviation activities outside the classroom and laboratory. Between 1926 and 1930, the fund created a "Model Air Line" and a special weather-reporting service along its airway, investigated blind flight, supported a worldwide safe airplane competition, sponsored two special air tours, published special reports and bulletins, and created a special medal award for aeronautics. Aside from education, there were other fields of endeavor where, once again, Guggenheim money pointed the way to future aeronautical development.

CHAPTER 6

The Guggenheim Model Air Line
and Weather Service

THE Daniel Guggenheim Fund for the Promotion of Aeronautics made three important contributions to the development of commercial passenger-carrying air-transport service in America. First, it created a "Model Air Line" between San Francisco and Los Angeles, run by Western Air Express using Fokker trimotor transports, which demonstrated successful, on-time, accident-free, and reliable service. The Model Air Line also benefited from the second Guggenheim fund contribution, establishment of a weather reporting service along the airline route that later served as a model for Weather Bureau reporting activities. The third contribution was the fund's research on blind flying, situations where the pilot could not rely on outside visual cues for reference.

The emergence of American airmail and passenger carriers helped create the proper environment for Guggenheim involvement in American air-transport affairs. Commercial aviation in the United States lagged far behind Europe until Congress passed the Air Mail Act of 1925, popularly known as the Kelly Act. This act opened the way for private airlines to carry the mail, and in October 1925 the Post Office Department awarded the first five contracts to private carriers, these going to Colonial Air Transport, the Robertson Aircraft Corporation, Varney Speed Lines, Western Air Express, and National Air Transport.[1] By the end of 1926, a dozen other feeder operators had joined the original five. These carriers all flew mail and some air express freight. Two, however, began flying passengers: Western Air Express (WAE) and Pacific Air Transport. The former operated a 660-mile mail service between Los Angeles and Salt Lake City, over Civil Air Mail (CAM) route 4, starting on April 17, 1926. After a month of operation, Western's president and general manager, Harris M. "Pop" Hanshue, decided the line was financially successful enough to offer passenger service in addition to flying the mail. Accordingly, Western Air Express began the nation's first scheduled passenger airline service on May 23, 1926. During the following year WAE's pilots covered roughly half a million miles in their single-engine Douglas M-2 and M-4 mailplanes, cruising at 110 mph with two passengers and a load of mail. The first year the line carried 125,000 pounds of mail and 350 passengers. The flights often involved danger. The CAM-4 Los Angeles-Salt Lake City route passed over barren desert with a stop at Las Vegas. High winds swept through the mountain regions, and at Los Angeles ocean fogs rolled in from the coast to blot out the field. Winter flights encountered snow and heavy icing, and while the pilots could obtain the latest weather reports from Los Angeles, Las Vegas, and Salt Lake City when they landed, their planes did not have the newly developed "wireless" aircraft radio equipment to receive weather reports in flight. Though the Douglas M-2's and M-4's had reliable Liberty engines and WAE frequently overhauled them, an engine failure over the rocky desert country could spell disaster.[2]

Remarkably, during its first year of operation, WAE cancelled only nine of its 730 scheduled trips, seven due to bad weather and two due to engine failure; no one was killed or injured, nor did WAE even suffer a crashed airplane. This fine record stemmed from WAE's careful maintenance, inspection, and flight operations programs, and from the skillful management of Hanshue. At this point, to help WAE maintain its safe and reliable service, the Guggenheim fund made plans for an equipment loan.

In later years, Harry Guggenheim credited his father, Daniel, with providing the impetus behind the fund's support of Western Air Express. Daniel Guggenheim frequently dropped in at the fund's office at 598 Madison Avenue, and persistently demanded that the fund do something for American air passengers. "We dodged the issue for a long while," Harry Guggenheim recalled, "and tried to satisfy him with the innumerable reasons why it could not be done. He flatly refused 'No' for an answer and his persistence and vision overcame all of our objections."[3] In response, Harry Guggenheim summoned the nation's leading contract airmail operators to a meeting in New York City on May 27, 1927. Present were Harris M. Hanshue of Western Air Express; Walter T. Varney and Charles Wrightson of

Varney Speed Lines; William B. Robertson and James D. Livingston of the Robertson Aircraft Corporation; L. H. Brittain of Northwest Airways; V. C. Gorst of Pacific Air Transport; George P. Tidmarsh of the Boeing Airplane Company; C. M. Keys, Carl B. Fritsche, and Paul Henderson of National Air Transport; C. H. Biddlecombe of Colonial Air Transport; William B. Stout and Stanley Knauss of Stout Air Service; William B. Mayo of the Ford Motor Company; Anthony Joseph of Colorado Airways; Reed Chambers of Florida Airways; Clifford S. Ball of Pittsburgh; G. S. Childs of the Pitcairn Company; and Assistant Secretary of Commerce for Aeronautics William P. MacCracken, Jr. At the meeting, Harry Guggenheim proposed that the fund subsidize equipment loans of new trimotor airplanes to the airmail operators as a means of promoting the inauguration of passenger-carrying airline service in the United States. The fund would establish one or more "thoroughly organized" passenger routes with radio communications and meteorological services approved by the Department of Commerce's Aeronautics Branch. This civilian "Model Air Line" experiment would be more extensive in organization and planning than the army's earlier "model airway" created for military service in 1922. The army experiment had catered to military needs only though some civilian pilots had flown over it. Peak military passenger loads during any single year barely topped the five hundred mark, and the "model airway" soon died out, despite its demonstrating the usefulness of such facilities as weather reporting stations.[4]

The airmail operators, on the whole, did not receive the Guggenheim proposal with favor. "All of the big shots of the air mail in that stage of development threw cold water on the idea of flying passengers," Guggenheim recollected. "In fact, only Hanshue and Varney had the vision to accept our proposition."[5] Cognizant of WAE's passenger service on the West Coast, Harry Guggenheim turned with favor towards Hanshue's Western Air Express as the chosen line for the Guggenheim experimental service. At a meeting of the fund's board of directors on June 16, 1927, the trustees approved a grant, not to exceed $400,000, for the purpose of making equipment loans "to promote the inauguration of passenger lines, on certain selected routes, in the United States."[6]

Guggenheim stipulated to Hanshue and WAE's operations manager, Corliss C. Moseley, that the company must select a multiengine transport aircraft capable of continuing a flight with one engine shut down. Hanshue wanted a plane with a 120 mph cruising speed, ten or more passengers and a thousand pounds cargo capacity, an endurance of six hours, and a ceiling of 16,000 feet. Consequently, Han-

shue and Moseley faced only two possible choices for such a multiengine airliner, aside from some proposed paper studies still in
design stage. These two were the Fokker F.VIIb-3m and the Ford
4-AT, both high-wing monoplane trimotors powered by three Wright
J-4 and J-5 220 hp Whirlwind radial engines. The F.VIIb-3m was of
all-wood construction, while the Ford 4-AT featured an all-metal
structure, with a distinctive corrugated external skin. In September
1927, Moseley visited various aircraft manufacturers and pilots, seeking their advice. All agreed that the choice really was between the
Fokker and Ford airplanes, and, while Ford was far ahead through
the use of all-metal construction, the Fokker had more desirable traits.
Moseley studied both aircraft carefully. The F.VIIb-3m was a stable
airplane, responsive to the pilot. In contrast, the Ford Tri-motor was
a handful for any pilot. As early airline pilot Ernest K. Gann recalls,
"A day's work in a Ford cockpit required resourcefulness and considerable muscle. Even in smooth air, flying a Ford became a chore,
if only because it was so difficult to keep in trim."[7] Further, should one
of the Ford's wing-mounted engines throw a propeller, it might enter
the cockpit or cut the plane's external control lines. The Fokker was
not as dangerous in this respect. Additionally, to meet the Guggenheim fund's requirement that the plane be capable of sustained flight
with one engine dead, Moseley asked both Fokker and Ford officials
if they could produce versions of their planes with three Pratt &
Whitney 425 hp Wasp radial engines replacing the three 225 hp
Whirlwinds. The Wasp was America's first aircraft engine greater
than 400 hp to enter general service and, in the words of engine researcher C. Fayette Taylor, was "the first large radial air-cooled engine of what may be called 'modern' design."[8] After his discussions,
Moseley believed that Ford would take longer than Fokker to produce
a Wasp-powered trimotor suitable to the requirements of the Guggenheim fund.[9]

   After comparing the Fokker to some proposed airplane design studies by Boeing, Douglas, Keystone, and Sikorsky, Moseley recommended that Western Air Express and the Guggenheim fund select
Fokker. At the beginning of October 1927, Harry Guggenheim met
with fund trustee Charles A. Lindbergh and aviation consultant
C. S. "Casey" Jones. At this conference, the three men agreed with
Moseley's recommendation that the fund and Western Air Express
give Fokker the task of developing the new passenger trimotor, essentially a much modified version of the earlier F.VIIb-3m.[10] Fokker
designated the new plane the F.X, but airlines and pilots designated
it the F-10 Super Trimotor. The new plane had Dutch-built F.VIIb-

3m wings, but featured a larger twelve-passenger fuselage built by Fokker's American company, Atlantic Aircraft Corporation, and three Wasp engines. The Fokker's plush mahogany cabin included upholstered seats, reading lights, and baggage racks. C. C. Moseley had persuaded Fokker to change the pilot's cockpit location to seat the pilot higher in the fuselage and slightly aft to give him greater forward and downward vision. By raising an adjustable seat, the pilot also had adequate rear vision, something completely lacking on earlier Fokker planes.[11]

On October 4, 1927, Western Air Express and The Daniel Guggenheim Fund for the Promotion of Aeronautics jointly announced that the Guggenheim fund would loan money to WAE to set up a model airline between Los Angeles and San Francisco using three Fokker F-10 trimotors cruising at 120 mph and covering the air distance of 365 miles between San Francisco's Oakland Airport and Los Angeles in three hours. The F-10's would leave each airport at 10:30 A.M., arriving at the other terminal at 1:30 P.M. Allowing an additional half hour at each end to travel between the terminal and the city, the journey could be completed in roughly four hours, instead of the thirteen and one-half hours then required by railroad service. WAE would furnish its passengers with an inflight lunch, the latest newspapers, market reports, magazines, and inflight radio listening. The Department of Commerce would assist the project by installing all available weather reporting and navigational aids along the length of the airway.[12]

The releases did not spell out the terms of the loan agreement. Actually, the Guggenheims always sought to avoid any arrangement that might appear as an attempt by the fund to profit financially from its transactions, or as an attempt by the fund to assist some institution or company to the disadvantage of its competitors. The WAE transaction was the closest the Guggenheim fund ever came to a commercial transaction. The purpose behind it was clearly to create a model airline that might, as its title indicated, serve as a model for subsequent passenger airline operations in the United States. When, through the error of an advertising manager, Western Air Express issued brochures picturing the airline as in a profit-making partnership with the Guggenheim fund, Harry Guggenheim quickly investigated to determine what Hanshue was up to, and the airline immediately withdrew the misleading advertisement. Under the terms of the Western Air Express–Guggenheim agreement, the fund would loan the airline $155,000, to be repaid over a two-year period at 5 percent interest. The money covered purchase of three Fokker F-10 trimotors at $50,000 each, plus incidental expenses. Early in December 1927, Western Air Express, the Guggenheim fund, and the Atlantic Aircraft Corporation signed a contract for three F-10 airplanes, and on December 6, 1927, Guggenheim vice-president Rear Adm. Hutchinson I. Cone sent Anthony Fokker the fund's check for $50,000 as initial payment. By February 15, 1928, the first F-10 was two-thirds complete, with the second aircraft half complete, and the third aircraft close behind.[13]

The first F-10 completed an uneventful maiden flight at Atlantic's Teterboro, New Jersey, airfield, on March 21, 1928. The plane displayed good controllability, a maximum speed of 145 mph, and a cruising speed of 125 mph. On March 23, Fokker took the controls himself, making a trial flight with a full load of passengers. WAE president Hanshue took delivery of the first F-10, resplendent in scarlet finish, on April 24, 1928, and put it into service with the other two trimotors on the Los Angeles–San Francisco run the next month. The advance publicity and subsequent public reaction presaged the fanfare surrounding Concorde SST service between Europe and America a half-century later; indeed, WAE even provided its customers with similar VIP treatment, including exclusive Cadillac transportation service at Los Angeles and Oakland. On May 26, the "Model Air Line" began service. Agreeably, the experiment got off to a good start. Thousands of people at Los Angeles and Oakland saw the simultaneous departures of northbound and southbound F-10's, filled with passengers who had paid fifty dollars for the trip. During the three-hour flights, passengers munched cold chicken lunches served by the F-10 copilots, and dozed in the comfortable seats. The trimotors passed in flight at the precise halfway mark, and then continued on to land on schedule at their destinations. A new era in air transportation had begun. WAE subsequently bought two additional F-10's for expanded service, and, after extending its route network, purchased twenty-one additional aircraft based on the F-10, known as the F-10A. These had wider-span American-built wings, higher performance, and provisions for advanced Wasp engines. The F-10 and F-10A Super Trimotor series saw extensive service with American airline and airmail operators until the death of Knute Rockne on March 31, 1931, brought to a close the era of the Fokker trimotor in American service.[14]

Furnishing suitable airplanes was only one part of the model airline assistance program. Another, and farther reaching, aspect in-

volved creation of a special weather service along the San Francisco–
Los Angeles air route. In the absence of any means whereby a pilot
could safely guide his aircraft through fog or clouds to his destination,
the best available assistance came in the form of organized weather
reporting services, informing him of expected weather conditions
over his flight route. Too many pilots had taken off only later to find
their destinations shrouded in clouds or fog. The more prudent among
them turned back, seeking a clear alternate field; the more reckless,
sometimes enticed by a beckoning hole in the clouds or fog, attempted
to fly through to their destinations, frequently adding to fatality
statistics.

Actually, the state of aviation weather forecasting prior to 1926 was
poor. The Weather Bureau issued three daily forecast reports, and,
if the airfield a pilot flew from had radio equipment, the pilot could
obtain a report of weather conditions earlier in the day. The time between the report and his departure often spelled the difference between an accurate and inaccurate forecast. Pilots did not have inflight radio communications enabling them to learn of changing
weather conditions while they flew to their destinations. Prior to the
Air Commerce Act of 1926, the Weather Bureau operated with the
same aviation weather facilities it had utilized during the First World
War.[15] In July 1926, Congress passed a deficiency bill granting the
Weather Bureau $75,000 to establish and maintain twenty-one ad-
ditional weather balloon stations along some civil airways to provide
more up-to-date information. The Weather Bureau noted that "if a
pilot is to leave at 2 for a 4-hour flight, a general forecast issued at
8 a.m. is of little use to him; what his experience has shown that he
needs is information at 1:45 p.m. as to conditions then prevailing,
and a prediction, based upon these conditions, for the next 5 hours."[16]

Even before beginning its mail service between Los Angeles and
Salt Lake City, Western Air Express had informed the Weather
Bureau that it believed the existing weather reporting services along
the route to be inadequate, asking for more reporting stations.[17] The
airline, then, welcomed the Guggenheim fund's intention to furnish
a trial weather reporting service over the San Francisco–Los Angeles
route for a period of one year. The Guggenheim weather reporting
service plan dated to the creation of the Daniel Guggenheim Committee on Aeronautical Meteorology, which Harry Guggenheim and
the fund trustees established in August 1927 to make meteorologists
and pilots aware of each others' specialties. Harry Guggenheim had
discussed organizing a meteorological committee with F. Trubee
Davison, Edward P. Warner, William P. MacCracken, Jr., the three

assistant secretaries for aeronautics in the War, Navy, and Commerce departments, and also with Charles F. Marvin, the chief of the Weather Bureau, all of whom enthusiastically endorsed the idea. So, with the cooperation of these agencies, the fund created a special five-man meteorological committee, composed of Carl Gustaf Rossby, chairman; Willis R. Gregg, Weather Bureau; Maj. William R. Blair, War Department; Lt. F. W. Reichelderfer, Navy Department; and Thomas H. Chapman, Commerce Department.[18]

All of these individuals later achieved prominence in meteorology, and Gregg and Reichelderfer became chiefs of the Weather Bureau. Most interesting of these men, however, was Carl Gustaf Rossby, a fun-loving Swedish scientist. Rossby came to the United States in 1926 from Sweden, where he had studied the new science of air mass analysis under its discoverer, Vilhelm Bjerknes. He worked for eighteen months with the Weather Bureau, trying to convince reluctant officials to adopt the novel method of weather forecasting. Rossby left the Weather Bureau under criticism after issuing forecasts without first consulting his superiors. On Reichelderfer's advice, the Guggenheim fund quickly selected Rossby for the fund's meteorological committee. Years later Patrick Hughes of the Environmental Science Services Administration described Rossby as "perhaps the most brilliant theoretical meteorologist of the 20th century."[19]

Rossby invited Jerome C. Hunsaker to meet with the Guggenheim meteorological committee on September 15, 1927, to discuss the feasibility of meteorological information services for commercial aviation. Hunsaker had left naval service in November 1926 to join the staff of Dr. Frank B. Jewett at Bell Telephone Laboratories as assistant vice-president and research engineer, in charge of all research on aviation radio communication.[20] At this meeting, Rossby informed Hunsaker that he believed airways should have meteorologists at each airport and trained observers placed every sixty miles along the airway, with a few observers reporting weather conditions as much as fifty to seventy-five miles on either side of the flight path. Rossby further recommended that the Guggenheim fund equip a section of the airway system with weather reporting services at its own expense, as a method of proving the feasibility of such a system.[21] By mid-October the meteorological committee had decided to install a trial weather reporting service on a section of the American airway system, although members still were uncertain where to locate it. Weather Bureau officials wanted an experimental service covering many states, but this was clearly beyond the financial capabilities of the Guggenheim fund. The fund's meteorological committee prepared elaborate plans for a trial reporting service from Iowa City in the west, to St. Louis in the south, and Buffalo in the north. The eastern portion was to include service from Boston to Baltimore. Though Hunsaker had Bell Telephone Laboratories prepare a tentative outline of the equipment requirements for this proposal, Guggenheim fund officials, because of time and cost requirements, finally decided to incorporate the meteorological reporting service only along the Western Air Express model airline from San Francisco to Los Angeles.[22]

By early 1928, Harry F. Guggenheim and the members of the Guggenheim meteorological committee were busy making final plans for the San Francisco–Los Angeles weather service. The basic outline of the service involved a series of observation stations reporting to the two terminals at Los Angeles and San Francisco. These stations would report on the weather conditions three times a day to the two terminals, where meteorologists would inform departing pilots what weather conditions they might encounter on their flights. The meteorological network would serve all airmen, not just those of Western Air Express. Additionally, planes having radio receiving equipment—and all WAE Fokker F-10's did—could receive inflight reports of weather conditions, especially warnings of any weather changes. Pilots who did not have such equipment could fly over specially designated ground points during their flights where ground observers would spread out canvas strips indicating weather conditions. For example, San Francisco meteorologists often asked pilots flying non-radio-equipped planes from San Francisco to Los Angeles to fly over Bakerfield's weather reporting station to ascertain weather conditions at Los Angeles's Vail Field. At Bakersfield, the pilot might see three canvas strips laid out in a "U" indicating that Los Angeles had ceiling unlimited conditions. However, he might see two parallel horizontal canvas strips, indicating that Los Angeles was overcast, with a cloud ceiling of 1,000 to 2,000 feet, or two strips in the form of cross, indicating that he should land at Bakersfield immediately for a detailed weather report.[23]

In March 1928, Harry Guggenheim informed the federal government's Air Coordination Committee, consisting of F. Trubee Davison, William P. MacCracken, Jr., and Edward P. Warner, that The Daniel Guggenheim Fund for the Promotion of Aeronautics intended to organize an aviation weather service along all the important airway routes between San Francisco and Los Angeles. Jerome Hunsaker had arranged through the Pacific Telephone and Telegraph Company for free telephone service between the reporting stations and the terminals, and the Guggenheim fund supplied Carl Gustaf Rossby to direct the weather reporting service. By late May 1928, Hunsaker had recommended that the Guggenheim fund manage the Los Angeles–San Francisco weather service for one year, from June 1928 through June 1929, at which time he hoped that the federal government's Weather Bureau would assume control of the system. Rossby had estimated that the weather reporting system might cost the Guggenheim fund $28,130 to run for one year; in fact, the actual cost came to slightly less, $27,561.22. Rossby arranged with WAE president Harris Hanshue for the meteorological telephone reporting network to enter service on May 21, 1928, five days before Western Air Express began its "Model Air Line" passenger service between Los Angeles and San Francisco. This provided time to check out the system and its operators and allowed pilots to become familiar with the system before using it in their commercial operations.[24]

The Guggenheim fund could not have chosen a better location for their trial weather service, for the airways from Los Angeles to San Francisco provided a variety of weather conditions. The air routes from Los Angeles passed northwest between the Santa Monica and Sierra Madre ranges, crossed the San Fernando Valley, and proceeded up the San Joaquin Valley via a pass at Lebec in the Tehachapi Mountains, and on through the coastal hills to Oakland. An alternate route, without beacon lights, diverged from the main lighted route at Lebec, passing over Buena Vista Lake and continuing to the San Benito River, following the river and the Southern Pacific railroad line to San Jose, and then up San Francisco Bay to Oakland. The principal danger to flying these routes consisted of fog, clouds, and general low visibility. In the mountainous areas of the Sierras, low visibility meant great danger, the ever-present hazard of flying into hills and mountains while encountering fog. California experienced two types of fog. The first was a night fog from irrigated valleys and the San Francisco Bay area, usually appearing during the winter months on calm nights inland from the coast. The second type was a coastal ocean fog, especially prevalent in the summer months and usually appearing in afternoons, moving slowly inland from the ocean, often burning off or taking on the appearance of low clouds. Fog thus posed a year-round problem, though aviators learned to cope with it by flying inland routes in the summer, and coastal routes in the winter.[25]

As originally established, the Guggenheim meteorological service along the Model Air Line consisted of twenty-two reporting stations connected via telephone to Los Angeles and San Francisco. These two major terminals had radio equipment to transmit inflight weather reports. Each station submitted a weather report three times daily, at 9:35 A.M., 11:05 A.M., and at 12:35 P.M. If Los Angeles or San Francisco terminals requested, a station might make extra reports at thirty-minute intervals. On these reports, the ground observers gave wind direction (the direction from which the wind blew) and velocity, weather conditions (fair, haze, smoke, fog, rain, showers), amount of clouds and cloud forms, cloud ceiling, horizontal visibility, temperature, and pressure. A typical station report thus might read, "Lebec: southeast, strong, fair, overcast, nimbus, five hundred, unlimited, fifty-six degrees, twenty-six point twelve." Rossby, in his instructions to ground observers, emphasized that their reports must be punctual, accurate, and as brief as possible.[26] The heavy demands placed on the experimental weather reporting service by three air transport companies—Western Air Express, Pacific Air Transport, and Maddux Air Lines, all of which operated a Los Angeles to San Francisco service—as well as numerous airmail and private fliers, soon forced the Guggenheim fund to extend the service, adding a further eighteen reporting stations, increasing the number of reporting stations from twenty-two to forty. Further, at the request of these air transport companies, Rossby increased the number of daily reports from three to four, and then to six, and used pilot balloon stations to acquire information on winds at cruising altitudes. Eventually, the Model Air Line had six pilot balloon stations, one each at San Francisco, Los Angeles, San Diego, Lebec, Fresno, and Hollister, three operated by the Guggenheim fund, two operated by the Weather Bureau, and one managed by the city of San Francisco. Rossby also added weather report collection facilities at Fresno and Bakerfield, raising these locations to full equality with San Francisco and Los Angeles.[27]

After beginning on May 21, 1928, the weather service quickly proved its worth. In addition to the Weather Bureau and Department of Commerce, the army and navy extended the Guggenheim fund their cooperation. The navy supplied theodolites to track weather balloons, and the army furnished Rossby with an assistant, Lt. Willis R. Taylor, who flew Rossby to remote weather reporting sites and helped him recruit observers from meteorologists, airmen, and airport operators along the projected airways.[28] Less than a week after the experimental meteorological service began operations, no less than five Los Angeles bound pilots called ground stations by radio for weather conditions around Los Angeles, and within a month C. C. Moseley of Western Air Express was able to send Rossby reports from his pilots endorsing the new weather reporting service and citing instances when it enabled them to detour storms or reduce their flying time. Lt. Col. G. C. Brant, commandant of the Army Air Corps base at Crissy Field, stated, "The Guggenheim Experimental Airways Weather Service has done more to raise the morale of the Army Flying Corps than anything else that has happened since I became associated with it. Formerly a pilot did not know what was ahead; now he knows and is prepared."[29] The Guggenheim experimental service later furnished the Naval Air Station at San Diego with a teletype receiver giving the navy access to weather service reports.[30] Historian Donald R. Whitnah has credited Guggenheim meteorological activities as being "the major source of aid to the Pacific Coast expansion."[31] With the Guggenheim experimental weather service handling the heavy air traffic in southern and central California, the Weather Bureau was free to expand its Pacific coast weather aviation services further north to Seattle.[32]

In August 1928, Carl Gustaf Rossby left the fund's experimental meteorological service headquarters at Vail Field to return east and join the faculty of MIT as director of MIT's Guggenheim-created meteorology program. Before leaving, Rossby placed the meteorological service under the control of Edward H. Bowie, the Weather Bureau's district forecaster at San Francisco. Local officials were highly impressed with Rossby's management of the service during the short time he acted as director. G. B. Hegardt, port manager for Oakland, California, the northern terminus of the service, wrote Harry Guggenheim that Rossby "certainly had succeeded in making the weather department chief officials of this district enthusiastic over the service . . . they are now thoroughly sold on the proposition, and look forward, with a great deal of pleasure, in taking over and operating it."[33]

Two major questions faced Bowie during his tenure as director of the experimental meteorological service. One involved extending the weather reporting service to cover night flight operations, and the other concerned ensuring that the Weather Bureau would assume control of the experimental weather service after the one-year Guggenheim program ended. During the fall and winter of 1928, Bowie recommended night weather reports, using a ceiling light projector to obtain cloud height data at night. The ceiling light projected an angled beam into the air while, five hundred feet away, a ground observer used an alidade to measure altitude, placing the sights of the alidade on the spot of light on the cloud layer. He could then read the height of the cloud layer from the graduated quadrant on the alidade. Harry Guggenheim quickly authorized Bowie to establish night reporting services along the Model Air Line and the night reports soon proved their worth. C. Eugene Johnson, operations manager for Western Air Express's rival, Pacific Air Transport, reported that his pilots "found it to be invaluable. . . . All in all, we believe it a most important addition to our weather reporting service on this run, and are decidedly appreciative of the efforts expended in the gathering of this data."[34] Military pilots also found the night reports useful.

Bowie further increased the efficiency of the reporting service by utilizing telephones for local weather reporting, and teletype machines for long-distance reporting. The teletype printer was more efficient than using slower long-distance telephone reporting networks. Bell Telephone Laboratories' vice-president Jerome C. Hunsaker believed that the key to accurate and prompt weather reporting lay in teletype communications from reporting stations, together with air-to-ground and ground-to-air radio communications equipment. He arranged for Pacific Telephone and Telegraph to furnish the Guggenheim fund's experimental service with teletype equipment, and it clearly demonstrated its superiority to the slower and more complex telegraph and telephone reporting methods. Hunsaker's prediction of the suitability of teletype communications to weather reporting was valid. Within two years after entering service in 1928, teletype communications covered eight thousand miles of American airways.[35]

When Rossby left for MIT, the Guggenheim fund arranged for Bowie and the Weather Bureau to assume control of the service, using Guggenheim funds. The agreement stipulated that the Weather Bureau and federal government were under no obligation to continue the weather service after it expired on July 30, 1929. By the late fall of 1928, Harry Guggenheim and other individuals were hard at work to ensure that the federal government would take over the weather service. In California, Bowie authorized a local aviation promoter, R. E. Fisher, the chairman of the California Aeronautical Committee, to begin a letter-writing campaign to California's senators and congressmen urging them to vote for appropriations measures providing for continuations of the Los Angeles–San Francisco service. Harry Guggenheim himself asked Assistant Secretary of Commerce for Aeronautics William P. MacCracken, Jr., to use his influence to continue the weather service with federal funding and under federal supervision once the fund's activities expired. Coming in the post-Lindbergh era when congressional support for aviation ventures took a marked upswing, their efforts met with success. The Weather Bureau received appropriations to continue the California weather service after June 30, 1928. The Guggenheim experimental meteorological service had served as a prototype for all future Weather Bureau weather-reporting services along America's airways.[36]

The airway meteorological service greatly influenced nonaviation enterprises as well. The frequent daily forecasts, for example, enabled meteorologists to issue highly accurate rain warnings during the summer and fall of 1928 to California fruit growers, so they could remove fruit being sun-dried before rains destroyed it. The United States Forest Service in California used radio reports from the Guggenheim meteorological service to provide weather information useful in combating and preventing forest fires. One meteorologist assigned to the Forest Service in the Santa Barbara National Forest reported that meteorological service reports enabled him to channel a fire "as one would herd a bunch of sheep" into a basin where waiting fire-fighters put it out.[37] Finally, the Automobile Club of Southern California leased a teletype printer from Pacific Telephone and Telegraph to enable tourists and vacationers to plan their outings with precise weather information. Subsequently, when fund officials campaigned for the federal government to assume control of the service, the automobile club became an active supporter of the plan. As with other Guggenheim fund activities, the experimental meteorological service generated benefits not foreseen when fund trustees authorized the weather-reporting program. Both the Guggenheim Model Air Line and the experimental weather service served as examples for future airway management. The two endeavors came at a crucial time in the development of American air transport, for the number of airline passengers rose from 18,679 in 1927 to 385,000 in 1930. By 1935 the figure was doubled, almost 800,000.[38]

The third contribution the Guggenheim fund made to commercial aviation was research on solving the problems of fog or blind flying. This involved creation of a special flight research laboratory at Mitchel Field, Long Island, acquisition of specially instrumented research airplanes, and a comprehensive flight research program. Once again, Guggenheim efforts in this direction met with success. The story of that success provides one of the most important episodes in the technological development of aviation.

CHAPTER 7

The Guggenheim
Assault on Blind Flight

BETWEEN September 1926 and October 1929, the Guggenheim fund undertook research on the problems of blind flight, especially fog flying. Such research aimed at producing ground and airborne instrumentation enabling the pilot to take off and land his aircraft without recourse to any visual cues aside from those provided by his cockpit instruments. Complete blind flying involved solving three major problems. The first was point-to-point navigation while in fog or above clouds; the second involved maintaining a safe attitude by using instrument readings to provide cues for control changes necessary to maintain straight and level flight; and the third required providing ground facilities that would enable a pilot to land or take off in very poor visibility conditions. In the mid-1920s none of these measures were really possible. Flying then was commonly termed "contact flying," for the pilot flew in constant sight of the ground, following known roads or railroads. The more skillful airmen, such as airmail pilots, did undertake long-distance flights over unfamiliar country, relying on their compasses for ascertaining direction, but on the whole, as Charles A. Lindbergh recalled, flight instructors warned their students, "A good pilot doesn't depend on his instruments." In early 1917, for example, Harry Guggenheim's flight instructor had pointed to a training plane's instruments and said, "See those instruments? Pay no attention to them. In the first place, they are not accurate, and I want you to get the feel of the ship regardless of instruments."[1]

Within a decade all this had changed: a pilot who flew without implicit trust in his instruments was a foolish one. Airlines could fly on instruments virtually from the moment of lift-off to touchdown. Nationally, the United States had a network of air traffic control stations, which the Federal Bureau of Air Commerce first established in July 1936, to monitor and direct airliner flight traffic patterns. Airline pilots flew into airports with cloud ceilings sometimes as low as one hundred feet, using instrument approach techniques as they followed invisible radio beams generated by radio range beacons. Further reflecting the change from visual "head out of the cockpit" flying to "under the hood" instrument techniques, the Bureau of Air Commerce deemphasized installing lighted airway beacons, and placed greater emphasis on installing radio range beacons and training commercial pilots to use the new radio navigation facilities.[2] Airplane accidents in inclement weather continued, but, as technology developed to cope with bad weather and night flying, such accidents increasingly reflected bad judgment on the part of the pilot.

Even before the advent of true blind flying instruments, some pilots of better than average skill taught themselves to fly limited instrument-only flights using just airspeed, altimeter, compass, and turn-and-bank indicators for reference. The turn-and-bank indicator, developed during the First World War by Elmer Sperry, warned the pilot of any divergence from straight flight and enabled him in a limited way to navigate his airplane while in clouds and fog without inadvertently entering a banked or spiraling position. During one test flight in 1921, Army Lt. J. Parker van Zandt flew a De Havilland D.H. 4B equipped with such an indicator through heavy fog and clouds from Moundsville, West Virginia, to Washington, D.C. During the daring one and one-half hour flight, two escorting Martin bombers not so equipped had to turn back.[3] One winter night while Lindbergh flew the mail, a bad snow storm caught his airplane near Peoria, Illinois, forcing him to ascend blind through clouds lest he remain too low and crash into woods around the Illinois River. During the blind flight, Lindbergh relied solely on his altimeter, turn-and-bank, and airspeed indicators, using them to guide his efforts during recovery from two stalls, the first induced by letting the plane's airspeed drop, and the second by maintaining too steep an angle of attack during recovery from the first stall. He recalled, "I'd learned that above all else it was essential to keep the turn indicator centered and the air-speed needle high. . . . I taught myself to fly by instruments that night."[4]

Pilot reliance upon instruments rather than the "feel" of the airplane, ran counter to contemporary training. Instructors warned students not to trust their instruments. Tragically, this advice was completely unsound, for safety in blind flight required implicit trust in one's instruments, even to the point of deliberately ignoring all other sensory evidence. In blind flight, the body had none of its usual visual references to guide it and let it know for certain what position it occupied. Vertigo could induce spatial disorientation so that a pilot might believe his aircraft was flying in a turn when, in fact, it was flying straight and level. "Vertigo," one veteran airman wrote, "has been a flight hazard since the first aviator flew into a cloud, happily discovered that he didn't get wet, and then stalled and spun out the bottom."[5] A pilot flying in marginal clear weather conditions where the horizon was vague or indistinct, or making abrupt head-turning movements while maneuvering his plane through turns and banks, often encountered vertigo. Without recourse to proper instruments giving him the plane's actual position, he might make unnecessary control "corrections," perhaps with fatal results.

In 1926, Air Corps Maj. David A. Myers proved decisively that a pilot must not trust his senses over his instruments. Myers had pilots sit in a Jones-Barany revolving chair with their eyes closed. If the rotation rate became constant, a pilot could not tell which way the chair was rotating. If the researcher slowed the rotation of the chair to a lower rate, the pilot being tested invariably thought the rotation had stopped. Finally, when the researcher actually stopped the chair, the pilot believed that the chair was now rotating in the opposite direction! Another Air Corps aeromedical researcher, Capt. William C. Ocker, added an instrument panel with turn-and-bank and magnetic compass indicators to the chair, and shut off the subject pilot from the outside. As the chair spun, most pilots at first refused to believe what the turn-and-bank indicator read, relying instead on their own misled senses.[6]

Part of the key to safe blind flying lay in developing radio navigation devices so that the pilot could guide his craft along its journey by following directional signals from ground radio beacons. As early as 1907, German radio researchers had patented the radio beacon concept, later adopted by the Commerce Department's Bureau of Standards. The bureau's radio beacon consisted of two loop antennae crossed at a ninety-degree angle. One generated an N Morse signal (−.), while the other generated an A Morse signal (.−). Midway between the N and A signals, the two signals merged, generating a monotone equisignal beam that fanned out from the beacon. Thus, the radio beacon field, if viewed from above, looked as in Figure 1:

FOUR-COURSE LOW-FREQUENCY RADIO RANGE

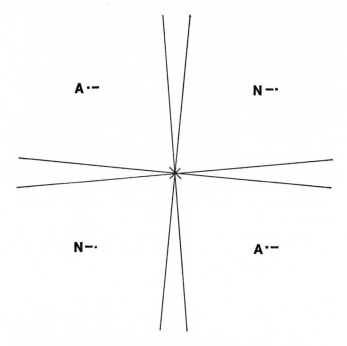

Pilot listens for equisignal (monotone),
then flies down the beam.

Figure 1

In 1920, the Bureau of Standards, acting at the request of the War Department, undertook development of an aural airborne direction finder, using signals from a two-antenna radio beacon. As the pilot flew down the equisignal, he could determine if he was deviating from his course by the amount of A or N signal he heard. If he heard a clear monotone, he was on course. Flight trials at Washington, D.C., and later at McCook Field, Ohio, indicated the feasibility of such a radio beacon, but the Bureau of Standards delayed this work to research other projects. They did not reemphasize radio beacon research until 1926, when the bureau's Radio Division authorized experimental beacon installations at College Park, Maryland, and Bellefonte, Pennsylvania, as a result of pressure from the Commerce Department's newly created Aeronautics Branch. The test beacons operated on a frequency band of 285 to 315 kilocycles.[7]

The Bureau of Standard's Aeronautical Research Division began active work on aeronautical radio problems starting on July 1, 1926, under the direction of J. Howard Dellinger, Harry Diamond, and Francis W. Dunmore. By the end of the year, bureau research pilots were flying a test De Havilland D.H. 4 at College Park airfield with an experimental visual indicator in the cockpit that showed the pilot when he was flying on the equisignal. This test instrument consisted of a radio receiver connected to two vibrating white reeds placed parallel to one another. If the pilot flew on the equisignal course, the reeds appeared equal in length. If he flew too far to the left of the equisignal, the left reed appeared taller than the right reed, and, if he flew too far to the right of the equisignal, the right reed appeared taller than the left. To remind the pilot, the instrument's face carried the note, "longest reed shows side off course."[8]

VISUAL COURSE INDICATOR
COCKPIT DISPLAY

**PLANE TO LEFT   PLANE EXACTLY   PLANE TO RIGHT
OF EQUISIGNAL   ON EQUISIGNAL   OF EQUISIGNAL**

Figure 2

This visual radio direction indicator was an important advance, for it freed the pilot from total reliance on the almost equally new aural beacon system. Using the aural system, the pilot listened for the Morse A and N, and adjusted his course until the two signals merged into the steady equisignal monotone, indicating he was flying "on the beam." Quite naturally, this was often a tiring experience, and, if static was present on the beam frequency transmissions, the pilot could become greatly fatigued. Though the aural system worked quite well, the reed visual cockpit indicator enabled the pilot to keep track of his course in relative quiet, without recourse to crackling, static-filled receivers. The left reed vibrated at 86.7 cycles per second, and the right reed at 65.0 cycles per second. As long as the pilot flew so the two reeds appeared with equal length, he knew the plane was on course on the equisignal beam. Actually, the pilot did not always want to keep exactly on the equisignal "equal reed" course; if, for example, he found stormy weather in his projected flight path, he could deviate from the planned course, either to the right or left, and then use the reeds to guide him back to the equisignal, flying until once again the two reeds exhibited equal length. Further, the pilot knew exactly when he arrived over the ground beacon, because the radio signals did not radiate directly upwards above the beacon. Using an aural indicator, the pilot flew into a "cone of silence" when over the beacon station. Using a visual indicator, the pilot noticed a sharp deflection in his reed indicators as he passed above the station. Thus, if the station was located at an airport, the pilot could precisely navigate from one field to another, even if he could not see the ground from his plane.[9]

Dellinger, Diamond, and Dunmore continued their research on radio beacons, and by the end of 1927, the Bureau of Standards felt confident enough to support an actual operational trial of the radio beacon system using scheduled flights by aircraft of National Air Transport over the New York to Cleveland airway. During December 1927, and the first two months of the new year, NAT aircraft demonstrated successful utilization of the beacon system, using equipment furnished by the Bureau of Standards. In February 1928, bureau research pilots were routinely flying 130-mile flights from and to the research station at College Park field, using experimental models of the visual reed indicator to guide their aircraft. By the beginning of 1928, then, the Bureau of Standards had demonstrated three important advances in aeronautical radio. These were the radio beacon system, the visual reed course deviation indicator, and the ground-air radio communications system.[10]

The pilot was no longer completely at the mercy of bad weather and fog. He could fly from point to point using radio navigation, and ground communications personnel could warn him of weather conditions ahead on his flight path. Still, one danger remained: How could a pilot land his aircraft at an airfield without visual guidance right down to the runway? Could he land his plane while flying completely blind? These were questions that the Bureau of Standards eventually investigated, but the basic solution to the blind flying and landing problem finally came not from the Bureau of Standards, but from The Daniel Guggenheim Fund for the Promotion of Aeronautics.

In June 1926, Harry Guggenheim had recommended to the fund trustees that the Guggenheim fund "encourage perfection of control in a fog," and "finance a study and solution of fog flying." The trustees responded by creating a small subcommittee chaired by Rear Adm. Hutchinson I. Cone to study fog and blind flying, with representatives from the War, Navy, and Commerce departments. Further, they appropriated an initial grant of $417.95 to Harvard meteorology professor Dr. Alexander McAdie for a report on methods of fog dispersion.[11] Three months later, in September 1926, Harry Guggenheim organized another informal committee composed of Edward P. Warner, F. Trubee Davison, William P. MacCracken, and various Post Office and Weather Bureau representatives. This committee, with Harry Guggenheim as chairman, decided to investigate fog dispersion, "development of means whereby flying fields may be located from the air regardless of fog," development of accurate altimeters to give the precise height of aircraft above the ground, development of special "fog flying" instruments to better enable the pilot to maintain his aircraft in stable flight, and research on the "penetration of fog by light rays."[12] In a related activity, the fund trustees also agreed to study ice formation on airplanes while in flight.

The radio work of the Bureau of Standards obviated the need for research on how to locate airfields swathed in fog; if the airfield had a radio beacon and the pilot had a radio receiver, one simply flew down the equisignal (commonly called the "beam" by pilots) until he reached the cone of silence. The matter of landing, however, remained unsolved. Simple in clear weather, even at night, landing at a fog-shrouded airport became a complex problem. It involved locating the airport, descending through fog or cloud cover while relying on the cockpit magnetic compass, turn-and-bank indicator, airspeed indicator, and altimeter, and then breaking into the clear, visually lining up on the runway, and descending to a landing. But many times, fog extended all the way down to ground level, leaving the pilot only two options: he could fly around and attempt to locate an alternate landing site, perhaps running out of fuel in the process, or he could risk a descent in an often vain attempt to land safely. These conditions led Jerome C. Hunsaker, a vice-president of the Bell Telephone Laboratories, to write, "safe landing in fog is not today possible and no means are in sight to make it so."[13]

Scientists in the United States and abroad had made various attempts to guide airplanes down to a safe landing while above a fogged-in or clouded-in airport. Scientists in England installed a string of captive balloons in a descending line from the airfield perimeter to the runway, indicating the line of approach. This method, of course, was makeshift in the extreme, for fog and cloud depth often extended far above the balloon height, and the balloons themselves could pose a collision danger. Another more promising method involved the use of so-called "leader cables." These were electrified cables extending from the ends of the runway; they generated a magnetic field which cockpit instruments could sense. Using his cockpit indicator, the pilot then flew down this magnetic track, which led him right to the runway threshold.

The leader cable, however, had several problems. First developed for guiding ships into foggy harbors, it could serve only as a *localizer*, leading the pilot to the runway. It could not indicate his glide slope approach angle, and the pilot could not determine his actual horizontal distance from the runway threshold, since the leader cables did not have any sort of vertical marker beacons to indicate distance to the end of the runway. There were operational problems as well. Scientists arranged the cable in a racetrack pattern, with the runway on one leg of the track. The pilot picked up the cable's magnetic field on his instrumentation, followed it on the downwind leg, turned on the base leg, turned on his final approach, and then began his descent to the runway. It was all very complex, and turning the airplane in the midst of clouds or fog, with recourse only to the leader cable indicator, magnetic compass, turn-and-bank indicator, airspeed indicator, and altimeter, was no easy matter. The Electrical Research Station of the British Air Ministry began investigations on leader cables in 1921, and first test-flew the system in 1926. Subsequent testing in England, France, and at the army test center at Wright Field indicated the system was far from perfect, and that much work remained before the leader cable method would be suitable—if ever —for routine air transport operations.[14]

After studying the balloon and leader cable methods, the Guggenheim fund rejected them as unsuitable. In the interim, fund trustees pressed for further study of fog dispersal and methods of developing precision altimeters. The latter presented serious difficulties. The standard barometric altimeter suffered from lag: for example, during a descent, an immediate altimeter reading might indicate altitude ten seconds *before* the reading, thus giving a misleading indication of height, and forcing the pilot to subtract a compensatory "fudge factor" to get an indication of his true height. This situation led 1st Lt. Albert F. Hegenberger, a noted Army Air Corps engineering test pilot, to declare in 1928, "The present service altimeter because of its lag and other errors and cramped scale can be considered undependable for altitudes lower than several hundred feet."[15] Accordingly, the Guggenheim fund issued three research grants to scientists investigating precision altimeter development. The first grant, for $2,500, went to Prof. C. J. Elias of the Technical University of Delft to develop an acoustic echo-sounding altimeter. Elias began his research in December 1927, and in April 1929, KLM, the Dutch national airline, began flight-testing the Elias acoustic altimeter on trips between London and Amsterdam. The tests proved disappointing, for the sensitivity of the altimeter was not as great as expected.[16]

The second grant on acoustic altimeter research went to Prof. L. P. Delsasso of the University of California at Los Angeles. Delsasso received a $2,000 Guggenheim grant, which he used to study the sound spectrum emitted by an airplane in flight. He began his research in December 1928, with a view to acquiring sound pitch data that could be used in the design of an acoustic altimeter indicating altitude on the basis of reflected noise signals from the ground. This involved developing an acoustic analyzer, which Delsasso constructed in 1929 and used to acquire information on the sound "signature" of commercial and military airplanes. He presented the results of his research at a meeting of the Acoustical Society of America at Chicago, in December 1929. Unlike the generally similar Elias work at Delft, Delsasso did not actually construct a prototype acoustic altimeter.[17] A third altimeter study grant of $3,750 went to Prof. William L. Everitt at Ohio State University.[18] Everitt proposed an altimeter design capable of beaming a radio signal and then computing the altitude above ground on the basis of its pitch change. He began his research in October 1929, and by the end of the fund's activities in 1930, his research still remained in the theoretical stage.*

In related activities, the fund issued a grant of $17,000 to Dr. S. Herbert Anderson of the University of Washington enabling him to take a leave of absence for two years from his teaching position, so that he could work with army officials on fog flying problems at Wright Field, and gave Dr. William C. Geer $10,000 to conduct icing research at Cornell University. Icing often accompanied fog or cloud flying, especially at high altitude, or in winter flying. Ice formation on an airplane sometimes blocked engine carburetors, or built up to unacceptable thicknesses on the plane's wings and fuselage, dangerously increasing its weight, raising its stall speed, and adding to

---

* Everitt was, in the long run, closer to a practical solution than Elias or Delsasso. When scientists developed radar, simply projecting a radio beam off an object and timing its return, they had the basis for the precision radar altimeter which appeared during World War II.

drag. Geer, a chemist, started his ice formation research in July 1929. By the end of the year, Geer had experimented with several methods of reducing ice buildup. He recommended either spreading a thin oil film over the wing (an impracticable idea), or using rubber "overshoe" strips along the leading edges of the wings that would alternately expand and contract, thus cracking ice as soon as it formed, and letting the airstream around the plane whip it away. Geer took this latter idea to C. W. Leguillon of the Goodrich Company. Goodrich went ahead with development, proving the deicer boot concept on two experimentally modified planes flown in 1931 and 1932. The concept appealed to Boeing design engineers and to Thorp Hiscock of Boeing Air Transport, and when the Boeing 247 appeared in 1933, it had rubber leading-edge deicer boots, the first production aircraft so equipped. Another method of ice removal that Geer suggested and which gained subsequent acceptance was heating the leading edges of the wings and tail surfaces to prevent ice formation. Though more complex than using a deicer boot, this method worked well.[19]

After Dr. S. Herbert Anderson received his grant from the Guggenheim fund, he joined the Air Corps Materiel Division at Wright Field and started working with Lt. Albert Hegenberger on the design of aircraft instruments and test equipment for fog research. Anderson began his work at Wright Field in July 1928, and soon undertook research on penetration of fog by infrared light and radio waves, leader cable installations, gyroscopic stabilization of aircraft instruments, and altimeter research. Visible light had poor penetration characteristics, and mail pilots, for example, had often found that they could not see a brightly lit airport although ground personnel could clearly hear the roar of their planes' engines. To test the transmission of light through fog, Anderson, aided by Dr. James Barnes of Bryn Mawr College, developed experiments using a small fog chamber built from standard steel steam piping. Anderson tested penetration of thin and thick fogs by red, yellow, green, and blue visible light, and by infrared light. In each case, the infrared light penetrated more deeply than the visible light. By the end of the fund, Anderson still had not come to any definite conclusions, though he advocated continued infrared research. Nevertheless, army officials believed the work well worthwhile; Brig. Gen. William E. Gillmore, director of the Air Corps Materiel Division, wrote to Harry Guggenheim, stating, "It is splendid that your fund is doing work of this sort that means so much to the proper development of aeronautics."[20]

All of this research on altimeters, light transmission, and ice prevention, contributed greatly to the ultimate victory over fog and inclement weather as a block in the path of commercial air operations. The climax of the fund's activity in blind flying research came when Lt. James H. Doolittle, an Army Air Corps test pilot on loan to the Guggenheim fund, completed the world's first successful "blind" flight, from takeoff through landing. Like other pioneering flights before and since, his achievement that damp morning over Long Island crumbled another barrier to safe flying. It was truly the dramatic highpoint of the entire fund's existence.

On June 22, 1928, Harry F. Guggenheim had announced a most important change in the organization of The Daniel Guggenheim Fund for the Promotion of Aeronautics. From that date onward, the fund would "transfer its emphasis from the work of assisting commercial aviation and stimulating public interest in its development, to the consideration of fundamental aeronautical and aerodynamical problems."[21] He further stated, "From now on, the Fund will concentrate upon the scientific problems involved in the mechanical structure of the airplane and the study of environmental conditions necessary for safe operation, particularly meteorology and the problem of fog-flying."[22] The next month, Harry Guggenheim decided to undertake an actual fog-flying flight research program using experimental airplanes and test pilots. While the fund selected the type of aircraft it required, Harry Guggenheim asked Maj. Gen. James E. Fechet, chief of the Air Corps, to assign a service pilot to work with the fund on special duty for a period of one year. Fechet assented, and asked Brig. Gen. William E. Gillmore to recommend some qualified test pilots. Gillmore recommended five men, all exceptionally well qualified.[23] They were Maj. Rudolph W. Schroeder; Edmund T. Allen, a civilian test pilot with Boeing; J. Parker van Zandt, another civilian test pilot; Capt. Edwin E. Aldrin; and Lt. James H. Doolittle, then on leave to South America flying as a demonstration pilot for the American government. Doolittle was the most colorful of them, as well as the most skilled. Fechet assigned him to work with the Guggenheim fund, after he returned to North America.[24]

James Harold "Jimmy" Doolittle was a public figure with an aviation following exceeded only by that of Charles Lindbergh. Few indeed were those who had not heard of the stocky pilot's exploits: first man to fly across the country in less than a day, first man to fly an outside loop, winner of the Schneider Trophy seaplane race in 1925, winner of the Air Corps' Mackay Trophy for 1926. Born in California but raised in Alaska, Jimmy Doolittle had learned to fly during World War I. His friendly and outgoing personality masked a strong will and scholarly mind. In 1925, Doolittle, then age twenty-eight, received a Sc.D. in aeronautical engineering from the Massachusetts Institute of Technology. The scientific Doolittle, noted for his rigorous and methodical preparations before any experimental flight, was a side of the test pilot the public rarely saw or appreciated; to them he was a daredevil, an image that has, unfortunately, persisted in subsequent writings.

Early in August 1928, Harry F. Guggenheim publicly announced that the Guggenheim fund would establish a "Full Flight Laboratory" to study fog flying under actual bad weather conditions. He further stated that Charles Lindbergh would serve as a special adviser to the program, though Lindbergh did not actually undertake this role. By December 1928, the Guggenheim fund had arranged for the cooperation of the War, Navy, and Commerce departments, the General Electric Company, and the American Telephone and Telegraph Company. Fund trustees had voted an appropriation of $70,000 for the laboratory, including $26,000 for two airplanes, a Vought O2U-1 Corsair (civil registration X-61E), and a Consolidated NY-2 (civil registration NX-7918). The trustees tentatively hoped to demonstrate successful blind flying at some airfield near New York, and then select a commercial airway for actual commercial flight demonstrations.[25]

Both the Vought O2U-1 and the Consolidated NY-2 were single-engine two-seat biplanes originally designed for military service, the former a naval carrier-based observation plane, and the latter a navy primary trainer. Each plane was well suited to the fund's needs. The O2U-1 was a fast 150-mph airplane useful for long-range research flights and ferrying equipment. The NY-2 was essentially a naval version of the army's PT-1 trainer. It had a wing span of forty feet, and a broad and rugged landing gear with special oleo shock absorbers that gave it excellent landing characteristics even in full stall and high-descent-rate touchdowns. The NY-2 could fly at 98 mph, and had positive inherent stability flight characteristics; indeed, the only fault of the PT-1/NY-2 series was that they bred overconfidence in the student pilots who flew them. Doolittle had technicians convert the rear cockpit of the Guggenheim NY-2 into a blind-flying instrumentation test-bed, with a special canvas hood that could isolate the pilot from all outside references. A "check pilot" could fly in the front cockpit, to make certain that the plane did not enter a dangerous flight condition while under test by the rear seat pilot.[26]

Jimmy Doolittle accepted the NY-2 from the Consolidated factory

On January 16, 1926, philanthropist Daniel Guggenheim created The Daniel Guggenheim Fund for the Promotion of Aeronautics, an act that transformed aviation in the United States . . .

The Guggenheim fund trustees: men of vision who shaped the course of American aviation. Left to right, standing: Secretary J. W. Miller; F. Trubee Davison; Elihu Root, Jr.; Hutchinson Cone; Charles Lindbergh; Harry Guggenheim, the fund president; Robert Millikan. Left to right, seated: John D. Ryan; Daniel Guggenheim, the fund's creator; Orville Wright; William Durand. Not shown are A. A. Michelson, Dwight Morrow, George W. Goethals, and Emory S. Land. Courtesy of Paul Iudica, Mason Studio, Port Washington, New York

In aerospace education, the fund endowed schools and universities around the nation, strengthening existing programs and building new ones . . .

Dr. Theodore von Kármán came to the United States in December 1929 to direct the Guggenheim Aeronautical Laboratory at the California Institute of Technology. The greatest aerospace scientist of his generation, von Kármán subsequently played a leading role in American aeronautical research and education. Bringing him to America was one of the Guggenheim fund's major successes. Courtesy of the National Air and Space Museum

Many noteworthy aircraft have undergone their initial wind tunnel trials in Guggenheim-sponsored laboratories. Here is a model of the famous Lockheed Constellation airliner awaiting a test in a wind tunnel at the University of Washington's Aeronautical Laboratory. Courtesy of the University of Washington Aeronautical Laboratory

To encourage passenger-carrying civil aviation, the Guggenheim fund established an experimental airway on the West Coast in cooperation with Western Air Express . . .

One of Western Air Express's Fokker F-10 trimotors being readied for flight. As much fanfare surrounded the beginning of the Model Air Line experiment between Los Angeles and San Francisco as was associated with the beginning of transatlantic Concorde SST service nearly a half-century later. Courtesy of the Sherman Fairchild Collection, National Air and Space Museum

Practical commercial air transportation demanded reliability and safety, especially in bad weather and fog conditions. The Guggenheim fund set out to solve the problem of blind flying . . .

To undertake a study of special blind flying instrumentation and techniques, the Guggenheim fund established a "Full Flight Laboratory" at Mitchel Field and equipped a modified Consolidated NY-2 trainer as a blind flying research aircraft. Courtesy of the National Air and Space Museum; model by Robert C. Mikesh

At the time, the NY-2 was the world's most extensively instrumented blind flying research aircraft. The rear cockpit contained the blind flying test instrumentation, and could be covered by a special hood so that all external visual references were eliminated. A safety pilot rode in the front cockpit. Courtesy of the National Air and Space Museum; model by Robert C. Mikesh

The NY-2, a rugged aircraft, was ideally suited for the blind flying trials. The fuselage contained the special radio and blind flying equipment, and a profusion of aerials surrounded the plane. Courtesy of the National Air and Space Museum; model by Robert C. Mikesh

The Army Air Corps detailed Lt. James H. "Jimmy" Doolittle, the foremost test pilot of his day, to pilot the NY-2 on its blind flying investigations. On September 24, 1929, Jimmy Doolittle accomplished what many thought impossible: a controlled blind flight, from takeoff through landing, using only cockpit instrumentation and without external references. Courtesy of the National Air and Space Museum

Earlier, in a flight that fully demonstrated the dangers even an accomplished pilot could face when flying blind without adequate instrumentation, Doolittle had narrowly escaped injury when he crash-landed the Guggenheim fund's Vought O2U-1 Corsair. Bad fog conditions had prevented him from finding and landing at Mitchel Field. After flying about until he ran low on gas, Doolittle finally had no choice but to pick a spot and set the plane down. The Corsair was a total loss. Courtesy of Gen. James H. Doolittle and the Doolittle Collection, via Edward Jablonski

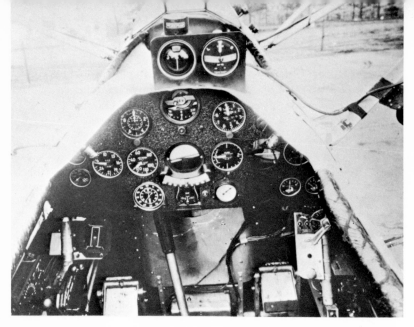

After numerous trial installations, the Guggenheim blind flying research team selected this arrangement of instruments as the most desirable. The Sperry artificial horizon, Sperry gyrocompass, Kollsman precision altimeter, and the visual reed radio indicators are all visible in this photograph of the final test instrument panel installed in the NY-2's rear cockpit. Courtesy of the National Air and Space Museum

Fate struck the NY-2 a cruel blow, for shortly after Jimmy Doolittle's historic blind flight, the plane was severely damaged in a collision with a streetcar in Buffalo, New York, while being transported to Consolidated for maintenance. After repairs, the NY-2 was delivered by the Guggenheim fund to the Army Air Corps for further blind flying trials at Wright Field. Courtesy of the National Air and Space Museum

Spurred to action by the number of accidents in which pilots lost control of their aircraft and crashed, the Guggenheim fund sponsored development of "safe" aircraft . . .

Harry Guggenheim kept abreast of the latest technical developments in aeronautics. His interest in the Cierva Autogiro (shown here in low-speed flight) led him to emphasize development of airplanes having good slow-flying characteristics without sacrificing practical utility, a lifelong quest that first manifested itself in the Daniel Guggenheim International Safe Aircraft Competition. Courtesy of the National Air and Space Museum

Harry Guggenheim, Charles Lindbergh, and H. I. Cone meet with safe aircraft competition officials. Left to right: Prof. Alexander Klemin, NYU; army test pilot Lt. Stanley Umstead; Admiral Cone; Harry Guggenheim (looking at a circling airplane); Charles Lindbergh; test pilot Thomas Carroll; army field manager Capt. Walter Bender; F. K. Teichmann, NYU. Courtesy of the National Air and Space Museum

The Cunningham-Hall Model X was one of many unorthodox—and unsuccessful—entries in the Guggenheim safe aircraft competition. Courtesy of the National Air and Space Museum

The graceful Handley Page HP 39 Gugnunc, photographed at Mitchel Field during the safe aircraft competition. Note the short-chord engine cowling added for the competitive flight trials. The extensive flap surfaces and the near-sesquiplane configuration are readily apparent. Courtesy of the National Air and Space Museum

The Curtiss Tanager cabin biplane, winner of the Daniel Guggenheim International Safe Aircraft Competition. Courtesy of the National Air and Space Museum

With its slats, flaps, and floating ailerons clearly visible, the Tanager clambers aloft steeply, easily passing over an imaginary thirty-five-foot obstacle, a feat only the Gugnunc or an Autogiro could have duplicated. Courtesy of the National Air and Space Museum

The Tanager in level flight. Courtesy of the National Air and Space Museum

Back in Britain after losing to the Curtiss Tanager, the Gugnunc saw extensive service as a STOL research aircraft. Here it drifts by the camera, flaps down and slats fully extended. Courtesy of the National Air and Space Museum

The technical lessons learned from the Guggenheim safe aircraft competition found expression in the STOL aircraft of the 1930s, such as this Ryan YO-51 Dragonfly whisking aloft with full-span flaps and slats. Courtesy of the National Air and Space Museum

The fund also sought to promote a positive image of aviation in the minds of Americans by a series of activities, including nationwide tours . . .

In October 1926, the Guggenheim fund sponsored a nationwide tour of Arctic explorer Richard Byrd's airplane, the Josephine Ford, *to promote public use of the air mail and to encourage airport development. Courtesy of the National Air and Space Museum*

The Guggenheims quickly grasped the importance of Lindbergh's Atlantic flight, and arranged for him to fly the Spirit of St. Louis *around the country to promote civil aviation. Between July 20 and October 23, 1927, Lindbergh visited eighty-two cities in the forty-eight states. The fund conservatively estimated that thirty million people saw his plane, though newspaper reporters believed the true figure to be closer to fifty million. Courtesy of the Dewell Collection, National Air and Space Museum*

The team that helped make Lindbergh's national tour a success. Left to right: Donald Keyhoe and Philip Love, Aeronautics Branch, Department of Commerce; Charles Lindbergh; "Doc" Maidment, Wright Aero Corporation service representative; Milburn Kusterer, Guggenheim fund advance man. Courtesy of the Carruthers Collection, National Air and Space Museum

In 1930, after the conclusion of the Guggenheim fund, Daniel Guggenheim pledged his financial support for an experimenter who dreamed of sending rockets into outer space . . .

The place: Auburn, Massachusetts. The date: March 16, 1926. The man: Dr. Robert Hutchings Goddard, physics professor at Clark University and rocket experimenter. The time: minutes before the world's first flight of a liquid-fuel rocket. Soon, an empty launch frame will be all that is left, and the "Kitty Hawk of rocketry" will be history. Courtesy of the National Air and Space Museum

Harry Guggenheim continued his father's support of Robert Goddard's work by a series of grants from The Daniel and Florence Guggenheim Foundation. Harry Guggenheim and Charles Lindbergh, another Goddard champion, are pictured here during a visit with the rocket pioneer at his Roswell, New Mexico, test site on September 23, 1935. Left to right: Goddard assistant Albert Kisk, Harry Guggenheim, Robert Goddard, Charles Lindbergh, Goddard assistant Nils Ljungquist. Courtesy of Mrs. Esther C. Goddard and the National Aeronautics and Space Administration

The payoff: a Goddard rocket climbs upwards from its launch tower at Roswell, August 27, 1937. Courtesy of Mrs. Esther C. Goddard and the National Aeronautics and Space Administration

Harry F. Guggenheim, president of The Daniel and Florence Guggenheim Foundation, pictured as he spoke at the opening of the Robert H. Goddard rocket exhibit at the American Museum of Natural History in New York City, April 21, 1948. Courtesy of The Daniel and Florence Guggenheim Foundation Collection, National Air and Space Museum

at Buffalo, New York, on November 3, 1928, and flew it to the Army Air Corps base at Mitchel Field, Long Island, the next day. Three weeks later, on November 21, 1928, Vought delivered the O2U-1 to the fund. In the meantime, Harry Guggenheim had arranged with Fechet and other Air Corps officials for use of a hanger at Mitchel Field, where the fund planned to establish its Full Flight Laboratory. The army also furnished an excellent mechanic, Cpl. Jack Dalton, to maintain the fund's two airplanes. Doolittle test-flew the two fund aircraft in November and December. Though he liked both planes, he complained about the NY-2's slow speed to Consolidated president Reuben Fleet. A flight from Mitchel Field to College Park, Maryland, took a full five hours. "On one occasion," Doolittle wrote, "while we were flying low over a road and into a head wind, a green automobile overtook and passed us. Hurt my pride no end."[27] Doolittle ferried the NY-2 to the Radio Frequency Laboratory, a private firm at Boonton, New Jersey, for installation of a voice radio system. It remained at Boonton until technicians completed equipment installation in late January 1929.

Mitchel Field already had a standard 125-mile-range army aural radio beacon installation located a quarter mile north of the field, but Doolittle believed this installation would be satisfactory only for long-range navigation, and that a visual cockpit indicator system would be best for blind landing research. Accordingly, early in 1929, Bureau of Standards Radio Section engineers, led by Harry Diamond and in cooperation with the Guggenheim fund, began installation of two other beacon aids, a low-powered 15-mile-range "landing" beacon triggering a cockpit visual reed indicator for "localizing" purposes, namely, to enable the pilot to fly right across the center of the field down the landing approach path, and a vertical marker beacon to indicate the beginning of the safe landing area. These beacons were similar to ones under test at the Bureau of Standards experimental radio development center at College Park, though bureau technicians did not complete installation of the equipment at Mitchel Field until August 1929. They placed the localizer landing beacon to the east of Mitchel Field, outside the boundary lights, and the landing area marker beacon along one leg of the localizer homing range, on the west side of the base as in Figure 3.

Accordingly, the test NY-2 carried two cockpit vibrating reed beacon indicators, one for the homing landing beacon "localizer," and one for the landing area marker beacon. Using this visual system, Doolittle would first locate Mitchel Field by following the reed homing beacon indicator. He would follow this homing localizer

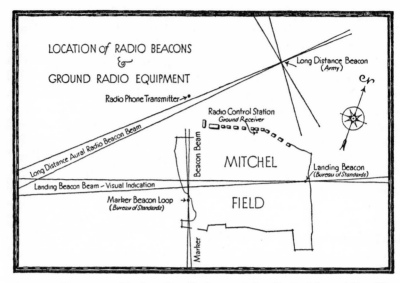

Source: *Equipment Used in Experiments to Solve the Problem of Fog Flying* (New York: Daniel Guggenheim Fund, 1930), p. 22.

Figure 3

right down the approach leg towards the center of the field. As the plane approached the landing area marker, the visual marker indicator's single reed would begin vibrating and rapidly build up to maximum amplitude, then die away as the plane passed directly over the marker, then again reach maximum amplitude as the plane began to pull away, and then slowly fade away. As soon as Doolittle had reed indications that he was lined up on the homing approach path localizer and passing over the landing area boundary marker, he would initiate a steady power-on descent at an indicated airspeed of 60 mph, approximately 15 mph above the NY-2's stall speed. The wide oleo shock-absorbing landing gear could accept the 60 mph touchdown and up to 700-feet-per-minute descent rates (11.6 feet/second) without damage, a tribute to Consolidated's NY-2 design team.[28]

On January 18, 1929, Harry Guggenheim announced that the Guggenheim fund had begun preliminary experiments in fog flying at the Mitchel Field Full Flight Laboratory. The next month, the fund arranged for Prof. William G. Brown of MIT's Aeronautics Department to join Doolittle at Mitchel Field and help direct the blind flying research program. Brown, a former instructor and old friend of

Doolittle's, remained with the Full Flight Laboratory in charge of all ground operations for the blind flying investigations, and also for the Guggenheim safe airplane competition, held in late 1929. To assist Doolittle and act as flight test safety pilot (riding in the front cockpit of the NY-2 while Doolittle flew blind in the rear cockpit), the army furnished another service test pilot, Lt. Benjamin S. Kelsey. "His piloting help, criticism of tests carried out, sound technical counsel, and ever pleasant personality contributed greatly to the results achieved," Doolittle later recalled.[29]

During preliminary flight trials, Doolittle discovered that the NY-2's standard flight instruments were, in some cases, inadequate for the task of navigating a plane with absolute precision through a fog. In particular, three difficulties existed. First, the plane's existing altimeter was not sufficiently precise to enable a pilot to know accurately his exact altitude, especially at low altitude. The gearing in the barometric altimeter was not sensitive enough for the task, and it suffered from lag, thus failing to provide the pilot with an instantaneous reading reflecting changes in altitude. Second, the plane's magnetic compass likewise could not furnish the information needed for accurate blind flying control. When turning from aircraft headings near north, the compass, because of magnetic influence, would indicate an *opposite* turning motion.

For example, if a pilot flew towards north, then began a *right* turn to east, the compass would first indicate a *left* turning movement. As the right turn to east continued, the compass would stop indicating a left turn, and would correctly indicate a right turn, but by now, its readings would be lagging behind the plane's actual easterly heading. Once the plane was established on its easterly course, the magnetic compass would catch up, but this lag, of course, reduced the pilot's chances for accurate, precise navigation. In fact, in shallow banked turns from a northerly heading, the compass might still falsely indicate that the plane was flying on its previous course, although the turn swung through an angle of twenty degrees or more. Eventually, as the turn progressed, the instrument would catch up, but once again lag was the critical problem. Turning west or east from southerly headings produced navigation difficulties of equal magnitude. In these instances, the magnetic compass would indicate the correct direction of the turn, but would *lead* the aircraft, indicating that the plane was making a faster turning movement than, in fact, it was. Clearly, scientists would have to develop a satisfactory substitute for the magnetic compass, if fog and blind flying were to be feasible. The third difficulty involved the NY-2's turn-and-bank indicator, for this instrument, while useful in blind flying, only indicated rate of turn, not degrees of bank. A major task of the Guggenheim fund would be to encourage the development of substitutes for the magnetic compass and the turn-and-bank indicators, as well as more accurate altimeters.[30]

Doolittle took this task upon himself and soon had three satisfactory instruments suitable for use in the NY-2 blind flying experiments. First, Doolittle set out to develop a precision altimeter. Realizing that the acoustic and radio altimeter research programs the Guggenheim fund supported were long-range development efforts little suited to the Full Flight Laboratory's needs, the popular pilot decided to see if an instrument company might be willing to attempt development of a more precise barometric altimeter. Earlier, a representative of the Bureau of Standards, aware of Doolittle's interest in altimeter development, had called the pilot and notified him that Paul Kollsman, a German-born instrument engineer, had submitted a new barometric altimeter to the Bureau of Standards that was far superior to any existing barometric design. Doolittle determined to contact Kollsman. Paul Kollsman and his brother E. Otto Kollsman were natives of Freudenstadt, in the Black Forest region of Germany. In 1928 they organized the Kollsman Instrument Company in New York City. Paul Kollsman had long believed that the major difficulty with existing altimeter designs lay in poor or inaccurate gear design. Thus, he turned to Swiss watchmakers for his gearing—after first stipulating that they redesign their gear-cutting machinery to produce even finer design tolerances.

Doolittle visited Kollsman, explained his problem, and asked to try out the new Kollsman altimeter. The engineer quickly gave his approval, and Doolittle completed the first test flight of the barometric altimeter on August 30, 1929, using the fund's Vought Corsair. During the flight, Kollsman sat in the Corsair's rear cockpit, the test altimeter in his lap. It performed perfectly, over twenty times as sensitive as a standard altimeter, responding immediately to any changes in air pressure and thus changing its height reading. Doolittle had found an instrument accurate to within five or ten feet, not just to fifty or one hundred feet. He had technicians install the altimeter in the fund's test NY-2.[31]

Now Doolittle set out to solve the two major instrumentation problems: developing a suitable course indicator without the weaknesses of the magnetic compass, and developing an advanced turn-and-bank indicator that would accurately indicate the degree of aircraft banking during turns. He sought assistance from Elmer Sperry, the foremost aircraft instrument developer of the time, and his son, Elmer Sperry, Jr. The elder Sperry, then age sixty-eight, had established a distinguished reputation in engineering by his development of aircraft instruments using gyroscopic control. In 1917, for example, he had developed an automatic control system for a prototype flying bomb built by the Curtiss company. In 1918 he had developed a turn-and-bank indicator, a prototype gyrocompass for the navy, and a gyro-stabilized bombsight. Sperry believed that his company had a special obligation to develop instruments enabling a pilot to navigate his craft in all weather conditions with precision. Writing his son Lawrence in 1920, Sperry stated, "We have absolutely got to solve this problem; if we die in the attempt and could have registered a single notch in advance, it seems to me that it would be well worth while."[32] The Sperry family did pay a tragic price for their success: on December 13, 1924, Lawrence Sperry crashed into the English Channel while flying a tiny Sperry Messenger biplane.

Doolittle had examined two German-made gyroscopically controlled compass and turn-and-bank instruments, the Anschütz and Gyrorector, but rejected them as unsuitable because of their bulk and a tendency for their gyros to "tumble." What he needed was an advanced form of compass and an instrument to show an "artificial horizon" reference so that the pilot could realize what his bank and pitch angles were during turns. Doolittle sketched a rough drawing of the proposed instrument and showed it to the elder Sperry. The old inventor examined the drawing, essentially a picture of a directional gyroscope superimposed on an artificial horizon, and then announced that while his company could indeed make such an instrument, Doolittle might find it easier to rely on two instruments. One would be a directional gyrocompass, and the other an artificial horizon. He assigned his son Elmer Jr. to work with Doolittle and MIT Prof. William Brown at the Guggenheim fund's Full Flight Laboratory. Young Sperry brought along another company engineer, Preston Bassett, to help develop the two gyroscopic instruments.

The first instrument developed was the Sperry artificial horizon to complement the standard turn-and-bank indicator. In clear visual flight, most pilots at that time simply relied on viewing the horizon line to determine the proper attitude of their airplane in flight. The Sperry artificial horizon indicator, in its final form as used in the Guggenheim tests, had a fixed airplane symbol (a mounted horizontal bar representing an airplane in wings-level flight) superimposed over a horizon bar controlled by a gyroscope. As the plane, for example, entered a left turn, the horizon bar would change position, indicating the left bank angle of the airplane, as in Figure 4.[33]

OPERATION OF THE SPERRY
ARTIFICIAL HORIZON

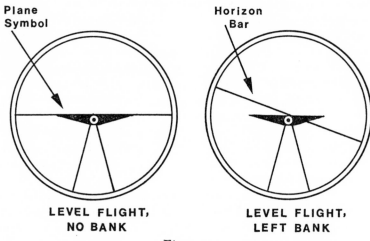

Figure 4

Using the artificial horizon, the pilot now knew exactly his plane's precise movements during a turn: the artificial horizon let him know the bank and pitch angles of his airplane, while the turn-and-bank indicator provided him with his rate of turn. But he still lacked a good directional course indicator to replace the magnetic compass. The device Elmer Sperry, Jr., developed to meet this need was a directional gyrocompass. Unlike the standard magnetic compass, it was not a magnetic instrument. Instead, it consisted of a card with compass indications printed on it attached to a gyroscope-controlled gimbal. The pilot would use his magnetic compass to set the instrument, first making certain that the magnetic compass was not under any error-causing influence. He accomplished this by setting the directional gyro only when the airplane was in straight and level unaccelerated flight conditions. The gyro stabilized the compass card, so that it indicated the course the pilot wished to follow. If he drifted off course, the indicator needle on the instrument revealed the amount of his drift, and the pilot could then correct his course until once again the proper course heading showed on the instrument.

Elmer Sperry, Jr., and Jimmy Doolittle tested the Sperry directional gyro during a series of test flights along sections of the Long Island Railroad near Mitchel Field. Doolittle would fly over a section of railroad track, ascertaining the compass heading and setting the directional gyro. Then, he would fly around the countryside and return to that particular section of track to see if the gyro had drifted off course. In this manner of continuing developmental flight tests, Doolittle and Elmer Sperry, Jr., refined the instrument, making it less susceptible to drifting off course because of bearing friction. Eventually, when both men were satisfied that the Sperry artificial horizon and the Sperry directional gyro were ready for operational testing, they installed both instruments in the rear cockpit of the fund's NY-2 test-bed. The NY-2, with its Kollsman sensitive barometric altimeter, Sperry artificial horizon and directional gyro, and extensive radio navigation instrumentation was now the most advanced blind-flying research airplane in the world.[34]

Doolittle used the NY-2 strictly for research flying, relying on the fund's faster Vought O2U-1 Corsair for ferry trips to various contractors or government agencies. This airplane helped Doolittle to keep up his flying proficiency while the NY-2 had new instrumentation installed or was otherwise grounded. The Vought Corsair, however, did not have any blind-flying instrumentation, and this limitation forced Doolittle to crash-land his aircraft during one cross-country flight.

On March 15, 1929, Doolittle made a night takeoff from Buffalo in fair weather, planning to maintain "contact" (visual) navigation all the way to Mitchel Field. To avoid mountains, he followed a cross-country route via Rochester, Syracuse, Utica, Schenectady, Albany, and then down the Hudson River. After Doolittle passed Albany, bad weather closed in on the plane. He had already used half of his fuel supply, and thus did not have enough to return to Buffalo where the weather was improving. Growing concerned, Doolittle resorted to following the lights of a southbound New York express train racing along the Hudson River Valley. When it disappeared from view, he began following the bank of the river. For a moment he thought of landing at the West Point parade ground, but decided to press on to Mitchel Field because the weather still remained flyable.

Over New York City he broke out into the clear, but fog completely shrouded the entire East River area; Doolittle realized that he could not go on to Mitchel Field. Governor's Island was swathed in fog, and fog had now enclosed the Hudson River as well. Doolittle flew over the Battery, intending to crash-land in Battery Park, but a man ran out as the plane descended and waved him off. He climbed back into the night, decided to crash-land in the Hudson River, and then rejected this plan for "the water looked uninviting."[35] He had one last chance: cross over to Jersey City and attempt a landing at Newark Airport. But here, too, fog had imprisoned the field.

With the Corsair's gas gauge reading empty, Doolittle climbed through the fog into the clear night air, attempting to fly westward away from the urban areas until he could parachute over sparse countryside. At this point, near Elizabeth, New Jersey, the pilot spotted a revolving air route beacon light and a reasonably flat area next to it suitable for an emergency landing. Still uncertain as to whether it was a field or a lake, Doolittle flicked on the Corsair's landing lights and began a descent. He flew low over the area, snagging a tree top and tearing the fabric on the plane's left lower wing. The O2U-1 staggered on and Doolittle turned around, located the best-looking clear spot, and set the plane down "by wrapping the left wing around a tree trunk near the ground," completely wrecking the Corsair. Doolittle, who fortunately escaped without injury, subsequently stated, "The moral of the story is that with the NY-2 mounting blind landing equipment and the Full Flight Laboratory radio station alerted at Mitchel, this would have been a routine cross-country flight with 'no sweat.' "[36]

Jimmy Doolittle's eventful flight demonstrated how even a skilled pilot became a prisoner of weather conditions unless his aircraft had proper instrumentation. The fund trustees replaced the wrecked Vought O2U-1 with a more advanced O2U-2 Corsair, this having a revised wing and tail structure. Like its predecessor, it received the civil registration number X-61E. Doolittle used this aircraft to test the Kollsman altimeter and the two Sperry gyroscopic instruments before installing them in the fund's NY-2.

By mid-September 1929, the NY-2's rear test cockpit contained all the specialized instruments necessary for blind flight, including an experimental Western Electric–Bell Telephone Laboratories radio voice transmitter with a sixty-five-foot trailing wire reel antenna and headset, a Radio Frequency Laboratory radio receiver and Morse code transmitter, Bureau of Standards' vibrating reed localizer homing range and marker beacon indicators, a Sperry directional gyro and artificial horizon, and a Kollsman altimeter. During the summer of 1929, Doolittle flew hundreds of simulated blind landing approaches at Mitchel Field, following the reed indicators until they told him he was on the localizer and over the landing area boundary marker beacon and then beginning his letdown, using his artificial horizon to ensure he was in a wings-level position before touchdown. Tests of the landing area boundary marker beacon revealed that this system lacked sufficient power to be useful, and it was not used on subsequent Guggenheim blind flight trials. Instead, Doolittle would approach Mitchel Field from the east, watching his reed indicators until they showed he was over the localizer beacon. Then he would begin his letdown. As he gained proficiency, Doolittle found he could land the plane completely blind, setting it down without so much as a landing bounce. After having tested the landing system in clear weather, Doolittle and Harry Guggenheim believed that it was time to test the blind-flying research aircraft under actual bad weather conditions.[37]

Mitchel Field often had bad morning fogs, especially in the spring and fall. Since the Guggenheim fund was also interested in fog dispersal, attempts were made to check various methods of dispersing fogs from around airfields. The most promising method seemed to be applying heat, thus driving off the fog by warming the air. This was the idea of E. C. Reader, owner of a gravel pit in Cleveland, Ohio. Reader noticed that whenever he operated the pit's blowtorch heater to dry gravel and sand, any fog in the immediate area broke up. He proposed to the Guggenheim fund that this method of fog dispersal be tested at Mitchel Field. Harry Guggenheim, ever on the alert for a useful idea, quickly invited him to New York, and the navy's Bureau of Aeronautics expressed interest in his theory.[38] Reader waited fruitlessly for a suitable fog for several months, then got his chance on September 24, 1929, when a thick damp fog rolled in from Long Island Sound, blanketing Mitchel Field.

That morning, Jack Dalton, the army maintenance chief on the fund's two airplanes, awoke and quickly noticed that the fog was pea-soup thick, perfect for testing Reader's gravel heater. Dalton called Doolittle and Reader to the field, and also notified Harry Guggenheim who began a long drive to Mitchel Field from his home at Port Washington. In an optimistic frame of mind, Reader lit the burner, but its flame made little impression on the fog, perhaps because, unlike at the Cleveland gravel pit, the heater lacked a mineral mass to store and reflect the heat over a broader area. Disappointed, he shut down the heater. Years later, during the Second World War, a similar idea worked well, vindicating Reader's earlier work.* That morning

* During World War II, British scientists used rows of gas burners along runways at three emergency and ten operational airfields to clear away fog.

in September 1929, the stage was set for one of the most important experimental flights in aviation history.[39]

The fog gave Jimmy Doolittle an idea. Almost without thinking about it, the stocky pilot ordered Dalton to ready the NY-2 for flight, while technicians manned the voice radio system and turned on the localizer landing beacon. Mechanics pushed the experimental biplane out of its hanger and warmed up its 220 hp Wright R-790-8 radial piston engine. The engine coughed to life, and then settled down to a steady throb. Doolittle climbed in, taxied out into the middle of Mitchel Field, added full throttle, and took off to the west. The little NY-2 disappeared from view almost from the moment its wheels left the ground. Below, various spectators, including Elmer Sperry, Jr., and Doolittle's wife, Josephine, could clearly hear the airplane, but could not see it. Aloft, Doolittle, fog swirling around him, concentrated on following his localizer landing beacon reed indicator, as well as the artificial horizon and directional gyro. He swung over Mitchel Field at five hundred feet and then landed, ten minutes after takeoff, having completed the first flight where a pilot guided his airplane through a fog to a precision landing, by relying on his instruments.[40]

As Doolittle touched down, Harry F. Guggenheim arrived by car from Port Washington, accompanied by other fund representatives, including fund vice-president, Capt. Emory S. Land, USN. By 11:00 A.M., the early morning fog was lifting, and Guggenheim, delighted with the results of Doolittle's pioneering ten-minute flight, decided that Doolittle should make another flight, this time with the cockpit completely enclosed from the outside by the canvas hood, an unquestionable demonstration of the fund's accomplishment. Just on the rare chance that the lifting fog might have enticed some pilot to take off, Guggenheim stipulated that Lt. Benjamin S. Kelsey ride in the NY-2's front cockpit to take control of the plane should a potential in-flight collision situation develop. The two pilots climbed into the plane; Guggenheim stood on the plane's lower wing and closed the blind flying canvas hood over Doolittle's head. Inside the cockpit, Doolittle switched on his cockpit instrument illumination lights and checked the instrument panel. Outside, his wife, Guggenheim, and Elmer Sperry, Jr., along with the commanding officer of

This method received the acronym FIDO (Fog Intense Dispersal Of) and by war's end, it had enabled about 2,500 fighters and bombers to land visually on fog-free runways. The USAAF preferred to train its Eighth Air Force bomber crews to land and take off blind without FIDO, and by May 1945, two of the Eighth's bomber groups were fully qualified for blind flying. FIDO subsequently appeared on some postwar civil airfields.

Mitchel Field and about fifty other spectators, watched expectantly.[41]

Kelsey sat inside the front cockpit, his hands resting on the outside of the cockpit away from the plane's controls, in full view of the anxious onlookers. As they watched, the NY-2 began to move, its wheels bumping over the damp ground. Inside the covered rear cockpit, Doolittle lined the plane up for takeoff by watching his visual reed localizer indicator and steering until the plane was on the landing beacon localizer path, pointing west. Then he added full throttle. Guggenheim and the others saw the NY-2 accelerate rapidly across the field, with Kelsey still sitting motionless in the cockpit, his hands resting outside the plane. It lifted off into the sky, climbing away to the west, from Mitchel Field. Doolittle let the plane climb along the localizer path until it reached one thousand feet. Five miles from the field, he leveled off and initiated a 180 degree left turn, leveling out on an easterly heading on the localizer beam. He flew east for seven miles, then initiated another 180 degree left turn, once again heading west on the localizer beam, now two miles away from Mitchel Field.

Doolittle carefully watched his visual reed landing approach path localizer indicator. He began a gradual descent from one thousand feet as he flew west along the localizer beam, leveled off at two hundred feet, and continued along the localizer until he passed directly over the landing beacon. The localizer reed indicator momentarily stopped vibrating, showing that the NY-2 was over the landing beacon. Doolittle now began a steady descent at 60 mph and held this until touchdown. A perfectionist, the pilot was not completely happy with the flight. "Actually," he recalled, "despite previous practice, the final approach and landing were sloppy." Fifteen minutes after takeoff, the NY-2's wheels brushed the turf at Mitchel Field. For the first time in aviation history, a plane had taken off, flown a precise flight path, and landed, controlled by a pilot observing only his cockpit instruments, without recourse to external visual references. Kelsey still sat in the cockpit, his hands clasped behind his neck.[42] In just ten months of flight research, The Daniel Guggenheim Fund for the Promotion of Aeronautics had reached a milestone in aeronautical research and development.

As expected, reaction was immediate and enthusiastic. Guggenheim quickly dashed off a telegram to Orville Wright, noting, "It is significant that the achievement is realized through the aid of only three instruments which are not already the standard equipment of an airplane."[43] He also prepared a news release for immediate distribution. It sketched the general development of the Guggenheim program and predicted that with quantity production of refined models of the

three new "fog-flying" instruments, commercial all-weather operations would become routine. Mindful of his parents' interest in the
fund's activities, Guggenheim scribbled across one of the releases,
fresh from the press, "Dear Father & Mother. This is the story. Love,
Harry."[44]

Charles H. Colvin, manager of the Pioneer Instrument Company,
remarked of the flight that "an aviator, placing full faith in his flight
and navigation equipment, accomplished one of the outstanding feats
of 1929 flying. . . . We believe the effect of the flight will be far-
reaching enough to exert a tremendous influence upon flying and
aviation of today."[45] Leading foreign aeronautical periodicals such
as Britain's *The Aeroplane* favorably commented on the flight.[46] Explorer Richard E. Byrd sent Harry Guggenheim a congratulatory
telegram from his camp on the Antarctic ice cap, adding, "I know of
nothing that has done as much for the progress of aviation as your
organization."[47]

Just over a week after Jimmy Doolittle's pioneering flight, the
fund's historic NY-2 test airplane suffered a grievous blow. The fund
had flown the NY-2 back to Consolidated in Buffalo for minor modifications and a periodic inspection. On October 3, 1929, a Buffalo
street car collided with the NY-2's flatbed truck while the NY-2 was
en route through the city from the airfield to the Consolidated plant.
The collision left only the plane's outer wing panels and cockpit intact; rebuilding required virtually a new airplane. Consolidated returned the NY-2 to flight status by November 16, but the Guggenheim
fund scarcely used it after the accident.[48] Instead, with the closing
of the fund on the horizon, fund vice-president Emory S. Land in-
quired if the army might want the airplane for further blind-flying
flight tests. In March 1930, Brig. Gen. Benjamin D. Foulois, chief of
the Army Air Corp's Materiel Division at Wright Field, notified Land
that "the Air Corps is desirous of continuing the experimental work
which has been done by the Fund in connection with fog flying and
appreciates the cooperative spirit shown by the Fund."[49] Accordingly, the Guggenheim fund's attorneys settled all claims on the various parties involved in the accident for a sum of $1.00, and on May
5, 1930, Lt. Albert Hegenberger ferried the NY-2 to Wright Field.
The plane became government property, operated by the Ohio National Guard.[50]

In April 1930, after the Guggenheim fund had closed, the fund trustees issued the final blind-flying report of the Full Flight Laboratory, discussing in detail the various instruments and equipment utilized in the Mitchel Field experimental work. With the principles of successful blind flying adequately demonstrated, the Bureau of Standards and the military services continued blind-flying research with a view to making it routine. Recognizing that some airmen might still prefer the old "seat of the pants" feel to trusting their instruments, the Guggenheim fund, in its final annual report, cautioned, "Any pilot who is not competent to fly by instruments alone has not yet finished his training."[51] In June 1930, the Army Air Corps added a blind flying course to the curriculum of the Air Corps Advanced Flying School at Kelly Field. The next month, on July 21, Marine Corps pilots Capt. Arthur H. Page and Lt. V. M. Guymon demonstrated just how practical blind flying could be. Page piloted a Marine O2U Corsair "blind" from Omaha, Nebraska, to Anacostia Naval Air Station, outside Washington, D.C., via Chicago and Cleveland. The flight covered nearly one thousand miles. Guymon, the safety pilot, only took control for the landings after Page, sealed in the hooded front cockpit without external references, had brought the Corsair down to two hundred feet on final approach.[52]

Cognizant of the advantages of radio navigation beacons, the Aeronautics Branch of the Department of Commerce had nine aural beacons in service by November 1929, marking the flight route from New York City to Omaha, and from Key West to Havana, Cuba. The branch had seven prototype visual (reed indicating) beacons under construction for use on the New York to Atlanta route, and planned to place a further thirty-five aural beacons in service on the nation's airways within a year.[53] Point-to-point airline navigation via radio beacon facilities soon became routine, along with radio communication and weather reporting services.[54]

The Aeronautics Branch and the Bureau of Standards teamed to develop further blind-landing aircraft aids, while the army conducted its own blind-flying research under the direction of Lt. Albert Hegenberger, using the donated Consolidated NY-2. Within a month after the Doolittle flight, the Bureau of Standards had a high frequency "bent" landing beam under development, which would enable the pilot to fly right down this beam (a glide slope beam) to a landing. This was an important progressive development coming after the localizer and marker beacon, for now the pilot could locate the airfield, follow the localizer down the approach, pick up the marker beacon, and then, instead of making a steady precalculated descent, following only the localizer signals to remain on the runway center line, he could follow the glide slope beam itself down the proper descent path to touchdown. Harry Diamond, the Bureau of Standard's radio aids for aviation pioneer, first developed the glide slope "bent beam" in 1930. The following year, the Bureau of Standards equipped a two-seat single-engine Curtiss Fledgling biplane with cockpit glide slope indicator equipment, initiating a series of development flights at College Park, Maryland, and Newark, New Jersey.[55]

The Aeronautics Branch designated James L. Kinney as project test pilot on blind flying research, and he made many blind flying tests, often under an enclosed hood, sometimes with Clarence Young, the Assistant Secretary of Commerce for Aeronautics, riding along as emergency safety pilot. The Fledgling trials indicated the feasibility of using a cockpit glide slope indicator on final approach, and the Aeronautics Branch purchased a larger single-engine Bellanca monoplane to extend the tests. Finally, on March 20, 1933, Kinney and Diamond believed that everything was ready for a long-range test, flying from College Park to Newark under actual bad weather conditions. That day, Kinney took off from College Park airfield, with Harry Diamond and William La Violette, a mechanic, as passengers. He made the takeoff and subsequent flight by instruments alone. As he approached Newark Airport, navigating by visual and aural radio beacons, he picked up the field's localizer, passed over the field boundary marker, and then descended on the glide slope beam, anxiously following his cockpit glide slope beam indicator. Kinney came safely down the "bent beam," landing in weather conditions that had grounded all other planes.[56]

Kinney's research certainly marked the logical extension of the blind-flying trials initiated by Jimmy Doolittle. With the development of the localizer, the fan marker, and the glide slope "bent beam," the three essential elements to an all-weather instrument landing system were readily at hand. The first Federal Instrument Landing System (ILS) went into airways operation in 1941 at six locations: New York, Kansas City, Chicago, Cleveland, Los Angeles, and Fort Worth. By 1947, thirty-five ILS facilities were in operation at airports along the nation's airways, and American airliners routinely flew in weather that would have grounded them less than two decades earlier.[57]

The Army Air Corps also followed up on the Guggenheim research. On May 9, 1932, Albert Hegenberger, then an Air Corps captain, made the first solo blind flight, enclosed within the cockpit "under the hood" and without a check pilot aboard, from takeoff to landing.[58] For this and some further research he directed on blind-landing procedures, Hegenberger received the 1934 Robert J. Collier Trophy, one of aviation's most prestigious awards. Previously, the army had made another advance towards reducing the pilot's burden during blind flight, by making tests over the fall of 1929 on a Ford C-9 Tri-motor cargo plane equipped with a prototype Sperry-built automatic pilot. Though the test equipment often broke down, Air Corps experts considered the results extremely promising, because the automatic pilot clearly reduced the tension normally associated with blind flying, so that the human pilot could relax while checking his instrument readings. Automatic pilots eventually became standard on military and civilian aircraft, especially bombers, transports, and airliners.[59] Finally, on August 23, 1937, at Wright Field, Air Corps Capts. Carl J. Crane, George V. Holloman, and civilian project engineer Raymond K. Stout, completed the first automatic blind landings, following up these initial tests with additional blind-landing research, their efforts winning them the Air Corps' Mackay Trophy for 1937. Complete blind-flying ability including precision takeoffs and automatic landings, had arrived.[60]

The trustees of The Daniel Guggenheim Fund for the Promotion of Aeronautics appropriated a total of $120,250 for research related to blind flying. At the time of the fund's first grant, only a pilot trapped by weather or one who was completely irresponsible attempted to fly through fog or heavy cloud to a landing. By 1930, this had all changed. Doolittle and the Guggenheim fund, with the cooperation of the Bureau of Standards and private industry, had demonstrated that with sufficient training and flying a properly instrumented airplane, an airman could overcome the elements between the airplane and its destination. Within the next decade, blind flying operations became routine for military and airline aircrews. The basic artificial horizon, directional gyro, and the precision altimeter, all developed and placed in operation by the Guggenheim fund's Full Flight Laboratory, gained acceptance around the world, appearing on subsequent aircraft.

The end of the Guggenheim blind-flying research program did not spell the end of the Full Flight Laboratory, however. On the contrary, the Full Flight Laboratory, over the fall and early winter of 1929, was busier than ever with another Guggenheim project, the Daniel Guggenheim International Safe Aircraft Competition, established in April 1927 "to achieve a real advance in the safety of flying through improvement in the aerodynamic characteristics of heavier-than-air craft, without sacrificing the good practical qualities of the present-day aircraft."[61]

CHAPTER 8

The Daniel Guggenheim International Safe Aircraft Competition

THE Guggenheim safe aircraft competition had its origins in Harry Guggenheim's and Hutchinson Cone's trip to Europe in the spring of 1926. While in Europe, Guggenheim studied methods of reducing aircraft takeoff and landing speeds, and ways to increase aircraft stability and control especially during spins. The Cierva Autogiro and the Handley Page wing slat impressed him as offering two ways that aviation safety might be increased. The Autogiro gave promise of ending stalling accidents, while the Handley Page wing slat, fixed to the leading edge of a conventional airplane's wing, reduced stall speeds and increased aircraft stability and control. During his stay in England, Guggenheim confided to Major R. H. Mayo, a leading British aeronautical engineer who later became the fund's British representative, that he believed "safety was the vital necessity to civil aviation."[1]

When he returned to the United States, Guggenheim recommended to the trustees that the fund concentrate its efforts on promoting safety in aviation, and he suggested that the fund establish an international safe aircraft competition in which such devices and advances as the wing slat and flap and the Cierva Autogiro could receive full trial.[2] At the fund's meeting on June 2, 1926, the trustees gave their tentative approval to the safe aircraft competition plan.[3]

During his discussions with Guggenheim, Mayo summarized five deficiencies in the operational characteristics of airplanes in the mid-1920s, all of which pertained to low-speed stability, control, and handling qualities. These deficiencies included high landing speeds and long landing rollouts, excessively long takeoff runs, inability to perform steep descents and ascents during landing approaches and climbs following takeoff, and poor behavior characteristics during stalls. Mayo believed that the Cierva Autogiro, the Handley Page wing slat, and the Hill tailless airplane could circumvent these difficulties. His views, together with the observations of Guggenheim and Cone, led the trustees to recommend an "Open International Aircraft Competition," with an appropriation between $150,000 and $200,000.

The trustees summed up the necessity for such a design demonstration by stating that most aircraft crashes were caused by a plane reducing its speed to below the stalling point while flying at low altitudes. During the first seven months of 1926, for example, Britain's Royal Air Force suffered twenty-six fatal accidents with forty-seven deaths from crashes due to stalling and subsequent loss of control. Other accidents occurred when pilots attempted to land at high speeds, to avoid stalling, on small confined landing strips. Just as the goal of Guggenheim blind-flying research had been to solve the problem of fog flying, the goal of the safe aircraft competition became one of reducing stall speeds through mechanical means.[4]

Announcement of the planned competition brought favorable response from the aeronautical community. The authoritative journal *Aviation* stated "the allocation of $150,000, and possibly $200,000, as prize money for this competition is likely to bring out some very real advancement, since these sums are sufficient to draw the attentions of the best minds of the world, along quite elaborate lines of experimentation."[5]

Throughout the summer of 1926, Guggenheim supervised the preparation of suitable contest rules. Generally, these rules stipulated that the contest aircraft meet minimum flying standards, including a landing speed no greater than 30 mph, a maximum 100-foot landing run, and a minimum level flight speed of 35 mph. The tentative rules also required the aircraft to have full controllability to the point of stall, and stable behavior characteristics while in a stalled attitude. At Guggenheim's request, Alexander Klemin, R. H. Mayo, and Archibald Black drew up the tentative rules, and then, in September 1926, submitted them to leading American and European aeronautical experts.[6] With the tentative rules went a questionnaire from Guggenheim asking if the existing aeronautical state-of-the-art could produce an airplane qualifying under the rules, whether such an aircraft would be "a distinctly markedly safer aircraft than existing types," and would it be possible to design an aircraft that could qualify under the rules, yet "at the same time defeat the object of the competition," a veiled euphemism for any possibility that the contest might produce an *unsafe* plane.[7]

At the outset, some American and foreign engineers and developers preferred emphasizing structural as well as aerodynamic design criteria in the safe airplane competition. Grover Loening, a well-known American airplane developer, recommended that the competition emphasize "the development of the 'crash-proof' airplane," one with a rugged shock absorbing structure, and capable of operating on land or water. He suggested that this had already been accomplished through the development of the Loening OA-2 Amphibian. In later correspondence, Loening reaffirmed his belief that, to meet the aerodynamic requirements of low stalling and landing speed, competition designers would have to construct extremely light and flimsy entries. Though he later attempted to enter a helicopter design in the competition, Loening remained a generally hostile critic of the Guggenheim safe aircraft investigation.[8] Georg Madelung, the Guggenheim fund's German representative, also believed that the competition should investigate structural developments. Mayo, during discussions with French engineers, found them preoccupied with the danger of inflight fire, to the point that they actually suggested that the competition should direct its full attention to elimination of inflight and postcrash conflagrations.[9] Though Harry Guggenheim and his technical advisers considered all these suggestions, they finally decided to continue emphasizing aerodynamic as opposed to structural problems.

By the spring of 1927, the fund's officials had threshed out a final form of the competition rules. To assist the fund in formulating meaningful requirements, F. Trubee Davison, the Assistant Secretary of War for Aeronautics, assigned Lt. Edwin E. Aldrin of the Army Air Corps to serve as the army's official representative and technical adviser to the fund. Test pilot Maj. Rudolph W. "Shorty" Schroeder, Lt. James Doolittle, and J. B. Hill, an airmail pilot, also advised the fund on the proposed rules. During a special dinner held at the Yale Club in New York City on April 29, 1927, Harry Guggenheim revealed the final details of the safe airplane competition. Those attending, including virtually all the corporate and governmental leaders of America's aircraft industry, heard Guggenheim announce a $150,000 competition, consisting of a $100,000 first prize, with five special $10,000 prizes for safety given to the first five aircraft to meet the minimum flying requirements. Guggenheim referred to the deaths on April 26 of Lt. Comdr. Noel Davis and Lt. Stanton Wooster as a demonstrable justification for the safety competition. While making a trial flight in a Keystone Pathfinder aircraft named the "American Legion" prior to attempting a New York-to-Paris flight, the two men perished when the overloaded trimotor biplane stalled and crashed shortly after takeoff from Langley Field, Virginia. The competition's committee of judges included Orville Wright, F. Trubee Davison, Edward P. Warner, William P. MacCracken, Jr., Comdr. Richard E. Byrd, and NACA's Dr. George W. Lewis. The competition's three technical advisers were Alexander Klemin, Lt. Edwin E. Aldrin, and Maj. R. H. Mayo.[10]

The final draft of the rules represented a blend between purely technical requirements and practical piloting matters. To qualify for the competition, all aircraft entered had to meet the following minimum requirements: achieve a maximum speed of at least 110 mph at sea level; attain a four-hundred-feet-per-minute climb rate at one thousand feet; maintain level and controlled flight at a speed no greater than 35 mph; demonstrate a power-off gliding speed of 38 mph or less; perform a steady glide to landing over a thirty-five-foot high obstruction with a landing roll no greater than three hundred feet from the base of the obstruction; and demonstrate a takeoff within a three-hundred-foot run, then pass over a thirty-five-foot obstruction located five hundred feet from the takeoff roll starting point. The competition required that each entry have sufficient inherent stability to permit "hands off" flying at any throttle setting and any airspeed from 45 mph to 100 mph for a full five minutes in gusty air. Each entry had to have a useful load of five pounds per engine horsepower. Entries would receive extra points for bettering these initial requirements. For example, for every mile per hour that an entry could fly less than 35 mph in level flight, the plane would receive an additional two points. The fund announced it would accept entries from any nation for the competition starting on September 1, 1927, and that the competition would close on October 31, 1929, or on a date prior to that time if the fund's officials decided that the objectives of the competition had been carried out.[11]

From the outset, these requirements favored development of a single-engine airplane with such devices as wing slats or flaps, a light though rugged structure, and accommodations for a pilot and one passenger. A multiengine entry simply offered too many problems, such as asymmetric control in the event of one engine failing, a natural tendency towards high landing and stalling speeds, and inability to operate from a confined landing and takeoff area. With but one exception, all the entries in the Guggenheim competition were single-engine aircraft having various unique and often freakish design features. The design competition opened in September 1927, and in the fall of 1929, the flight trials began. Then, only two of the many entries successfully passed all the basic flying requirements, becoming eligible for the actual safety competition.

By October 31, 1929, twenty-seven companies in the United States and abroad had entered the Guggenheim competition. Twenty-one of these came from the United States, five came from Great Britain, and one came from Italy. Circumstances limited the actual number of aircraft that appeared for the tests to fifteen, fourteen American and one British. Of these fifteen, three withdrew before flight-testing, two crashed during preliminary trials, and eight failed to meet any of the qualifying requirements. Only two airplanes advanced to the safety tests: these were the American-built Curtiss Tanager and the Handley Page HP 39 Gugnunc, a British entry. Of these two, the Tanager went on to win the Daniel Guggenheim International Safe Aircraft Competition with its first prize of $100,000.[12]

The two aircraft that passed the preliminary requirements showed surprisingly similar design approaches. The other thirteen airplanes, however, were more diversified, and represented various ingenious and not so ingenious methods of improving low-speed aircraft stability and control. The majority of entries were biplanes, but some unusual monoplanes also appeared; they all failed to pass the preliminary trials. One such aircraft, designed by Heraclio Alfaro, featured broad trailing edge flaps. During testing, however, the plane had poor lateral (turn and roll) control at low speeds, as well as insufficient range of elevator movement for pitch control at low speeds. Further, it failed to attain the minimum high speed of 110 mph, and fund officials thus disqualified it. A similar design, the Taylor Brothers Model C-2, also failed to meet the high-speed requirement, and it did not qualify for the competition. Maj. Rudolph Schroeder and John Wentworth sponsored development of yet another monoplane featuring a variable-camber parasol wing with trailing edge flaps, and a complex variable-pitch propeller for maximum engine performance. During preliminary flight-testing by "Shorty" Schroeder himself, it entered an uncontrolled power-on spiral at five hundred feet, just missed a hospital, and crashed in a street. Schroeder crawled from the wreckage and lamely explained that his lack of injuries proved the plane was a safe one. James McDonnell, an up-and-coming young designer, entered a two-place low-wing monoplane informally called the Doodlebug; it, too, crashed, due to structural failure, injuring McDonnell.[13]

The biplane entries were, in effect, all variations on the same theme. They all were two-seat aircraft with single engines and generous wing areas. Most had flaps or some special "safety" device the designers hoped would improve low-speed stability, control, and handling qualities. Many had poor stability and control characteristics at low speeds, and others could not attain the 110-mph minimum high speed or the 35-mph level flight low speed. The only aircraft to come close to the Tanager and HP 39 in performance was the Command-Aire 5-C-3, but it failed to meet the minimum flying speed requirement, being incapable of flight below 46 mph. The most bizarre biplane design was the Cunningham-Hall Model X. It had a large lower wing and a smaller upper wing; the upper wing served primarily as a mounting point for the plane's ailerons for lateral control, as well as a key structural member in the wing truss. The lower wing had a flap built into its ventral surface. When the pilot lowered this flap, it changed the camber of the lower wing, increasing the wing's lift. Struts connected to the ailerons on the narrow-chord upper wing also drooped the ailerons as the flap on the lower wing extended downwards. The pilot controlled this unique drooped aileron and flap combination via a small handwheel in the cockpit. Despite its intriguing features, the Cunningham-Hall Model X had no chance of winning the Guggenheim competition. It was underpowered, had a minimum flying speed of 44 mph, and had bad lateral-directional control characteristics.[14]

The first five companies to respond to Harry Guggenheim's call for entries had been British: De Havilland, Gloster, Cierva, Handley Page, and Vickers. Their quick response prompted some to fear that the American competition might be an entirely European affair.[15] As events turned out, this was not so, though Harry Guggenheim and other fund officials welcomed British entries. They especially hoped that the Cierva Autogiro or the Hill Pterodactyl tailless airplane might make their appearance in American skies. At one time these hopes seemed fulfilled, for the Cierva Autogiro Company, Ltd., of Great Britain and the Pitcairn-Cierva Autogiro Company of the U.S. both submitted entry forms, but the actual design development and construction of the aircraft took too long. Britain's Westland Company, involved in prototype development of G. T. R. Hill's tailless Pterodactyl aircraft, took no notice of the Guggenheim competition, and thus neither the Autogiro nor Pterodactyl participated in a competition which, in part, they had helped inspire. French companies emphasized structural rather than aerodynamic research, and thus did not enter the Guggenheim contest, and Germany's aircraft industry, severely hampered by economic conditions and the Versailles Treaty, was in no position to enter. One Italian firm, the Società Italiana Ernesto Breda, registered a design, but was unable to complete it in time for entry in the Guggenheim competition. Thus, the Daniel Guggenheim International Safe Aircraft Competition remained an American and British affair.[16]

The final confrontation between the Tanager and the HP 39 Gugnunc concluded a two-year design effort by the Curtiss and Handley Page companies, and a year of preparing for flight-testing by the Guggenheim safe aircraft committee itself. Harry Guggenheim decided to use the facilities of the Full Flight Laboratory at Mitchel Field, and the army furnished Capt. Walter Bender to serve as field manager for the safe aircraft competition. Alexander Klemin, one of the competition's technical advisers, threw the full support of New York University behind the Guggenheim project, and the school provided three technical observers, Otto Lunde, K. F. Rubert, and Frederick K. Teichmann. MIT furnished another observer, Prof. William G. Brown. Edwin Aldrin, the army's technical adviser to the competition, provided an army test pilot for the trials, Lt. Stanley Umstead, and the Guggenheim fund acquired the services of two other well-known test pilots, E. W. Rounds of the navy's Bureau of Aeronautics, and Thomas Carroll, a well-known research pilot formerly with the National Advisory Committee for Aeronautics. Mayo later stated that the pilots "were all three men of exceptional skill and experience and their handling of the various planes with their novel flying features was beyond criticism."[17] During 1928, Carroll made a series of check flights in a De Havilland Moth to furnish the fund with data useful in planning the actual flight operations of the competition. The Bureau of Standards sent various instrument experts to Mitchel Field to check that the instrumentation used in flight-testing the various entries operated properly.[18]

    While the various aircraft companies struggled to meet the demands of the Guggenheim requirements, some engineers and pilots claimed that the required performance specifications, such as a 35-mph or lower minimum level flight speed, or a three-hundred-foot takeoff distance, were unrealistic and unattainable for all except

freakish and impractical aircraft. To demonstrate that the requirements could be met with success if designers paid close attention to
new aeronautical developments, Klemin wrote a two-part series of
articles for *Aviation*, the United States' oldest and most respected
aeronautical journal, explaining the rules and relating new technical
developments to them. In the articles, Klemin concluded that "there
should be no insuperable difficulty in designing an airplane that
would meet requirements of the competition." He cautioned that
any such aircraft must have some method of increasing the lift of
the wing and ensuring stability and control at low speeds. He differed to a minor degree with Harry Guggenheim over the advantages
of the Hill Pterodactyl tailless airplane, arguing that if the Pterodactyl
incorporated slats and flaps instead of its radical tailless configuration,
it would lose many of its advantages, and thus a more conventional
design with a tail, as well as wing slats and flaps, could perform just
as well. In particular, Klemin foresaw the poor damping characteristics of tailless designs when they develop longitudinal (pitching)
oscillations, a problem that plagued subsequent tailless and flying
wing designs. He concluded that an airplane satisfying the competition requirements would "possess a real commercial value," and added
that "the competition offers incentive to research . . . and is certain
to induce progress."[19]

The best method of improving the lifting characteristics of an airplane's wing at low speeds appeared to be use of the wing flap and
leading edge wing slat. The flap, essentially a section of the wing's
trailing edge hinged to open downwards, increased the lift of a wing,
thus improving lift characteristics at takeoff and landing. For the
first time, the Guggenheim safety competition linked flaps to the
goal of short and low-speed landings; they have been recognized as
indispensable ever since. The slat, a "little wing" mounted on the
leading edge of a plane's wing, could open and create a gap between
itself and the wing through which oncoming airflow would stream,
preventing the air moving over the top of the wing from breaking
away in turbulence and subsequently causing loss of lift. The slat
enabled a pilot to climb more steeply at low speeds, for example just
after takeoff. When a wing reached a certain angle of attack relative
to the airstream, the airflow over the top of the wing would break
away, not joining with the airflow under the wing when both met at
the wing trailing edge. The wing would lose its lift and stall. The
airplane would usually drop precipitously, with a tendency to spin
to the left or right. At high altitude, this presented little problem for
a well-designed airplane and well-trained pilot; the pilot could re-

cover from the spin into a dive, pick up airspeed, and then pull out from the dive into level flight. At low altitudes, however, the plane might smash into the ground before the pilot could effect recovery. Loss of engine power just after takeoff, or a poorly judged attempt to stretch a landing glide, could cause a stall at low altitudes. The slat, by "tricking" the wing into "believing" it was operating at a lower angle relative to the airstream (and hence a "higher" speed), delayed this onset of airflow disruption over the wing, reducing stall speeds. Its use during spins often brought about immediate recovery, greatly increasing the confidence of pilots in their airplanes.

AIRFLOW AROUND AN UNSLATTED AND SLATTED WING AIRFOIL SECTION

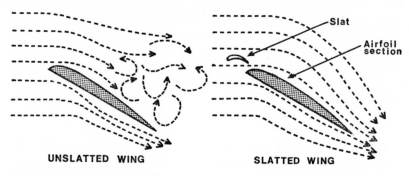

UNSLATTED WING   **SLATTED WING**

Wing is already stalled with flow sep-   Wing is still unstalled. Flow separa-
aration above the wing.   tion has not yet occurred.

Note: Airspeed and angle of attack are assumed constant for both wings.

Figure 5

The wing slat, one of the most important devices ever developed in the technical history of aviation, stemmed from the work of two men, Frederick Handley Page and Gustav Lachmann. In 1918, Handley Page, a noted British aircraft developer, had cut spanwise slots in model wings and then tested the slotted wings in a wind tunnel. He hoped that the slotted wings would smooth the airflow over the wing, preventing airflow burbling that occurred prior to a stall. The slots did improve lift, and when he located the slots near the wing's leading edge, the wing's lift jumped by 60 percent. Handley Page then went one step further, mounting a retractable slat on the leading edge of the wing so that when extended it created the necessary gap or slot. This marked the birth of the Handley Page wing slat. Gustav

Lachmann, a German pilot and theoretical aerodynamicist, had been severely injured in 1917 when his plane stalled and crashed. During his hospital recuperation he reasoned that a series of slots cut into a wing would enable the wing to continue generating lift even at steep angles of attack where an unslotted wing would clearly stall. He persuaded Ludwig Prandtl at Göttingen to perform wind-tunnel tests on a model wing having two slots. Prandtl, to his surprise, found the slots increased the wing's lift by 63 percent.[20]

By 1921, Lachmann and Handley Page had reached similar conclusions on the value of the wing slot and retractable wing slat, and the two men, who up to this time had worked separately, joined forces to work on slatted wing development. The wing slot, while an efficient innovation, was a fixed and open gap in the wing. At high speeds it increased drag without offering any high-speed compensatory advantage. Therefore, the Handley Page retractable wing slat seemed more attractive, for it could be extended at low speeds where it was needed, and then retracted flush against the leading edge of the wing at high speeds when it was not required. Handley Page, on the right track with the retractable slat, then made its operation completely automatic. He reasoned that a pilot, at the point of the stall, had his full attention occupied by flying the airplane, and could not spare the time or effort to operate some control linkage to extend the slat. Handley Page discovered that, at steep angles of attack, the air pressure at the wing's leading edge could itself open the slat, resulting in automatic wing slat extension.[21]

One of the most enthusiastic supporters of the Handley Page automatic wing slat was another early British aircraft pioneer, Geoffrey de Havilland. De Havilland equipped one of his Moth light airplanes with the Handley Page device, and flew a test demonstration program. He verified that the slats reduced aircraft stall speed, and that, in the event that a pilot let the airspeed drop to the stall point, the subsequent stall was gentle, and the pilot could easily recover, even if a spin developed. In most cases, when completely stalled with the slats extended, the aircraft would sink down a steep descent path, but in a level or slightly nose-high attitude. Any lateral control instability, such as wing dropping, was negated by the slats. Encouraged by de Havilland's flight research, Gustav Lachmann provided the single-engine Albatros C-72 commercial transport biplane in 1926 with slotted wings, the first commercial aircraft so equipped. Its successful operations further encouraged Handley Page and Lachmann, who began selling the patent rights for the device to various governments, including the United States. The U.S. Navy's Bureau of Aeronautics was deeply interested in the advantages offered by the slat and slot, and requested the Curtiss Aeroplane & Motor Company to undertake further slat and slot development. This eventually led to the subsequent legal controversy between Curtiss and Handley Page over their entries in the Guggenheim International Safe Aircraft Competition, when the British designer claimed patent infringement by Curtiss.[22]

Handley Page had been one of the first designers to enter the Guggenheim competition; the fund had accepted his entry on October 1, 1927, and the company had set right to work developing its proposal. As ultimately completed, the Handley Page HP 39 Gugnunc was a trim biplane with full-span retractable wing slats on the leading edges of both the upper and lower wings. The lower wing had full-span trailing edge flaps, and the upper wing also had a broad flap area, broken only for ailerons mounted on the outer portions of the wing's trailing edge. For maximum lift during steep climbs, high angles of attack, and during stall approaches, Handley Page and his design team had linked the leading edge slats to the flaps. Now, when the air pressure opened the slats, the forward movement of the slats pulled the flaps down. The HP 39 had a rectangular fuselage constructed from spruce longerons and struts, and covered with plywood sheeting; the wings and tail surfaces were of conventional wood and fabric construction. The pilot sat in a front cockpit, and an observer occupied a rear cockpit also equipped with full flying controls. The plane had a long stroke steel tube oleo landing gear to absorb the impact of landing at high descent rates, and the wheels had brakes to reduce landing roll.

The wings were almost of sesquiplane configuration, for the upper wing, spanning 40 feet, was much broader and of greater chord than the lower wing. The top wing had a wing area of 205 square feet, while the lower wing had an area of only 88 square feet. A Warren truss strut arrangement joined the upper and lower wings, with N type outer interplane struts, and A type struts joining the wing center section to the fuselage. Overall length of the airplane was 25 feet 9 inches, and the height was exactly 9 feet. Cockpit instrumentation consisted of an airspeed indicator, altimeter, tachometer, oil pressure gauge, and an oil temperature gauge. The pilot had a control stick for elevator and aileron surface deflection, and pedals to move the rudder. He could adjust the stabilizer angle via a sliding lever, and had another lever for brake operation. The HP 39 had a five-cylinder air-cooled Armstrong Siddeley Mongoose III radial engine rated at

155.6 hp at 1,850 rpm driving a two-bladed wooden propeller with a diameter of 7.54 feet.[23]

The origins of the "Gugnunc" appellation lay in a popular British comic strip, "Pip, Squeak, and Wilfred," which appeared in the *Daily Mirror* newspaper. One of the strip's main characters, Wilfred the rabbit, spoke a nonsense language containing the words "gug" and "nunc." The immense popularity of this serial had caused some individuals to form a charitable organization, the Wilfredian League of Gugnuncs. At some point, staff members of *Flight*, a leading British weekly aeronautical journal, dubbed the HP 39 the Gugnunc, no doubt because the sobriquet fitted nicely with its Guggenheim origins. Gugnunc was never an official designation, but it soon caught on and was more widely known than the HP 39 design bureau number.[24]

Handley Page completed the sole HP 39 Gugnunc aircraft registered G-AACN in April 1929, and it completed its maiden flight on April 30, 1929, at Cricklewood Aerodrome, piloted by Maj. James Cordes, a Handley Page test pilot. The plane proved to have superlative handling characteristics. Stall onset, instead of bringing sharp nose dropping, with perhaps wing dropping and entry into a spin, led instead to a virtually horizontal wallowing motion in a steep descent path, from which the pilot could easily recover. Clearly the Gugnunc flew very well. Cordes and Squadron Leader T. H. England completed its preliminary trials, moved on to easily pass Certificate of Airworthiness tests at Martlesham Heath, and then disassembled and crated the airplane for its journey to the United States. Cordes and the Gugnunc left for America aboard the liner *Minnewaska*, arriving in New York in mid-September. By September 24, the plane was at Mitchel Field; Handley Page technicians assembled the Gugnunc and had it ready for its first check flight by October 3, 1929. Later that month, after Cordes had completed some familiarization flights in the HP 39 following its reassembly, the Gugnunc's principal rival flew into Mitchel Field. This was the Curtiss Tanager, a trim black and red biplane.[25]

The Curtiss Tanager, the final winner of the safe aircraft competition, was a bigger and heavier airplane than the lithe Gugnunc. Curtiss had taken two and a half years to develop the Tanager, starting in May 1927 just after Harry Guggenheim had publicly announced the competition at the Yale Club dinner. Theodore Paul Wright, the Curtiss company's chief engineer, directed the design evolution, supervising a design team consisting of Robert R. Osborn, project engineer and chief designer; Arne Vinje, assistant designer; William H. Miller and Robert E. Johnson, project aerodynamicists; Raymond C. Blaylock, chief of structural analysis; E. J. Ashman and R. G. Buzby, specialists in aircraft weight; and H. R. Moles, in charge of drafting and shop work. In May 1927, C. M. Keys and F. H. Russell, president and vice-president, respectively, of the Curtiss company, asked T. P. Wright and the Curtiss engineering department if the company could design an aircraft capable of meeting the stringent Guggenheim requirements. The engineering department, after studying the competition rules, concluded that the company could design such a plane, but that since the competition involved overcoming stiff aerodynamic problems, the development process would necessitate much preliminary wind-tunnel testing and aerodynamic research.[26]

Eventually, the development of the Tanager cost Curtiss $105,000, a sum that the Guggenheim first prize, plus an additional $10,000 safety award, just covered. Much of the costs stemmed from an intensive wind-tunnel research program that Curtiss began in September 1927, using a company tunnel to test various types of wing flap and wing slat devices. By April 1928, after hundreds of tests, Curtiss aerodynamicists had concluded that a plane equipped with wing slats in conjunction with wing flaps and an odd device, the "floating aileron," could win the competition, provided that structural designers reduced aircraft weight to a minimum. In April 1928, Curtiss notified the Guggenheim fund of its intention to enter the design competition, and asked for further elaboration of certain rules that were not completely clear. Curtiss then decided to build a practical aircraft, and not simply a high-performance exotic entry to last just through the competition, since company engineers believed that this would constitute a violation in spirit of the contest. The company wind tunnel tested five different designs, each having wings with Curtiss C-72 airfoil cross sections, with leading edge slats and trailing edge flaps.[27]

On each of the biplane designs, the lower wing also had a unique feature known as a floating aileron, which, like a regular aileron, maintained lateral (roll) control. To overcome the problem of poor lateral control at low speeds and to prevent yawing induced by differential aileron operation, with consequential unequal lift and drag on opposing wings, Curtiss engineers placed the aileron on the wing tip, rather than on the trailing edge of the wing. Further, each aileron had a symmetrical airfoil section, and its rotation point was located behind the leading edge. During operation, the ailerons moved with respect to one another, but "floated" freely on their pivots with respect to the plane. For example, a five-degree upward angle on one aileron automatically resulted in a five-degree downward angle on the other. Because the ailerons were of symmetrical airfoil cross section, and because the upward and downward deflection angles were always equal, the lift and drag characteristics on both wings were equal, enabling the Tanager to roll without yawing. Curtiss estimated that the Tanager's ailerons were 50 percent more effective at low speeds than normal ailerons, with their yawing problems.[28]

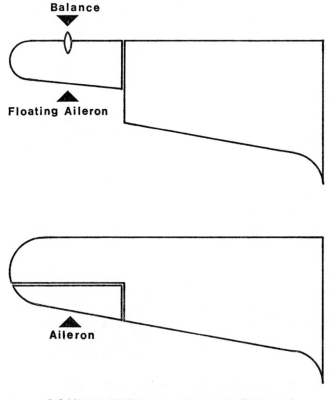

CONVENTIONAL AND FLOATING AILERON CONFIGURATIONS

Figure 6

The Tanager, in its final configuration, was a larger, more practical and comfortable aircraft than the Handley Page Gugnunc. The

Tanager was a biplane with a fully enclosed cockpit and cabin, rather than the open cockpits of the HP 39. A pilot and passenger could sit in tandem, with room for a third seat. The top wing had full-span automatic leading edge slats and trailing edge flaps; unlike the Gugnunc, the flaps did not automatically extend when the slats opened. Rather, the pilot operated the flaps manually. The slats opened automatically when the wing's angle of attack reached twelve degrees. The lower wing also had leading edge slats and trailing edge flaps, but also had, at its tips, the Curtiss floating ailerons. The total wing area was 333 square feet, and the wing spanned forty-three feet eleven inches. The plane was twenty-six feet eight inches long and eleven feet four inches high. Like the Gugnunc, the Tanager was basically of wood and fabric construction, though its fuselage consisted of duralumin and steel tubing covered with fabric. It had a steel tube split-axle, long-stroke oleo landing gear to absorb the impact of high landing loads, and the wheels had brakes to reduce further the landing roll. Powered by a six cylinder Curtiss Challenger radial engine producing 176 hp at 1,830 rpm, the Tanager could carry a useful load of 880 pounds. The cockpit instrument panel had an air-speed indicator, altimeter, tachometer, oil pressure gauge, oil temperature gauge, and compass. The pilot controlled the elevators and ailerons via a control stick, had rudder pedals for rudder control, and could adjust the movable stabilizer and flaps via cranks. The wheel brake controls were mounted on the rudder pedals.[29]

Curtiss test pilot Paul Boyd completed the first flight of the Tanager on October 12, 1929. The company had completed only one of the craft, which received a special experimental registration, X-181M. During its initial flights, Boyd noted no serious handling problems, other than a tendency for the plane to cruise better with slightly more stabilizer trim adjustment required than tunnel tests had predicted. Pleased by the initial flight test results, Boyd delivered the airplane to the Guggenheim Full Flight Laboratory at Mitchel Field on October 29, 1929. There it joined the Handley Page HP 39 Gugnunc for actual trials.[30]

Handley Page and the Gugnunc design staff had not greeted the development of the Curtiss Tanager with neutral emotions. They felt, in some ways rightly so, that the Tanager was capitalizing on a Handley Page invention. Popular interpretation of the Guggenheim competition had led many individuals to assume that each company involved would enter an airplane having one outstanding design feature. Thus, many hoped, Cierva would enter an Autogiro, Hill a tailless Pterodactyl, and Handley Page a plane equipped with slats and flaps. By this reasoning, the Curtiss company's chief contribution could be the floating aileron. Wisely, the Guggenheim fund, at Harry Guggenheim's insistence, had taken no position on issues of patent infringement. The only position the fund took concerned the actual copying of design features by one competitor from another. Fund officials had written into the rules that "the employment of design features which, in the opinion of the Fund, are copied from the design of another competitor, may render the aircraft ineligible for entry."[31] Guggenheim had asked that this provision be included because he believed that designers might be presenting designs for testing at any time from 1927 through 1929, and he wished to prevent a later competitor from gaining any advantage from the work of an earlier one. In the case of the Tanager and Gugnunc, both aircraft had been under simultaneous development, and Curtiss and Handley Page had both announced their intention to use a slotted and flap-equipped design from the outset.[32]

The subsequent brouhaha between Handley Page and Curtiss company officials generated the only serious ill will during any of the Guggenheim fund's activities, and led, eventually, to a postcompetition legal squabble between the two companies. "It was a pity that Harry Guggenheim had to leave for Cuba before the end of the competition," fund technical representative R. H. Mayo later recalled. "His presence during the early stages of the tests had created an atmosphere of goodwill which persisted to the end in spite of the breezes tending to dissipate it."[33] Though safe aircraft committee member Orville Wright recommended that the Curtiss entry be permitted to fly in the competition only if it had its slats locked closed, Harry Guggenheim decided that the fund should not declare one of the entries ineligible after having accepted it for trial. In any case, the situation was not clear-cut: Curtiss engineers charged Handley Page designers with violating Curtiss patents, and Alfredo Leigh, designer of the Brunner-Winkle Bird, claimed to have invented the wing slat before Handley Page.[34]

Fund technical advisers and judges had little doubt after seeing the Tanager and Gugnunc during preliminary flight demonstrations that the contest boiled down to which aircraft was better engineered. Had the Tanager flown with restrictions placed on its slat operation, undoubtedly the Gugnunc would have given the better performance. The point of the contest was to demonstrate superior technology, not to determine who would get a production contract.[35] Therefore, such a penalizing of Curtiss would have hurt the overall purpose of the side the scope of the competition, though they were vital to questions involving commercial production and sale of the planes involved.*

Harry Guggenheim had hoped originally to have the safety contest underway in June 1929, but the majority of entries, including the Gugnunc and Tanager, did not arrive until late September and early October, with the result that test flights were often postponed because of marginal weather conditions. One by one, the various aircraft arrived at Mitchel Field, flown by company pilots. After company demonstration flights, frequently watched by Daniel Guggenheim himself, the fund's three test pilots would fly the planes. At first, none of the entries were able to pass the stiff safety tests; then the Gugnunc arrived.

In a further attempt to reduce drag and to increase the speed of the airplane, Handley Page engineers had hastily equipped the Gugnunc with a narrow-chord Townend engine cowling, essentially a ring around the cylinder heads. (Curtiss had likewise manufactured a NACA engine cowling for the Tanager, but did not use it in the actual Guggenheim trials.) Thus equipped, the Gugnunc made its first American demonstration flight on October 3, 1929. Test pilot James Cordes' exhibition left little doubt that the HP 39 was a strong contender for the first prize. With the engine snarling, Cordes lifted the little airplane off the ground after a short run, then climbed steeply. He performed a succession of low-speed maneuvers, including tight turns at about 40 mph, then accelerated to over 100 mph before performing a steep descent and landing, the plane rolling to a halt within one hundred feet. Later in the day, safety competition test pilots Stanley Umstead and Thomas Carroll flew the Gugnunc and discovered that they could handle the docile airplane almost as skillfully as Cordes could, despite their lack of familiarity with it.[36]

Three weeks after the Gugnunc completed its first demonstration flight, the Curtiss Tanager arrived at Mitchel Field, flown directly from the company to the test site. Test pilot Paul Boyd's subsequent demonstration of the aircraft drew immediate comparison with that of the Gugnunc. Boyd turned the plane over to the fund's three test pilots in November, and they began flying the Tanager to see if it

* After the competition, Handley Page sued Curtiss for patent infringement. Reports had previously suggested that the Curtiss entry might be mass-produced. Handley Page, with the technical advice of Theodore von Kármán, won the suit in federal court, and Curtiss did not market the Tanager. See Theodore von Kármán with Lee Edson, *The Wind and Beyond*, p. 114.

met the qualifying regulations. Charles A. Lindbergh, a fund trustee and unofficial adviser on the safe aircraft competition, also flew the plane shortly after it arrived at Mitchel Field, making a succession of short takeoffs and landings with steep climbs and glides. Like the rival Gugnunc, the Tanager had no difficulty meeting the competition requirements, although it was a larger and heavier airplane, and so it moved on to the safety tests.[37]

During the testing of the Tanager and Gugnunc, the Guggenheim competition officials permitted some leeway in the regulations to provide for unusual or extenuating factors. For example, the Handley Page entry did not really meet the qualifying requirement that adequate accommodation exist for both a pilot and observer. The Gugnunc's cockpits were so small and narrow that a pilot and passenger could not wear parachutes while flying in the plane, and the pilot had severely restricted mobility. Nevertheless, because the plane had so many interesting aerodynamic features and because it was a foreign entry, competition officials unanimously agreed to keep the Gugnunc in the contest. In another case, both the Tanager and HP 39 failed to attain the required engine-off steep glide angle of "not less than sixteen degrees." This regulation necessitated placing the aircraft in a stall, and thus was really a test of aircraft controllability and handling characteristics during a stalled descent. When the steepest angle the two aircraft could attain was roughly 12 to 13 degrees, competition officials realized that the original requirement that the flight path and horizon form an angle of not less than 16 degrees was unrealistic and impractical. Accordingly, they lowered the regulation to no less than 12 degrees. The Gugnunc could attain 12.8 degrees, just barely meeting the requirement, while the Tanager came in at a steeper and more desirable 13.2 degrees. Handley Page and Curtiss officials were happy that neither of the planned two Autogiro entries had shown up for testing, for the Autogiro almost certainly could have descended at an angle of 16 degrees or more, forcing Guggenheim competition officials to retain the original requirement.[38]

Foggy and rainy weather kept the Tanager and Gugnunc grounded during much of November. Nevertheless, by early December, the Curtiss entry led its British rival, having successfully completed fourteen of the eighteen scheduled tests, the Gugnunc having passed twelve.[39] The Gugnunc failed in two tests, that of landing in a confined space, and maintaining a gliding speed of not more than 38 mph. In the first test, the Gugnunc and Tanager had to glide without power over a thirty-five-foot-high obstruction, land, and come to a stop within three hundred feet from the base of the obstruction. This simulated complete engine failure necessitating an immediate forced landing in a restricted area surrounded by such obstructions as trees or buildings. The test emphasized controlled approaches with high sink rates and heavy touchdowns. It strained the landing gears of the Tanager and Gugnunc to the utmost, and both aircraft suffered damage. But while the Tanager simply suffered bent fittings, the Gugnunc's gear partially collapsed on two occasions.

In subsequent testing, out of fear of structural failure, safety competition pilots landed the British plane at a lower sink rate, necessitating a higher landing approach speed. Thus flown, the Gugnunc could not pass the test; it consistently landed and completed its landing roll in 320 feet—still outstanding, but more than the 300-foot maximum, and inferior to the Tanager's 293-foot landing and rollout mark.[40]

The second test that the Gugnunc failed to pass was maintaining a 38-mph gliding speed for three minutes while all engine power was off. In each case, competition test pilots found that the HP 39, when trimmed in this condition, glided earthwards at about 40 mph—its final competition figure was 39.7 mph. This puzzled and worried James Cordes and other Handley Page representatives, who claimed a three-minute power-off gliding speed of 33½ mph, based on exacting tests at Britain's Martlesham Heath, and who believed that disassembling and then rerigging the aircraft in the United States might have changed its aerodynamic characteristics. It is possible that by installing the Townend ring, Handley Page adversely altered the performance characteristics of the aircraft, increasing the Gugnunc's maximum speed, but "cleaning up" the plane so much that its minimum gliding speed increased. If so, then the company, in an understandable attempt to wring maximum performance from the aircraft, actually contributed to its defeat. (Curtiss engineers might well have faced a similar problem had they flown the Tanager with the NACA cowling they had built for it. One may speculate that they recognized this possibility and consequently never flew the Tanager with the cowling.) Despite efforts to remedy the situation, the Gugnunc could not attain the requisite 38 mph, though Curtiss managed to attain 37.1 mph in their Tanager.[41]

The Gugnunc had other undesirable characteristics as well. If the pilot deliberately stalled the Gugnunc, the nose tended to drop downwards. Sometimes, as the nose dropped below horizontal due to the stall, the automatic slats would respond to changes in air pressure and retract, thus also raising the flaps at a critical time when both slats and flaps were needed to improve aircraft stability and control.

Like many other conventional designs, the Gugnunc would then dive earthwards picking up speed until the pilot had sufficient airspeed to regain control effectiveness and pull out of the dive. This could be most serious in a low-altitude stall. The Tanager, with manually operated flaps, did not have this problem. Indeed, the Gugnunc tended, when stalled, to lose altitude, pick up sufficient airspeed for the pilot to recover, and then, as the pilot raised the nose, stall again, "continuing this cycle apparently indefinitely."[42] Its directional stability characteristics at low speeds also deteriorated, and, just above stall speed, the Gugnunc tended to "hunt" with its nose. In contrast, the Tanager, perhaps because of its tail design, was much more stable near its stalling speed, and the floating ailerons greatly improved its lateral control characteristics, minimizing any tendency to yaw. Thus, in several critical low-speed stability and handling characteristics, the Curtiss Tanager performed significantly better than its British rival.[43]

By Christmas 1929, the Curtiss Tanager had passed all of the Guggenheim safety tests, while the Handley Page HP 39 had failed two, disqualifying itself for the $100,000 first prize. In all other respects, the Gugnunc had performed excellently, being the only fixed-wing aircraft, aside from the winning Tanager, that could have possibly approached the stiff standards of the Guggenheim competition. On January 1, 1930, Capt. Emory S. Land, vice-president of the fund, announced that the board of judges, headed by pioneer Orville Wright, had declared the Tanager the winner.[44] The final point score was 22.9 for the Tanager and 21.9 for the Gugnunc.[45] The closeness of the competition brought forth acid comments from C. G. Grey, feisty editor of *The Aeroplane*, Britain's most respected aeronautical journal. Edward P. Warner, editor of the American aeronautical weekly *Aviation*, responded with equally biting replies.

Grey argued that officials had unfairly applied the competition rules to the detriment of the Gugnunc. In several letters and an editorial, Warner rebutted Grey's charge, calling it an "oddly distorted account," and stating that the Curtiss Tanager "showed a brilliant general conception, and ingenuity and care in detail design. It bore the fruits of extended research. It won the competition by making the best showing under the rules as they were drawn—and as they were drawn, so were they applied."[46]

The final tabulated results indicated just how close the Gugnunc and Tanager had been (see Table 1).[47]

The Tanager had already won an initial safety prize of $10,000 after passing all the safety requirements, and on January 6, 1930, Capt.

TABLE 1

RESULTS OF SAFE AIRCRAFT COMPETITION

	Required	Tanager	Gugnunc
Maximum speed (in mph)	110 or more	111.6	112.4
Rate of climb at 1,000 ft (in ft/min)	400 or more	700	730
Minimum horizontal speed (in mph)	35 or less	30.6	33.4
Minimum gliding speed (in mph)	38 or less	37.1	39.7[a]
Landing run (in feet)	100 or less	90	82
Landing run over obstruction (in feet)	300 or less	293	320[a]
Takeoff run (in feet)	300 or less	295	290
Takeoff run over obstruction (in feet)	500 or less	500	440
Flattest glide (in degrees)	8 or less	6	7.2
Steepest glide (in degrees)	12 or more[b]	13.2	12.8
Useful load (in lbs)	5 per hp[c]	880	778

[a]Indicates requirements Gugnunc failed to meet.
[b]Requirement changed from 16 or more to 12 or more.
[c]Both aircraft met minimum requirements exactly, based on 176 hp for Tanager, 155.6 hp for Gugnunc.

Emory S. Land presented Clement M. Keys, president of the Curtiss Aeroplane and Motor Company, with a fund check for $100,000. More than three hundred representatives of the aircraft industry attended the ceremony, held at the Guggenheim's Full Flight Laboratory at Mitchel Field, Long Island. They heard Land announce, "There is nothing revolutionary about the winner but there are a number of evolutionary ideas transplanted from the design board to the air. . . . American aviation may well be proud of these results."[48]

Land also criticized the popular press image of the competition as a contest to develop a "foolproof" plane. "No one in the fund expected to obtain a 'foolproof' plane," Land said. "There isn't any such animal. Moving masses cannot be made 'foolproof,' but they can be made safe. Old man Kinetic Energy can always do damage to a fool."[49] Fund test pilot Stanley Umstead added emphasis to Land's words by demonstrating the Tanager's capabilities before the assembled throng and declaring after landing, "It is the safest airplane I ever flew."[50] Theodore P. Wright, the Curtiss company's chief engineer received recognition for his leadership of the Tanager design effort when the Society of Automotive Engineers presented him with their annual Wright Brothers Medal award.[51]

At the awards ceremony, which in effect marked the public closing of all the Guggenheim fund's activities, Land had also predicted that "the seed planted by this competition will bear fruit for the next decade."[52] He was correct. The Guggenheim fund released the final report on the Daniel Guggenheim International Safe Aircraft Competition in March 1930. The report summarized the conclusions that could be drawn from the competition, including the obvious one that "the advantages of slots and flaps in lowering the minimum speed were clearly demonstrated." They certainly had been; with its slots closed and flaps up, the Tanager could attain a minimum level flight speed of 41.5 mph. As good as this was, with slots open and flaps down, this minimum level flight speed dropped still further, to 30.6 mph. Because many of the other aircraft had disqualified themselves before even becoming eligible for the special safety tests, the competition did not obtain enough information to make any sort of reasoned judgment on the value of such things as variable area and variable camber wings, variable incidence wings, or the use of wing spoilers in place of ailerons for the purpose of lateral control. The variable incidence wing appeared subsequently on such aircraft as the Vought F8U Crusader with good success, and the wing spoiler became a standard feature on high-performance turbojet aircraft. Variable area wings (but of different conception than those on the Guggenheim aircraft) won acceptance on such designs as the Bell X-5, General Dynamics F-111, and Grumman F-14. These were applications, however, that the competition's judges and technical advisers could hardly have foreseen.[53]

The Tanager and Gugnunc soon disappeared from the headlines after the safe aircraft competition ended. The Tanager crashed during a crosswind takeoff at Wichita, Kansas, fortunately without injuring its pilot, while on a publicity trip around the country. The accident demonstrated the vulnerability of light STOL aircraft having low wing loadings to gusts. Though apparently rebuilt, the Tanager was then lost in a hangar fire, an unworthy end.[54] The Gugnunc, after protracted legal difficulties, arrived back in England in mid-1930, exchanging its civil registration for Royal Air Force registration K-1908. For the next few years, Air Ministry test pilots flew the plane at Farnborough's Royal Aircraft Establishment in a low-speed research program. It also appeared in military flying displays at Hendon in formation with a Cierva Autogiro and the Westland/Hill Pterodactyl—truly as unique a group of airplanes as have ever flown together. Finally, Handley Page and Armstrong Siddeley Motors Ltd. presented the Gugnunc to the Science Museum in London on July 19, 1934. The Science Museum displayed it until 1939, and then put it in storage.[55]

The major accomplishment of the Daniel Guggenheim International Safe Aircraft Competition was that it formulated the requirements for short-takeoff-and-landing (STOL) aircraft long before many in the aeronautical community realized such a need existed. Without question, the modern STOL airplane today, with its profusion of high-lift devices, owes its conception in part to the Guggenheim competition of 1927–29. The six recommended devices deemed worthy by the fund of further study became virtually indispensable equipment on subsequent STOL aircraft: leading edge slots or slats, automatic or manually controlled flaps, floating ailerons, long stroke oleo landing gear, an adjustable stabilizer capable of operation over an extreme range of settings, and brakes to reduce landing roll.[56]

In the late 1930s, several STOL aircraft appeared on the aviation scene, such as the Bellanca YO-50 and Ryan YO-51. The most outstanding, as well as most famous, was the German-built Fieseler Fi 156 *Storch*, designed as a utility and liaison aircraft for Hitler's *Wehrmacht*. *Storch* and STOL are synonymous, and this little two-seat airplane could land in fifty feet and virtually hover in a steady breeze. One rescued deposed dictator Benito Mussolini from a tiny space behind his hotel prison on a mountaintop on September 12, 1943. Yet these aircraft differed little aerodynamically from the Guggenheim conceptions of over a decade earlier. All were high-wing single-engine two-seat monoplanes with leading edge slats and trailing edge flaps, and long stroke landing gears. All could fly in the 110–130 mph class, but this was not as impressive, when one remembered that the *Storch* had a 240 hp engine, and the YO-50 and YO-51 could each muster between 420 and 440 hp, a far cry from the 155–176 hp of the Gugnunc and Tanager.[57]

The continuing progress in developing more powerful lightweight piston engines, as well as the aerodynamicist's general tendency to "clean up" aircraft design, resulted in the biplane configuration gradually giving way to the heavier high-wing STOL monoplane. Initiated well before World War II, this trend continued into the postwar world with the appearance of such aircraft as the Prestwick Pioneer and the Koppen-Bollinger Helioplane. The Guggenheim safe aircraft competition directly influenced the Helioplane, which first flew in 1949. Otto C. Koppen, professor of aeronautical engineering at the Guggenheim school at the Massachusetts Institute of Technology, had kept in close touch with the progress and goals of the Guggenheim competition. After the competition ended, he determined to keep working for the development of stall- and spin-proof airplanes. In 1948, in conjunction with Prof. Lynn Bollinger of the Harvard Business School, Koppen decided to modify a standard Piper Vagabond single-engine high-wing light monoplane into a STOL testbed. Koppen did all the design work, adding full-span trailing edge flaps, leading edge automatic slats, modifying the fuselage, and attaching a special broad two-bladed propeller to the 85 hp Continental piston engine.[58]

The resulting aircraft could fly at speeds as low as 27½ mph, take off in sixty feet (at only 73 percent power), and cruise as fast as 108 mph. The plane could not spin and could not stall; at 30 mph the Helioplane's wing was still fourteen degrees below the stall angle. First flown in a secret early morning test in April 1949 by Koppen himself, the Helioplane quickly caught the imagination of many aeronautical scientists, and it served as an initial test vehicle for later more powerful piston and turboprop-propelled successors, such as the superlative Helio Courier and Helio Stallion, the most outstanding single-engine STOL aircraft of the 1960s.[59]

The postwar STOL revolution was successful because it rested on a solid technical foundation dating to the Guggenheim competition. The Helio Courier, together with such aircraft as the Pilatus Porter, achieved the potential that Harry Guggenheim and his advisers had hoped such aircraft might reach. Once again well-spent Guggenheim money had helped generate a breakthrough by spurring research and development and by supporting full-scale in-flight demonstrations of new aircraft. Perhaps slow to take root, the ideas, inventions, and innovations revealed during that testing over Long Island attained their fullest expression three decades later, in the age of supersonic flight.

CHAPTER 9

Improving Aviation's Image

DANIEL and Harry Guggenheim were always conscious of the need to improve the image of aviation, which the reckless and careless aviator had done much to tarnish. The fund, by encouraging research and development, by promoting aeronautical education, and by demonstrating successful passenger-carrying airline service, helped convince the American public to accept the prospect of commercial air operations. But the fund also embarked on other, more dramatic, ways of spreading the gospel of aviation safety. The most elaborate of these were the two air tours of the United States by Charles A. Lindbergh and Floyd Bennett, the personal pilot of polar explorer Richard E. Byrd. The fund also supported local airfield and town marking projects, and issued special news releases, publications, and reports on a variety of aeronautical subjects. It sponsored the first national aviation safety conference held in the United States, and created a special Guggenheim medal fund to honor pioneers in aeronautics around the world.

Harry Guggenheim believed that "reliability" tours around the country demonstrating successful aircraft operation could help erase the reckless image of aviation and replace it with one emphasizing safety, regularity, and reliability. Guggenheim did not originate the air tour idea. Edsel Ford and Harvey Campbell had promoted air tours to stimulate the growth of air travel, their efforts leading to the first Ford reliability air tour in September 1925.[1] In June 1926, Harry Guggenheim had recommended to the fund trustees that the fund promote a series of reliability tours, including a round-the-country flight by a seaplane.[2] His opportunity for a nationwide tour came in June 1926, when Comdr. Richard E. Byrd arrived to a hero's welcome in New York City after his pioneering polar flight the previous month. Harry Guggenheim had decided that such risky demonstrations of aircraft reliability as transatlantic flights might cost the fund too much money, as well as chance disaster, with a consequential deleterious effect on aviation safety. For this reason, he had refused to assist several flyers who approached the fund with plans for transatlantic crossings. Byrd, however, was a different case. Byrd and his pilot, Floyd Bennett, were national heroes, credited with making the first flight over the North Pole. After Byrd and Bennett had landed back at their base camp at King's Bay, Spitzbergen, following their polar attempt, Harry Guggenheim dashed off a telegram reading, "Your courage in face of tremendous handicaps is an inspiration to all those interested in the development of commercial aviation. You have demonstrated to the world the increasing dependability of modern aircraft."[3] Shortly after the two airmen arrived back in the United States, Harry Guggenheim asked if Byrd would fly around the country in his plane, the Fokker trimotor *Josephine Ford*, to promote the cause of commercial air transportation. Byrd quickly assented, but, because of his naval duties and his plans to fly the Atlantic, he could not go along on the trip. Instead, Floyd Bennett, who had flown the plane for Byrd, agreed to make the swing around the country.[4]

Harry Guggenheim arranged the Byrd tour in conjunction with the Aeronautics Branch of the Department of Commerce. William P. MacCracken, Jr., the Assistant Secretary of Commerce for Aeronautics, offered his department's full support, provided the Guggenheim fund paid the tour's expenses. The trustees of the fund appropriated $20,000, and instructed Donald Keyhoe to act as the Aeronautics Branch's representative and as tour manager.[5] Keyhoe and the Guggenheim fund quickly worked out the itinerary of the Byrd tour. The plane would leave Washington, D.C., on October 7, flying to New York. It would then proceed to Ohio, Indiana, Illinois, Missouri, Nebraska, Colorado, Utah, Nevada, California, Arizona, New Mexico, Texas, Louisiana, Arkansas, Tennessee, Alabama, Georgia, the Carolinas, Virginia, and back to Washington, D.C. "The specific objective of this program," Harry Guggenheim wrote, "is the promotion of the establishment of airports and the encouragement of the public in the use of the established air mail routes."[6]

The Byrd tour got under way on October 7, 1926, when Floyd Bennett took off from Bolling Field, and flew to Mitchel Field with Harry Guggenheim, Edward P. Warner, and William P. MacCracken riding as passengers. Then it left for Albany. Over the next six weeks, the plane droned its way across the country, arriving back at Bolling

Field, Washington, D.C., on November 23, 1926. In the course of the tour, the *Josephine Ford* had flown 7,000 miles and had landed at forty-five cities, besides flying over dozens of others and hundreds of towns. At each stop, an average of 12,000 people inspected the plane, a grand total of about 540,000 having seen it on the ground nation-wide. At each stop, Bennett would give a short talk on the possibilities of commercial aviation, emphasizing that the plane was not a unique experimental aircraft, but simply a standard Fokker trimotor suit-able for passenger service that had been successfully modified to meet the rigors of Arctic flying. Additionally, Bennett and Keyhoe made radio broadcasts and granted interviews to the press.[7]

Bennett and Keyhoe concluded that the tour had clearly shown that the public was not in the least familiar with aviation. In his re-port of the tour, Keyhoe wrote, "In very few of the cities visited was the populace familiar with the large three-motor ship, and the com-ments of the crowd clearly showed that they had no conception that an airplane was anything but the old pre-war type."[8] High school and university students, as well as local businessmen, seemed most in-terested in the commercial possibilities of air transportation.[9] During the visits, local authorities regarded the tour with suspicion until they realized that the Guggenheim fund was paying all expenses, and that the townspeople did not have to contribute towards the venture. Then, their mood changed completely and they often asked if the fund would sponsor a return tour back to the same cities. The fund was undecided about such activities until Lindbergh burst upon the aeronautical scene.[10]

Charles A. Lindbergh was an obscure midwestern airmail pilot un-til he decided to fly across the Atlantic in a single-engine monoplane in order to win the $25,000 prize offered by Raymond Orteig of New York City for the first New York to Paris nonstop flight. The adulation and publicity that attended his successful flight in the Ryan NYP *Spirit of St. Louis* plane has been unequaled for any American since; the confetti that the office workers of New York City showered on his entourage cost the city $16,000 to clean up.[11] His flight did more to popularize flying and demonstrate how far aviation had come since the Wright brothers than any venture the Guggenheims could have supported.

Harry Guggenheim had met the tall, lean airman in the spring of 1927, shortly after Lindbergh had arrived at Curtiss Field, Long Island, with the *Spirit of St. Louis*. Looking at the sparse cockpit of the plane, Guggenheim thought, "This fellow will never make it. He's doomed!" Introduced to the young pilot, Guggenheim said with forced cheerfulness, "Well, when you get back to the United States, come up to the Fund and see me," though he never expected to see Lindbergh again.[12] Despite his misgivings, Guggenheim posed with Lindbergh for a publicity photo in front of the little monoplane.[13]

To Harry Guggenheim's surprise and pleasure, Lindbergh safely made his way across the Atlantic. No sooner had he arrived back in the United States, however, than many reporters and popular writers began calling Lindbergh "Lucky Lindy," or, in extreme cases, "The Flying Fool." The flight across the Atlantic had required courage, great skill, and careful planning. Lindbergh was no daredevil taking a foolhardy gamble hoping he would succeed. His flying of the plane had clearly indicated his scientific approach to aviation: he had cautiously tried out the craft, measuring its flying qualities and handling characteristics, proceeding step by step in a test program that was as carefully executed as any other at that time. Now, Harry Guggenheim realized, a danger existed that the thorough preparations for Lindbergh's flight, with their implications for future air transport, might go unnoticed in the craze surrounding the pilot. What better way to ensure that these implications would not be forgotten than by sponsoring a flight around the country?

After his return from Europe, Lindbergh had spent much of his time at Falaise, Harry Guggenheim's Long Island home, where the younger Guggenheim let him stay while Lindbergh wrote *We.* Harry and his advisers, especially lawyer Henry Breckinridge, closely guarded Lindbergh against any commercial ventures that might hurt the airman, including one attempt by publisher William Randolph Hearst to sign up the pilot for an aviation film costarring Hearst's close friend Marion Davies.[14] Fund trustee Dwight Morrow was also concerned lest Lindbergh be exploited for someone else's profit, and he had urged Harry Guggenheim to find some spot for the pilot within the Guggenheim fund. When Harry Guggenheim enquired about having Lindbergh tour the country as Byrd had done, Morrow responded that the fund should pay the pilot $50,000 for his services. The financier justified such a large payment by stating that Lindbergh could certainly earn much more "if he accepted any of the many offers which pour in upon him. . . . Colonel Lindbergh's position has been perfect in not wanting to capitalize his advertising value," Morrow wrote. "I do not feel, however, that the Foundation, which has a definite work to do in the promotion of aviation, should take advantage of this feeling on Colonel Lindbergh's part."[15] On July 19, 1926, Harry Guggenheim and Charles A. Lindbergh signed a contract paying the pilot $50,000 for flying the *Spirit of St. Louis* around the country.[16] Another $18,721.27 went to cover the costs of the tour.

As with Byrd, the Department of Commerce Aeronautics Branch extended its full cooperation. Once again, Donald Keyhoe went along as tour manager, and the Aeronautics Branch also furnished an escort airplane piloted by Branch inspector Philip Love. The Guggenheim fund sent along an advance man, Milburn Kusterer, to make arrangements in each city prior to Lindbergh's arrival.[17] Harry Guggenheim announced that the nationwide tour, to all forty-eight states, would accomplish three ends: stimulate popular interest in aviation, encourage the use of existing commercial mail and passenger air services, and promote the development of airports and air communications.[18]

Lindbergh and the rest of the tour group left Mitchel Field on July 20, 1927, and did not complete their nationwide tour until three months later, when the *Spirit of St. Louis* flew back to Mitchel Field on October 23. By the time of Lindbergh's return, he had visited eighty-two cities, flown 22,350 miles, and dropped 192 messages as he flew over towns where his schedule prohibited landing. The *Spirit of St. Louis* had touched down in all forty-eight states, and while the Guggenheim fund conservatively estimated that 30 million people had seen the plane, most newspapers estimated 50 million people had seen it as it toured the country. On the same day as Lindbergh's return to Mitchel Field, Postmaster General Harry New notified the Guggenheim fund that, while it was difficult to determine the exact impact of Lindbergh's tour on the growth of airmail, "There is, without a doubt, a substantial encouragement which has been given to the use of air mail by Colonel Lindbergh's tour." In April 1927, for example, mail carriers flew 96,925 lbs. of mail; in May, the month of Lindbergh's Atlantic flight, this had risen to 99,107. In June, it jumped to 118,746, and in September 1927, mail planes transported over 146,000 lbs. of mail.[19] William P. MacCracken credited the Lindbergh tour with increasing use of the air mail, inspiring municipalities to acquire or improve existing airports, and demonstrating the reliability of current airplanes.[20]

With only minor exceptions, the Lindbergh tour went as planned. One incident early in the tour threatened the purpose of the entire trip. At one field, as Lindbergh prepared to take off, a photographer, camera in hand, dashed out in front of the plane. Because of the design of the *Spirit of St. Louis*, Lindbergh could not see directly forward from the cockpit. He advanced the throttle, the Ryan's Wright Whirlwind engine roared, and the silver propeller scythed through the air. A mechanic realized that the newsman was totally ignorant of the danger, and that Lindbergh did not know the man was in front of the plane. He shouted a warning as Lindbergh passed by: fortunately, the pilot heard the message above the roar of the engine, and he jerked back the throttle. The *Spirit of St. Louis* came to a halt, its propeller less than three inches from the cameraman. Shaken, Lindbergh descended from the plane, just as the near victim began to laugh. "Do you know you just missed being killed?" Lindbergh asked. "We're trying hard to complete this tour without hurting anyone. But if everyone acted as you did we wouldn't get very far. The other photographers waited as they were asked to do. You took a foolish risk, and nearly got killed," Lindbergh added. "Don't ever cross in front of an airplane again."[21] Greatly disturbed by the near tragedy, Lindbergh ordered Guggenheim tour advance man Milburn Kusterer to tighten airfield security to prevent repetitions from occurring in the future.

This was the only instance on the tour when anyone came close to being killed or injured, although, at some airfields, overenthusiastic crowds broke through security lines. One other event, however, also posed some inherent danger and forced the only delay on the trip: while flying from Boston, Massachusetts, to Portland, Maine, Lindbergh encountered thick fog and heavy rain that forced him to divert from his scheduled flight plan and land at Concord, New Hampshire. Philip Love, flying to Portland but not in formation with the *Spirit of St. Louis*, managed to reach the Maine border, but wisely set his plane down in the first clear patch of ground he flew over. For the next few hours Love fretted over Lindbergh's safety. Then came word that Lindbergh had safely landed at Concord. Lindbergh later stated that he had managed to reach Portland, and that he had circled over the city for 3½ hours trying to find a hole in the fog before giving up and heading westward to clear ground. The next day, Lindbergh flew to Portland from Concord, though fog again threatened the success of the flight. The delayed arrival at Portland was the only time that the *Spirit of St. Louis* deviated from its planned schedule. This experience indicated the necessity of perfecting blind flying methods.[22]

Despite the rigorous schedule of flying, Lindbergh insisted on keeping the tour on time. The tight schedule did tire the pilot, and photographs taken of Lindbergh after he arrived at some cities, his eyes rimmed by the marks of his flying goggles, gave him a haggard and even sick appearance. Immediately reporters raised the alarm that Lindbergh was sick, perhaps seriously so. Harry Guggenheim and William MacCracken quickly had Lindbergh examined, and then announced that he was in excellent health. Lindbergh's own mother attested to her son's good physical condition, and MacCracken even had his father, a Chicago M.D., examine the pilot. The rumors of ill health disappeared, and the tour went on.[23]

Besides landing at large cities, Lindbergh dropped 192 "Greetings" messages over smaller towns. These messages, printed on an elaborate scroll, had the signatures of Lindbergh, Harry Guggenheim, and William MacCracken. The message read in part, "We feel that we will be amply repaid for all of our efforts if each and every citizen in the United States cherishes an interest in flying and gives his earnest support to the air mail service and the establishment of airports and similar facilities."[24] The *Spirit of St. Louis* arrived back at Mitchel Field on October 23, 1927. Ahead lay Lindbergh's goodwill tour to Mexico, and Central and South America, and, finally, a return to the United States and enshrinement of the plane at the Smithsonian Institution.

During his tour, Lindbergh spoke before civic and business groups on the importance of having towns clearly marked so that the pilot could tell from the air where he was. Many smaller towns and cities asked the pilot to fly over them on the way to his next destination, and, as a "fee," Lindbergh usually extracted the promise that the city officials would paint the town's name on some prominent building or landmark.[25] This early effort at town marking proved highly successful, and it led to another of the Guggenheim fund's programs, a concerted effort to promote the marking of towns across the country. In August 1927, the Department of Commerce launched a voluntary program of town marking, recommending that townspeople paint the town's name in six-foot-high yellow letters on black tile, shingle, tin, or slate roofs. Secretary of Commerce Herbert Hoover sent personal letters to state governors urging them to support such efforts.[26] All in all, however, the states did not prove responsive to the call. A year later, the Guggenheim fund set out to accomplish the same end.

The Guggenheim roof-marking program opened in October 1928. Harry Guggenheim announced that the fund, in conjunction with the Post Office Department, would contact eight thousand postmasters nationwide. The announcement climaxed a two-month study by Guggenheim and Milburn Kusterer, in conjunction with F. Trubee Davison, the Assistant Secretary of War for Aeronautics, Edward P. Warner, the Assistant Secretary of the Navy for Aeronautics, and William P. MacCracken. Davison, Warner, and MacCracken all issued short public statements stressing the importance of town marking as an essential step in establishing a national air transport system. Rufus Rand, the chairman of the Aeronautics Committee of the American Legion, promised that organization's full support, and R. E. Fisher, a California aviation booster, convinced a local paint manufacturer to provide free paint to mark all the cities in California. The Guggenheim fund issued a circular letter requesting all towns of between one thousand and fifty thousand population to identify themselves by painting the town name in ten-to-twenty-foot-high letters on roofs, with a large arrow pointing north, and a smaller arrow indicating the direction of the local airfield.[27]

Harry Guggenheim enlisted the support of prominent public figures and organizations behind the roof-marking campaign. Postmaster General Harry S. New lent the fund his personal signature die for signing circulars sent to Post Office officials around the country. Will Rogers, the noted humorist, also volunteered his services, for he was a keen air sportsman. W. W. Atterbury, the president of the Pennsylvania Railroad, offered his support as well. Harry Guggenheim was particularly happy to receive Atterbury's support, because lost pilots often followed railroads in an attempt to find their way, and a town name painted on a railroad station was thus of higher significance than one in the open country. In addition the American Legion, the Kiwanis, Lions, and Rotary clubs also urged members to designate their towns. Local American Legion posts even branched out and volunteered to paint place names on the roofs of neighboring communities.[28]

The Guggenheim marking campaign was an unqualified success. By December 1929, Milburn Kusterer was able to report to Harry Guggenheim that 4,074 communities had completed identifying themselves, 2,000 more were in the process of doing so, and another 2,000 had reported to the fund that they were marked prior to October 1928, when the campaign began. The total number of identified communities in the country numbered more than 8,000. This fund action, coming in a time before the advent of large-scale radio navigation aids and federally run airway communications systems, quickly drew approval from pilots and airline managers. Each town that responded to the Guggenheim request received a signed certificate from Charles A. Lindbergh. The certificate served as an inducement to cooperate, and, once sent, as a reminder to maintain the roof marking as a permanent contribution to aeronautics.

The fund awarded 7,800 of the certificates, and only nine hundred communities failed to place a marker. Nationwide, midwestern and Pacific coast states were most responsive, due chiefly to the Standard Oil Companies of Indiana and California, which directed their community plants to identify local towns. The Ford Motor Company also sponsored the Guggenheim roof-marking campaign, and the state of Ohio, in response to the Guggenheim program, passed an ordinance making it obligatory for towns and cities to place markers. Nearly two thousand communities not on the fund's original listing joined the program during its existence. As a measure of the Guggenheim interest, the fund sent more than 51,700 letters and 68,000 bulletins on marking to postmasters and other local officials. The entire roof-marking campaign cost the Guggenheims $15,803.35.[29]

In addition to the marking program, Harry Guggenheim also had another project for which he always sought support. This was a plan to create airfields at ten-mile intervals in each direction so that a plane, if it suffered engine failure, would never be more than seven miles, diagonally, from a landing field. If the plane were at an altitude of five thousand feet, it would rarely be out of gliding distance from a landing field. Guggenheim pointed out that by 1929 the United States had 28,500 square miles of roads and highways, and that the amount of land devoted to railroads boosted this figure to 50,050 square miles. If communities, perhaps in conjunction with the state and federal governments, built airfields ten miles apart having 1,200-foot runways, the total land area nationwide for these airfields would only require 1,544 square miles. "One has but to fly over even the most thickly populated areas here in the East to realize how comparatively easily and cheaply land could be made available for a nationwide system of landing fields," Guggenheim wrote. "Following close on the heels of the realization of such a system, flying would be the safest means of rapid transportation and become universal in America with its concomitant economic and social advantages."[30] Privately, Guggenheim probably realized that such a proposal had little chance for adoption. States and local communities might sponsor marking campaigns, but after the onset of the depression, few if any would be willing to undertake such a massive program of airfield development, despite its unquestioned value. Airports and airfields continued to spring up across the country, but in a haphazard and unsystematic manner.

During the life of the fund, Harry Guggenheim supervised the publication of a variety of bulletins and reports on aviation matters. Many of these were news releases prepared by the Ivy Lee public relations firm. Others, however, cogently examined important matters and aspects of air transportation and commercial aviation.[31] The fund published a total of thirteen bulletins. Some of these explained the rationale behind fund activities, such as the grants to Caltech and Stanford, or the safe airplane competition. Others discussed aeronautical education, how flying schools should be organized, and how an expanding aviation market required more trained mechanics. Some promoted use of the air mail, and one illustrated how airplanes were performing valuable work in aerial photography, crop dusting, forest fire patrols, power line patrols, and exploration flights. Still others discussed technical problems such as aerial navigation using sun and star sightings, the hazard of lightning to planes, and the problem of air sickness. The Guggenheim fund also published an "Aviation Notes" series, which digested important articles, news, and regulations for the airman.

In addition to its bulletins and notes, the Guggenheim fund also published a series of pamphlets, most of which covered aspects of the fund's programs, such as the rules of the safe airplane competition, or the fund's blind flying research. Some of the pamphlets, however, treated wide-ranging studies that the Guggenheim fund had supported. Four of the pamphlets concerned developments in European aeronautics. In September 1927, Virginius E. Clark, a noted aeronautical engineer and designer of the famed Clark Y airfoil, toured Europe at the request of the Guggenheims to study contemporary manufacturing and design techniques in European airplane construction. Clark visited England, France, Germany, and Italy, stopping at various aircraft manufacturers. Hugo Junkers' duralumin construction techniques impressed Clark, as did the Handley Page leading edge slat. The Guggenheim fund printed several hundred copies of his report, and sent them to the NACA, the Navy Bureau of Aeronautics, the Engineering Division of the Army Air Corps, some technical colleges and universities, and American aircraft manufacturers. Raymond Ware of the Thomas-Morse Aircraft Corporation wrote to fund vice-president Hutchinson Cone, calling the report "the most comprehensive survey of the activities abroad in metal construction of aircraft that we have seen."[32]

The next year, Brig. Gen. William E. Gillmore, director of the Air Corps Engineering Division, toured Europe to study European airline operations. Like Clark's report, Gillmore's study received wide distribution, and, within the year, Harry Guggenheim arranged for fund representatives in Europe to prepare a comprehensive report on the safety and accommodation of European passenger airplanes. This report compared vision, lighting, knee and head space, fire prevention techniques, and design and structural details of various transport aircraft. The representatives recommended that American manufacturers benefit from the European experience by designing passenger aircraft with fuel tanks in the wing, not fuselage, without wooden components in engine compartments, with internal fire extinguisher equipment, and with seat belts.[33] In 1929, Clarence M. Young, director of the Aeronautics Branch within the Department of Commerce, toured Europe to investigate airport management and administration. Young visited the major airports in Europe, including Croyden in England, Le Bourget in France, and Templehof in Germany, and submitted a report on airfield operation. The report covered such topics as landing fees, radio communications installations, authority of the pilot to cancel flights on his own, without requiring permission from higher authority, and airport ownership. This report was influential on future Aeronautics Branch airport development policy. The Guggenheim fund produced over one thousand copies, and distributed them to American passenger and mail carriers, military officials, and local Chambers of Commerce across the nation.[34]

One Guggenheim study had significant impact on an area vital to commercial aviation: the problem of a transport pilot getting medical insurance. Prior to the Guggenheim fund's insurance activities, many aeronautical observers stated that the one hindrance to American air transportation was the lack of organized aviation insurance.[35] Insurance companies had no accurate figures on pilot mortality and accident rates upon which to base any insurance program. Faced with a lack of information, some companies adopted the simple expedient of not offering any insurance to pilots at all. In early 1929, Harry Guggenheim, in conjunction with the fund trustees, decided to examine the entire issue of aviation insurance with a view to generating reliable statistical information that American insurance companies could use in preparing insurance programs. The study would also examine the status of aviation insurance in the rest of the world.

On the recommendation of F. Trubee Davison, Harry Guggenheim turned to Army Air Corps Capt. Ray A. Dunn to prepare the insurance report. Dunn was a good choice for the job. A professional pilot since 1917, he was an expert on insurance, and had studied insurance matters for over five years.[36] Davison offered Guggenheim and Dunn full access to all pertinent Army Air Corps records, as did William P.

MacCracken for the Department of Commerce, and David S. Ingalls, who had replaced Edward P. Warner as Assistant Secretary of the Navy for Aeronautics. Dunn began his study in June 1929, and by the end of the summer, he had visited every major insurance company in the country, as well as gathering all available government information on casualty figures for military and civil aviators. Because of the depth of the subject, and his own natural tendency to examine it in detail, Dunn did not complete the full report until early 1930, despite the pleas of the fund trustees that he expedite his work. The results were well worth waiting for. His final report contained thirty-one charts giving previously unavailable flying and fatality statistics. Dunn discovered that only 109 American companies wrote aviation insurance policies for pilots and passengers, and that they lacked uniform statistical data upon which to base requirements for writing and issuing policies. Dunn pointed out that, with the majority of airmen lacking insurance coverage, the general public automatically assumed that insurance companies had studies that showed flying to be unsafe. In fact, such studies did not exist, and, as a result, people in the insurance industry simply guessed about the probability of a pilot having an accident. The public, in most cases, drew the understandable if erroneous conclusion that flying was especially hazardous, and, as a consequence, many people chose not to fly, thereby retarding the growth of the air transport industry.[37]

Dunn did not neglect mentioning that some companies, through ignorance, minimized the risk in flying, and gave out policies to reckless or unqualified individuals. In the 2½ years prior to 1929, underwriting companies had paid out over $3.5 million in death benefits on 465 airmen. Yet, Dunn did not believe that such statistics justified the often exorbitant rates charged pilots by insurance companies, or the outright refusal of others to insure airmen. The statistics he presented clearly showed that fatalities for both military and civilian pilots were dropping from year to year, and they also indicated the degree to which federal air regulation through the Air Commerce Act of 1926 had succeeded in making the airways safer.

The Actuaries Society of America had formed a special aviation committee to investigate aviation insurance, but after completing its research, this special committee did not make any recommendations. Dunn suggested that the various insurance companies establish a central statistical archives where the records on aviation risks could be assembled. He further suggested that the insurance companies consult with representatives of the aircraft industry and air transport carriers before writing policies. Though insurance companies did not bother with the central records depository suggested by Dunn, they did take greater notice of aviation statistics and such factors as the reduction in the numbers of nonlicensed pilots flying around America. Dunn's study did not cause an immediate turnabout in insurance company practices. Nevertheless, from the generally favorable insurance industry response to the Guggenheim fund, it is clear that the study played a significant role in encouraging insurance companies to examine their industry in light of the new field of air transportation.[38]

While the Guggenheim fund sponsored a variety of publications and reports to promote aviation, the organization also supported various national meetings for the same purpose. In September 1928, Harry Guggenheim completed final preparations for a national safety conference on aeronautics, the first of its kind ever held in the United States. He arranged for the fund to co-host the meeting in conjunction with the National Safety Council's Seventeenth Annual Safety Congress in New York City. The safety conference got under way on October 1, and lasted for five days. The various sessions covered meteorology, the public and flying, passenger safety, aviation legislation, fire prevention, radio navigation and blind flying, airport and airway development, airplane control characteristics, and aviation medicine.

This conference set the pattern for future conferences and stressed the importance that the Guggenheim fund placed upon aviation safety. All the major figures in American aeronautics attended: Jerome Hunsaker, Alexander Klemin, Theodore P. Wright, F. C. Hingsburg, J. H. Dellinger, Rear Adm. William Moffett, Maj. Gen. James Fechet, A. F. Hegenberger, C. E. Rosendahl, Edward P. Warner, Samuel W. Stratton, William P. MacCracken, F. Trubee Davison, Charles A. Lindbergh, Joseph S. Ames, and Emory Land. Authors presented thirty-seven papers, which the Guggenheim fund published as a separate volume, and local newspapers presented the highlights of the conference. Attendees heard speakers extol the virtues of the long-range passenger dirigible, call for uniform standards of medical examination for aircrews, analyze the growing role of radio for communications and navigational purposes, and discuss the value of various devices to make aircraft safer. Harry Guggenheim was highly satisfied with the results of the conference, and continued his interest in aviation safety long after the fund closed down. After the Second World War, he created the Cornell-Guggenheim Aviation

Safety Center in New York City, which carried on the earlier work on aviation safety undertaken by the fund. This included calling special symposia and conferences on the subject of aviation safety.[39]

The Guggenheim fund undertook one other aviation promotion venture, but, unlike the others, this took the form of a special aviation award, a gold medal named in honor of Daniel Guggenheim. The medal project, another of Harry Guggenheim's ideas, received approval from the fund trustees at a meeting on June 16, 1927. Daniel Guggenheim promised $15,000 as a tentative appropriation for the medal, to provide an annual income necessary to cover the annual award of the medal and all incidental expenses. Since the medal would be awarded after The Daniel Guggenheim Fund for the Promotion of Aeronautics ceased, the trustees had to form a special organization, The Daniel Guggenheim Medal Fund, Inc. The Guggenheim fund incorporated this new organization in New York on October 3, 1927. By that time, Harry Guggenheim had drawn up and secured the services of a board of directors for the medal fund. The board included William F. Durand, Elmer A. Sperry, Edwin E. Aldrin, Edward P. Warner, E. T. Jones, Arthur Nutt, Howard E. Coffin, and P. G. Zimmermann. These men selected Sperry to serve as president of the medal fund. As originally established, the medal fund was a joint endeavor between the Guggenheim fund, the Society of Automotive Engineers, and the American Society of Mechanical Engineers. The medal fund would award the medal annually "to a person in recognition of some notable achievement performed by him which shall tend to the advancement of aeronautics," with no restrictions because of race, color, nationality, or sex.[40]

Daniel Guggenheim contributed the $15,000 pledge in March 1928, and the medal fund directors set about selecting a suitable medal design. Eventually, they chose a gold medal, having the *Spirit of St. Louis*, a dirigible, and a balloon, all in flight. In the background were clouds, the sun, rain, and stars. On the reverse, in the midst of a circular three-wing design, were the words "for great achievement in aeronautics." By 1929, five additional directors, one each from England, Germany, France, Italy, and Japan, had joined the medal fund. The board of directors, after conferring on suitable candidates, unanimously decided on May 1, 1929, to present the first Daniel Guggenheim Medal to aviation pioneer Orville Wright. Wright received the medal in Washington, D.C., on April 8, 1930, during ceremonies at the celebration of the fiftieth anniversary of the founding of the American Society of Mechanical Engineers.[41]

The Daniel Guggenheim Medal soon became one of aviation's most prestigious and coveted awards, and has continued to be regarded as such. On August 15, 1938, the medal directors reorganized the corporation and placed it under the United Engineering Trustees, Inc. The new corporation's board of directors was known as The Daniel Guggenheim Medal Board of Award, and acted as a committee of the United Engineering Trustees.[42]

The winners of the Daniel Guggenheim Medal, from 1929 through 1976, have been:[43]

1929	Orville Wright	1953	Charles Lindbergh
1930	Ludwig Prandtl	1954	Clarence Howe
1931	Frederick Lanchester	1955	Theodore von Kármán
1932	Juan de la Cierva	1956	Frederick Rentschler
1933	Jerome Hunsaker	1957	Arthur Raymond
1934	William Boeing	1958	William Littlewood
1935	William Durand	1959	George Edwards
1936	George Lewis	1960	Grover Loening
1937	Hugo Eckener	1961	Jerome Lederer
1938	Alfred Fedden	1962	James Kindelberger
1939	Donald Douglas	1963	James McDonnell, Jr.
1940	Glenn Martin	1964	Robert Goddard
1941	Juan Trippe	1965	Sydney Camm
1942	James Doolittle	1966	Charles Draper
1943	Edmund Allen	1967	George Schairer
1944	Lawrence Bell	1968	H. Mansfield Horner
1945	Theodore Wright	1969	H. Julian Allen
1946	Frank Whittle	1970	Jakob Ackeret
1947	Lester Gardner	1971	Archibald Russell
1948	Leroy Grumman	1972	William Mentzer
1949	Edward Warner	1973	William Allen
1950	Hugh Dryden	1974	Floyd Thompson
1951	Igor Sikorsky	1975	Dwane Wallace
1952	Geoffrey de Havilland	1976	Marcel Dassault

In all these ways, the Guggenheim fund undertook to create a positive image of aviation in the minds of the public. Harry Guggenheim, on his own, often spread the gospel of aviation. He attended banquets and luncheons, speaking before various civic and business groups. He would stress how airplanes could bring nations and peoples together by improving communications and commerce.[44] In a book of essays on aviation he wrote, "The airplane gives to man a new freedom, eliminating the geographical barriers of river, sea, mountain and desert between him and his kind, and thus eliminating those prejudices and misunderstandings which have jeopardised human relations in the past."[45] He also attended various international meetings, and served as a member of the League of Nations' Committee of Experts on Civil Aviation, when that group submitted a report on international disarmament as it related to the development of civil aviation. The committee met in Brussels in February 1927, and endorsed proposals that nations separate civil aviation administration from their military services, and participate in international civil air transport conventions.[46] Eventually, such proposals led to creation of the International Civil Aviation Organization (ICAO) in 1947.

Harry Guggenheim also sought to promote aviation by persuading financiers to place the growing aircraft industry on firm financial footing. To this end, he often corresponded with businessmen and financiers in quiet, unpublicized promotion efforts that fund trustee Charles Lindbergh considered highly important. Additionally, he warned the public about becoming overconfident and investing in foolish ventures. Speaking before one audience, he stated, "The greatest danger at the moment may arise from the promotion of ill-advised economically unsound aviation enterprises . . . the conservative investing public should be extremely wary of investing its money . . . until the science, art, and operation as a whole have been more thoroughly perfected."[47]

He was also aware of the special responsibility the press had in reporting aviation events. In November 1928, Guggenheim wrote to newspaper editors around the country stressing the need for accurate and thoughtful reporting of aviation news, especially items on aviation safety and aircraft accidents. This early attempt to promote accuracy met with little success, and one aviation writer later stated, "Aviation writing in the late 1920's was not aviation writing at all; it was Broadway theatrical writing. . . ."[48] A full decade after Guggenheim's earlier efforts, in 1938, a group of newspaper and magazine journalists who were also aviation enthusiasts met and formed the Aviation Writers Association. This group, led by Devon Francis of The Associated Press, did much then and subsequently to ensure accuracy in aviation reporting, largely by impressing editors with the need for having staff reporters who understood and who could intelligently communicate the technical and commercial aspects of aeronautics.[49] It was yet another example, however, of how Harry Guggenheim had promoted causes and advocated policies that did not attain fruition until they became self-evident to many in the aviation community.

CHAPTER 10

Prelude to Space:
The Guggenheims and Aviation Development
since 1930

EARLY in September 1929, Harry Guggenheim informed the Guggenheim fund trustees that he believed the fund had fulfilled its founding
purposes. It had promoted aeronautical education, assisted aeronautical research, promoted the development of commercial aircraft, and
furthered the utilization of aircraft by business, industry, and transportation firms. Several fund projects remained unfinished, such as
the safe aircraft competition, blind flying research, and the grant to
a southern university. During its brief existence, the fund had gone
through two stages: first, to promote air-mindedness and education;
and second, after June 1928, to undertake research on specific aeronautical problems. Guggenheim noted that the general public had
swung from a state of indifference towards aviation to one of intense
enthusiasm. "There are now established on a solid basis aeronautical
engineering and research centers in different geographical sections
of this country second to none in the world," he wrote. "These centers trusteed to great universities evolving with humanity itself will
provide an everlasting stream of men and ideas for the ever-changing
problems of the new science of aeronautics."[1]
    The trustees agreed with Guggenheim's assessment, and at a special
meeting in mid-October 1929, they decided to conclude the fund's
activities about January 1, 1930. Actually, the fund did not shut down
its operations until February 1, 1930. "The work of the Fund," Harry
Guggenheim wrote, "now passes into other hands."[2] Gradually, the
trustees of the fund drifted back to their regular vocations. By the
time of the fund's closing, Harry Guggenheim had his hands full
mediating between various Cuban political factions. His father out-
lived the fund by seven months. Emory S. Land, who had replaced

169

Hutchinson I. Cone as the fund's vice-president, resumed a brilliant naval career. Robert A. Millikan devoted his full attention to Caltech, and William F. Durand once again retired—until the National Advisory Committee for Aeronautics asked him to supervise American turbojet engine development in 1941. Cone, who had left the fund to become head of the U.S. Shipping Board, but remained a fund trustee, quit the aviation scene for his first interest, the sea and shipping. A. A. Michelson and Dwight Morrow both died in 1931. Elihu Root, Jr., and John D. Ryan returned to law and finance. F. Trubee Davison remained as Assistant Secretary of War for Aeronautics until 1933, then became president of the American Museum of Natural History. Charles A. Lindbergh, appointed a trustee in 1927, resumed his pioneering long-distance flights, in company with his wife, the former Anne Spencer Morrow. Orville Wright continued as America's elder statesman of aviation, guarding the family's aeronautical achievements against all critics.[3]

America's aviation community greeted the closing of the Guggenheim fund with admiration for its accomplishments yet with regrets at its passing. During its existence the fund had won plaudits from aeronautical authorities and societies around the world. Herbert Hoover, while secretary of commerce, had written in 1928 that the fund had "accomplished more for aviation in the last two and a half years than any other factor we have had at work in the situation." He emphasized that it had saved the government from research work that private organizations were better able to perform.[4] The National Advisory Committee for Aeronautics remarked upon the closing of the fund that "thanks to the inspiration of Mr. [Daniel] Guggenheim and his leadership, the fund was one of the most important factors in accelerating the development of aviation during the years 1926 to 1929, and American aeronautics is greatly indebted to him."[5] NACA also praised the blind flying and ice formation research undertaken by the Guggenheim fund, and added that "the work of the Guggenheim Fund in the field of education in aeronautical engineering has been outstanding."[6]

Years later, aircraft developer Grover Loening, a contemporary critic of the Guggenheim safe aircraft competition, nevertheless concluded that the fund had done its work "admirably."[7] Charles A. Lindbergh said, "The Guggenheim Fund was timely, well directed, and of extraordinary benefit to aeronautical progress," further remarking, shortly before his death in 1974, that "The Daniel Guggenheim Fund for the Promotion of Aeronautics was the first important boost that aviation in the United States had. . . . Putting all this money in an infant industry had a tremendous psychological effect."[8] Alexander Klemin considered the Guggenheim fund's activities "a story of splendid interest," and added, "to my mind, the fund built the foundations of a great many of the achievements of modern aeronautics."[9]

Because of the fund's successes, Daniel Guggenheim had granted it an additional $300,000 to supplement its original $2,500,000, raising the total capital of the fund to $2,800,000. During its four-year existence, the fund authorized grants totaling $2,876,857.20 and actually expended $2,663,749.52 on various projects, most of which went into educational activities.[10]

These appropriations were:

Education

California Institute of Technology	$350,000.00
Stanford University	195,000.00
University of Michigan	78,000.00
Massachusetts Institute of Technology	230,000.00
University of Washington	290,000.00
Georgia School of Technology	300,000.00
Guggenheim Airship Institute	250,000.00
Air Law Institute	11,666.67
Library of Congress	140,000.00
Committee on Elementary and Secondary Aeronautical Education	45,000.00
Ground School Instructor's Course, New York University	11,722.00
Meteorological Course, New York University	500.00
Meteorological Program, Massachusetts Institute of Technology	34,000.00
Meteorological Textbook by Prof. E. W. Woolard, George Washington University	6,000.00
Graduate School of Business Administration, Harvard University	15,000.00
Aerial Photography Program, Syracuse University	60,000.00
Durand Aeronautical Encyclopedia	60,000.00
Tour of the United States by Theodore von Kármán	4,500.00
Support for Two University Conferences	5,000.00
Society for the Promotion of Engineering Education	2,500.00
Fellowships for Aeronautical Study Abroad	6,500.00

Scientific Research

Support for Expeditions to Greenland by the University of Michigan	$10,000.00
Research on Two-Cycle Aircraft Engines	2,000.00
Committee on Aeronautical Meteorology	10,000.00
Experimental Meteorological Service along the Model Air Line	27,500.00
Support of Altimeter Research in The Netherlands	2,500.00

Research on Light Transmission through Fog | 17,000.00
Financing an Aerologist for the Byrd Antarctic Expedition | 3,840.00
Support of the Full Flight Laboratory at Mitchel Field, Long Island | 85,000.00
Support of Acoustic Research at the University of California | 2,000.00
Research on the Formation of Ice on Aircraft, Cornell University | 10,000.00
Support of Altimeter Research at Ohio State University | 3,750.00
Support of Reports Discussing Research Results and Inventions | 2,500.00

Commercial Development and Aviation Promotion

Guggenheim Safe Aircraft Competition | $200,000.00
Equipment Loan to Western Air Express | 155,000.00
National Tour of the Byrd Arctic Airplane | 20,000.00
National Tour by Charles A. Lindbergh | 68,000.00
Guggenheim Town Marking Program | 16,000.00
Guggenheim Grants to the National Aeronautic Association | 22,000.00
Promotion of the U.S. Air Mail | 2,500.00
Guggenheim Grants to the New York Airport Committee | 700.00
Guggenheim Grant to the International Civil Aviation Conference | 250.00
Promotion Tour for South American Delegates | 200.00
Report on European Aircraft Manufacturing Practices by Virginius E. Clark | 500.00
Report on European Aviation by William E. Gillmore | 1,000.00
Report on European Aviation by Clarence M. Young | 1,000.00
Report on the Status of Aviation Insurance by Ray A. Dunn | 2,200.00
Support for the Daniel Guggenheim Medal Fund | 19,028.53

Educational and Public Information

Support for the Royal Aeronautical Society, Great Britain | $25,000.00
Support for the Aero Club de France | 28,000.00
Support for the Aero Club von Deutschland | 15,000.00
Support for the Associazione Italiana di Aerotecnica | 20,000.00
Support for the First National Aeronautical Safety Conference | 2,000.00

Note: The fund paid an additional $227,367.28 to cover additional expenses including salaries, publication fees, and rental fees.

Yet, massive though this effort was, it did not mark the end of Guggenheim philanthropic support of the flight sciences. Because of Daniel and Harry Guggenheim's interest in aviation, Guggenheim money supported aeronautics long after the original Guggenheim fund had disappeared. Such assistance continued into the dawn of manned exploration beyond the earth.

Daniel Guggenheim's generosity in endowing aeronautics had always carried beyond the confines of The Daniel Guggenheim Fund for the Promotion of Aeronautics. In 1927, he had contributed $25,000 to finance what was ultimately an unsuccessful search for the lost Atlantic fliers Nungesser and Coli. He made a personal grant of $480,000 in 1928 to the Chilean government to sponsor a school of aeronautics.[11] In 1930, after the Guggenheim fund had closed, he gave his personal support to an almost unknown rocket experimenter in Worcester, Massachusetts: Dr. Robert Hutchings Goddard. A professor of physics at Clark University, Goddard had begun studying rocket propulsion before the First World War. In 1919, the Smithsonian Institution published his speculative and farsighted report, "A Method of Reaching Extreme Altitudes," in which he advanced the idea of using multistage rockets to undertake high-altitude research. Goddard had received a patent on his multistage idea in July 1914, and in his report he theorized that a large multistage rocket could reach the moon. This speculation caused little serious study and lots of public ridicule. In the early 1920s, Goddard gave up his study of solid-fuel rockets, because they could not, at that time, provide continuous and smooth power. He turned instead to liquid-fuel rockets, taking a notable step forward in the history of astronautics.[12]

Goddard at first considered using liquid hydrogen and liquid oxygen, little realizing that this combination, nearly a half-century later, would help send the first men to the moon. Because of the severe problems in acquiring, storing, and using liquid hydrogen, Goddard searched for acceptable substitutes, finally selecting liquid oxygen as an oxidizer and gasoline as a suitable fuel. By December 1925, he was testing rocket engines on static test stands burning "lox" and gasoline. Finally, he believed he was ready for the big step: test firing a free-flight rocket using liquid propellants. He constructed a strange-looking open-framework rocket having the rocket engine mounted on the top of the frame. On March 16, 1926, a cold, blustery day, Goddard, his wife Esther, Clark physics professor Dr. P. M. Roope, and Henry Sachs, a Clark machinist, ventured out to the farm of Effie Ward, a distant Goddard relative who let the professor fire his rockets on her farm and store his equipment in a henhouse. Just after noon, the little band completed all preparations for the launching. Sachs ignited the engine; Goddard waited for 90 seconds, and then launched the rocket. It sputtered aloft, flew 184 feet, and then, 2½ seconds after lift-off, fell to earth. The "Kitty Hawk of Rocketry" had occurred.[13]

After this modest beginning, Goddard pressed onward with flight trials of liquid-fuel rockets. By 1929 he had an advanced model undergoing ground testing. Finally, on July 17, 1929, Goddard and his small group set out for the Ward farm with the new rocket. It was over 11 feet tall, weighed thirty-five pounds empty, and carried a small package of meteorological instruments. Once again Henry Sachs ignited the rocket, Goddard pulled on a release cord, and the test vehicle roared up a 60-foot launching tower. The rocket left the tower, climbed 20 feet, executed a sharp turn, climbed an additional 10 feet, and then plunged to the ground, 171 feet away from the tower. Goddard and his crew were picking up the pieces when police cars, two ambulances, and private automobiles converged on the farm, attracted by the noise of the flaming rocket. The resulting publicity once again brought ridicule, as the Boston Globe thundered " 'Moon Rocket' Man's Test Alarms Whole Countryside."[14] But more importantly, it brought Goddard into contact with aviator Charles A. Lindbergh, and, ultimately, with Daniel Guggenheim.

During a cross-country commercial survey flight in 1928, Lindbergh had contemplated the future course of aviation. He concluded that reaction-driven aircraft would eventually replace propeller-driven planes. In mid-1929, Lindbergh visited with engineers of the Du Pont Corporation at Wilmington, Delaware, and sought their advice on whether rocket propulsion for airplanes might be feasible. The Du Pont engineers flicked their slide rules and concluded that a rocket engine having the power of a Wasp piston engine for one minute's operation would require four hundred pounds of black powder igniting in a firebrick-lined combustion chamber, and that the chamber pressures might be too high for the firebrick to withstand. Any idea of using rockets for flight beyond the earth's atmosphere was out of the question. Here matters lay for several months, until after Goddard had fired his "moon rocket."[15]

One day in November 1929, Charles Lindbergh was at Harry Guggenheim's home at Falaise discussing the problems and prospects of rocket flight with Guggenheim. Suddenly Caroline Guggenheim, Harry's second wife, broke into the conversation and began reading a newspaper item concerning Goddard's experiments at the Ward farm. Harry Guggenheim then suggested that Lindbergh check on Goddard's activities.[16] The young aviator discussed Goddard's work with C. Fayette Taylor of MIT, and then telephoned the rocket experimenter at his home in Worcester, on November 22, 1929. Favorably impressed, Lindbergh visited Goddard the next day, and within a few days, the two men journeyed back to the Du Pont Corporation. Once again Du Pont engineers discouraged further research on rocket propulsion, and Lindbergh informed Goddard that he would next ask the Carnegie Institution for funds to carry on Goddard's rocket research.[17]

Lindbergh persuaded John C. Merriam, the president of the Carnegie Institution, to meet with Goddard in Washington, D.C. Goddard met Merriam on December 10, and by the end of the month, the Carnegie Institution had authorized a grant to Goddard of $5,000. The money came at a critical time in Goddard's research, for the professor realized that his experiments with liquid-fuel rockets had shown others around the world the possibilities of rocket propulsion. German ordnance experts, in particular, saw the rocket as one means of evading the limitations of Versailles. Goddard believed he needed as much support as possible, considering himself a "little dog with a great big bone."[18]

Unknown to Goddard, further help was on the way. Charles Lindbergh, convinced that Goddard was on the right path, was not content to let the matter of financial backing rest in the hands of the Carnegie Institution and the Smithsonian, both able to grant only comparatively small amounts. Instead, he approached Daniel Guggenheim in the spring of 1930, after The Daniel Guggenheim Fund for the Promotion of Aeronautics had closed shop. The elder Guggenheim, as enthusiastic as ever about blazing new ground in aeronautics, asked Lindbergh if he believed Goddard's work might advance the frontiers of aeronautical science. Lindbergh replied that one could never be certain about such matters, but that Goddard knew more about rocketry than anyone else in the United States. Daniel Guggenheim, without further hesitation, pledged $100,000 for Goddard's work, in a move Lindbergh later termed "highly visionary and very courageous." Goddard would receive $25,000 per year for the first two years. Then, if his progress appeared satisfactory, the grants would continue at $25,000 per year for another two years. By early June 1930, Daniel Guggenheim, Charles Lindbergh, attorney Henry Breckinridge, Clark University president Wallace W. Atwood, and Goddard had worked out the details of the grant, and Daniel Guggenheim announced it to the public on July 10, 1930.[19]

The rest of the Goddard story is well known. Goddard and his wife left for the Mescalero Ranch, north of Roswell, New Mexico, where he set up a launching tower, work shop, and static test site for running rocket engines on the ground. He remained at Roswell, with but one major absence, for the next decade. In 1932, his initial Guggenheim grants came to an end, not because of dissatisfaction with his work, but simply because the funding had come from Daniel

Guggenheim's personal account, and after the philanthropist's death in 1930, settlement of the estate took a long time. Further, the stock market crash had eroded the Guggenheim fortunes. From 1932 through 1934, Goddard once again assumed the mantle of a physics professor at Clark, though his interests and hopes remained fixed on New Mexico. Then, in the fall of 1933, at Harry Guggenheim's and Charles Lindbergh's instigation, Guggenheim money again flowed to Goddard. The Daniel and Florence Guggenheim Foundation advanced $2,500 for Goddard's use at Clark, and then, in August 1934, resumed full support of Goddard's work in New Mexico, with a grant for $18,000 covering one year's work. Goddard moved back to Roswell the next month.[20]

While at Roswell, Goddard continued his advances in rocket development by being the first to use deflector vanes in a rocket's exhaust to guide the rocket, by developing gyroscopic stabilization for rockets, and by launching the first liquid-fuel rocket to exceed the speed of sound, the latter taking place on March 8, 1935. He also developed small turbine-driven pumps to furnish the rocket engines with propellants. Goddard's breadth of vision was such that future rocket and missile designers found they could not design, manufacture, or operate a rocket-propelled vehicle without infringing on one or more of Goddard's patents. During his Roswell stay, Lindbergh and Harry Guggenheim often visited the Mescalero Ranch to see how Goddard was getting along and to provide support and encouragement.

In May 1940, Harry Guggenheim arranged for Goddard to meet with representatives of the army and navy to see if his rocket research could benefit national defense. Goddard met with the service representatives on May 28, 1940, but they expressed little interest; indeed, the army representative suggested that future army development should concentrate on improving trench mortars. Over the next few months, however, army and navy officials asked Goddard to assist them in the development of liquid-fuel rocket motors to assist heavily loaded aircraft during takeoff. This complemented the work that Frank Malina and his group were undertaking on solid-fuel jet assisted takeoff (JATO) units at Caltech's Guggenheim Aeronautical Laboratory (GALCIT).[21]

In September 1941, Goddard stopped his private research and began work on contracts from the army and navy. In July 1942 he moved to the navy's Engineering Experimental Station at Annapolis, Maryland, where he served as director of rocket research for the navy's Bureau of Aeronautics. Much of his time was occupied with designing liquid-fuel JATO units. Certainly it was important work, but, in the opinion of fellow rocketeer G. Edward Pendray, "like trying to harness Pegasus to a plow."[22] Goddard's eyes were on rocket-propelled missiles and spacecraft. He successfully developed a variable-thrust rocket engine that Curtiss-Wright later used in developing their XLR-25 rocket engine for the postwar Bell X-2 supersonic research airplane. Then, in June 1945, Robert Goddard entered Johns Hopkins hospital in Baltimore for surgery on throat cancer. Doctors performed a laryngectomy on July 5. He remained active and, though he could not speak, he filled pages with notes. Late in July, Harry Guggenheim, on active naval service as a navy commander, wrote Goddard at the hospital and promised his full assistance to the rocket pioneer after the war. "Your job is to get your mind off everything but your health," Guggenheim wrote, "and when that has been recovered, we'll make a fresh start on the great future ahead."[23] But such was not to be. On August 9, Goddard slipped into a coma. He died the next day, at the age of sixty-two.[24]

Two of the most significant scientific and technological advances of the Second World War were the atomic bomb and the guided missile. Even as Goddard lay dying in Baltimore, the citizens of London and Antwerp were busy clearing debris from their shattered cities, which German V-2 missiles, the grown-up nephews of Goddard's earlier rockets, had devastated. While military leaders contemplated a wedding of the atomic bomb to the ballistic missile, many other aeronautical scientists looked to the time when rocket power might place men in orbit around the earth, or propel long-range commercial aircraft. Two years after Goddard's death, Harry Guggenheim concluded that the current state of rocket research resembled that of aviation after World War I. And, he reasoned, as his father's fund had helped to put American aviation on its feet, so might philanthropy now advance the field of rocketry. Since the war, many Americans had learned a little of Goddard's work, and, Guggenheim believed, this growing public awareness coupled with well-organized rocket research centers might go far in putting rocket research on solid ground.

In 1947, Harry Guggenheim, through The Daniel and Florence Guggenheim Foundation, asked Dr. G. Edward Pendray, an American rocket pioneer and senior partner of Pendray and Company, to undertake a survey determining the principal needs in the field of rocketry. Pendray submitted his report in 1948. He had sent out 105 questionnaires to leading engineers and scientists. Over 80 percent of those who responded predicted that the rocket would see increased service in aeronautics, and 26 percent responded that the next decade might well bring about the development of orbital spacecraft. Almost all who responded stressed the need for advanced education and research in rocketry and related fields. Pendray's conclusions coincided with those Harry Guggenheim had reached in private consultation with such aeronautical leaders as Jerome C. Hunsaker. Harry Guggenheim had suggested that such educational centers might require an endowment of about $500,000. Hunsaker agreed, adding that the Guggenheims might not want to place too much money aside for research purposes, as the federal government could be counted on to support rocket research through such agencies as NACA. The main impetus should be, first and foremost, on education.[25]

Over the summer of 1948, Harry Guggenheim and his advisers pondered where to establish the centers. Guggenheim finally selected two locations: Princeton University in the East, and the California Institute of Technology in the West. On December 14, 1948, The Daniel and Florence Guggenheim Foundation announced the two grants, creating a Robert H. Goddard professorship at each school. The Guggenheims provided $239,000 per center for the first seven years of operation, and additional travel and expense funds brought the total sum for the two centers to $500,000. Both centers honored Daniel and Florence Guggenheim, being known respectively as The Daniel and Florence Guggenheim Jet Propulsion Center at Princeton University, and The Daniel and Florence Guggenheim Jet Propulsion Center at the California Institute of Technology.[26]

Actually, Caltech had had a Jet Propulsion Laboratory since 1943, when Frank J. Malina, H. S. Tsien, and Theodore von Kármán had begun issuing reports bearing that title. The group officially became the Jet Propulsion Laboratory, GALCIT, on November 1, 1944. The title dated from the GALCIT-Air Corps jet propulsion research project, where von Kármán and Malina had decided to use the word "jet" rather than the more fanciful-sounding and antagonistic "rocket." By 1945, GALCIT's Jet Propulsion Laboratory (JPL) had produced several successful liquid- and solid-fuel rockets, including the Private and WAC Corporal series. All that the Guggenheim grant did at Caltech was simply provide for a Robert H. Goddard professorship, though ultimately JPL left GALCIT and became an independent branch of Caltech.[27]

Shortly after receiving the Guggenheim grants, Caltech and Princeton selected their Robert H. Goddard professors. Dr. Hsue-Shen Tsien, a former von Kármán student teaching at MIT, joined JPL at Caltech. Dr. Luigi Crocco went to Princeton. Tsien brought with him a good background in rocket propulsion and supersonic aerodynamics dating from his prewar days at Caltech.* Crocco had a thorough knowledge of early Italian rocket experimentation, for his father had been one of Italy's outstanding aeronautical researchers. Both centers immediately accelerated their research work on rocketry. In 1950, for example, Hsue-Shen Tsien felt confident enough to predict that "the requirements of a transcontinental rocket liner [are] not at all beyond the grasp of present-day technology."[28] Indeed, shortly after the Guggenheim grant to Caltech's JPL, a JPL-developed WAC Corporal, riding on the nose of a captured V-2 first-stage booster, became the first man-made object to enter space. Launched from the White Sands Proving Ground on February 24, 1949, virtually in Goddard's old haunts, the WAC Corporal separated from the V-2, ignited, and shot up to 244 miles altitude.[29]

In the years following the creation of the two Guggenheim centers, the Jet Propulsion Laboratory at Caltech made notable contributions to the development of actual "hardware" such as unmanned lunar and planetary space probes. Princeton's center concentrated more on developing studies and texts on rocket and missile technology, rocket propulsion, and aerospace vehicle design. In the 1950s, the Jet Propulsion Laboratory at Caltech developed the Corporal and Loki missile systems, and during 1954–55 collaborated with the Army Ballistic Missile Agency on early satellite proposals. When the United States launched its first unmanned satellite, Explorer I, it utilized JPL-derived solid-fuel upper stages and instrumentation. By the late 1950s and early 1960s, JPL supervised development of the Ranger, Pioneer, Surveyor, and other space probe projects. In 1976, JPL Viking unmanned spacecraft soft-landed on the planet Mars. JPL gained worldwide attention by its development and management of the NASA Deep Space Network (DSN).[30]

Harry F. Guggenheim did not forsake the airplane entirely for the rocket. In the 1930s, first as ambassador to Cuba and later as a private

* Tsien left JPL in 1955 for the People's Republic of China. Subsequent reports indicate that Tsien, as Chien Hsueh-Sen, played a major role in getting China's satellite and ballistic missile programs off the launch pad. Dr. W. D. Rannie replaced Tsien as Goddard professor at JPL.

sportsman pilot, he often flew his own plane around the country and retained his interest in new "safe" aircraft prototype designs. In the 1930s, he helped test-fly two such unique airplanes—a French Nieuport Delage design, and one built by American enthusiast Waldo Waterman—in an experimental demonstration sponsored by the Department of Commerce.[31] During World War II, Guggenheim returned to active naval aviation service, rising from the rank of lieutenant commander to captain. He commanded the naval air station at Mercer Field, Trenton, New Jersey, and later flew on air strikes against Okinawa as a combat observer aboard Grumman-General Motors TBM Avenger attack aircraft launched from the carrier U.S.S. *Nehenta Bay.*

After the war, "Captain Harry" Guggenheim continued his quest for aviation safety. He had always maintained a close friendship with Theodore P. Wright, the project manager of the Curtiss Tanager, following the 1929 Guggenheim safe aircraft competition. In 1948, Wright left his position as administrator of the federal government's Civil Aeronautics Administration to become president of the Cornell Aeronautical Laboratory, affiliated with Cornell University. Cornell Aero Lab, incorporated in March 1948, was one of the first aerospace research and development "think tanks" to spring up across the country. Its personnel were interested in everything from supersonic aerodynamics to aviation safety. In April 1949, Dr. Clifford C. Furnas of Cornell Aero Lab announced that while statistics indicated commercial airplanes were safer than automobiles, private pleasure aircraft had far worse safety records. In 1946, one out of every eighty-five registered private planes was involved in a fatal accident. Furnas added that aviation safety required major research on increasing pilot aids, preventing postcrash fires, and reducing crew and passenger fatalities by improving passenger and crew seat restraint equipment and interior design.[32] Theodore Wright, who had already discussed aviation safety with Harry Guggenheim, proposed on December 12, 1949, that Guggenheim collaborate with Cornell's Committee for Air Safety Research to found a center for aviation safety.

Already receptive to the recommendation, Harry Guggenheim suggested that the organization be broad in its support and influence, and not closely tied with any one institution. By the late summer of 1950, Guggenheim and Wright had worked out preliminary plans in consultation with Cornell's administrators. On September 18, 1950, The Daniel and Florence Guggenheim Foundation announced creation of The Daniel and Florence Guggenheim Aviation Safety Center at Cornell University, known more familiarly as the Cornell-Guggenheim Aviation Safety Center. The foundation provided $180,000 in an initial grant to the center, created "for the improvement of aviation safety, to the end that progress in safety will keep pace with advances in speed and efficiency, and flying will be the safest form of transportation."[33] Wright assumed the chairmanship of the center, and Jerome Lederer, a graduate of NYU and the founder of the Flight Safety Foundation, became the center's director. Lederer's connection with the Flight Safety Foundation, which issued information bulletins and undertook limited research, complemented the activities of the Cornell-Guggenheim Aviation Safety Center. The Guggenheims also added a distinguished panel of advisers, including NACA chairman Jerome C. Hunsaker, Air Force chief of staff Gen. Hoyt S. Vandenberg, and Donald W. Nyrop, administrator of the Civil Aeronautics Administration.[34]

By 1960, the center had undertaken research on collision avoidance, crash fire prevention, occupant protection, private flying, airline safety, human factors research, altimeter and instrumentation error, and in-flight explosions. Among its first activities, the center compiled a list of more than 1,500 safety research projects underway around the country. The list also indicated a number of gaps that existed in the field of aviation safety. One such area was research on vertical-take-off-and-landing and short-take-off-and-landing aircraft (V/STOL). In 1954, Harry Guggenheim, remembering the Guggenheim safe aircraft competition, requested the aviation safety center to study VTOL and STOL aircraft that could land safely in small restricted landing areas. The result was an important study by Jerome Lederer and R. M. Woodham entitled *Safety through Steep Gradient Aircraft*, which reviewed the technical development and current prospects of a variety of helicopters, convertiplanes, and STOL aircraft.[35] The report stressed the suitability of rotary and fixed-wing V/STOL aircraft for short-range intercity airline operations, provided such aircraft could be equipped with adequate engine power and stability and control systems. V/STOL developments since 1954 have borne out the predictions of the report, as military services have adopted the helicopter and such VTOL aircraft as the Hawker Siddeley Harrier, while many small civilian operators utilize such STOL passenger planes as the De Havilland DHC-6 Twin Otter and Dornier Do 28.[36]

The Cornell-Guggenheim Aviation Safety Center also supported a variety of specialized publications dealing with design errors that jeopardized aircraft safety and the importance of human factors research in aircraft operation. One such note dealt with the non-fatal crash of a high-performance military fighter. During the takeoff roll, the pilot found that he could not pull back on the control stick. The fighter ran off the end of the runway and sustained major damage, fortunately without injuring the pilot. Postaccident investigation indicated that the pilot had placed his clipboard under the seat, exactly as the designers had intended, but it had slipped forward and wedged between the seat and the control stick. A design note recommending the clipboard storage position be changed and emphasizing careful attention to detail went out immediately.[37] The center also promoted a series of meetings to increase the interchange of ideas in aviation safety and aviation medicine.

In 1961, Theodore P. Wright stepped down as chairman of the Aviation Safety Center, and Lederer replaced him with Elwood R. Quesada, former administrator of the Federal Aviation Agency. The Guggenheim Aviation Safety Center continued its work until June 30, 1968, when the center closed its operations. By that time, Quesada, Lederer, Guggenheim, and Wright believed that it had fulfilled its original goals. Comparative transportation accident fatality statistics supported their conclusion. In 1967, 132,088,000 passengers flew on U.S. scheduled airlines, compared to 19,103,000 in 1950. In 1950, the fatality rate per 100 million passenger miles flown by domestic airlines was 1.15. In 1967 it had dropped to 0.30. The fatality rate for scheduled international airlines had dropped from 2.05 per 100 million passenger miles in 1950 to 0 in 1967. These figures were far better than comparable statistics for private passenger automobiles. As with many other Guggenheim endeavors, their support of aviation safety had led to greater emphasis and research on accident prevention by private and federal aeronautical scientists and such agencies as the Federal Aviation Administration, National Aeronautics and Space Administration, and the military services.[38]

Though its assistance to Robert H. Goddard, Caltech, and Princeton, and the creation of the Cornell-Guggenheim Aviation Safety Center were the largest aerospace projects endorsed by The Daniel and Florence Guggenheim Foundation, the foundation also extended its support to aviation and the aerospace sciences in other ways. On February 18, 1957, the foundation announced creation of the Harvard-Guggenheim Center for Aviation Health and Safety at the Harvard School of Public Health, with an initial grant of $250,000. This center, under the direction of Dr. Ross A. McFarland, a noted specialist in aviation medicine, specialized in studying such areas as the medical problems of aircrew members, susceptibility of pilots to stress, and dangers of emergency cabin depressurization.* Earlier, on October 23, 1953, the foundation established The Daniel and Florence Guggenheim Institute of Air Flight Structures at Columbia University with an initial grant of $329,000. This institute had responsibility for graduate training in aerospace vehicle design, serving as a clearinghouse for information on structural problems, and acting as a center for structural research. In July 1961, the foundation also created The Daniel and Florence Guggenheim Laboratories for the Aerospace Propulsion Sciences at Princeton University.

Nor did the foundation ignore public education. In 1948, in conjunction with the American Museum of Natural History, it prepared a traveling exhibit on the life and accomplishments of Robert H. Goddard and, a decade later, funded a special Goddard rocket collection at the pioneer's old Roswell test site. In 1960, at the suggestion of Theodore von Kármán, the foundation helped support the creation of the International Academy of Astronautics (IAA), an outgrowth of the International Astronautical Federation. The IAA is devoted to the peaceful exploration and utilization of space, and consists of several hundred carefully selected engineers, scientists, lawyers, and social scientists from around the world. It holds annual meetings and presents The Daniel and Florence Guggenheim International Astronautics Medal to outstanding contributors to the art and science of astronautics. Recipients of this award, first granted in 1961, have been:

1961	Sir Bernard Lovell	1970	Andrian Nikolayev
1962	James Van Allen		Vitaly Sevastyanov
1963	Marcel Nicolet	1971	Luigi Broglio
1964	Wallace Fenn	1972	Reimer Luest
1965	Mstislav Keldysh	1973	Maxime Faget
1966	Robert Gilruth	1974	Hilding Bjurstedt
1967	Jacques-Emile Blamont	1975	Oleg Gazenko
1968	Zdenek Svestka	1976	Marcel Barrere
1969	Charles Berry		

The foundation also donated The Daniel and Florence Guggenheim Space Theater to the American Museum of Natural History for

* Dr. McFarland died Nov. 7, 1976, at Dublin, New Hampshire, age seventy-five. He was Daniel and Florence Guggenheim Professor Emeritus of Aerospace Health and Safety at Harvard.

use in conjunction with the Hayden Planetarium and, in 1964, issued a ten-year grant to the National Air and Space Museum of the Smithsonian Institution to aid in the development of exhibits and other museum activities. In addition to the organizations aided by The Daniel and Florence Guggenheim Foundation are numerous individuals who have received Daniel and Florence Guggenheim Fellowships. By this generous program, the foundation is again sowing the seeds of future aerospace development, as the earlier Daniel Guggenheim Fund for the Promotion of Aeronautics did in the 1920s.[39]

Harry Frank Guggenheim died quietly at Falaise on January 22, 1971, at the age of eighty. Oddly, most obituaries cited him for founding *Newsday*, the nation's largest suburban newspaper, and for assisting Robert H. Goddard, rather than for his earlier work as president of The Daniel Guggenheim Fund for the Promotion of Aeronautics. The death of Harry Guggenheim signaled a close to the early research and promotion era of American aviation. Orville Wright, the patriarch of aeronautical scientists around the world, had died in 1948. Except to insiders, Harry Guggenheim was an unknown compared to Wright, but in his own way, this aviator, financier, diplomat, publisher, and philanthropist had made an everlasting mark on the aerospace sciences.

Daniel and Harry Guggenheim were born in an era when those who advocated powered flight were treated as simpletons. Yet Daniel lived to see the European and American land masses joined by an aerial bridge, and Harry witnessed the landing of men on the moon. The spectacular aeronautical achievements in the twentieth century, from the Wrights and Goddard through the first transoceanic flights, the introduction of the turbojet engine, the first flights faster than sound, and finally, the "one small step" of Neil Armstrong at Tranquility Base, all rested on a broad base of scientific research, education, and experience. Public support of aeronautics had been necessary to the creation of this base. The unique contributions of the Guggenheims, both father and son, had assisted the educational and scientific side of aeronautical development, and the promotion and public relations side as well.

The Guggenheim schools by 1942 were generating graduates who would contribute to the Allied victory over the Axis powers. By the 1960s, those schools, and the new centers aided by The Daniel and Florence Guggenheim Foundation, were generating graduates who would contribute to another victory: that of man over the world of space. In comparison with the challenges of the universe and even the solar system, the triumphs of the 1960s and 1970s grow pale. The first steps had been taken, and they would continue. It took centuries before man learned to fly within the docile atmosphere of the earth, but less than seven decades after Kitty Hawk and a mere four decades after Goddard's first experiments, man reached beyond his planet to set foot upon earth's satellite. The 120-mph 12-passenger Fokker tri-motors of the 1920s gave way to the 595-mph 374-passenger Boeing 747 of the late 1960s. By the 1970s, air transport planners awaited the introduction of the 1,450-mph Mach 2 + Anglo-French Concorde and the Soviet Tu-144 SST, aircraft Daniel Guggenheim could little have imagined when he set his great fund for aeronautics in motion. Writing on the value of aeronautical research, Harry Guggenheim stated in 1930 that "the experiments of pioneers like the Wright brothers found fitting expression in the achievements of today, and these, in turn, may be taken as indications of the developments still ahead of us."[40] Unknowingly, he had also expressed the importance of the Guggenheim contributions to flight.

Appendixes

INTRODUCTION

WRITING in 1949, Dr. Vannevar Bush, the wartime head of the Office of Scientific Research and Development, remarked that during the interwar years, Americans were living in "a new industrial country. With it went a considerable advance in American science, fundamental and applied. We had always leaned on Europe for our basic science, devoting our attention rather to applications and gadgetry, but now sound extensive basic research programs began to appear. These were centered in our universities and research institutions, private and state-supported."[1]

The United States owed much of its technical aeronautical growth to the activities of the National Advisory Committee for Aeronautics (NACA) and the Bureau of Standards, as well as to private industry and the impetus afforded by the army and navy. A great amount of support and research also came from the Guggenheim-supported and established schools. They furnished graduates who assumed positions of key responsibility in the aircraft industry, federal government, and military services, and they often undertook fundamental research and development work in aeronautics. A brief survey of Guggenheim school activities prior to American entry in the Second World War clearly indicates the wide-ranging scope of their programs.

APPENDIX I

The Impact of the California Institute of Technology on American Air Transport and Aeronautical Development, 1926-41

INDISPUTABLY, the Guggenheim school at the California Institute of Technology became the best known and most important of the Guggenheim-funded schools.[1] By 1940, this institution had already earned a major share of the credit in getting American air transport off the ground, and its students, scientists, and engineers, under the able and paternal direction of Theodore von Kármán, were already investigating the feasibility of flight faster than sound and the potential of the rocket engine. Its wind tunnels ran day and night, testing for hundreds of hours the new products of America's aviation industry, many of which later contributed greatly to Allied air supremacy in the Second World War. Then there was applied research: studying the effects of wing fillets in reducing wing-fuselage aerodynamic interference, examining behavior of flying wing and tailless aircraft configurations, developing aircraft instrumentation and test procedures, measuring the stall characteristics of highly tapered wings, and analyzing the flow of air around bridges and wind-run electrical generators, to name just a few of the topics examined.

The Guggenheim fund sent Caltech an initial check for $25,000 on November 12, 1926, to begin construction of the aeronautics building, and by the following June, the framework of the building was already emerging from its excavation.[2] By the end of 1927, the Guggenheims had sent the last of the $180,000 allocated for building construction to Caltech. In the meantime, however, Millikan had apologetically notified Harry Guggenheim that the estimated cost was far below the sum required; Caltech needed at least $225,000 to build the school, not $180,000. All through the spring of 1928 the money issue dominated correspondence between the fund and Caltech.

Finally, Millikan submitted a progress report to the fund on June 10 showing that the school and the fund had borne about equal shares of the costs of construction. At a special meeting of the board of directors on June 15, 1928, the trustees, at the suggestion of Harry Guggenheim, approved an additional appropriation of $45,000 for Caltech, raising the total Caltech grant from $305,000 to $350,000, and increasing the building appropriation from $180,000 to $225,000.[3]

The Caltech Guggenheim complex really consisted of two separate components. One was research-oriented, the Guggenheim Aeronautical Laboratory of the California Institute of Technology, later known worldwide as GALCIT. The second was the Daniel Guggenheim School of Aeronautics, devoted to aeronautical education. The single building housed both, and the university completed it in 1928. Late in that year, Theodore von Kármán made his second visit to the United States, and while at Caltech, where he gave a series of lectures to aeronautical engineering students, he was asked by Millikan if he would be willing to direct the Guggenheim Aeronautical Laboratory at the school. Von Kármán showed interest in the offer, remarking that because of the vast size of the country, the future of aviation would certainly be in the United States. Millikan wanted von Kármán for the Caltech laboratory because "he shows a rare combination of exceptional theoretical grasp with practical insight into, and a physical approach to, the problems of aeronautics."[4] Harry Guggenheim urged Millikan to persuade von Kármán to leave Germany and come to Pasadena, stating, "His association with you would be an outstanding achievement for you and the country, and should lay the foundation for extraordinary results."[5]

Actually, von Kármán was reluctant to come to America, because he was nearly fifty years old, the social position of a professor in America was lower than that of a professor in Germany, and because his mother did not want him to leave. "She was obsessed," von Kármán recalled years later, "with the European upper-class belief that only misfits and family black sheep settled in America."[6] Political events decided his future for him, however. With the rise of antisemitism and the growing strength of Adolf Hitler's Nazi party, even von Kármán, despite his position and reputation, was not safe. In July 1929, Millikan again offered von Kármán the position of GALCIT director, adding that Caltech soon would be assisting in another Guggenheim fund activity, the creation of an Airship Institute in Akron, Ohio. In October 1929, von Kármán consented to come to America. He left Germany for Pasadena, together with his mother and sister, in December 1929.[7]

Caltech's aeronautics faculty in 1930 consisted of von Kármán, Frank Wattendorf, a Boston-born student of von Kármán's from Aachen, Clark B. Millikan, Harry Bateman, Arthur L. Klein, Ernest E. Sechler, W. Bailey Oswald, F. F. McFadden, Frank Moyers, and two visiting instructors from Göttingen, Walter Tollmien and Reinhold Seifert.[8] These men undertook personal research in a variety of areas, including aerodynamics, propulsion, and structural design. During the first ten years GALCIT concentrated its activities on two areas: structural research and aerodynamics.[9] Additionally, a small group of graduate students investigated rocket propulsion, sowing the first germinating seeds of the future GALCIT Jet Propulsion Laboratory. Early in its existence, Caltech's aeronautics department formed a partnership with the Douglas Aircraft Company at Santa Monica, the school hiring Arthur E. Raymond, Douglas's assistant chief engineer, to teach courses in structural design. In 1932, Caltech graduate Dr. W. Bailey Oswald went to Douglas as the firm's chief aerodynamicist, a position he held through the war years and into the 1950s. In 1934, Caltech added courses in meteorology under the direction of Irving Krick, who formed a partnership with von Kármán, studying the phenomenon of air turbulence and the effects of weather upon it. Krick first gained prominence when he demonstrated that a combination double vortex formed by two opposing air masses off the New Jersey coast had brought about the loss of the navy dirigible airship *Akron* together with seventy-three of its crewmen on April 4, 1933.[10]

GALCIT engineers and students emphasized research that could be applied to aircraft designs under development, and the school, with the Douglas company, had a good opportunity to demonstrate this in the design of the Douglas DC-1. The progenitor of the Douglas DC-3, the most successful commercial airplane ever built, the DC-1 pushed American air transport development a full decade ahead of Europe. The story of the DC-1, and its evolution into the DC-2 and, ultimately, its influence on the Douglas Sleeper Transport, the DC-3, is well known. Its Caltech GALCIT connection, however, is not so well remembered, and yet it was GALCIT research in structures and aerodynamics that made the aircraft the success it was.

Three events influenced the development of the DC-1: the death of Knute Rockne in a Fokker F-10 trimotor, the development of the Boeing 247 transport, and advances in structural design. The Fokker

F-10 was a three-engine all-wooden transport based on Fokker's earlier F.VII-3m airplane; it owed its development to the Guggenheim fund and Western Air Express. The F-10, and later the F-10A, served in many American airlines, including Western Air Express, Pan American, and Transcontinental & Western Air, the forerunner of Trans World Airlines (TWA). The Aeronautics Branch, under Assistant Secretary of Commerce for Aeronautics Clarence M. Young, who had replaced William P. MacCracken, had long regarded the wooden Fokkers with suspicion, believing them susceptible to dry rot, and was, in fact, on the point of issuing a grounding order when tragedy struck. On March 31, 1931, a Transcontinental & Western Air Fokker F-10, en route from Kansas City to Wichita, Kansas, fell from a cloud deck, its wing tumbling after it, and smashed into a farm near Bazar killing all eight persons abroad, including Notre Dame's legendary football coach, Knute Rockne. Young immediately grounded all Fokkers in airline service and, following an unpublicized meeting with representatives from airlines flying the planes, restricted the planes to nonpassenger airmail service, provided the pilots wore parachutes.[11] Fokker airplanes soon disappeared from American skies, not to return for another thirty years, when the Fokker F-27 entered commercial service.

With the exception of the Ford Tri-motor, a rugged all-metal airplane that gave its passengers a safe, though noisy and often uncomfortable, flight, American airlines really had few aircraft to turn to. Curtiss had the eighteen-passenger twin-engine Model 18 Condor biplane transport, a civil version of the Curtiss XB-2 Condor bomber, in limited service with Eastern Air Transport and TWA. Both the Condor and the Ford Tri-motor were in the 115 mph class. Neither had comfortable, spacious interior cabins, and while both represented advances over previous air transport aircraft designs, they were not economical enough in operation to earn money simply by hauling passengers. If the airlines had not had airmail contracts from the Post Office Department, they could not have continued operation without some other form of subsidy.

Only the Boeing company had a design on paper that seemed indicative of the future: this was the Boeing Model 247, a twin-engine airplane powered by two 550 hp Pratt & Whitney Wasp radial engines, the heir of an earlier design, the Boeing Model 200 Monomail. A monoplane, the 247 was based on the experimental Boeing XB-9, which boosted army bomber speeds from 100 to 185 mph. The Model 247 incorporated many revolutionary advances, including variable-pitch propellers to optimize fuel consumption and make the most of engine power both at low and high speeds, during takeoff, cruise, and landing; all-metal stressed-skin internally braced construction, giving the plane a smooth skin and reasonably low drag, especially in comparison with the trimotor and biplane transports then in service; and a retractable landing gear and wing-mounted engine nacelles with low-drag NACA engine cowlings, which also reduced drag and thus improved speed, payload, and range capabilities. Boeing had developed the plane specifically for United Air Lines, a corporate cousin of the Boeing company. UAL was the heir to the old Boeing Air Transport, and part of a Boeing conglomerate, the United Aircraft and Transport Corporation. Boeing's 247 could carry two crew members and ten passengers, the passengers sitting in individual armchair seats. The plane had a galley and toilet. In short, the Model 247 represented virtually a quantum leap over the Fokker and Ford trimotors, with their slow speeds, drafty cabins, and roaring noise.[12] Its design features soon became standard on all advanced transport aircraft.

TWA was in trouble almost from the moment that the Aeronautics Branch grounded their Fokkers. In early 1932, UAL had ordered fifty-nine Model 247's from Boeing and, TWA management learned, Boeing would not sell TWA any of the new aircraft until the company had filled the United order. In short, Boeing was looking after its own; Transcontinental & Western Air would have to look elsewhere. Jack Frye, TWA's vice-president in charge of operations, quickly assembled TWA's engineering staff, and the men drew up design specifications for a new transport airplane. It must be an all-metal trimotor monoplane, carry at least twelve passengers in a sound-proof comfortable cabin, have two crew members, a minimum top speed of 185 mph, a payload of at least 2,300 pounds, and a range of 1,080 miles. On August 2, 1932, Frye sent these specifications to five aircraft manufacturers, stating that TWA "is interested in purchasing ten or more trimotored transport planes." Only Donald W. Douglas, founder and president of the Douglas Aircraft Company of Santa Monica, California, consented to take on the task.[13]

Douglas had graduated from MIT's aeronautics course in 1914, then joined the Connecticut Aircraft Company, switching to the Glenn L. Martin company, the Aviation Section of the Army Signal Corps, and back to Martin, and finally in 1920 he left for California, where he started up his own firm. Douglas was an engineer of unusual ability, and a man who, by nature, was inclined to accept challenges, provided they were not foolhardy. After receiving Frye's message, he called a meeting of the company design staff and together they drafted a letter of acceptance. Then, in a second engineering conference, Douglas and company chief engineer James H. "Dutch" Kindelberger, meeting with Arthur E. Raymond and other engineers, mapped out a plan of attack. They agreed to build a twin-engine plane, since after the Rockne accident, many travelers were skeptical about any trimotor. Further, the plane would have an all-metal internally braced structure, a low wing, retractable landing gear, wing flaps to help reduce landing speeds, and closefitting NACA cowlings for the wing-mounted engines. TWA consultant Charles A. Lindbergh further insisted that the plane be capable of taking off with a full load from any airfield along TWA's routes on just one engine. Douglas agreed to meet these requirements, and on September 20, 1932, the aircraft company signed a development contract for a prototype.[14]

One of the outstanding features of the new aircraft designated the Douglas DC-1, for "Douglas Commercial," was its all-metal construction. All-metal construction was not new in 1932; in 1915, Hugo Junkers, a professor of mechanical engineering at Aachen's Technische Hochschule, in conjunction with Theodore von Kármán, had designed an all-steel cantilever monoplane, the Junkers J 1. Junkers then turned to using lighter duralumin tubing covered by a duralumin corrugated skin, and produced a succession of all-metal transport aircraft including the F 13, G 24, and W 34. In 1929 he had built a gigantic four-engine all-metal transport, the G 38, having a 144-foot wing span and a length of 76 feet. It weighed nearly 53,000 pounds at takeoff.[15] Other early advocates of all-metal construction were Adolf Rohrbach, Claude Dornier, the Short brothers, and William Stout. The DC-1 incorporated some novel all-metal design techniques that placed it in advance of all previous metal transports.

In 1932, Douglas gained control of the Northrop Corporation, formed and directed by John K. Northrop, a man well known for his advocacy of flying-wing aircraft. Northrop, in 1929, had designed a low-wing single-engine six-passenger monoplane having all-metal construction, called the Alpha. The Northrop Alpha featured a North-rop innovation called multicellular wing construction. Multicellular wing construction consisted of a flat metal external skin supported by numerous spars and ribs. Northrop shaped aluminum sheets into channel sections, and then riveted these together. The "walls" of the channels served as spars, running from the wing root to the wing tip, while the "top" and "bottom" of the channels served as attachment points for the external skin. Northrop then added sheet aluminum inserts to form wing ribs. Multicellular construction provided several major advantages over other metal construction techniques, including ease of construction, inspection, maintenance, and repair; extreme lightness in relation to structural rigidity and strength; and very small unsupported areas. One famous anecdote illustrates the load-carrying capabilities of the Alpha's multicellular wing. In 1929, a Northrop Alpha crashed while on a test flight. Northrop inspected the airplane and decided it was beyond repair. Nearby a road crew was working; Northrop asked a steamroller operator to flatten the wing, making it easier to scrap. The roller operator drove his vehicle back and forth over the wing. While Northrop watched in pleased astonishment, the roller failed to crush the wing, or even make an appreciable dent. Photographs taken of the event proved some of the best publicity pictures Northrop ever had.[16]

Northrop's Alpha had been one of the first airplanes GALCIT had put through its ten-foot wind tunnel. Further, GALCIT graduate student Ernest E. Sechler, later a professor of aeronautics at Caltech, had reviewed research on using thin metal sheets as structural members while a student in a von Kármán seminar. Although some engineers had predicted that such sheets would collapse under loading, Northrop, Sechler, and von Kármán demonstrated that multicellular construction did not fail even after buckling, and, indeed, it still retained about 90 percent of its prebuckling strength. After operating the Alpha in scheduled service, TWA stipulated such construction on the DC-1. Douglas did so, using the Alpha wing as a design guide. Multicellular construction was responsible for the DC-3's longevity in airline and military service, and it was a happy result of the partnership of John K. Northrop and the Guggenheim-created GALCIT.[17] Northrop had also developed the Alpha with a low mounted wing that passed completely below the fuselage, thus preventing the loss of interior space normally occupied by the wing "carry-through" structure. The Boeing 247, for all its advances, still had its wing spar structure running through the passenger cabin, cramping accommodations near the wing and forcing passengers to climb over it when entering or exiting from the aircraft. On the DC-1 and its successors, the DC-2 and DC-3, the spar structure passed entirely below the fuselage, which, in effect, was a tapered cylinder on top of the wing.

Equally important with structural design, however, is an airplane's aerodynamic design. Proper aerodynamic design can permit greater payload, increase range, and increase cruising speed. It requires careful attention to detail, and hundreds of hours of wind-tunnel testing followed by extensive prototype flight-testing. One example serves to illustrate just how important smoothing the airflow and reducing the drag of an airplane can be. For years, designers had mounted radial piston engines on the nose of an airplane without regard for the drag generated by airflow around the engine. Indeed, radial engine drag often amounted to one-third of the total airframe drag. Then, in 1927, H. L. Townend of the British National Physical Laboratory mounted a narrow "ring" around the engine, sharply reducing engine drag. In the United States, National Advisory Committee for Aeronautics scientists went one step further, enclosing the engine in a close-fitting low-drag cowling. After hundreds of tests in the NACA Langley Laboratory Propeller Research Tunnel, NACA engineer Fred E. Weick announced development of the "NACA cowling" in November 1928. Flight tests of the cowling mounted on an Army Curtiss AT-5A advanced trainer boosted the airplane's speed from 118 mph to 137 mph, the equivalent of adding an additional 83 hp. It also greatly improved engine cooling. By 1932, industry spokesmen estimated that the NACA cowling had saved the industry approximately $5 million. It won for NACA the 1929 Robert J. Collier trophy, American aviation's most prestigious award, and the NACA cowling became standard on future American aircraft, including the Boeing 247 and Douglas DC-1, DC-2, and DC-3.[18]

From the outset, Douglas aimed at exceeding the performance of the rival Boeing 247. On one wall in the Douglas plant at Santa Monica was a huge cutaway drawing of the 247 with the admonition, "Don't Copy It! Do It Better."[19] Company president Donald Douglas reminisced years later, "It was the challenge of the 247 that put us into the transport business."[20] Douglas already had some advantages, such as the low wing below the fuselage, which made the plane more comfortable and more likely to win favor with the public. Another was the TWA specification that called for a minimum of twelve passengers. Boeing had made a serious error in designing the 247 for just ten passengers, for this boosted seat-costs per mile. Likewise, the absence of wing flaps on the 247 necessitated a lower payload to meet safe takeoff and landing criteria. The DC-1, with its greater passenger capacity and wing flap installation, was thus inherently a more attractive airliner for air transport operations.[21] But the final advantage in favor of Douglas was the aerodynamic design refinement undertaken in GALCIT's ten-foot wind tunnel.

GALCIT testing contributed greatly to the success of the DC-1 aircraft and its ultimate triumph over the rival Boeing 247. GALCIT wind-tunnel testing, under the direction of Theodore von Kármán and with the assistance of Dr. W. Bailey Oswald, A. L. Klein, and Dr. Clark B. Millikan, revealed early stability problems that redesign quickly cured. During GALCIT testing on the Northrop Alpha, von Kármán, A. L. Klein, and Clark Millikan had discovered that the plane buffeted violently at speeds around 200 mph. They traced this problem to airflow interference at the junction of the wing and the fuselage. Here, the airflow slowed and formed turbulent eddies that disturbed the airflow over the tail surfaces, causing the airplane to buffet. Von Kármán, Klein, and Millikan found that installation of a smoothly shaped metal fairing smoothed the airflow and prevented airflow separation, thus eliminating buffeting. Since the Alpha wing was similar to that on the DC-1, they added a wing fairing to the DC-1, von Kármán himself climbing into the GALCIT ten-foot tunnel, putty in hand, to modify the shape of the test model.[22] Douglas had built a 1/11-scale model, and all through the fall and winter of 1932, it "flew" two hundred test runs in the GALCIT 200 mph wind tunnel.

Douglas engineers tried no less than three wings and six different wing flap arrangements before testing the final configuration. To cure a longitudinal stability problem, GALCIT researchers increased the sweepback on the wing's leading edge, changing the location of the plane's center of gravity. This problem had not shown up on previous engineering calculations, and had GALCIT tests not uncovered it, the DC-1 during flight-testing might well have proven a failure. Finally, as a result of GALCIT advice, Douglas installed NACA cowlings on the engines, with streamlined engine nacelles linking the engines to the leading edge of the wings.[23]

Boeing had completed the first flight on the 247 on February 8, 1933; the DC-1, piloted by Douglas test pilot Carl A. Cover, took to the air almost five months later, on July 1, 1933, eleven months after Jack Frye's letter to Donald Douglas. The first flight was not a success, for carburetor trouble nearly caused total engine failure, and Cover just managed to limp back to the airfield and land without accident. Subsequent flight-testing, however, revealed that the hours of careful wind-tunnel study at Caltech had turned the DC-1 into a winner. The 247 could carry ten passengers at 150 mph cruising speed; the DC-1 could carry twelve at 185 mph, and for a longer distance.[24] Overnight, even before the 247 entered large-scale airline service, the DC-1 had relegated it to obsolescence.

In February 1934, the DC-1 made headlines nationwide when Edward V. "Eddie" Rickenbacker and Jack Frye flew the DC-1 from Glendale, California, to Newark, New Jersey, in thirteen hours and four minutes, a new transcontinental record. President Franklin Roosevelt's executive order forbidding the airlines to carry the mail,

and turning over responsibility for airmail service to the Army Air
Corps had triggered the Rickenbacker-Frye demonstration, the last
airline airmail flight before F.D.R.'s executive order took effect. During the flight, Rickenbacker and Frye flew high over bad weather,
including the infamous "Hell Stretch" of the Alleghenies, arriving in
Newark two hours ahead of schedule. Rickenbacker and Frye had set
out to demonstrate that only the airlines could carry the mail with
any degree of safety and reliability, since their pilots were generally
more experienced than junior service pilots. Further, the airline aircraft, such as the DC-1, were usually better equipped and suited to
carry mail than the pursuit and bomber aircraft used on a makeshift
basis by the army.

For example, the DC-1 on its cross-country journey utilized a
Sperry-built automatic pilot for automatic guidance during 90 percent of the flight, the first commercial airplane so equipped. Rickenbacker termed the army airmail service "legalized murder."[25]
Though Rickenbacker's remark was an overstatement, there is no
doubt that the army, despite President Roosevelt's and Postmaster
General James Farley's statements to the contrary, was not equipped
or able to carry the airmail safely. Within a month of starting service,
the army lost ten airmen in airmail related accidents. As a result of
the fatalities and public outcry, Roosevelt suspended the service on
March 10, 1934, and eventually Farley authorized new airmail-
carrying contracts with the airlines. Once more, the airlines carried
the mail, safely and reliably.[26]

Despite its success, Douglas did not put the DC-1 into production.
Rather, at the behest of TWA, the company enlarged the airplane
slightly, increasing passenger load to fourteen, and added more
powerful 720 hp Wright Cyclone engines. The new airplane became
the DC-2, and in the prewar years it saw widespread service with
TWA, American Airlines, Eastern Airlines, General Airlines, Pan
American, Pan American-Grace (Panagra), KLM, and Swissair. In
1934, a KLM DC-2 came in second, behind a specially built racing
airplane, the De Havilland D.H. 88 Comet, in the MacRobertson air
race from England to Australia, but way ahead of a Boeing 247D entered by Roscoe Turner. TWA's DC-2's could fly the Newark-Pitts-
burgh-Chicago route in five hours; United's 247's required an extra
thirty minutes. Further, the DC-2 carried more passengers in roomier
accommodations significantly cheaper than the rival Boeing plane.[27]
Yet Cyrus Rowlett "C.R." Smith, the hard-driving chieftain of American Airlines, was not satisfied. Smith wanted to compete on equal
footing with TWA and United, and he decided that the best way to

do so was to introduce a DC-2 "Sleeper Transport," for night flights to the west coast. He contacted Douglas engineers, who promised a design study, then obtained a $4.5 million loan from Jesse Jones' Reconstruction Finance Corporation. Douglas began engineering studies on the new plane, tentatively designated the DST—Douglas Sleeper Transport. Naturally, this involved crafting another 1/11-scale model, and testing it in GALCIT's wind tunnel at Pasadena.[28]

Once again, GALCIT wind-tunnel studies saved the Douglas company from possible disaster. Douglas initially conceived of the DST as a stretched and widened DC-2 with a larger wing and redesigned landing gear capable of carrying twenty-one passengers in three rows of seven seats, two rows together separated by an aisle from the third row. Thus, the DST had a 50 percent increase in passenger capacity over the DC-2. Wind-tunnel tests by A. L. Klein and W. Bailey Oswald in the 200 mph GALCIT ten-foot tunnel revealed a wallowing instability problem generated by changes in the location of the plane's center of gravity; Klein and Oswald changed the DST's wing airfoil section, shifting the center of gravity, and turning the DST into a safe and stable airplane. Caltech ran more than three hundred wind-tunnel tests on the airplane before test pilot Carl Cover, on December 17, 1935, the thirty-second anniversary of the Wright brothers flight, completed the first flight of the DST. The DST, later designated DC-3, first went into service with American Airlines on June 7, 1936. It proved easier to fly than a DC-2, and 1,200 hp Pratt & Whitney engines gave it greater power. It could carry 50 percent more passengers than the DC-2, yet it had an operating cost only 3 percent greater than its predecessor. Its seat-mile costs were roughly one-third to one-half less than those of the DC-2.[29]

The DST/DC-3 dominated domestic air transport in the United States and abroad until the early 1950s. By 1938, for example, Douglas had orders for 803 DC-3's, and they carried 95 percent of America's civil air commerce.[30] A military cousin, the C-47, likewise dominated military air transport, contributing greatly to the success of such operations as the Normandy invasion, the aerial supply of China via the Himalayan "Hump," and the return to the Philippines. The DC-3 still operates around the world with many smaller air arms and airlines. American and foreign manufacturers built roughly 13,000 DC-3 and C-47 aircraft; Japan's Nakajima company produced approximately 45 aircraft for Dai-Nippon Airways, and Boris Lusinov supervised construction of about 2,000 PS-84 (later Li-2) models of the DC-3 for the Soviet Air Force and Aeroflot.

Altogether, the DC-3 was responsible for completing an airframe revolution that placed American air transport ahead of its international rivals, who since have attempted, without success, to dethrone the United States from its position of leadership. It was the first airplane that could pay for its operation simply by flying passengers, without recourse to airmail contracts or government subsidy. A successor to the DC-1 and DC-2, it owed much of its technical excellence to the engineering staff of the Guggenheim Aeronautical Laboratory, California Institute of Technology. It was perhaps the greatest of GALCIT's many contributions to air transport technology.[31]

Though GALCIT, in the prewar years, undertook numerous research studies in other areas, including tailless aircraft research for flying wing advocate John K. Northrop, and research into the causes and nature of air turbulence, its most far-reaching research was that undertaken by a group of GALCIT faculty and graduate students on rocket propulsion research. This is, in fact, the beginning of what later became the world-renowned Jet Propulsion Laboratory.

In 1934, The Daniel and Florence Guggenheim Foundation had already been assisting Dr. Robert H. Goddard, the American rocket pioneer. Many scientists still regarded rocketry as akin to science fiction, despite Goddard's having fired a liquid-fueled rocket in March 1926, the "Kitty Hawk" of rocketry. On June 11, 1928, German test pilot Friedrich Stamer had made the first manned rocket flight in history, a one-mile journey in a rocket-propelled glider, using solid-fuel rocket boosters, from the Wasserkuppe in the Rhön mountains. In 1934, Frank J. Malina, a young graduate student, came to GALCIT on a scholarship in mechanical engineering from Texas A & M College. Malina began working part-time as an assistant in the GALCIT wind tunnel. During 1935, Malina, working on a master's thesis on propeller behavior, found his attention turning increasingly to rocket propulsion. By this time, GALCIT engineers recognized that the piston engine propeller-driven airplane was rapidly approaching the peak of its technological development, and they began looking to jet propulsion—either by gas turbine or by pure rocket—as a way of getting around this technological block. Further stimulus for rocket research came from Caltech meteorologist Prof. Irving Krick, who was investigating cosmic ray measurements at high altitudes. Krick and his students used balloons for their studies, but Malina recognized that the rocket, if properly developed, had the potential to greatly exceed the altitude capabilities of the meteorological research balloon.[32]

In March 1935, at one of Theodore von Kármán's weekly seminars, GALCIT graduate student William Bollay presented a report in which he outlined the progress made in rocket aircraft development and theory by German rocket pioneer Eugen Sänger. Sänger argued that rocket-propelled high-speed aircraft were feasible, a statement guaranteed to produce much controversy in aeronautical circles, and published his views in what eventually became a rocketry classic, *Raketenflugtechnik*. Bollay repeated his oral report on Sänger's activities before a local Los Angeles meeting of the Institute of the Aeronautical Sciences, and it attracted the attention of several journalists. The resulting accounts in newspapers brought two rocket enthusiasts to GALCIT, John W. Parsons, a "self-taught chemist with considerable innate ability," von Kármán recalled, and Edward S. Forman, a rocketeer who fabricated rocket engines and inventions for Parsons. In February 1936, Parsons and Forman convinced Malina and Bollay to design and develop a high-altitude sounding rocket propelled by either a solid or liquid fuel rocket engine for Krick's cosmic ray research. So it was that by 1936, three groups of Americans were investigating rocket propulsion and designing rocket vehicles: Robert H. Goddard's tiny band at Roswell, New Mexico; G. Edward Pendray's small American Rocket Society group in New York state, and the budding group at Caltech's GALCIT.[33]

After less than a month of study, Malina and Bollay concluded that too little information existed to permit the design of such a rocket. Malina decided to obtain formal approval of the group's activities from Caltech, and approached Dr. Clark B. Millikan for permission to continue rocket studies. Malina proposed that Caltech let him complete his doctoral dissertation on rocket propulsion. Millikan's initial reaction was cool; he proposed that Malina would be better off with a good job in the aircraft industry. Malina next visited von Kármán who gave Malina approval to complete his doctorate on rocket propulsion. Malina, Bollay, Parsons, and Forman accordingly formed the GALCIT Rocket-Research Project, the first serious university-supported rocket research project in America. In May 1936, GALCIT graduate student Apollo M. O. Smith joined the team, and he and Malina began an investigation of the theoretical flight performance of a sounding rocket.[34] In August 1936, Malina met with rocket pioneer Robert H. Goddard, during a brief visit by Goddard to Caltech. Goddard had reluctantly gone to Caltech at the behest of Harry Guggenheim, to meet Robert A. Millikan, who was anxious to

secure a collaboration between Goddard and the burgeoning aeronautical research center at Pasadena. Goddard felt uneasy, fearful
that he might lose control over his research. During the cordial meeting, Malina made arrangements to visit Goddard's research laboratory
at Roswell, New Mexico. He visited Goddard at Roswell at the end
of the month, but though the visit was made as pleasant as possible,
Goddard was clearly unwilling to show Malina his laboratory or to
discuss fully his work, writing Millikan later that "I naturally cannot
turn over the results of many years of investigation, still incomplete,
for use as a student's thesis." Goddard did offer Malina a position in
his laboratory after Malina finished his degree at Caltech.[35]

Between October 1936 and January 1937, the Caltech rocket research group tested its first rocket motor, fueled by gaseous oxygen
and methyl alcohol, in the Arroyo Seco, behind Devil's Gate Dam
outside Pasadena. Coincidentally, Goddard himself had used this site
during World War I for smokeless powder rocket experiments with
Clarence N. Hickman, and it was very close to the future site of the
postwar Jet Propulsion Laboratory. By November 1936, they were
able to run the engine for twenty seconds without something going
wrong. Malina decided to get official backing for a rocket laboratory
on campus; in March 1937, A. M. O. Smith and Malina completed
their theoretical study of a sounding rocket. Their calculations demonstrated that such a rocket could soar to several hundred thousand
feet, and von Kármán, impressed by the paper, authorized the
GALCIT rocket research group to conduct limited tests of rocket
engines on campus.[36]

The next month, April 1937, Weld Arnold, an assistant in Caltech's
Astrophysical Laboratory, donated $1,000 to the rocket group and
joined the project as a photographer. At the same time, Hsue-Shen
Tsien, a graduate of the Chiao Tung University in Shanghai, China,
and holder of an M.S. in aeronautical engineering from MIT, joined
the Caltech rocketeers. Tsien, who had a great impact on American aeronautical development and also, apparently, on rocketry in
the People's Republic of China, was one of von Kármán's outstanding pupils. Arnold and Tsien completed what became known as
GALCIT's original rocket research group, consisting of Malina, Bollay, Parsons, Forman, Arnold, and Tsien. This group continued its
theoretical studies of rocket propulsion in conjunction with practical
experimentation on rocket engines. After a minor explosion during
the test of an engine using methyl alcohol for fuel and nitrogen di-
oxide as oxidizer, Caltech students dubbed the Malina group the

"Suicide Squad." During this period, however, the group conducted some of the first tests in America on the use of a storable liquid oxidizer in a rocket engine, leading to the later widespread usage of red fuming nitric acid (RFNA) in rocket engine applications.[37]

Though Malina and other group members had expected that their first successes in rocketry would involve sounding rockets for cosmic ray and meteorological research, the first major contribution the GALCIT rocket team made was to jet-assisted takeoff (JATO), using rocket boosters to propel heavily loaded aircraft from the ground. In December 1938, Malina prepared a report on jet propulsion for Air Corps chief Henry H. "Hap" Arnold and the Committee on Army Air Corps Research of the National Academy of Sciences (NAS). At this time the term "jet propulsion" was a catchall phrase for any research on using a stream of high-pressure gas for thrust. As a result of Malina's report, in January 1939 NAS awarded GALCIT a $1,000 contract for JATO research, later adding $10,000 on July 1, 1939, for research to give aircraft "super-performance," including faster level-flight speeds, higher rates of climb, and JATO takeoff assistance.[38]

The grant made to GALCIT on July 1, 1939, by the National Academy of Sciences Committee on Army Air Corps Research marked the beginning of Army Air Corps interest in rocket-boosted and rocket-propelled aircraft. The service created the Army Air Corps Jet Propulsion Research Project with Theodore von Kármán as director, together with Frank Malina, John Parsons, and Edward Forman. Yet, so many scientists held rocketry in such low repute that when MIT aeronautics director Jerome D. Hunsaker heard of GALCIT's rocket research project, he told von Kármán, "You can have the Buck Rogers job." Vannevar Bush, later director of NACA and the father of the modern computer, once remarked to von Kármán and Robert Millikan, "I don't understand how a serious scientist or engineer can play around with rockets."[39] In July 1940, the Army Air Corps assumed sponsorship of Caltech's rocket research from the National Academy of Sciences.[40]

GALCIT's JATO studies led to the first manned rocket flight in the United States. Malina, Parsons, Forman, and other GALCIT rocket investigators had begun studying both solid-fuel and liquid-fuel rocket motors capable of supplying sufficient thrust to enable an airplane to take off and reach an altitude high enough so that the plane could continue to fly without rocket assistance. Such engines, researchers believed, should provide full thrust for ten to thirty seconds.[41]

Malina, Parsons, and Forman directed studies on developing a restricted-burning rocket propellant. Like a cigarette, the charge burned at only one end, producing a constant, prolonged thrust. The design and fabrication of these charges, however, involved some difficult technical problems. For example, heat transfer from the burning charge to the long steel cylinder walls housing the charge threatened to ignite the entire charge at once, possibly bursting the cylinder like an exploding bomb, thus destroying the aircraft. If the propellant crumbled or cracked under combustion, exposing more propellant surface area to ignition, the internal pressure would again rise rapidly, exploding the containing cylinder and the remaining charge. To overcome these problems, GALCIT researchers developed special insulating liners between the charge and the cylinder walls to reduce potentially dangerous heat transfer. They also molded the powder "sticks" that composed the charge in a hydraulic press under great pressure. Throughout the spring of 1940, GALCIT researchers pursued their JATO investigations. Numerous test stand failures caused von Kármán, at one point, to derive a group of four differential equations to determine if it were possible to develop a slow-burning solid fuel rocket motor. Malina solved the four equations, demonstrating that there were no theoretical roadblocks on the path to a solid-fuel rocket engine. Heartened, GALCIT investigators continued their research. Finally, they arrived at a usable engine and propellant.[42]

The new propellant was GALCIT 27, an amide powder developed by Parsons, and forced into a steel cylinder container having a rocket nozzle at the end. The entire unit weighed 10.7 pounds, and the GALCIT 27 propellant accounted for 2 pounds. It produced 28 pounds of thrust for twelve seconds. A hydraulic press forced the charge into the cylinder under a pressure of eighteen tons. In the event that the internal pressure generated by the igniting propellant reached dangerous levels, the motor had a "fail-safe" feature, whereby the bolts holding the nozzle on the cylinder would give way, and the entire nozzle would fly off, preventing the charge from bursting.[43] By January 1941, GALCIT JATO development was so well advanced that the Army Air Corps Air Materiel Command at Wright Field authorized continued research and flight tests of the JATO units on a small airplane under AMC Aircraft Laboratory project MX-121. In January 1941, Clark Millikan, by now a rocket enthusiast himself, and Caltech scientist Homer J. Stewart completed an aerodynamic study of how JATO would affect an airplane's takeoff and climb characteristics. Their calculations showed that the airplane should have a greatly reduced takeoff roll. In the summer of 1941, the army furnished a small single-engine Ercoupe for the JATO tests, along with a test pilot, Capt. Homer A. Boushey, Jr. Boushey had previously served as army liaison between GALCIT and Wright Field.[44]

Between August 6 and 23, 1941, Boushey conducted sixty tests with the GALCIT 27 rockets at the army's air base at March Field, near Pasadena. At first he took off on conventional power, using the plane's engine and propeller, and then ignited the rocket boosters, mounted in pairs of three or six underneath the wings. Finally, on August 12, Boushey was ready to make the first American rocket-assisted takeoff. With the propeller engine ticking over, Boushey taxied out and then began to accelerate down the runway, with a small Piper Cub off the Ercoupe's left wing following suit. As the Ercoupe accelerated, Boushey ignited six of the GALCIT rocket boosters. The little plane, with a hissing roar, leapt into the air at a steep angle, trailing a streamer of gray smoke, and reached an elevation of several hundred feet before the Cub had even attained flying speed. "None of us," von Kármán recalled later, "had ever seen a plane climb at such a steep angle."[45] Now von Kármán, Boushey, Millikan, Malina, Parsons, Forman, and GALCIT researcher Martin Summerfield turned to completing the first American flight on rocket power alone. Technicians removed the Ercoupe's propeller, and installed twelve rocket units. On August 23, 1941, all was ready. A truck towed the Ercoupe via a rope to a speed of 25 mph, and Boushey ignited the rockets. Under a total thrust of 336 pounds, the Ercoupe shot aloft. Then the engines burned out, and it coasted back down to the runway, its flight a complete success.[46]

GALCIT's JATO demonstrations convinced army and navy officials of the importance of solid-fuel rocket boosters for takeoff assistance. JATO assistance had shortened the Ercoupe's takeoff run from a normal 580 feet to 300 feet, a saving of 48.3 percent, and had reduced takeoff time from 13.1 seconds to 7.5 seconds.[47] Because of their need to operate heavily loaded aircraft from the restricted confines of an aircraft carrier's deck, the navy had even greater interest in JATO than the army. At the request of the navy's Bureau of Aeronautics, Caltech's GALCIT began research on solid-fuel JATO motors capable of producing two hundred, five hundred, and one thousand pounds thrust, using new and improved fuel combinations called GALCIT 46, GALCIT 53, and GALCIT 61-C. Naturally GALCIT did not have the facilities to undertake mass production of these booster units, so on March 19, 1942, von Kármán, Frank Malina, Andrew Haley, John Parsons, Edward Forman, and Martin Summerfield established the Aerojet Engineering Corporation, which produced JATO units and other rocket engines for use during the war, and became one of the aerospace giants in the postwar era. Both the Army Air Forces and U.S. Navy utilized JATO on aircraft before the war's end, and by V-J Day, JATO was an expression familiar to all service airmen.[48] There were other notable rocketry contributions by GALCIT during the wartime years, such as development of the widely used 5-inch "Holy Moses" high-velocity aerial rocket (HVAR), the 11.75-inch "Tiny Tim," and various shore bombardment rockets.[49]

Two other projects undertaken by Caltech's GALCIT illustrate the broad interests of its director, Theodore von Kármán, and also the ability of the laboratory to assist researchers and developers operating outside the aeronautical industry. One was the development of the Smith-Putnam wind generator. The wind generator was the brain-child of Palmer C. Putnam, a Boston engineer. In the early 1930s he proposed constructing a large windmill in New England to generate electricity and had succeeded in obtaining the backing of a com-mercial turbine manufacturing firm, the S. Morgan Smith Company, together with the aid of various experts, including a structural engineer from MIT and a Norwegian meteorologist. In 1939, Putnam asked von Kármán for Caltech's assistance. Under von Kármán's direction, GALCIT instructor Dr. William Sears and grad-uate student Duncan Rannie completed various generator configura-tion studies and ran model tests in Caltech's ten-foot tunnel; Stanford's Guggenheim Aeronautic Laboratory also tested wind turbine models. New England was a good choice for such a wind generator, for it has some of the highest recorded wind velocities in the world. On April 12, 1934, the recorded wind speed at the peak of Mount Wash-ington reached an incredible 231 mph, a world's record. GALCIT also made studies of suitable sites, finally choosing a 2,000-foot hill in central Vermont near Rutland known as Grandpa's Knob. The final windmill design selected on the basis of Caltech wind-tunnel studies was a two-bladed rotor spanning 175 feet. Each blade weighed eight tons and was as large as the wing of a transport. S. Morgan Smith completed construction of the Smith-Putnam wind generator in August 1941. The large rotor, rotating at twenty-nine revolutions per minute, required lengthy trials and structural modifications. Finally, on March 3, 1945, the generator went into service operation—but not for long. The prolonged testing had induced structural fatigue (known but uncorrected because of wartime material shortages), and twenty-three days later, early on March 26, one blade separated from the shaft, sailing 750 feet down Grandpa's Knob. It was an inauspicious start for a farsighted idea; during its brief operation, the generator produced 1.25 megawatts of electrical power as the wind turned its blades. Three decades later, in the midst of growing concern over environmental protection and the decline of fossil fuels, the abortive experiment at Grandpa's Knob is attracting serious examination, and many aerodynamicists and environmentalists see wind generators as one practical way to overcome a growing energy crisis.[50]

The second nonaeronautical endeavor undertaken by GALCIT was an investigation of the Tacoma Narrows Bridge collapse. On the morning of November 7, 1940, the suspension bridge, a 2,800-foot span across Puget Sound in Washington State, began oscillating in a 42-mph wind. At just after 10:00 A.M., the vertical oscillations gave way to a corkscrew, spiraling motion that whipped the bridge deck through angles of forty-five degrees, so that lamp posts appeared almost horizontal. For about forty-five minutes the bridge structure withstood the violent stresses. Then part of its center span gave way, followed shortly by the rest of the center section. The bridge, built at a cost of $6,400,000 and opened to traffic on July 1, 1940, had earned the nickname of "Galloping Gertie" because of its tendency to oscillate vertically as much as four feet in light winds. GALCIT director Theodore von Kármán believed that the collapse might be due to the formation of vortices, swirling horizontal columns of air formed by the airflow striking the bridge. These vortices would stream downwind and then periodically detach or "shed" themselves from the bridge structure, setting up a lateral oscillation exactly like that which wrecked the bridge. Von Kármán had first studied vortex formation while a graduate student under Ludwig Prandtl at Göttingen in 1911, and his analysis of their behavior earned him a worldwide reputation. Now he placed a rubber model of the Tacoma Narrows Bridge in front of a small fan; the model oscillated. Recognizing that aerodynamic forces might have led to the collapse of the bridge, government officials appointed von Kármán to a special investigatory committee studying the bridge collapse. He was the only aerodynamicist; the remaining members were all civil engineers. The fallen Tacoma bridge had eight-foot vertical metal plate sidewalls. Von Kármán reasoned that the airflow formed vortices from the top and bottom of these plates which shed in a periodic manner, setting up a

continuous oscillation that induced structural failure. He proved his
hypothesis with a series of wind-tunnel tests on a model of the bridge
in the GALCIT ten-foot wind tunnel conducted by GALCIT researchers Louis G. Dunn and Duncan Rannie. As a result of von Kármán's
studies, civil engineers gained an appreciation for the importance of
aerodynamics in bridge design. Subsequent suspension bridge designers have avoided the vortex problem by abandoning solid plate
sidewalls in favor of an open-sided network, and by cutting slots in
the deck of the bridge to equalize the air pressure above and below
the deck.[51]

Thus within a decade of its establishment, the Guggenheim Aeronautical Laboratory of the California Institute of Technology had
already greatly contributed to growing American mastery of air transport development and had become one of the world centers of aeronautical research, the ideal academic counterpart to the various
federal government agencies pursuing aeronautical research and development. Much as the University of California at Berkeley became
a major center of nuclear research, Caltech's GALCIT became the
United States' leading university center of aeronautical instruction
and research. Its faculty members worked closely with the federal
government and private industry. Private companies such as Douglas,
North American, Northrop, Hughes, Vultee, Consolidated, and Lockheed regularly tested their new designs in its wind tunnels. In part,
the crucial role of Caltech in prewar American aeronautics was due
to the unique personality of Theodore von Kármán, the greatest aerospace scientist of his generation. The most important factor, however,
was the foresight of Daniel and Harry Guggenheim in endowing Caltech in 1926, and, together with Robert A. Millikan, in persuading
von Kármán to come to the United States. With the massive federal
support of aeronautical research and development that took place
during World War II, the importance of Guggenheim funding to
Caltech took on a diminished role. Before the war, however, it was
crucial. Caltech's school of aeronautics could not have made its contributions to aeronautical technology without the assistance that the
Guggenheims provided through their grant of $350,000. The money
spent in Pasadena spurred aeronautics around the world.

APPENDIX 2

Aeronautical Progress
at the Other Guggenheim Schools, 1926-41

THE glamorous accomplishments of GALCIT do not diminish in any way the more esoteric advances in aeronautical research and education undertaken at the other Guggenheim schools. Like GALCIT, these various schools sent their graduates to the federal government or private industry, and by 1941 Guggenheim school alumni figured prominently on the design and research teams of every major American aircraft company and every important aviation branch of the federal government. Like GALCIT, these schools also contributed to numerous projects directly and indirectly related to aeronautics.

The first of the Guggenheim-supported schools, predating the activities of The Daniel Guggenheim Fund for the Promotion of Aeronautics, was the Daniel Guggenheim School of Aeronautics at New York University which opened officially on October 27, 1926, with an enrollment of fifty-seven students. By the end of 1927, New York University had spent approximately $186,000 of the Guggenheim endowment for a two-story building, a nine-foot wind tunnel and other equipment. The tunnel was capable of 90-mph wind speeds generated by an eight-bladed cast aluminum alloy propeller driven by an electric motor. It complemented the earlier four-foot low-speed wind tunnel presented to the school by Glenn Curtiss before the Guggenheim grant. In 1928, airplane manufacturer Sherman M. Fairchild established a $3,000 two-year fellowship at the school for engine research and to find a qualified individual to direct establishment of an engine laboratory. A subcommittee formed from aircraft industry leaders and consisting of Fairchild, Charles L. Lawrance, Arthur Nutt, Frederick Rentschler, and L. M. Woolson selected K. F. Rubert, a Cornell and NYU graduate, to hold the fellowship. Rubert subsequently di-

rected the development of the NYU aircraft engine laboratory, completed in 1930 and used primarily for instruction and graduate thesis
research.[1]

In 1932, NYU enlarged the aeronautics building to permit class
instruction in aircraft maintenance and rigging. Four years later, the
school added a 150-foot-long towing basin for seaplane hull model
testing, the only one then available at any university in the country,
and established the Richard F. Hoyt Memorial Seaplane Fellowship
in 1938. The first fellowship recipient, John D. Pierson, used the towing basin to analyze seaplane porpoising, presenting the results of his
research in a paper delivered to the Institute of the Aeronautical
Sciences in 1939. The same year, forty-five sponsors created the $7,000
Juan de la Cierva Memorial Fellowship in honor of the Spanish Autogiro pioneer. The Cierva Fellowship sponsored research on rotary-
wing aircraft, and it paralleled courses in rotary-wing aerodynamics
that Alexander Klemin had instituted at NYU in 1937. Chairman of
the fellowship committee was W. Wallace Kellett, a pioneering developer of the Autogiro in America. By 1944, slightly less than $3,000
remained in the fellowship fund, the rest having been expended in
grants of $720 per year. In the summer of 1941, the school completed
its prewar expansion by adding on a third story to the aeronautics
building, financed by combining $15,000 remaining from the Gug-
genheim grant with a $15,000 gift from an anonymous donor.[2]

During the years 1923 to 1932, Alexander Klemin directed, in the
words of Frederick K. Teichmann, one of the school's first graduates,
a "one-man school." Gradually the faculty grew, and by 1933 Klemin
had a staff of ten instructors, a figure that generally remained un-
changed until American entry into the Second World War. Klemin
remained at New York University until 1941, when for reasons of
health he stepped down as aeronautics department chairman. Prof.
Charles H. Colvin succeeded him and directed the school over the
next two years. Then, in 1943, Frederick K. Teichmann assumed the
chairmanship of the department of aeronautical engineering, holding
this position until 1955.[3]

Klemin and von Kármán shared many of the same qualities; each
would often become so engrossed in a problem that he would lose
track of time or place. Though sometimes brusque, each took a deep
personal and paternal interest in his students. Each man also had no
patience for those less energetic than himself, or those who were unwilling to accept innovation and change. Klemin recognized that
while the aircraft industry desired aeronautical engineers trained as
broadly as possible, the time would come when the industry would

require the services of skilled specialists. Accordingly, in the early 1930s, he broadened the program of aeronautics at NYU to include courses in materials and methods of aircraft construction, aviation law, meteorology, air transportation, aircraft radio, and rotary-wing aerodynamics.

In November 1924, Klemin had presented the first American paper on helicopter aircraft before a meeting of the American Society of Mechanical Engineers. He became a staunch advocate of the Autogiro and helicopter, at a time when these vehicles were regarded as freak contraptions incapable of contributing to air transportation. In the 1930s, however, the helicopter, an aircraft which, unlike the Autogiro, could hover motionless in the air because its rotor was directly connected to the engine, made significant progress. In 1935, for example, French designers Louis Breguet and Rene Dorand developed and flew a Gyroplane Laboratoire, a single-engine helicopter utilizing two coaxially-mounted rotors, which set a rotary-wing aircraft speed record of 67 mph, recognized by the Fédération Aéronautique Internationale. In 1936 the Germans flew the Focke-Achgelis FW 61, which placed Germany in the lead of helicopter development. Two years later, Igor Sikorsky a Russian émigré, persuaded the United Aircraft Corporation to pursue helicopter development. Sikorsky had built a series of highly successful seaplanes, and had experimented with helicopters as early as 1909, while in Russia. In 1939 he constructed the VS 300, and after trying various combinations of main and tail rotors, he successfully flew the VS 300 for the first time on May 13, 1940. The Army Air Corps and NACA, which had actively studied Autogiro and helicopter design in the 1930s, threw their full support behind Sikorsky, and the lead in helicopter development passed to the United States. "Sikorsky" and "helicopter" became virtually synonymous terms.[4]

Klemin, who foresaw the possibilities of helicopters and Autogiros long before these events awakened general interest in rotary-wing flight, put his ideas into practice by initiating a series of courses in helicopter aerodynamics and making wind-tunnel studies of helicopters, Autogiros, and one particularly interesting design, the Herrick Convertoplane. The Convertoplane was a biplane whose top wing could serve both as a wing and as a two-bladed rotor, depending on the wishes of the pilot. Designed by Gerard P. Herrick and Ralph H. McClarren, the Convertoplane first flew in 1937, piloted by George Townsend, successfully performing an inflight transition from biplane to rotor operation. Klemin's paper "Principles of Rotary Aircraft," presented before the Franklin Institute in November 1938, resulted in industry-wide approval of NYU's helicopter and Autogiro research. Together with the de la Cierva fellowship, this led to introduction in 1940 of a specialized graduate-level series of courses in the aerodynamics and design of rotary-wing aircraft, the first offered anywhere in the world.[5]

Like Caltech, NYU opened its wind tunnels to private industry. In the years before World War II, all the major East Coast aircraft manufacturers tested their prototype designs in the NYU tunnels. Some companies, such as Sikorsky, Chance Vought, Seversky, and Grumman, all located in the New York-Connecticut area, used NYU for the bulk of their tunnel research. Grumman, for example, tested models of the F4F Wildcat, the navy's first monoplane fighter, in NYU's nine-foot tunnel. Occasionally, NYU's tunnels tested other vehicles and structures besides aircraft. Several railroad locomotive manufacturers and rail companies tested new streamlined locomotive designs in the NYU tunnels, and civil engineers ran tests on telephone cable resistance and vibration in wind, the aerodynamic characteristics of the perisphere and trylon shape used at the 1939 World's Fair in New York, and air loads on buildings and bridges. Later NYU entered the new field of environmental studies when aerodynamicists ran tests on smoke plumes and their dispersion from industrial plants, aimed at reducing harmful air pollution. Klemin and NYU faculty members used the small four-foot tunnel for tests on lift-increasing devices for aircraft, including Zap, Wragg, and Fowler flaps. The Fowler flap, which aeronautical engineers adopted worldwide, especially for the design of multiengine transport and bomber aircraft, underwent much theoretical study in NYU tunnels.[6]

Beginning in 1927, graduates of NYU's aeronautics department received the degree of Aeronautical Engineer (A.E.). The school presumed that each graduate already possessed a B.S. degree in mechanical engineering, and the A.E. degree largely represented completion of industrial work followed by a thesis. It approximated an M.S. degree in engineering. In 1937, to avoid confusion with the designation system for state-licensed professional engineers, NYU dropped the A.E. degree, and replaced it with a Bachelor of Science degree specialized in aeronautical engineering (B.S.A.E.). By 1939, the American aviation industry, including every important aircraft manufacturer in the country, employed over 285 graduates from the Guggenheim school at New York University. Others directed aeronautical research and development or aircraft procurement with such governmental bodies as the National Advisory Committee for Aeronautics, the Materiel Division of the Army Air Corps, the Navy Bureau of Aeronautics, and Civil Aeronautics Authority (CAA). Still others taught aeronautical engineering at schools and universities around the country. By 1941, then, the Guggenheim grant to New York University had caused the germinating seed planted by Alexander Klemin and Collins Bliss in the early 1920s to flourish into an institution capable of both supplying the aircraft industry and federal government, especially on the East Coast, with well-trained graduates, and providing the industry with the research facilities necessary for basic research. While it would be foolish to attribute NYU's rise to aeronautical prominence solely to the Guggenheim fund, it could not have advanced as far as it did without the Guggenheim money.[7]

During its first decade of existence, the Guggenheim Aeronautic Laboratory at Leland Stanford University continued its pre-Guggenheim grant tradition of emphasizing research on aircraft propellers. The director of the laboratory, E. P. Lesley, supervised all laboratory experimental work and propeller design, assisted by Alfred S. Niles, who specialized in teaching aircraft structural design and stress analysis, and Elliott G. Reid, who gave courses in aerodynamic theory. Like New York University, Stanford offered courses in aeronautical engineering that presupposed a major in mechanical engineering, and thus the aeronautical engineering degree offered at Stanford compared to a M.S. in engineering. From the outset, Stanford aeronautics instructors managed an ambitious program of research. By December 1927, one year after the Guggenheim grant, Stanford had six major research projects underway investigating propeller performance characteristics, analyzing propeller behavior during yawing maneuvers, measuring the rotational velocity of propeller slipstreams, studying boundary layer aerodynamics, measuring the induced drag of wings having high aspect ratios, and measuring the profile drag of airfoil sections. To facilitate Stanford's research, the navy donated two nonflyable aircraft, a thick wing all-metal single-engine three-seat naval observation plane, the Martin MO-1, and a small government-built biplane, the TS-3. Stanford used the planes for instruction in aircraft construction, rigging, and control.[8]

Lesley, Reid, and Niles, with the occasional advice and assistance of William F. Durand, supervised Stanford's aerodynamic research and teaching over the next decade, aided by teaching assistants. During that time, Stanford trained 217 students in aeronautics. Forty of the students were aeronautical majors who received the degree of Engineer in Mechanical Engineering (Aeronautics), requiring two full years of graduate work plus a thesis. Like New York University, prewar Stanford graduates dispersed throughout the aircraft industry and federal government. Primarily, however, Stanford remained a center of propeller research. By 1939, NACA had published twenty-two propeller research reports generated by Stanford research, an average of one per year for every year the school had conducted propeller research, including eleven student theses. Stanford also experimented with coaxially mounted, contrarotating "tandem" propellers to reduce propeller torque, testing this installation in its eight-foot wind tunnel before the army flight-tested this arrangement on an experimental Curtiss P-36 Hawk pursuit plane. Lesley, who retired in late 1939, believed the research on tandem propellers to be the most important propeller research Stanford ever conducted. Though relatively rare, this propeller arrangement later appeared with notable success on some high-speed propeller-driven aircraft, especially turboprop designs.[9]

The Committee on Graduate Instruction of the American Council on Education approved Stanford in 1934 as one of only three institutions in the United States adequately staffed and equipped for work leading to the doctorate in aeronautical engineering. The other two were the Massachusetts Institute of Technology, and Caltech. Stanford remained somewhat aloof from the aircraft industry until 1939 because senior university officials refused to permit the aeronautical laboratory to open its wind tunnels for industrial research. Finally, in 1939, largely from pressure by William F. Durand, Stanford opened its tunnel facilities to industry research whenever they were not in operation for instruction or university research. The first commercial work undertaken in the Stanford wind tunnel was for the S. Morgan Smith Company's proposed Vermont air turbine, a project to which Caltech's GALCIT contributed heavily. Next, the school tested the engine nacelle and cowling installation for a proposed North American bomber which became the famed B-25 Mitchell. In September 1939, NACA selected Sunnyvale, California, as the site for a new major West Coast aeronautical laboratory. This became the Ames Aeronautical Laboratory, later NASA's Ames Research Center. NACA selected the Sunnyvale site, six miles from Stanford, because it wanted a research center close to the gigantic

West Coast aircraft industry, yet not so close as to become involved in routine aircraft development rather than basic research. Sunnyvale, near San Francisco, offered just the right combination of facets: it was a major army-navy air base, near a good university, and it was north of the Los Angeles aircraft manufacturing complex. When Ames opened in the midst of the Second World War, many of its workers used Stanford to upgrade their academic training. Slowly a partnership formed between the university and the laboratory that still remained strong in the mid-1970s.[10]

By 1941, Stanford, like the other Guggenheim schools, had done its share in advancing aeronautical education and research. One project completed on campus deserves special mention. At the instigation of the Guggenheim fund, William F. Durand prepared a six-volume aeronautical encyclopedia entitled *Aerodynamic Theory: A General Review of Progress under a Grant of the Guggenheim Fund for the Promotion of Aeronautics*, published by Julius Springer Verlag in Berlin from 1934 through 1936. During his trip to the United States in the fall of 1926, Theodore von Kármán had met with Daniel Guggenheim at Hempstead House and suggested that the Guggenheim fund sponsor a series of aeronautical handbooks that scientists and engineers could use for ready reference.[11] Von Kármán's suggestion met with the interest of Daniel and Harry Guggenheim, who contacted various American authorities in aeronautics to see if such a project would be worthwhile. The response was cool, most consultants believing the state of aviation technology not far enough advanced to warrant a general technical encyclopedia which was, as Jerome C. Hunsaker phrased it, "a thing the Germans do well and we not at all."[12] Hunsaker believed, however, that an encyclopedia on the aeronautical sciences was necessary, because "we have developed practical design men who are ignorant of much of the fundamental basis for their practices, (manufacturer's design staff) and others who do not appreciate the structural and dynamical principles involved (wind-tunnel experimenters)."[13]

In October 1927, Harry Guggenheim asked Dr. William F. Durand to make a general survey of aeronautical theory and practice and then recommend whether or not the fund should support such an encyclopedia.[14] Durand worked for several months, and soon found that "designs and methods of construction were changing too rapidly, things were moving so fast that an encyclopedic treatment would be out of date before the work could be completed."[15] By June 1928, Durand had concluded that there was "a core of fundamental theory springing from the theory of fluid mechanics" that would not change in time. He therefore recommended that the fund prepare an encyclopedic treatment on "aerodynamic theory and the experimental data relating thereto." Such a work, he estimated, would require six volumes and cost about $45,000 to publish.[16]

The trustees of The Daniel Guggenheim Fund for the Promotion of Aeronautics received Durand's report with favor, and approved publication of the encyclopedia, provided that Durand himself direct and edit the work. Durand decided to go abroad and study the question in consultation with outstanding European aeronautical scientists. He sailed for Europe on April 4, 1929, aboard the *Leviathan*. While in Europe, Durand met with von Kármán, and also with scientists Ludwig Prandtl and Adolf Betz. Together the men hammered out the general outline of the proposed work. The final plan called for twenty divisions within the encyclopedia prepared by twenty-five authors. Durand concluded that his initial estimate of $45,000 was too low and that $60,000 was a more realistic figure. At a meeting held on October 1, 1929, the fund trustees approved an appropriation of $60,000 for the encyclopedia, which occupied Durand's full attention for the next seven years. In preparation for the closing of the fund in 1930, Durand arranged for the unspent portions of the money to go to Stanford, which would administer the money for the completion of the manuscript. In the event that Durand would be unable, from illness or death, to complete the work, it would go to NACA for completion.[17]

Finishing the project was no simple matter. Durand had arranged for publication with an American publisher who subsequently turned the encyclopedia down "due to a feeling of uncertainty as to prospective sales."[18] By an odd twist, a German publisher, Julius Springer, next offered to assume all the risks of publication, and Durand delivered the manuscript to him. Publication took from 1934 through 1936. The encyclopedia in final form occupied six volumes and a total of 2,200 pages. Durand had to review galley and page proofs sent to America from Berlin, undertaking tedious correspondence with the various authors involved. After publication, aeronautical engineers hailed the encyclopedia as a standard reference for years to come. In fact, Durand, together with von Kármán, planned to update the work as early as 1939, but the outbreak of World War II brought their plans to an end. Because of the need of the book by engineers during the Second World War, Caltech undertook photoduplication of the volumes. Though it did not cover jet or rocket propulsion, nor deal with astronautics, Durand's *Aerodynamic Theory* even in the 1970s

remains a valuable reference work, still much sought after by practic-
ing engineers.[19]

––––––––––––––––

The University of Michigan's major contribution in the prewar
years to American aviation was in training a small group of outstanding youg engineers who later joined the American aircraft industry,
rising to direct major American aeronautical and aerospace projects.
During this same time, the school also used money from The Daniel
Guggenheim Fund for the Promotion of Aeronautics to study aircraft
engines and send an expedition to Greenland to study North Atlantic
weather conditions. The first Daniel Guggenheim Professor of Applied Aeronautics at Michigan was Lawrence V. Kerber, appointed
in March 1927. Kerber, a Michigan alumnus, class of 1918, had previously been in charge of Air Corps aerodynamic research at McCook
and Wright fields, Dayton, Ohio. While at McCook, Kerber, in conjunction with another Michigan graduate, W. F. Gerhardt, wrote
A Manual of Flight Test Procedure, which became the first major
standard reference work for test pilots and project engineers. In
August 1928, with the approval of the Guggenheim fund, Kerber left
Ann Arbor for Washington, D.C., where he directed the engineering
section of the Commerce Department's Aeronautics Branch. Kerber
enjoyed his work in the Commerce Department so much that, in July
1929, he resigned from the Guggenheim chair and joined the federal
service full time, remaining with the Aeronautics Branch and the later
Bureau of Air Commerce and Civil Aeronautics Authority for the
next decade, before joining the Lockheed Aircraft Corporation. Michigan replaced him as Guggenheim professor with Felix Pawlowski,
and then, in 1930, the school created a separate Department of Aeronautical Engineering, chaired by Prof. Edward A. Stalker who held
the chairmanship until 1942.[20]
    Kerber's example caused many Michigan students to gravitate to
the Bureau of Air Commerce where, as Michigan professor Milton J.
Thompson recalls, "They outnumbered by far those from other
schools."[21] Best known of the subsequent Michigan alumni at the
Civil Aeronautics Authority was Harold D. Hoekstra, who joined the
CAA in 1937, serving with it and the later Federal Aviation Administration, and chairing various committees, including some investigating jet airliner and SST feasibility. Michigan graduates also joined
the aircraft industry in great numbers, and some of them, such as
Raymond C. Blaylock (Curtiss), Robert J. Woods (Bell), and Clar-

ence L. "Kelly" Johnson (Lockheed), quickly moved into the forefront of industrial leadership.* This trend has continued since 1945 as well.[22]

One Michigan project undertaken with additional Guggenheim money was an investigation of two-cycle engines for aircraft, with fuel injection and supercharging for better performance at high altitudes. Michigan Prof. Edward A. Stalker believed that such an engine, in contrast to conventional four-cycle piston engines, had definite advantages, among which were more horsepower per weight, reduced mechanical complexity, and less maintenance and servicing requirements. Stalker persuaded the Guggenheims early in 1927 to issue a $2,000 research grant. His winning point was the claim that a two-cycle engine could double available power over a four-cycle engine of the same weight, increasing a plane's rate of climb and enabling it to operate from smaller airfields. George W. Lewis, NACA's director of aeronautical research, already had two-cycle research programs underway at Langley Laboratory, but he considered (correctly) Stalker's proposed design prone to failure due to inadequate cooling, incomplete fuel-air mixture combustion, and insufficient supercharging for maintaining power at altitude. Over the next year and a half, Stalker continued his basic research, but the complexity of the task thwarted any immediate beneficial results.† Finally, in July 1929, the Guggenheims closed the project, no nearer to completion than previously.[23]

In May 1927, The Daniel Guggenheim Fund for the Promotion of Aeronautics granted Dr. William H. Hobbs of the University of Michigan $5,000 to match $15,000 already appropriated by the university for a meteorological and geological expedition to Greenland. Hobbs, head of Michigan's geology department, had previously asked for Guggenheim fund assistance in February 1926 when he was outfitting a Greenland expedition for aerial surveying and me-

---

* For example, Blaylock helped design the Curtiss Tanager, winner of the 1929 Daniel Guggenheim International Safe Airplane Competition, within a year of his graduation from Michigan. Woods helped initiate the Bell X-1 supersonic research airplane program, the variable-sweep Bell X-5, and generated interest leading to the North American X-15. Kelly Johnson, whose world reputation in the aeronautical community ranks alongside that of Britain's legendary Barnes N. Wallis, spurred numerous Lockheed projects, including the XP-80, the XF-104, and the A-11.

† The two-cycle aircraft piston engine has always held great attraction for engine designers, and many such experimental models have appeared. The type generally has serious misfiring difficulties, as well as high fuel consumption. During the 1930s the German Junkers Jumo engine firm developed a two-cycle diesel engine that did see limited service on some German transports, and on the wartime Ju 86P reconnaissance aircraft.

teorological studies. The Guggenheims took no action because fund trustees saw no direct connection between aviation and the Hobbs Expedition, aside from his proposed aerial surveying program using amphibian and ski-equipped airplanes.[24] After his return from Greenland, Hobbs reported his findings and, in April 1927, again approached the Guggenheim fund, asking for assistance in funding a second expedition that would establish a permanent meteorological station on Greenland. At this time, Charles Lindbergh had not yet made his Atlantic crossing, but Hobbs emphasized that such a station would offer "the possibility of forecasting, probably with an interval of several days, the storms along the flight lanes between the United States and Europe."[25]

Harry Guggenheim turned to the navy and the Weather Bureau for advice, and Lt. Francis W. Reichelderfer, the navy's aviation aerologist and Charles F. Marvin, chief of the Weather Bureau, both recommended with cautious optimism that the Guggenheim fund support Hobbs.[26] Accordingly, on May 4, 1927, Harry Guggenheim granted $5,000 to Hobbs, to match another $15,000 Hobbs had raised on his own. Hobbs wasted no time, sailing for Greenland from Hoboken, New Jersey, aboard the steamship *Frederick VIII* on May 10, 1927. He returned from Greenland in the late fall, and presented a report on his work before the Guggenheim fund's Daniel Guggenheim Committee on Aeronautical Meteorology, chaired by Dr. Carl Gustaf Rossby. Rossby, a Swedish meteorologist brought to the United States by the Guggenheim fund, recommended that the fund grant Hobbs an additional $5,000 to continue Michigan's research on Greenland, and Hobbs did receive another $5,000 in early 1928 to make another trip to Greenland. At the same time, Rossby also suggested to Weather Bureau chief Charles F. Marvin that the United States or Danish governments undertake formal financial and scientific support of permanent meteorological installations on Greenland.[27]

William Hobbs's and Harry Guggenheim's advocacy of transatlantic weather reporting services came at a time when transoceanic air service was unknown. Harry Guggenheim wrote that the "ability to forecast weather conditions correctly in the Atlantic region will remove one of the principal obstacles to transatlantic airplane flights." But many meteorologists questioned the expense or trouble involved in creating North Atlantic shipboard or land-based weather stations for the express purpose of aiding commercial air transport operations over the ocean.

Weather Bureau chief Charles F. Marvin had asked Congress in 1927 for an appropriation of $100,000 to permit hiring additional forecasters and arranging for shipboard weather reports, all to assist airplane flights over the ocean. Congress rejected his request. Matters nearly came to a head in 1929, when the German passenger airship *Graf Zeppelin* crossed the Atlantic from New York to Friedrichshafen without benefit of reliable weather reporting services. Even as late as 1936, when another German Zeppelin, the *Hindenburg*, made its initial transatlantic flight, weather forecasters could offer only minimal assistance in predicting weather conditions over the ocean. Weather reporting stations on Greenland did eventually prove their great value to transatlantic flying, starting with aircraft transport and ferry operations between North America and Europe during World War II. Here again the Guggenheim fund had promoted a venture whose need, with the benefit of hindsight, was unquestionable.[28]

The Guggenheim grant of $230,000 to the Massachusetts Institute of Technology implied an obligation on the part of the school to maintain and expand on their program in aeronautics. Within a few years after the Guggenheim grant, the annual aeronautics budget at MIT rose from roughly $35,000 to over $100,000, directly traceable to the impact of the Guggenheim fund. As the Guggenheim grant to New York University stimulated additional grants from other individuals, the grant to MIT, in the opinion of Jerome C. Hunsaker, stimulated grants totaling $85,000 from General Motors chief Alfred P. Sloan and Henry M. Crane in 1928 for an engine laboratory. In 1938, the MIT Corporation, in conjunction with a number of private donors, erected a new wind tunnel next to the Guggenheim building, in honor of the Wright brothers, at a cost of $25,000.[29]

In 1933, Hunsaker rejoined the MIT faculty as chairman of the department of mechanical engineering. He also directed MIT's aeronautics program. At this time, the MIT aeronautics faculty consisted of R. H. Smith, Otto Koppen, Shatswell Ober, J. S. Newell, E. S. Taylor, J. R. Markham, and Manfred Rauscher. During the decade after the Guggenheim grant, MIT's aeronautics program graduated a number of students who later became influential members of the aeronautical community. They included John Stack, who joined NACA and later became one of the nation's supersonic pioneers and director of aeronautical research for the National Aeronautics and Space Administration (NASA), and Charles Stark Draper, who organized MIT's Instrumentation Laboratory (later renamed in his honor).

Between 1927 and 1939, MIT's aeronautics department awarded 294 B.S. degrees, 76 M.S. degrees, and 3 Sc.D. degrees. By 1939 MIT graduates included the chief engineers or engineering directors of the Curtiss-Wright, Glenn L. Martin, Pratt & Whitney, Vought, Hamilton Standard, Lockheed, Stearman, and Douglas firms. NACA's Langley Laboratory alone had fifteen MIT graduates on its staff.[30]

During the 1930s, MIT's aeronautics faculty directed student studies in such areas as vehicle design, structural analysis and design, flutter and aeroelasticity, propulsion, fluid mechanics, and instrumentation and automatic control. Manfred Rauscher developed test techniques whereby small models in low-speed wind tunnels could simulate airplane wing or control surface flutter at high airspeeds. Otto Koppen taught a seminar in airplane design problems, including air transport economics and airfield requirements. Charles Stark Draper, later chairman of MIT's aeronautics department, taught instrument design and, in individual research, developed blind flying instrumentation permitting blind landings, detonation indicators and recorders, and a vibration recording apparatus. Draper, the guiding light behind MIT's subsequent postwar work in automatic control of aircraft and spacecraft, developed during World War II the navy's Mark 14 gyroscopic lead-computing gun director, a device that made possible highly accurate antiaircraft fire for ship defense and helped break the back of the *Kamikaze* menace in 1944–45.[31]

On June 18, 1928, the Guggenheim fund granted MIT an additional $34,000 to establish a course in meteorology at the school for three years. The grant provided $10,000 for equipment, $12,000 for salaries, $6,000 for three $2,000 fellowships, and $6,000 for research.[32] The course came about through the effort of MIT professor Edward P. Warner, then the Assistant Secretary of the Navy for Aeronautics, and Carl Gustaf Rossby, the Swedish meteorologist brought to America by the Guggenheim fund. Warner emphasized in a series of letters to Harry Guggenheim that both military and commercial aviation required precise, accurate weather forecasting, with research on methods to determine upper air conditions. Such services would greatly benefit airship operation. Already the Weather Bureau faced an acute shortage of men trained in the science of air-mass analysis. Such a shortage, Warner believed, could become very serious and a definite block to aeronautical progress within a few years unless some institution in the United States undertook instruction in meteorology.[33]

Warner had the complete support of MIT president Samuel Stratton. MIT had already arranged with Harvard to offer limited graduate training in meteorology to naval officers, but the course lacked financial backing, and Warner confessed, "the results have not been entirely satisfactory."[34] Rossby, who also favored establishing a school of meteorology in the United States, was at the time directing the weather reporting services on the Guggenheim model airline on the West Coast. Harry Guggenheim secured Rossby's willingness to serve on any meteorological faculty assisted by the fund, and after bringing up the matter with Guggenheim fund trustees, he announced creation of the course in his letter to Samuel Stratton. Rossby reported to MIT early in September 1928, just before the start of the fall term. By this time, the creation of the three-year meteorological course at MIT had drawn favorable comment from aeronautical trade journals and from the military services. Warner then asked that Guggenheim undertake not simply aerological education but research as well. Guggenheim passed on Warner's suggestion to Rossby, remarking, "I heartily concur with his view."[35] To assist in creating the course, Rossby acquired the services of Dr. H. C. Willett, a meteorologist formerly with the Weather Bureau, and G. D. Camp, A. J. Montzka, and F. A. Arsenault, all of the MIT Meteorological Observatory at South Dartmouth, Massachusetts.[36]

Rossby began MIT's meteorological program in the fall of 1928 by having H. C. Willett offer an introductory course in meteorology. Next came a course in synoptic meteorology, a general nonmathematical discussion of atmospheric circulation and air mass and front analysis, based upon the Bjerknes Polar Front air mass theory. Along with this course, students took a laboratory course in which they learned to interpret weather maps, make weather observations, and prepare temperature pressure graphs for the upper atmosphere. The lab course also covered pilot balloon observations using hydrogen-filled pilot balloons tracked by theodolites. At night, researchers attached paper lanterns and small candles to the balloons. Although standard practice, the use of open flame near hydrogen-filled observation balloons must certainly have given the students pause for reflection. Potential meteorologists next took a course in dynamic meteorology, with much emphasis on quantitative interpretation of weather conditions, including study of hurricane and tornado formation. Students then undertook individual research in a meteorological seminar meeting two hours a week for two terms under the direction of Rossby himself. In 1929, with the assistance of the Goodyear Zeppelin Corporation and E. H. R. Green, MIT set up a research observatory on Green's estate, Round Hill, at South Dartmouth, Mass. Goodyear contributed a small nonrigid airship for radio and meteorological studies, and MIT hired several meteorologists to man the station and make observations. Much of Rossby's work at MIT consisted of laboriously plotting all the weather observations taken around the country to create a general picture of American climatological conditions.[37]

Rossby remained with MIT from 1928 until 1941, when he left to become assistant chief of the Weather Bureau in charge of research. In 1939, Hunsaker considered MIT's meteorological center, "perhaps the most progressive group in the world," adding that "its methods are sought out by visitors and students from many countries." Ten years after its creation, the Guggenheim-funded meteorological center had three professors, eight research assistants, and eighteen graduate students. MIT awarded its first M.S. degrees in meteorology in 1931; by 1939, the school had awarded a total of twenty-one M.S. and five Sc.D. degrees in meteorology. With additional funding from the Rockefeller Foundation, MIT undertook pioneer daily upper-air soundings by airplane from 1931 through 1934, developing techniques and instrumentation enabling the airplane to function as a meteorological research tool. The Weather Bureau later standardized these techniques and expanded on them. Individual research on American air mass analysis by H. C. Willett, based on Rossby's earlier work, became the basis for airline weather forecasting in the United States. MIT's meteorology program remained as a division of aeronautical engineering until 1945, when the institute set up a separate department of meteorology. By that time it had established its unique position as the most important academic center of weather studies in the United States. Guggenheim support of meteorological education and research, as exemplified by the creation of MIT's first courses in the subject, was clearly one of the fund's most important contributions.[38]

The University of Washington, in the years prior to World War II, did not break new ground in aeronautical research as did Caltech or MIT. Rather, it continued a tradition of providing the best engineering education in the Northwest, while maintaining an informal relationship with the Boeing company in Seattle, where most of Washington's aeronautical graduates pursued their careers.

The four-story Daniel Guggenheim Hall of Aeronautics, finished in Tudor-Gothic style, officially opened on April 11, 1930, at ceremonies attended by William E. Boeing, the president and founder of the Boeing Airplane Company. University officials, at the suggestion of Boeing and with the concurrence of Harry Guggenheim, appointed Prof. E. O. Eastwood, chairman of the mechanical engineering department, as director of aeronautics. Frederick K. Kirsten continued his work on cycloidal propellers. In 1930, the school graduated six students with Bachelor of Science degrees in aeronautical engineering. Three years later the school graduated twenty-six students, but because of the depression, class size dropped, and between 1933 and 1939 the average graduating class numbered roughly sixteen. Though some went into federal service or joined other aircraft companies, many joined Boeing, so many in fact that by the end of the decade a majority of Boeing's technical staff consisted of Washington-trained engineering graduates.[39] The Guggenheim Hall of Aeronautics housed two wind tunnels, a small tunnel demonstrating airflow around models and a larger tunnel used for research. The latter tunnel, designed by Kirsten and built by two senior students in aeronautical engineering, had a hexagonal cross section, an airspeed of 100 mph, and could accommodate models having a wing span of two feet. By 1934, however, the school needed a larger tunnel for research, as did the Boeing company. Accordingly, Boeing, the Washington state legislature, and the federal government through the Works Progress Administration appropriated funds for a new tunnel. The new tunnel, designed by Kirsten, featured a rectangular cross section measuring eight by twelve feet, and it could generate an airflow of 250 mph. Washington completed the tunnel in 1938, which went into immediate use, testing new aircraft designs for Boeing and other companies, including the radical Davis airfoil for Consolidated-Vultee. Among the aircraft that passed through the tunnel for testing were the North American AT-6, B-25, and P-51, the Chance Vought XOS2U-1, the Consolidated-Vultee B-24, the Grumman F4F-3, and all the Boeing designs of the prewar and war years.[40]

Between 1933 and 1942, the Boeing company became the nation's leading manufacturer of large multiengine bomber and transport aircraft. The company made its reputation on the XB-15, the B-17, and the B-29 bombers, and the Model 307 and 314 transports. All of these aircraft underwent their initial wind-tunnel testing in Washington's new 250-mph tunnel. Boeing's Model 299, the prototype B-17, served as a basis for the famed B-17 Flying Fortress, perhaps the best-known bomber of World War II. The XB-15, though grossly underpowered and a strictly experimental design, gave Boeing experience and confidence in the design and construction of large all-metal multiengine bombers, thus aiding the development of the Boeing B-29 Superfortress, the best heavy bomber of World War II, and the plane responsible for the ruination of Japan's wartime heavy industry. The Boeing Model 307 Stratoliner, a four-engine airplane based upon the B-17 design, was the first airliner to enter scheduled service equipped with a pressurized passenger cabin. Boeing built only ten 307's, one for Howard Hughes and the rest for Pan American Airways and TWA. One broke up and crashed in the Mount Rainier foothills during stability and control tests.* Following additional wind tunnel studies at the University of Washington, others entered passenger service. As late as the Vietnam War, two or three of the 307's still flew as courier aircraft between the various strife-torn nations of Southeast Asia with representatives of the International Control Commission.

Washington's wind tunnel also contributed to the discovery and cure of some potentially serious problems in new Boeing designs. The Boeing Model 314, a four-engine long-range flying boat based on the abortive XB-15, performed unsatisfactorily during its initial flight trials. Further testing in Washington's wind tunnel led Boeing designers to change the tail configuration from a single vertical fin and rudder to a triple vertical fin and rudder installation. After that, the 314 handled easily, becoming one of the most popular flying boat designs ever built. The University of Washington ran its first tests on the B-29 in January 1940, and during these initial trials the proposed wing design for the B-29 showed signs of airflow separation as the airflow airspeed over the wing approached the speed of sound. Boeing redesigned the wing's shape, ran more tunnel tests at Washington and Caltech, and corrected the problem.[41]

Since World War II, with rising numbers of graduates, students at the University of Washington have shown less preponderance on Boeing's design teams. Boeing, which now has its own wind-tunnel test facilities, still uses the University of Washington for low-speed wind-tunnel test work. Washington did much of the low-speed testing on the B-47 (the United States' first sweptwing jet bomber), the B-52, the original "Dash-80" Model 707 jet tanker/transport prototype, and, more recently, the ill-fated Boeing SST. Through its unique informal relationship with the Boeing company, the University of Washington contributed greatly to American multiengine bomber and transport development.[42]

* The 307 accident claimed the life of A. G. von Baumhauer, a Dutch engineer who had formerly been the Dutch representative of The Daniel Guggenheim Fund for the Promotion of Aeronautics.

The Georgia School of Technology had further to go in creation of an aeronautical engineering school and research center than any of the other Guggenheim schools, inasmuch as no previous courses or programs had existed at the southern school. The Guggenheim fund had selected Georgia Tech simply for the purpose of establishing an aeronautical school in the South, and the director of the aeronautics center, Professor Montgomery Knight, thus had the full burden of planning an undergraduate and graduate course program, arranging for research work, and insuring that the school's financial needs were met.[43] It is entirely to his credit, then, that by 1934 the school, which opened in January 1931, had two operating wind tunnels, a small one for instruction and a nine-foot 100 mph tunnel for research, and had graduated over fifty seniors who had become aeronautical engineering majors partway through their undergraduate training.[44]

With an upswing in the aeronautical industry as the 1930s progressed, Georgia Tech found that like other schools it had sufficient student interest in aircraft engineering to permit its aeronautical engineering department to continue.[45] By 1939, the school had granted 121 bachelor degrees in aeronautical engineering. Montgomery Knight and Georgia Tech president M. L. Brittain had no intention, however, of turning the school into a mass degree mill. The two men insisted on highly qualified graduates by admitting no more than eighteen juniors each year to the senior year aeronautical program. The result was a high order of scholarship, with a very favorable student-instructor classroom ratio.[46]

Education was but one aspect of the Guggenheim center at Georgia Tech, for the grant stipulated that the school would be an aeronautical research center with a research function as well. The school had two wind tunnels, and a wood and machine shop for model fabrication and instrument assembly. By 1935 it also had a Pitcairn PCA-2 Autogiro, donated in October 1934, for flight research. From the start, however, Georgia Tech was beset with financial difficulties. Under the original agreement, the city of Atlanta, Fulton County, and the state government were each to contribute $9,000 annually to support the school of aeronautics. Actually, neither the city, county, nor state contributed their share because of the depression and more pressing budget problems.[47] Instead of receiving $27,000 annually for research, the school received only between $2,000 and $3,500 for research purposes, and not until 1935 did the state meet its original commitment.

Even by 1939, Atlanta and Fulton County still could not provide their shares.[48]

It is surprising, therefore, that Georgia Tech completed as much research as it did, including helicopter studies, research on boundary layer aerodynamics, and an examination of plastic as a possible airframe structural material. That it did is due to Knight. Before coming to the school, he had worked for five years at NACA's Langley Memorial Aeronautical Laboratory at Hampton, Virginia. While with NACA, Knight specialized in aviation safety and the safety problems of conventional, fixed-wing airplanes. When he came to Georgia, Knight continued to pursue his interest in aircraft safety. He believed that while such innovations as wing slots and flaps improved fixed-wing aircraft safety, "there was a limit to such built-in safety imposed by the minimum speed requirements which made landing and take-off precision maneuvers." As with Alexander Klemin and other rotary-wing advocates, Montgomery Knight turned to investigating helicopters, with their vertical takeoff and landing capabilities, and Autogiros, with their ability to execute short takeoffs and landings. In this research, he was fortunate to have the three-seat Pitcairn PCA-2 Autogiro. A pilot on the staff of the school flew the Pitcairn Autogiro in a sixty-hour flight research program examining the general aerodynamic and stability characteristics of rotary-wing aircraft in flight.[49]

Knight next turned to developing various helicopter concepts. Aided by other faculty members and graduate students, Knight, by 1938, felt competent enough to undertake the design of a full-scale helicopter. The design he drew up had two radical features. First, the rotor had only one blade, counterbalanced by a counterweight. Knight believed that this single blade configuration offered maximum reliability, simplicity (fewer manufactured parts and lower manufacturing costs), and the elimination of problems when folding a rotor for helicopter storage or ground transport. Second, the helicopter had a "cold jet" rotor which operated in a manner similar to a lawn sprinkler. It rotated from expulsion of a high pressure air jet from the rotor tip. In the Georgia Tech helicopter, an engine-driven axial-flow compressor rotating at 7,000 rpm supplied pressurized air through a duct built into the hollow rotor blade, and expelled it through a jet nozzle built into the blade tip. Knight believed that the cold jet rotor offered several important advantages over the power-driven rotor. First, in a conventional helicopter with a motor-driven rotor, the mechanical drive between the rotor and the engine in the body generated a torque that produced a turning effect. This required installation of either a small tail rotor facing sideways to counter the torque, or else two main rotors rotating in opposite directions. For example, Sikorsky, in his helicopter designs, ultimately followed the first course. The German Focke-Achgelis FW 61 followed the double-rotor method. But in the Georgia Tech design, the absence of a mechanical linkage between the rotor and the engine had the distinct advantage of eliminating the tendency of the helicopter to turn. The lack of heavy drive shafts, gearing, or any free-wheeling or clutch mechanism resulted in lower weight, hence higher performance. Additionally, the air used for propulsion first passed over the piston engine driving the compressor, thus gaining heat as it cooled the engine cylinders. Then the compressor further heated the air. Therefore, as the air passed through the rotor before being expelled from the tip nozzle, it heated the blade slightly, preventing possible ice formation on the rotor blade, a serious potential danger in helicopter operations.[50]

The Georgia Tech cold-jet-rotor-driven helicopter remained a highly interesting paper study, for lack of adequate state funding prevented its further development. Tests in the nine-foot tunnel, and full-scale tests of the engine, compressor, and single rotor did demonstrate the complete feasibility of the design. Knight estimated the craft's top speed at 144 mph. Although the single-blade rotor, like attempts to use single-blade propellers, did not come into widespread use, the jet rotor did eventually see production. As early as 1915, two French researchers had experimented with a helicopter having a cold-jet-driven rotor, but it had crashed during its initial flight trials on March 31, 1915. Even before this, however, in 1842, British scientist W. H. Phillips successfully flew a model helicopter with a jet-driven rotor. During World War II, Friedrich Doblhoff, a German scientist, developed a series of helicopters powered by jet-driven rotors. He passed high pressure air mixed with fuel to the rotor tips, then ignited the mixture in small combustion chambers. This greatly improved the efficiency of the propulsion, and in the postwar years the British Fairey company adapted this hot jet rotor propulsion method for its Jet Gyrodyne and Rotodyne designs, as did a Dutch company, the Nederlandse Helicopter Industrie, during development of the H-3 Kolibrie.*

---

* Remotely related developments included helicopters mounting small rotor tip ramjets, such as the American Hiller Hornet, though these did not prove highly successful. The question of influence and invention also arises. It is, for example, unknown whether Knight knew of the French cold rotor experiments

The cold jet rotor, as pioneered by Georgia Tech, also proved worthwhile. In 1953, the Sud Aviation company of France developed the S.O. 1220 and 1221 Djinn, a two-seat helicopter with a two-bladed rotor driven by a cold jet rotor tip nozzle system drawing air from a Turbomeca Palouste air generator. The little Djinn, highly popular with its pilots, was capable of 78-mph airspeeds combined with great agility, and quickly entered service as a military trainer, spotter, and agricultural crop duster. It thus enjoyed the success that might have gone to Georgia Tech's novel design, had proper support and funding been available.[51]

After his appointment as director of research at the Daniel Guggenheim Airship Institute in Akron, Theodore von Kármán designated Dr. Theodore Troller of Aachen as the deputy director, in charge of the actual design of the institute. Troller, after conferences with representatives of the airship industry, drew up plans for a four-story building with twenty-five thousand square feet of floor space. One of the outstanding features of the research center was a 6½-foot wind tunnel blowing vertically with an airflow of 125 mph. The vertical wind tunnel was the joint idea of von Kármán, Dr. Karl Arnstein of the Goodyear-Zeppelin Corporation, and Dr. Wolfgang Klemperer, another German-trained Goodyear airship engineer. With a vertical wind tunnel having the airstream blowing upwards, researchers could suspend the airship model by a single suspension wire from the stern, the nose pointing downwards in the oncoming airstream, thus eliminating airflow interference present with usual wind-tunnel mounting methods and the consequent effect on drag measurements of the model. This vertical tunnel went into operation in 1932, the same year that Troller began exercising his duties as resident director of the laboratory.[52]

Von Kármán supervised the work of the Airship Institute until October 1934, when Caltech decided not to exercise its option of continuing direction of the institute. At that time, the University of Akron assumed full administrative direction of the institute, with Theodore Troller as director, and von Kármán as a scientific adviser. At about this same time, the institute added two other types of research apparatus, a whirling arm and a water tank. The whirling arm consisted of a long strut; it featured a long arm, with the model

in 1915, or whether Sud knew of Georgia Tech's interest when they developed the *Djinn*. The latter is doubtful.

mounted at the end. As the arm rotated in a circle, the model revolved with it, while researchers made their observations. The whirling arm at Akron had a radius of thirty-two feet from the model under test to the arm rotation point; it could generate rotational speeds at the model of 200 mph. Because the whirling arm offered an opportunity to perform certain tests not easily duplicated in a wind tunnel, such as tests of how an airplane or airship reacts as it passes through a vertical air gust, Troller added a gust tunnel which generated a vertical updraft for a distance of sixteen feet along the path of the model on the whirling arm. Researchers could then measure the changes in air loads, stability, and control experienced by the model as it passed from stable air into the vertical gust.[53]

In addition to the whirling arm with its gust tunnel modification, Troller added a water tank with a straight channel for the water eight feet wide and five feet deep, broken only by an opening for a horizontal jet of water perpendicular to the channel. Using this tank, Troller and the other airship researchers could expose an airship model to conditions simulating atmospheric gustiness. Relying on conventional research techniques, airship researchers would have to build, for example, a twelve-foot-long model of the *Akron* weighing only one pound, yet able to withstand dynamic air pressures of twenty pounds per square foot, a structual impossibility. In the water tunnel, an airship model could operate in conditions approximating the environment of a full-scale dirigible. As the model passed down the straight channel of the tank, the water jet installed perpendicular to the channel produced a gust; as with the whirling arm, researchers could observe and measure the gust loads on the model and its reaction to them.[54]

Besides undertaking aerodynamic research on airship design, the Airship Institute sponsored meetings and examined the operating conditions in which a Zeppelin flew. To continue their gust studies, researchers mounted special instrumentation at the top of a fifty-foot meteorological tower on the institute's roof, measuring temperature, wind direction, and the horizontal and vertical wind force. The navy later issued the Guggenheim Airship Institute a grant to conduct similar research using three towers at the dirigible station at Lakehurst, New Jersey. The institute also had a small laboratory for the study of structures, with x-ray equipment and a strength-testing machine for research on the metals used in aircraft and airship construction. Troller, as director, organized a number of conferences and forums on airship problems, including one notable conference in July 1935, coming on the heels of the *Macon's* crash into the Pacific.[55]

Great success did not come to the Airship Institute, however, as it had to the other Guggenheim-supported centers, though the decade from 1926 through 1937 marked the golden age of the rigid hydrogen- or helium-filled dirigible airship. During this time, the German Luftschiffbau Zeppelin company, under the skillful management of Hugo Eckener, developed the LZ-127 *Graf Zeppelin*. After several proving flights, Eckener took the *Graf Zeppelin* across the Atlantic from Friedrichshafen to Lakehurst, New Jersey, in October 1928, the first commercial flight across the ocean with paying passengers. The next year, in August 1929, Eckener flew the *Graf Zeppelin* around the world. He did not like using hydrogen, and, in the early 1930s, Eckener undertook development of an even larger airship, the LZ-129 *Hindenburg*, designed to use helium, available only in the United States. The Helium Control Act of 1927, however, forbade its export, and Eckener was unable to get it. Accordingly, the LZ-129 made its first flight on March 4, 1936, filled with hydrogen. It soon entered service on passenger runs to North and South America, and many aeronautical journalists predicted it would open a new era in air commerce. Germany was not alone in its advocacy of large airships. Great Britain developed two large hydrogen-filled rigid airships, the R-100 and R-101, and the U.S. Navy flew two advanced helium airships, the ZRS 4, U.S.S. *Akron*, and the ZRS 5, U.S.S. *Macon*, capable of launching and retrieving airplanes while in flight.[56]

Despite this bright promise, the story of the rigid airship is essentially tragic, and the Guggenheim Airship Institute reflected the decline of the dirigible. With the exception of the *Graf Zeppelin* and the R-100, both broken up for scrap, all of the airships mentioned previously met with violent ends. The British R-101, an engineering nightmare and prime example of technical mismanagement, crashed at Beauvais, France, in the midst of a storm on October 5, 1930; its hydrogen ignited, and in the ensuing conflagration, forty-eight people perished, including Sir W. Sefton Brancker, Britain's Director of Civil Aviation. Arguments that the R-101 was virtually an accident waiting to happen made little impression; wreckers broke up its rival, the well-designed and successful R-100, for scrap. On April 4, 1933, the Akron crashed into the Atlantic during a severe storm, killing seventy-three. Nearly two years later, on February 12, 1935, the *Macon* lost its upper vertical fin in air turbulence off Point Sur, California, and, leaking helium, plunged into the Pacific; fortunately, of its eighty-three-man crew, only two died. Then, on May 6, 1937, the LZ-129 *Hindenburg* exploded and burned at Lakehurst; of the ninety-seven passengers and crewmen on board, thirty-five died. The loss of the

Akron, Macon, and *Hindenburg,* combined with memories of the earlier *Shenandoah* disaster, spelled the end of the rigid airship in America. The horrible photographs of the *Hindenburg,* its bow jutting skyward even as a mushroom of flame devoured its stern and midsection, appalled most Americans, who immediately drew the unwarranted conclusion that the airship, by its very nature, was a flaming deathtrap.

After the *Hindenburg* disaster, the Airship Institute at Akron tottered on, providing studies that benefited the later development of nonrigid blimps used during World War II for antisubmarine and convoy escort patrol. The center extensively studied the loss of the *Macon,* using the water tank and vertical wind tunnel, as well as a large scale model of the *Macon* for structural analysis studies. These tests furnished Goodyear with safety data that the company later incorporated in its nonrigid airships.[57] The Airship Institute itself continued in operation until 1949 when the University of Akron discontinued its aeronautical engineering program. The building remained a monument to a bygone age. Though many airship advocates subsequently predicted a lighter-than-air renaissance for such diverse uses as transporting NASA spacecraft rocket boosters, hauling outsize cargo, or conducting environmental research, the rigid airship became simply a nostalgic attraction, despite the continuing cries for revival.

During the first decade of their existence, the Guggenheim schools and research centers contributed to the growth of American and world aviation in many ways. The schools studied heavier-than-air and lighter-than-air flight; fixed wing and rotary wing aircraft; propeller design and rocket engines; airline operation and piloting problems. Their graduates occupied, virtually without exception, the most important positions within the aeronautical community. While less obvious than the fund's grants directly assisting aeronautical science, the Guggenheim education programs had significant impact in bringing America into the air age.

Notes

ACKNOWLEDGMENTS

1. Waldemar A. Nielsen, *The Big Foundations*, p. 3.

CHAPTER 1

1. Alan Morris, *Bloody April* (London: Anchor Press, 1968), pp. 60–61; H. A. Jones, *The War in the Air*, vol. 3, pp. 341–42.
2. Donald R. Whitnah, *Safer Skyways*, pp. 9–10, 15–18.
3. Robert Casari, "A Christmas Fantasy: The Incredible Story of the Bullet," *Air Enthusiast* 5, no. 6 (Dec. 1973): 293–95, 303.
4. Dean C. Smith, *By the Seat of My Pants*, pp. 102–3.
5. Bradley to Hoover, Aug. 24, 1922, "Commerce—Bureau of Aeronautics Legislation, 1921–22," Commerce Papers, Hoover Library.
6. Ibid.
7. Aeronautical Chamber of Commerce of America, Inc., *Aircraft Year Book for 1923*, pp. 102–5; Aeronautical Chamber of Commerce of America, Inc., *Aircraft Year Book for 1924*, pp. 103–7; Don Dwiggins, *The Barnstormers*, p. 67; Robert C. Mikesh and Claudia M. Oakes, *Exhibition Flight*, pp. 1–4, 16–19.
8. Donald R. Whitnah, *Safer Skyways*, pp. 21–23, 26–27; Michael Osborn and Joseph Riggs, "Mr. Mac," pp. 61–77.
9. Dwiggins, *The Barnstormers*, picture of Seitz advertising poster, p. 131.
10. Charles A. Lindbergh, *The Spirit of St. Louis*, pp. 430–32.
11. R. E. G. Davies, *A History of the World's Airlines*, p. 11.
12. Ibid., pp. 11–13.
13. Ibid., pp. 14–15. See also Kenneth Munson, *Airliners Between the Wars, 1919–39*, pp. 26–27, 107–8.
14. Davies, *History of the World's Airlines*, p. 13.
15. Ibid., p. 17.
16. Frank T. Courtney, *The Eighth Sea*, pp. 121–22.
17. Davies, *History of the World's Airlines*, p. 43.
18. Data from Lawson biographical file, Smithsonian Institution National Air and Space Museum (hereinafter referred to as NASM). See also Frank J. Clifford, "Ham & Eggs Lawson," *FAA Aviation News* 9, no. 3 (July 1970): 12–13.

19. *Aircraft* 4, no. 4 (June 1913): 81. Beachey's foolhardy and reckless flying, culminating in his untimely death at San Francisco on March 14, 1915, did nothing to advance the technical development of aviation and contributed greatly to the public's lack of faith in airplanes and air transportation.

20. C. G. Grey, ed., *Jane's All the World's Aircraft*, p. 457a.

21. Clifford, "Ham & Eggs Lawson," pp. 12–13; Robert F. Brooks, "The Airliner and Its Inventor: Alfred W. Lawson"; Robert J. Schadewald, "A Forgotten Pioneer," *Air Line Pilot* 45, no. 11 (Nov. 1976): 11–13.

22. Alfred W. Lawson, *Lawson*, pp. 199–223; *Cleveland Plain Dealer*, Sept. 2, 1919; *The World*, Sept. 14, 1919; *New York Tribune*, Sept. 16, 1919; *Washington Post*, Sept. 20, 1919, and Sept. 22, 1919. See also "Lawson Air Liner Makes History," *Aerial Age Weekly* 10, no. 2 (Sept. 22, 1919).

23. Robert F. Brooks, "The Airliner and Its Inventor," in *Jane's All the World's Aircraft*, ed. C. G. Grey, p. 1836.

24. George Hardie, Jr., "The Airline That Might Have Been," *Historical Messenger of the Milwaukee County Hist. Soc.* 27, no. 1 (March 1971): 13–21.

25. Ibid.

26. Radio address of Postmaster General Walter F. Brown, on Station WRC, Washington, D.C., Sept. 23, 1931; "Post Office: Press Releases of the Postmaster General, 1931," Presidential Papers, Hoover Library; Rudolf Tuma, "Golden Anniversary—Air Mail Service," *Journal of the American Aviation Historical Society* 13, no. 2 (summer 1968): 79; Richard P. Hallion, "Commercial Aviation: From the Benoist Airboat to the SST, 1914–1976."

27. Address by Postmaster General Walter F. Brown before the Cleveland Chamber of Commerce, Cleveland, Ohio, Jan. 14, 1930, "Post Office—Correspondence—Jan.–Feb. 1930," Presidential Papers, Hoover Library. See also Lester D. Gardner, "The Development of Civil Aeronautics in America," Fourth International Congress of Aerial Navigation, Oct. 1, 1927, "Aviation—1927: Oct.–Dec.," Commerce Papers, Hoover Library.

28. Ibid.; Page Shamburger and Joseph Christy, *Command the Horizon*, pp. 103–5. This first transcontinental flight included the saga of mail pilot Jack Knight, who flew from North Platte, Nebraska, to Chicago via Omaha and Iowa City at night in ice and snow without a relief pilot to spell him. See Page Shamburger, *Tracks Across the Sky*, pp. 69–89.

29. Elsbeth E. Freudenthal, *The Aviation Business*, p. 75; Whitnah, *Safer Skyways*, p. 19.

30. Lester D. Gardner, "The Development of Civil Aeronautics in America"; radio address of Postmaster General Walter F. Brown over Station WRC, and his address before the Cleveland Chamber of Commerce.

31. Statement of Postmaster General Harry S. New before the Air Service Inquiry Board, October 13, 1925; "Aviation—President's Aircraft Board, 1925," Commerce Papers, Hoover Library.

32. Smith, *By the Seat of My Pants*, pp. 120–23.

33. Ibid., pp. 135–36.

34. Charles A. Lindbergh, *The Spirit of St. Louis*, pp. 4–9. Paradoxically, as in many airmail accidents where pilots had died, the mail was intact and undamaged. An excellent fictionalized account of flying the airmail, accurately depicting the problems and limitations facing airmail pilots, is Ernest K. Gann's *Blaze of Noon* (New York: H. Holt, 1946). Gann himself was an early commercial pilot.

35. Carroll V. Glines, *The Compact History of the United States Air Force*, pp. 115–16; Shamburger and Christy, *Command the Horizon*, pp. 129–31, 138–39. For an account of the loss of the Shenandoah, see Thomas Hook, *Shenandoah Saga*, pp. 174–88.

36. Herbert Hoover, *The Memoirs of Herbert Hoover*, vol. 2, *The Cabinet*

and the Presidency, 1920–1933, pp. 132–34; Harold Nicolson, *Dwight Morrow*, pp. 280–87; Whitnah, *Safer Skyways*, pp. 20–21.

37. War Department, Bulletin No. 8 (Washington, D.C., Aug. 18, 1926), pp. 4–16. See also memo entitled "Data re Army Air Corps," Aug. 23, 1929, "Aeronautics–Correspondence 1929–July–Sept.," Presidential Papers, Hoover Library. Also Grover Loening, *Takeoff Into Greatness*, pp. 179–80.

38. U.S. Department of Commerce and the American Engineering Council, Joint Committee on Civil Aviation, *Civil Aviation*, pp. 1–20; Freudenthal, *The Aviation Business*, pp. 77–79; Laurence F. Schmeckebier, *The Aeronautics Branch, Department of Commerce*, pp. 1–13.

39. Richard K. Smith, *First Across! The U.S. Navy's Transatlantic Flight of 1919*, pp. 85–189; Ted Wilbur and NC-4 Fiftieth Anniversary Committee, *The First Flight Across the Atlantic, May, 1919*.

40. Louis S. Casey, "The First Nonstop Coast-to-Coast Flight and the Historic T-2 Airplane," *Smithsonian Annals of Flight* 1, no. 1 (1964): 19–31.

41. Carroll V. Glines, *Compact History of the USAF*, pp. 102–4. Eugene M. Emme, *Aeronautics and Astronautics*, p. 18.

42. Maurice Holland and Thomas M. Smith, *Architects of Aviation*, pp. 26–44. Bane died in 1930 from a brain tumor. Frederick Neely, "Conquest of the Stratosphere," *Air Transport* 2, no. 3 (March 1944): 26–34; Douglas J. Ingells, *They Tamed the Sky*, pp. 10–15.

43. Public Law No. 271, 63d Cong., 3d sess., H. Rept. 20975.

44. *Forty-fourth Annual Report of the National Advisory Committee for Aeronautics: Final Report* (Washington, D.C., 1959), p. 10.

45. Ibid., pp. 8–24; George W. Gray, *Frontiers of Flight*, pp. 15, 276.

46. Richard P. Hallion, *Supersonic Flight*, pp. 9–10.

47. J. H. Dellinger, "Directional Radio as an Aid to Safe Flying." See also Rexmond C. Cochrane, *Measures for Progress*, p. 295.

48. Jerome C. Hunsaker, "A Survey of Air Transport and Its Communication Problems" (Bell Telephone Laboratories, July 1, 1927), pp. 6–7, Jerome C. Hunsaker Papers, box 10, Smithsonian NASM archives.

49. Ibid., p. 23.

50. Ibid., pp. 1–3.

51. Ibid., p. 3. See also Joint Committee on Civil Aviation of the U.S. Department of Commerce and the American Engineering Council, *Civil Aviation*, p. 148.

52. Kenneth Munson, *Airliners between the Wars*, pp. 56–57, 141–43; Lesley Forden, *The Ford Air Tours, 1925–1931*, pp. 1–21.

53. Munson, *Airliners Between the Wars*, pp. 54, 138–40; Holland and Smith, *Architects of Aviation*, pp. 127–44; William B. Stout, *So Away I Went.*

54. For example, see R. H. Mayo, "The Promotion of Aeronautics: A Review of the Work of the Daniel Guggenheim Fund" (unpublished manuscript, n.d., hereafter referred to as Mayo Manuscript), pp. 19–45, Papers of the Daniel Guggenheim Fund for the Promotion of Aeronautics (hereafter referred to as DGF Papers), Library of Congress, box 20.

55. Milton Lomask, *Seed Money*, p. 85.

56. G. Edward Pendray, ed., *The Guggenheim Medalists*, p. 11.

CHAPTER 2

1. Harvey O'Connor, *The Guggenheims*, pp. 18–20; Milton Lomask, *Seed Money*, pp. 12–14; Edwin P. Hoyt, *The Guggenheims and the American Dream*, pp. 3–15.

2. O'Connor, *The Guggenheims*, pp. 24–30; Lomask, *Seed Money*, pp. 15–18; Hoyt, *The Guggenheims and the American Dream*, pp. 17–20.

3. O'Connor, *The Guggenheims*, p. 34; Hoyt, *The Guggenheims and the American Dream*, p. 23.

4. O'Connor, *The Guggenheims*, pp. 42–61; also Lomask, *Seed Money*, pp. 20–21.

5. O'Connor, *The Guggenheims*, pp. 60–61.

6. Ibid., pp. 73–75; Lomask, *Seed Money*, p. 24.

7. O'Connor, *The Guggenheims*, pp. 73–81, 85–95; Lomask, *Seed Money*, p. 26; Hoyt, *The Guggenheims and the American Dream*, pp. 72–106.

8. O'Connor, *The Guggenheims*, pp. 109–11, 126–29.

9. Ibid., pp. 102–25; Lomask, *Seed Money*, pp. 26–27; Hoyt, *The Guggenheims and the American Dream*, pp. 113–28. ASARCO's headquarters today are still at the business center of the Guggenheim interests, 120 Broadway, New York City.

10. Tarbell quote from O'Connor, *The Guggenheims*, p. 322; Baruch quote from Lomask, *Seed Money*, pp. 24–25. See also Bernard M. Baruch, *Baruch*, pp. 39–40.

11. Herbert Hoover, *The Memoirs of Herbert Hoover*, vol. 2, *The Cabinet and the Presidency, 1920–1933*, p. 186; see also Eugene Lyons, *Herbert Hoover*, p. 144. His position as secretary of commerce paid $15,000 per year.

12. O'Connor, *The Guggenheims*, pp. 355–56, 414, 424–25; Lomask, *Seed Money*, pp. 27–28; Hoyt, *The Guggenheims and the American Dream*, p. 259.

13. O'Connor, *The Guggenheims*, pp. 424–25; Lomask, *Seed Money*, pp. 121, 291; Hoyt, *The Guggenheims and the American Dream*, pp. 290–91.

14. Lomask, *Seed Money*, pp. 33–36, 79–81; Mayo Manuscript, pp. 14–15, DGF Papers, Library of Congress; data from Harry Guggenheim biographical file, Smithsonian NASM; H. F. Guggenheim biographical sketch, April 20, 1929, "Aeronautics: National Advisory Committee for Aeronautics, 1929:Jan.–April," Presidential Papers, Hoover Library. Finally, see Albert Marquis, ed., *Who's Who in America, 1928–1929* (Chicago: The A. N. Marquis Company, 1928), p. 617.

15. See note 14 above.

16. Ralph D. Paine, *The First Yale Unit*, 1:5–171.

17. Paine, *The First Yale Unit*, 2:187, 214–41; Guggenheim biographical file, NASM; Lomask, *Seed Money*, p. 82; H. F. Guggenheim biographical sketch, April 20, 1929, "Aeronautics: National Advisory Committee for Aeronautics, 1929: Jan.–April," Presidential Papers, Hoover Library.

18. See note 17 above.

19. Lomask, *Seed Money*, p. 62.

20. Maurice Holland, *Architects of Aviation*, p. 85; MIT Alumni War Records Committee, *Technology's War Record* (Cambridge, Mass.: Murray Printing Co., 1920), p. 12.

21. See Robert P. Weeks, *The First Fifty Years*, p. 2; Smithsonian NASM, *The California Institute of Technology: Development* (Washington, D.C., n.d.), pp. 1–2; Shatswell Ober, *The Story of Aeronautics at M.I.T.*, pp. 6–11; W. F. Durand, *Adventures*, pp. 102–5.

22. Frederick K. Teichmann, *Report on the Daniel Guggenheim School of Aeronautics, Covering the Period 1923–1944* (New York University, April 1944), pp. 5–8, in Smithsonian NASM archives. Klemin to Collins, June 29, 1939, DGF Papers, box 21; Holland, *Architects of Aviation*, pp. 89–90; Daniel Guggenheim School of Aeronautics, New York University, *Pioneer Educator in the Air Age*, pp. 11–15.

23. Patrick to Brown, Feb. 26, 1925; Moffet to Brown, n.d.; Henderson to Brown, Feb. 26, 1925; DGF Papers, box 13. See also Klemin to Collins, June 29, 1939.

24. Klemin to Collins, June 29, 1939; G. Edward Pendray, *The Guggenheim Medalists*, pp. 12–13. Sources disagree as to whether or not Harry Guggen-

heim stipulated that his own relatives were not to be contacted. Available correspondence indicates that Brown, Bliss, and Carty assumed the Guggenheims would indeed be contacted, and Brown stated plainly that he was requesting the money from Daniel Guggenheim in his letter to Guggenheim, May 25, 1925, DGF Papers, box 13.

25. Klemin to Collins, June 29, 1939, DGF Papers, box 21.

26. Perishing to Carty, May 14, 1925, DGF Papers, box 13.

27. Brown to Daniel Guggenheim, May 25, 1925, DGF Papers, box 13.

28. Ibid.

29. Klemin to Collins, June 29, 1939. Another version has it that Harry Guggenheim showed the letter to his father preparatory to showing it to his uncles and members of the financial world. The old entrepreneur asked to think about it overnight, and the next day announced his intention of endowing the school on his own. Supporting documentation is stronger for the Klemin version.

30. Guggenheim to Brown, June 12, 1925, quoted in *Technical Notes to the Daniel Guggenheim School of Aeronautics* (New York: New York University, January 1931), p. 2.

31. Klemin to Collins, June 29, 1939; O'Connor, *The Guggenheims*, p. 425.

32. Brown to Wright, Sept. 24, 1925; Wright to Brown, Oct. 1, 1925. Both in Papers of the Wright Brothers, box 43. See also Klemin to Collins, June 29, 1939.

33. O'Connor, *The Guggenheims*, p. 425.

CHAPTER 3

1. Milton Lomask, *Seed Money*, pp. 83–84; Lee to HFG, Jan. 25, 1926; HFG to Lee, Jan. 28, 1926; Wright Papers, box 29.

2. HFG to Wright, Jan. 9, 1926, Wright Papers, box 29.

3. Lomask, *Seed Money*, pp. 84–85; Reginald M. Cleveland, *America Fledges Wings*, pp. 2–3; G. Edward Pendray, ed., *The Guggenheim Medalists*, p. 15.

4. HFG to Wright, Jan. 9, 1926; Daniel Guggenheim to Orville Wright, Jan. 14, 1926; Wright Papers, box 29.

5. Albert Marquis, ed., *Who's Who in America, 1928–29*, pp. 532, 617, 1523, 2282. See also Marvin W. McFarland, ed., *The Papers of Wilbur and Orville Wright*; and Harold Nicolson, *Dwight Morrow*.

6. Marquis, ed., *Who's Who in America, 1928–29*, pp. 686, 1473, 1797, 1819. See also Dorothy M. Livingston, *The Master of Light*; and W. F. Durand, *Adventures*.

7. HFG to Wright, Jan. 9, 1926; Wright to Daniel Guggenheim, Jan. 22, 1926; Wright Papers, box 29.

8. HFG to Hoover, Jan. 11, 1926; telegram, John Marrinan to HFG, Jan. 12, 1926; HFG to Hoover, Jan. 12, 1926; Daniel Guggenheim to Hoover, Jan. 16, 1926. All in "Aviation—Daniel Guggenheim Fund," Commerce Papers, Hoover Library. On Nov. 2, 1929, the Internal Revenue Service ruled The Daniel Guggenheim Fund for the Promotion of Aeronautics a nonprofit tax-exempt organization under the provisions of Section 103 (6) of the Revenue Act of 1928. See David Burnet to Daniel Guggenheim Fund for the Promotion of Aeronautics, Nov. 2, 1929, DGF Papers, box 17.

9. Daniel Guggenheim to Hoover, Jan. 16, 1926. This letter is reprinted in full in Reginald Cleveland's *America Fledges Wings*, pp. 3–7; and also in "Daniel Guggenheim Gives $2,500,000 to Foster Aviation," *Aviation* 20, no. 4 (Jan. 25, 1926): 106–7.

10. Hoover to Secretary of State Frank B. Kellogg, to H. C. MacLean, to C. E. Herring, to H. D. Butler, to C. H. Cunningham, to C. L. Jones, and to

J. F. Hodgson, all Jan. 15, 1926, in "Aviation—Daniel Guggenheim Fund," Commerce Papers, Hoover Library.

11. Guggenheim Brothers news release, "Status of Civil Aviation," Jan. 17, 1926. See also Guggenheim Brothers news release, "Mr. Daniel Guggenheim Establishes Fund for Promotion of Aeronautics," Jan. 17, 1926. Both in bound volume, DGF Papers, box 1.

12. Internal memo, Daniel Guggenheim Fund for the Promotion of Aeronautics, Jan. 19, 1926, bound volume, DGF Papers, box 1.

13. Daniel Guggenheim Fund for the Promotion of Aeronautics, *Tentative Report on Program*, p. 8.

14. Ibid., pp. 5–13.

15. Ibid., pp. 14–15. Leader cables and blind flying research will be fully discussed in Chapter 7.

16. Ibid., pp. 15–18.

17. "The Guggenheim Aviation Fund," *Aviation* 20, no. 4 (Jan. 25, 1926): 105.

18. Hoover to Daniel Guggenheim, Jan. 18, 1926. Department of Commerce news release, Jan. 18, 1926. Both in "Aviation—Daniel Guggenheim Fund," Commerce Papers, Hoover Library.

19. There are numerous letters to this effect in "Aviation—Daniel Guggenheim Fund," Commerce Papers, Hoover Library.

20. DGF news release, Feb. 2, 1926, bound volume, DGF Papers, box 1.

21. Report, HFG to DGF directors, May 1, 1926, "Aviation—Daniel Guggenheim Fund," Commerce Papers, Hoover Library. A less legible copy is in the Wright Papers, box 21.

22. Ibid.

23. Ibid. America did get such a center, when the Guggenheims persuaded Theodore von Kármán, a former Prandtl pupil, to head the Guggenheim school at the California Institute of Technology. See Chapter 4 and Appendix 1.

24. Report, HFG to DGF directors, May 1, 1926, "Aviation—Daniel Guggenheim Fund," Commerce Papers, Hoover Library. A less legible copy is in the Wright Papers, box 21.

25. Ibid.

26. Ibid. See also Oliver Stewart, *Aviation*, pp. 111–27; Ronald Miller and David Sawers, *The Technical Development of Modern Aviation*, pp. 79–86.

27. G. T. R. Hill, "The Tailless Aeroplane." For more information on Hill's tailless designs, see John W. R. Taylor and Maurice F. Allward, *Westland 50*, pp. 60–64. See also Oliver Stewart, *Aviation*, pp. 185–90.

28. Report, HFG to DGF directors, May 1, 1926. Also see R. H. Mayo, "The Promotion of Aeronautics: A Review of the Work of the Daniel Guggenheim Fund" (unpublished manuscript, n.d., hereafter referred to as Mayo Manuscript), pp. 13–14, DGF Papers.

29. Juan de la Cierva and Don Rose, *Wings of Tomorrow*, pp. 44–54, 99–111; Stewart, *Aviation*, pp. 85–110; Frank T. Courtney, *The Eighth Sea*, pp. 161–75. For American Autogiro research, see H. F. Gregory, *Anything a Horse Can Do*, pp. 35–87.

30. Cierva and Rose, *Wings of Tomorrow*, pp. 104, 109–10; Courtney, *The Eighth Sea*, pp. 164–166.

31. Courtney, *The Eighth Sea*, p. 168; *Report*, HFG to DGF directors, May 1, 1926.

32. Mayo Manuscript, pp. 125–42, DGF Papers.

33. Ibid., p. 15.

34. Donald R. Whitnah, *Safer Skyways*, pp. 22–29; Michael Osborn and Joseph Riggs, *"Mr. Mac,"* pp. 56–63.

35. Minutes, Special Meeting of the Board of Directors, DGF, June 2, 1926, Wright Papers, box 21.

36. HFG to directors, DGF, June 2, 1926, Wright Papers, box 21.
37. Ibid.
38. Ibid.
39. Minutes, Special Meeting of the Board of Directors, DGF, June 2, 1926.

CHAPTER 4

1. Guggenheim to Hoover, Jan. 16, 1926, "Aviation—Daniel Guggenheim Fund," Commerce Papers, Hoover Library.
2. Potter to HFG, Feb. 5, 1926, "Aviation—Daniel Guggenheim Fund," Commerce Papers, Hoover Library.
3. Ibid.
4. Letter and enclosure, Millikan to HFG, Dec. 24, 1925, DGF Papers, box 6; Robert A. Millikan, The Autobiography of Robert A. Millikan, pp. 240, 243–44.
5. Millikan to HFG, Dec. 24, 1925, DGF Papers, box 6.
6. Douglas to Millikan, Dec. 24, 1925, DGF Papers, box 6.
7. Enclosure to letter, Millikan to HFG, Dec. 24, 1925, DGF Papers, box 6.
8. Millikan, Autobiography, pp. 243–44. See also his introduction to Cleveland's America Fledges Wings, pp. vi–vii.
9. Shatswell Ober, The Story of Aeronautics at M.I.T., p. 4.
10. Ibid. See also Theodore von Kármán with Lee Edson, The Wind and Beyond, p. 124.
11. Smithsonian NASM, The California Institute of Technology: Development, p. 2; Robert A. Millikan, "A Résumé of the Activities to Date of the Daniel Guggenheim Graduate School of Aeronautics at the California Institute of Technology," transmitted via letter, Millikan to HFG, Dec. 2, 1927, DGF Papers, box 6; "Research Data Destroyed by Fire," Aviation 23, no. 7 (Aug. 15, 1927): 360.
12. HFG to Daniel Guggenheim, Jan. 6, 1926, DGF Papers, box 6.
13. Millikan to HFG, May 14, 1926; Millikan to secretary, DGF, April 25, 1926; telegram, HFG to Millikan, April 28, 1926; DGF Papers, box 6. See also Millikan to HFG, Jan. 29, 1926; and HFG to Millikan, March 4, 1926; Robert A. Millikan Papers, Millikan Library, California Institute of Technology.
14. Millikan to HFG, May 14, 1926, DGF Papers, box 6; HFG to Millikan, May 25, 1926, Millikan Papers, Caltech.
15. Wilbur to DGF trustees, May 13, 1926, DGF Papers, box 15; William F. Durand, Adventures, pp. 55, 102.
16. Minutes, Special Meeting of the Board of Directors, DGF, June 2, 1926.
17. HFG to Wilbur, June 7, 1926, DGF Papers, box 15; HFG to Millikan, June 7, 1926, DGF Papers, box 6. The original of the letter, HFG to Millikan, June 7, 1926, is in the Robert A. Millikan Papers, Caltech.
18. Von Kármán with Edson, The Wind and Beyond.
19. Ibid., pp. 120–21.
20. Millikan to HFG, July 7, 1926, Millikan Papers, Caltech.
21. Millikan to HFG, July 13, 1926, DGF Papers, box 6. Copy in Millikan Papers, Caltech.
22. HFG to Millikan, July 14, 1926, Millikan Papers, Caltech; HFG to Millikan, July 19, 1926, Millikan Papers, Caltech. Copy in DGF Papers, box 6.
23. Telegram, HFG to Durand, July 19, 1926, DGF Papers, box 6; Durand to HFG, DGF Papers, box 15.
24. Wilbur to HFG, July 19, 1926, DGF Papers, box 15.
25. Telegrams, HFG to Millikan and Wilbur, Aug. 7, 1926; DGF Bulletin #1, "Guggenheim Fund Makes Grants to Finance Study and Experiments in Aeronautics," DGF Papers, box 1. Minutes, Special Meeting of Executive Committee, DGF, Aug. 24, 1926, Wright Papers, box 21.

26. HFG to Millikan, Aug. 25, 1926, Millikan Papers, Caltech; copy in DGF Papers, box 6; HFG to Wilbur, Aug. 25, 1926, DGF Papers, box 15.

27. "Guggenheim Fund Endows Universities," *Aviation* 21, no. 6 (Sept. 6, 1926): 402.

28. Von Kármán with Edson, *The Wind and Beyond*, pp. 121–27; news release, DGF, Sept. 22, 1926, DGF Papers, box 1.

29. Von Kármán with Edson, *The Wind and Beyond*, pp. 121–27.

30. Ibid.

31. Ibid., p. 128; Von Kármán lecture schedule, DGF Papers, box 1; R. H. Mayo, "The Promotion of Aeronautics: A Review of the Work of the Daniel Guggenheim Fund" (unpublished manuscript, n.d., hereafter referred to as Mayo Manuscript), pp. 49–50, DGF Papers.

32. "Gift Advances Study of Aviation in University," *The Michigan Alumnus* 33, no. 11 (Dec. 18, 1926): 235–37.

33. Robert P. Weeks, *The First Fifty Years*, pp. 2–6.

34. See Edita Lausanne, *The Romance of Ballooning*, pp. 29, 45, 86–87.

35. Weeks, *The First Fifty Years*, pp. 1–8; Herbert C. Sadler, "Report upon the Course in Aeronautical Engineering: University of Michigan," July 23, 1926, DGF Papers, box 12; "Deaths: Edward A. Stalker," *Astronautics & Aeronautics* 12, no. 2 (Jan. 1974): 78; Wayne W. Parrish, ed., *Who's Who in World Aviation, 1955* (Washington, D.C.: American Aviation Publications, Inc., 1955), p. 314.

36. Cone to Cooley, Dec. 28, 1925; Cone to Stratton, Dec. 28, 1925; DGF Papers, box 12.

37. HFG to Sadler, May 18, 1926, DGF Papers, box 12.

38. Herbert C. Sadler, "Report upon the Course in Aeronautical Engineering: University of Michigan," July 23, 1926; Sadler to HFG, May 25, 1926; DGF Papers, box 12.

39. Minutes, Special Meeting of the Board of Directors, DGF, Oct. 26, 1926, Wright Papers, box 21.

40. HFG to Mortimer Cooley, Oct. 27, 1926; HFG to C. C. Little, Oct. 27, 1926; DGF Papers, box 12.

41. News release, DGF, Dec. 2, 1926, DGF Papers, box 1; "Guggenheim Fund Assists Michigan University," *Aviation* 21, no. 25 (Dec. 20, 1926): 1041–42.

In March 1927, Michigan selected Lawrence V. Kerber, a Michigan graduate who was in charge of the aerodynamic section at the Air Corps research center at McCook Field, for the Guggenheim Chair. In August 1928, with the approval of the Guggenheim fund, Kerber took a leave of absence to spend a year with the Aeronautics Branch, Department of Commerce. Kerber enjoyed his work with the Commerce Department so much that he resigned the Guggenheim Chair in July 1929; Felix Pawlowski subsequently became the new Guggenheim Professor at Michigan. See Herbert Sadler to HFG, March 10, 1927; Clarence M. Young (director of aeronautics, Department of Commerce) to HFG, Aug. 20, 1928; HFG to Young, Aug. 21 and Aug. 28, 1928; Sadler to HFG, Aug. 20, 1928, and July 8, 1929; HFG to Sadler, Aug. 28, 1928; DGF Papers, box 12. See also Weeks, *The First Fifty Years*, pp. 16–17.

42. Daniel Guggenheim to HFG, Dec. 16, 1926, DGF Papers, box 19; Harry F. Guggenheim, "The First Year of the Guggenheim Fund," *Aviation* 22, no. 1 (Jan. 3, 1927): 18.

43. Minutes, Annual Meeting of the DGF, Dec. 7, 1926, Wright Papers, box 21.

44. News release, DGF, Jan. 16, 1927, DGF Papers, box 1.

45. Cone to Stratton, Dec. 28, 1926; Stratton to Cone, Feb. 1, 1926; HFG to Stratton, May 18, 1926; DGF Papers, box 11.

46. Report, Capt. Washington I. Chambers, USN, to Navy Bureau of Navigation, March 13, 1913; and Maclaurin minority report; both in Washington Irving Chambers Papers, Library of Congress, box 7. The Taft Commission was one of the first important steps on the road to creation of NACA.

47. Richard P. Hallion, *Supersonic Flight*, p. 8.

48. Jerome Hunsaker, "Europe's Facilities for Aeronautical Research," *Flying* 3, no. 3 (April 1914): 75, 93; and no. 4 (May 1914): 108–9; Ober, *The Story of Aeronautics at M.I.T.*, pp. 6–8.

49. Ober, *The Story of Aeronautics at M.I.T.*, pp. 9–18; T. P. Wright, "Edward Pearson Warner, 1894–1958: An Appreciation," *Journal of the Royal Aeronautical Society* 62, no. 574 (Oct. 1958): 691–703; MIT Alumni War Records Committee, *Technology's War Record*, p. 12.

50. Taylor to HFG, April 24, 1926; HFG to Taylor, May 18, 1926; DGF Papers, box 11.

51. Robert Schlaifer and S. D. Heron, *Development of Aircraft Engines and Fuels*, pp. 440–93.

52. Stratton to HFG, May 25, 1926; Stratton to Cone, June 12, 1926; DGF Papers, box 11. MIT graduates included Edwin E. Aldrin, Virginius E. Clark, Donald W. Douglas, Walter Diehl, Leroy R. Grumman, and Maurice Holland.

53. Stratton to HFG, May 25, 1926, DGF Papers, box 11.

54. Stratton to Cone, June 12, 1926, DGF Papers, box 11.

55. Edward P. Warner to Cone, July 10, 1926; Cone to E. P. Warner, July 16, 1926; DGF Papers, box 11.

56. Everett Morse to Cone, Sept. 23, 1926; Cone to Morse, Sept. 25, 1926; DGF Papers, box 11.

57. HFG to Stratton, Oct. 27, 1926; Stratton to HFG, Oct. 22, 1926; DGF Papers, box 11; quote from Minutes, Special Meeting of the Board of Directors, DGF, Oct. 26, 1926.

58. Warner to HFG, Dec. 4, 1926; HFG to Warner, Dec. 7, 1926; HFG to Stratton, Jan. 13, 1927; Cone to Stratton, Jan. 19, 1927; Stratton to Cone, Jan. 26, 1927; all in DGF Papers, box 11. News release, DGF, Jan. 16, 1927, DGF Papers, box 1.

59. Minutes, Annual Meeting of the Board of Directors, DGF, June 16, 1927, Wright Papers, box 21. At this meeting, the trustees approved the expenditure of the additional $30,000.

60. Stratton to HFG, May 14, 1928; telegram, HFG to Stratton, May 29, 1928; *Boston Evening Transcript*, June 4 and 5, 1928, DGF Papers, box 11.

61. Jerome C. Hunsaker to HFG, Jan. 28, 1939, DGF Papers, box 21; Cleveland, *America Fledges Wings*, pp. 152–53.

62. Brownell to HFG, Feb. 16, 1926; HFG to Brownell, May 12, 1926; Roberts to HFG, May 21, 1926; Suzzallo to HFG, May 29, 1926; HFG to Roberts, June 7, 1926; DGF Papers, box 16.

63. Harold Mansfield, *Vision*, pp. 5–15; "Exhibits Giving Information about the University of Washington," Sept. 1927, DGF Papers, box 16; "A Retrospect on the Development of the Guggenheim School of Aeronautics at the University of Washington," Feb. 1939, DGF Papers, box 21.

64. Magnusson to HFG, Sept. 13, 1927; Spencer to HFG, n.d. (but Sept. 1927); HFG to Spencer, Sept. 26, 1927; DGF Papers, box 16.

65. Boeing to HFG, Oct. 5, 1927; HFG to Boeing, Oct. 14, 1927; DGF Papers, box 16. HFG gave Boeing the same reply he had given to Spencer and Magnusson.

66. J. P. Olding to M. Lyle Spencer, Nov. 30, 1927; Spencer to HFG, Dec. 22, 1927; HFG to Spencer, Jan. 3, 1928; DGF Papers, box 16.

67. HFG to Spencer, May 8, 1928; Spencer to HFG, May 11, 1928; HFG to Spencer, June 19, 1928; DGF Papers, box 16; news release, DGF, June 20,

1928, DGF Papers, box 1; Minutes, Annual Meeting of the Board of Directors, DGF, June 15, 1928, Wright Papers, box 21; *Seattle Interbay Tribune*, July 26, 1928; and *Seattle Post Intelligencer*, Aug. 10, 1928.

68. Spencer to HFG, Jan. 9, 1928; telegram, Spencer to HFG, Jan. 10, 1929; telegram, HFG to Spencer, Jan. 10, 1929; HFG to Spencer, Jan. 14, 1929; telegram, Spencer to HFG, Feb. 20, 1929; Land to Richardson, Nov. 9, 1928; Spencer to HFG, Jan. 23, 1929; HFG to Spencer, Feb. 1, 1929; HFG to Spencer, June 4, 1929; Spencer to HFG, June 22, 1929; Spencer to HFG, June 27, 1929; HFG to Spencer, July 5, 1929; DGF Papers, box 16. Eastwood to Land, March 5, 1930; Land to Eastwood, March 14, 1930; DGF Papers, box 3. See also "A Retrospect on the Development of the Guggenheim School of Aeronautics at the University of Washington."

69. Minutes, Special Meeting of the Board of Directors, DGF, Oct. 1, 1929, Wright Papers, box 21.

70. Minutes, Annual Meeting of the Board of Directors, DGF, Jan. 6, 1930, Wright Papers, box 21. News release, DGF, Oct. 29, 1929.

71. "The President Picks an Envoy," *Aviation* 27, no. 13 (Sept. 28, 1929): 649.

72. Land to James H. Kirkland, Jan. 8, 1930; Land to Edgar O. Lovett, Jan. 8, 1930; Land to M. L. Brittain, Jan. 8, 1930; telegram, Lovett to Land, Jan. 11, 1930; Brittain to Land, Jan. 11, 1930; W. G. Waldo to Land, Jan. 13, 1930; Lovett to Land, Jan. 16, 1930; George H. Denny to Land, Jan. 31, 1930; John Tigert to Land, Jan. 31, 1930; Julian A. Burruss to Land, Feb. 6, 1930; DGF Papers, box 3.

73. Durand to Land, Feb. 19, 1930; H. I. Cone to Land, Feb. 21, 1930; Millikan to Land, Feb. 27, 1930; telegram, Millikan to Land, March 1, 1930; telegram, Durand to Land, March 1, 1930; telegram, Land to Millikan, March 3, 1930; telegram, Land to HFG (in Cuba), March 4, 1930; DGF Papers, box 3.

74. Land to Brittain, March 3, 1930, DGF Papers, box 3. It is also reprinted in M. L. Brittain, *The Story of Georgia Tech*, pp. 158–59.

75. Brittain, *The Story of Georgia Tech*, pp. 156–59; Brittain to Land, March 5, 1930; L. W. Robert, Jr., to Land, March 5, 1930; Land to Brittain, March 14, 1930; DGF Papers, box 3. See also Montgomery Knight, *Daniel Guggenheim School of Aeronautics, Georgia School of Technology* (Atlanta, June 6, 1939), p. 1, in DGF Papers, box 21.

76. Hugh Allen, *The House of Goodyear*, pp. 269–99; Robinson, *Giants in the Sky*, pp. 221–23.

77. Zook to HFG, March 3, 1926; F. A. Collins to Zook, March 6, 1926; Zook to HFG, Oct. 25, 1926; HFG to Zook, Oct. 27, 1926; telegram, Zook to HFG, Nov. 5, 1926; Zook to DGF, Nov. 9, 1926; DGF Papers, box 4.

78. Letter and transmittal, Zook to HFG, Nov. 9, 1926; HFG to Zook, Nov. 12, 1926; Zook to HFG, Nov. 15, 1926; DGF Papers, box 4.

79. Moffett to HFG, Feb. 3, 1927, DGF Papers, box 4.

80. Memo, "Conversation held with President Zook of the University of Akron," Feb. 9, 1927, DGF Papers, box 4.

81. Zook to HFG, May 12, 1927, DGF Papers, box 4.

82. Minutes of meeting held at the University Club, Akron, Ohio, May 29, 1927. Transmitted with letter, Zook to HFG, June 18, 1927, DGF Papers, box 4.

83. Hunsaker to Emory S. Land, Feb. 13, 1929, DGF Papers, box 4.

84. For example, see letters, R. B. Moore to HFG, March 25 and 30, 1929, DGF Papers, box 4.

85. Note, Land to HFG, Feb. 15, 1929, attached to Hunsaker letter, Feb. 13, 1929, DGF Papers, box 4.

86. Copies of these questionnaires are in the DGF Papers, box 4.

87. Copies of the replies are in the DGF Papers, box 4. See also Robert A. Millikan to Theodore von Kármán, July 6, 1929, DGF Papers, box 4.

88. Millikan to von Kármán, July 6, 1929. See also Emory S. Land, memo on Airship Institute Conference, June 14, 1929, DGF Papers, box 4.

89. HFG to Millikan, Oct. 22, 1929; HFG to von Kármán, Aug. 8, 1929; von Kármán to HFG, Oct. 9, 1929; DGF Papers, box 4.

90. Quote is from Minutes, Special Meeting of the Board of Directors, DGF, Oct. 1, 1929, Wright Papers, box 21; Zook to HFG, July 2, 1929; Zook to HFG, Aug. 31, 1929; DGF Papers, box 4.

91. News release, DGF, Oct. 29, 1929, DGF Papers, box 2.

92. Letters, HFG to Zook and Millikan, Nov. 22, 1929; DGF Papers, box 4.

93. Minutes, Special Meeting of the Board of Directors, DGF, Oct. 1, 1929.

94. Von Kármán and Edson, *The Wind and Beyond*, pp. 160–61; Theodore Troller, "The Daniel Guggenheim Airship Institute," *Journal of Applied Physics* 9, no. 1 (January 1938): 24–29; Theodore Troller, "The Daniel Guggenheim Airship Institute," Feb. 21, 1939, DGF Papers, box 21.

95. This includes an additional appropriation of $45,000 granted to Caltech in June 1928 to cover a building cost overrun.

96. News release, DGF, Dec. 8, 1926; DGF Papers, box 1. This tabulates the results of a Guggenheim-sponsored nationwide survey of aeronautical education at universities and colleges.

CHAPTER 5

1. William F. Durand, *Aeronautic Education*, p. 10.

2. Ibid., pp. 6–9.

3. Minutes, Annual Meeting of the Board of Directors, DGF, Dec. 6, 1927, Wright Papers, box 21.

4. Withers to HFG, Dec. 15, 1927, and HFG to foreign representatives of the fund (Mayo, Baumhauer, Dollfus, Marieni, Madelung), Dec. 27, 1927; DGF Papers, box 7.

5. News release, DGF, Jan. 27, 1928, DGF Papers, box 1.

6. Meeting report, Executive Group Conference, Committee on Elementary and Secondary Education, Feb. 1, 1928; E. E. Aldrin to Walter S. Young, n.d. Minutes of the executive group, March 28, April 11, April 25, and May 9, 1928; Roland H. Spaulding, *Dictionary of Aeronautical Terms and Phrases*, DGF Papers, box 7.

7. Minutes of the executive group, May 9, 1928, DGF papers, box 7; R. H. Mayo, "The Promotion of Aeronautics: A Review of the Work of the Daniel Guggenheim Fund" (unpublished manuscript, n.d., hereafter referred to as Mayo Manuscript), pp. 145–48, DGF Papers.

8. Daniel Guggenheim Committee on Elementary and Secondary Aeronautical Education, *Report of Activities, Nov. 1, 1928–Sept. 1, 1929*, DGF Papers, box 7. Totals do not always tally exactly because some schools had combined programs.

9. Ibid.

10. Minutes, Special Meeting of the Executive Committee, DGF, July 22, 1929, Wright Papers, box 21; news release, DGF, May 24, 1929; NYU Summer School brochure, July 1–August 9, 1929; DGF Papers, box 2. Daniel Guggenheim Committee on Elementary and Secondary Aeronautical Education, *Report of Activities, Nov. 1, 1928–Sept. 1, 1929*, DGF Papers, box 7. See also Mayo Manuscript, pp. 149–50, DGF Papers.

11. "Deaths: Roland H. Spaulding," *Astronautics & Aeronautics* 12, no. 2 (Feb. 1974): 78.

12. Harold E. Mehrens, *Aviation in School and Community*, p. 2.

13. Minutes, Special Meeting of the Board of Directors, DGF, June 15, 1928, Wright Papers, box 21.

14. Ibid. News release, DGF, June 20, 1928, DGF Papers, box 1; Mayo Manuscript, pp. 166–67, DGF Papers.

15. Fred D. Fagg biographical file, Smithsonian NASM; Wigmore to Land, June 28, 1929, DGF Papers, box 4. See also De Forest Billyou, Air Law, pp. 1–3.

16. McCormick to Wigmore, June 11, 1929, DGF Papers, box 4.

17. Chicago Tribune, June 12, 1929.

18. Wigmore to Land, June 28, 1929.

19. Landis to Land, July 1, 1929, DGF Papers, box 4.

20. Breckinridge to Land, July 3, 1929, and Land to Breckinridge, July 2, 1929; DGF Papers, box 4.

21. Land to Landis, July 9, 1929, DGF Papers, box 4.

22. Land to Wigmore, July 6, 1929, DGF Papers, box 4.

23. Wigmore to HFG, July 10, 1929, DGF Papers, box 4.

24. Minutes, Special Meeting of the Executive Committee, DGF, July 22, 1929, Wright Papers, box 21.

25. HFG to Wigmore, July 23, 1929, DGF Papers, box 4.

26. Wigmore to HFG, July 27, and HFG to Wigmore, Aug. 1, 1929; DGF Papers, box 4.

27. Wigmore to HFG, Sept. 5, and Miller to Wigmore, Sept. 12, 1929; DGF Papers, box 4.

28. "Air Law Institute," Northwestern University Bulletin, 30, no. 11 (Nov. 11, 1929). Copy in DGF Papers, box 4.

29. Fred D. Fagg biographical file, Smithsonian NASM; New York Times, March 2, 1937; New York Herald Tribune, Oct. 5, 1937; Donald R. Whitnah, Safer Skyways, p. 87.

30. HFG to Pawlowski, May 31, 1928, DFG Papers, box 16.

31. Ibid. See also letter, Pawlowski to HFG, June 8, 1928, DGF Papers, box 16.

32. Witoszynski to John Jay Ide, June 22, 1928; Lewis to Land, Aug. 25, 1928; Land to Lewis, Sept. 5, 1928; Miller to Pawlowski, July 25, 1928; Pawlowski to Miller, Aug. 24, 1928; HFG to Pawlowski, Aug. 10 and Aug. 14, 1928; Land to Bankers Trust Company, New York, Aug. 29, 1928; DGF Papers, box 16.

33. Lewis to Land, Oct. 15, 1929, and Nov. 21, 1929, DGF Papers, box 16.

34. Pawlowski to HFG, April 25, May 13, and May 21, 1929; HFG to Pawlowski, April 30 and May 17, 1929; Land to Thompson, June 26, 1929; DGF Papers, box 16.

35. Paul E. Hemke obituary, Washington Star-News, May 29, 1974.

36. Hemke to Land, Aug. 9, Nov. 23, Dec. 26, 1928; Robinson to Land, Sept. 7, and Land to Robinson, Sept. 10, 1928; HFG to Hemke, Dec. 28, 1928; Jones to Hemke, Jan. 21, 1929; DGF Papers, box 10.

37. Land to Hemke, March 28, April 30, Oct. 23, 1929; Hemke to Land, April 25, Oct. 13, 1929; DGF Papers, box 10.

38. Hemke obituary, Washington Star-News, May 29, 1974. Hemke died May 25, 1974.

39. DGF, "Aerial Service," Bulletin #3, Jan. 7, 1927, DGF Papers, box 1.

40. Mitchell to HFG, March 24 and May 17, 1926; HFG to Mitchell, May 12, 1926; DGF Papers, box 15.

41. HFG to Mitchell, July 28, 1927, DGF Papers, box 15.

42. Marshall to HFG, Oct. 9, 1928; Land to Richardson, Nov. 23, 1928; Mitchell to HFG, Dec. 14, 1928, including enclosed report; HFG to Mitchell, n.d., and Dec. 20, 1928; DGF Papers, box 15.

43. Telegram, HFG to Flint, May 31, 1929; Sarason to Mitchell, Feb. 28, 1929; Land to Mitchell, March 26, 1929; Mitchell to Land, April 24, 1929; HFG to Mitchell, May 24, 1929; Flint to HFG, May 27, 1929; HFG to Flint, June 4, 1929; DGF Papers, box 15. See also Minutes, Special Meeting of the

Executive Committee, DGF, May 31, 1929, Wright Papers, box 21; *New York Sun*, June 11, 1929.

44. HFG to Flint, Oct. 18, 1929, DGF Papers, box 15; Minutes, Special Meeting of the Board of Directors, DGF, Oct. 1, 1929, Wright Papers, box 21.

45. Land to Putnam, Jan. 21, 1929, DGF Papers, box. 10.

46. Putnam to Land, Jan. 22, 1929, DGF Papers, box 10.

47. Ibid.

48. Telegram, HFG to Land, Jan. 29, 1929, DGF Papers, box 10.

49. HFG to Putnam, Feb. 1, 1929, DGF Papers, box 10.

50. Corbin to Abbot, Feb. 27, and Putnam to Land, Feb. 29, 1929; DGF Papers, box 10.

51. Telegram, Maggs Brothers to Putnam, Aug. 14, 1929. Land to Putnam, March 7, 1929; Putnam to Land, March 9, Sept. 21, 1929; Putnam to HFG, July 10, 12, 27, Aug. 22, Sept. 3, Oct. 2, 8, 1929; HFG to Putnam, July 11, Aug. 2, Oct. 1, 1929; Putnam to Durand, July 27, and Durand to Putnam, Aug. 20, 1929; DGF Papers, box 10. See also Minutes, Special Meeting of the Board of Directors, DGF, Oct. 1, 1929, Wright Papers, box 21.

52. HFG to Putnam, Oct. 29, 1929, DGF Papers, box 10.

53. Mellon to HFG, Nov. 6, 1929, DGF Papers, box 10. News release, DGF, Oct. 29, 1929, DGF Papers, box 2.

54. *Washington Post*, Dec. 27, 1929; news release, DGF, Dec. 31, 1929, DGF Papers, box 2; Land to Putnam, Dec. 9, 24, and Putnam to Land, Dec. 26, 1929; DGF Papers, box 10.

55. Albert F. Zahm, "The Division of Aeronautics of the Library of Congress," document 120, in *Aeronautical Papers: 1885–1945*, 2:916–17. Hereafter cited as *Zahm Papers*.

56. Ibid.

57. Ibid. Also, Albert F. Zahm, "Report of the Division of Aeronautics, Library of Congress, 1933," document 127, *Zahm Papers*, 2:949–50.

58. Mayo Manuscript, pp. 132–33.

59. Ibid., pp. 134–37. See also various letters in "*Aero Club von Deutschland*, 1928–29" folder, DGF Papers, box 4. The bibliographical guides are published in Aero Club von Deutschland, *Mitteilungen des von Tschudi-Archiv beim Aero Club von Deutschland gegrundet durch Stiftung des Daniel Guggenheim Fund*.

60. Pritchard to HFG, Oct. 25, 1927, DGF Papers, box 15; Mayo Manuscript, pp. 121–24, DGF Papers.

61. Mayo Manuscript, pp. 121–24, DGF Papers. See also Royal Aeronautical Society, *The Royal Aeronautical Society, 1866–1966: A Short History*.

62. Pritchard to Mayo, June 15, 1928, DGF Papers, box 15.

63. HFG to Pritchard, Jan. 4 and Dec. 18, 1928, and HFG to Mayo, Oct. 29, 1929; DGF Papers, box 15.

64. A. Crocco, "Report on the Work of the A.I.D.A. during 1928 with the Financial Assistance of the Guggenheim Fund for the Promotion of Aeronautics," Feb. 1929; Durand to HFG, Oct. 12, 1927; HFG to Marieni, Nov. 3, and Marieni to HFG, Nov. 19, 1927; HFG to Raffaele Giacomelli, Jan. 28, 1929; Land to Grocco, March 11, 1929; Grocco to HFG, April 4, 1929; DGF Papers, box 5. Mayo Manuscript, pp. 137–40, DGF Papers.

65. Figure based on DGF statement of appropriations and expenditures, Jan. 27, 1930, plus New York University grant; DGF Papers, box 18.

CHAPTER 6

1. R. E. G. Davies, *A History of the World's Airplanes*, pp. 44–45.

2. Ibid. Earl D. Osborn, "The Western Air Express," *Aviation* 23, no. 9

(Aug. 29, 1927): 474–75. Robert J. Serling, *The Only Way to Fly: The Story of Western Airlines, America's Senior Air Carrier,* pp. 14–55.

3. HFG to Reginald M. Cleveland, Jan. 12, 1940, DGF Papers, box 21.

4. Minutes, Annual Meeting of the Board of Directors, DGF, June 16, 1927, Wright Papers, box 21. See also "Guggenheim to Finance Passenger Service," *Aviation* 23, no. 3 (July 18, 1927): 151. "The Air Corps Model Airway," news release of the Department of Commerce, n.d.

5. HFG to Cleveland, Jan. 12, 1940.

6. Minutes, Annual Meeting of the Board of Directors, DGF, June 16, 1927, Wright Papers, box 21.

7. Ernest K. Gann, "The Tin Goose," *Flying* 95, no. 2 (Aug. 1974): 93, 96–101.

8. C. C. Moseley to HFG, Sept. 29, 1927, DGF Papers, box 6. Taylor quote from C. Fayette Taylor, *Aircraft Propulsion,* p. 46.

9. Moseley to HFG, Sept. 29, 1927, DGF Papers, box 6.

10. Conversation with Charles A. Lindbergh, July 22, 1974. Memorandum, HFG to Cleveland, Nov. 5, 1941, DGF Papers, box 21.

11. Moseley to HFG, Sept. 29, 1927, DGF Papers, box 6; also, Kenneth Munson, *Airliners Between the Wars, 1919–39,* p. 143.

12. DGF news release and WAE news release, Oct. 4, 1927, DGF Papers, box 1.

13. Various papers in "Western Air Express: Equipment Loan Documents 1927–1929" folder, DGF Papers, box 16. See especially Cone to Fokker, Dec. 6, 1927, and "Atlantic Aircraft Corporation F-10 Progress Report," Feb. 15, 1928.

14. Flight test reports, Fokker F-10 #1, March 21 and 23, 1928; Hanshue to DGF, April 24, 1928; flight test report, Fokker F-10 #2, April 27, 1928; King to DGF, May 9, 1928; DGF Papers, box 16. Munson, *Airliners Between the Wars, 1919–39,* p. 143. See also Robert J. Serling, *The Only Way to Fly,* pp. 68–76.

15. Donald R. Whitnah, *A History of the United States Weather Bureau,* pp. 169–80.

16. U.S. Department of Agriculture, "Weather Bureau to Aid Commercial Aviation," July 9, 1926; "Commerce: Bureau of Aeronautics Legislation 1921–22," Commerce Papers, Hoover Library.

17. Moseley to chief, U.S. Weather Bureau, Feb. 10, 1926, "Aviation: 1926," Commerce Papers, Hoover Library.

18. Questionnaire, DGF, Aug. 30, 1927, and news release, DGF, Sept. 15, 1927, DGF Papers, box 1. See also Jerome C. Hunsaker, "Memorandum for File," Sept. 19, 1927, Hunsaker Papers, box 6.

19. Patrick Hughes, *A Century of Weather Service,* p. 69; Milton Lomask, *Seed Money,* pp. 109–10; Whitnah, *A History of the United States Weather Bureau,* pp. 160–61.

20. Data from Hunsaker biographical file, NASA Historical Office.

21. Rossby to Hunsaker, Sept. 8, 1927; Jerome C. Hunsaker, "Memorandum for File," Sept. 19, 1927; Hunsaker Papers, box 6.

22. Jerome C. Hunsaker, "Memorandum for File," Oct. 27, 1927, Hunsaker Papers, box 6. Report, Rossby to Hunsaker, Nov. 1, 1927; Hunsaker, "Aeronautical Meteorology Telephone Communication Systems: Modified Plan," American Telephone and Telegraph Co., March 21, 1928; Hunsaker Papers, box 10.

23. Hunsaker to J. C. Bates, Feb. 1, 1928, and report "San Francisco-Los Angeles Air Passenger Service: Telephone Facilities to Weather Stations," n.d., Hunsaker Papers, box 10. See also Rossby, "Outline for Meteorological Service for the Airways Between Los Angeles and San Francisco," Feb. 1, 1928; draft

report, Edward H. Bowie, "Weather and the Airplane," Aug. 1929; DGF Papers, boxes 8 and 9.

24. Telegram, HFG to MacCracken, Davison, and Warner, March 9, 1928; Rossby to HFG, May 14, and Hunsaker to HFG, May 24, 1928; Rossby, "Outline for Meteorological Service," Feb. 1, 1928; DGF Papers, box 8. See also "Appropriations and Expenditures," Jan. 27, 1930, DGF Papers, box 18.

25. Rossby, "Outline for Meteorological Service," Feb. 1, 1928; Bowie, "Weather and the Airplane," pp. 1–11.

26. Rossby, "Instructions for Observers of the Experimental Meteorological Service," n.d., DGF Papers, box 6.

27. DGF, The Second Report of the DGF, 1928, pp. 24–27. See also various letters concerning airline in "Experimental Meteorological Service, Part I: California, 1928" folder, DGF Papers, box 8.

28. Reichelderfer to Cone, May 2, and Taylor to Brant, June 6, 1928; DGF Papers, box 8. Also report, Reichelderfer to Land, Aug. 25, 1928, DGF Papers, box 9.

29. Grant quote from Bowie, "Weather and the Airplane," p. 17. See also Rossby to DGF, May 29, and Morehouse to Moseley, July 31, 1928; DGF Papers, box 8.

30. Bowie to Davis, Feb. 2, 1929, DGF Papers, box 9.

31. Whitnah, A History of the United States Weather Bureau, p. 182.

32. For example, see Rossby to HFG, June 28, 1928, DGF Papers, box 8.

33. Hegardt to HFG, Aug. 23, 1928; DGF Papers, box 8. For Rossby transfer, see Bowie to HFG, Aug. 21, 1928; DGF Papers, box 9.

34. Johnson to U.S. Weather Bureau, San Francisco, Feb. 14, 1929; Bowie to Miller, Dec. 15, 1928; HFG to Bowie, Dec. 28, 1928; Rossby to HFG, Dec. 23, 1928; DGF Papers, box 9.

35. Bowie, "Weather and the Airplane," pp. 13–14. See also data in Hunsaker biographical file, NASA Historical Office, and Whitnah, A History of the United States Weather Bureau, pp. 184–85.

36. Memo of Understanding, DGF and Weather Bureau of the Department of Agriculture, Sept. 11, 1928; DGF Papers, box 9. HFG to MacCracken, Sept. 18 and Oct. 31, 1928; Fisher to Senator Hiram Johnson and eleven California representatives, Nov. 20, 1928; Fisher to MacCracken, Nov. 20, 1928; Bowie to HFG, Nov. 22, 1928; DGF Papers, box 8. MacCracken to HFG, Jan. 8, 1929; DGF Papers, box 9.

37. Bowie, "Weather and the Airplane," pp. 19–21.

38. Bowie, "Weather and the Airplane," pp. 19–21; news release, DGF, July 25, 1929, DGF Papers, box 2; Rossby to HFG, Jan. 4, 1929, DGF Papers, box 9. Much of this rapid growth was, of course, due to the Lindbergh impact. See also Grover Loening, Takeoff into Greatness, p. 186, and Robert J. Serling, The Only Way to Fly, p. 76.

CHAPTER 7

1. Charles A. Lindbergh, The Spirit of St. Louis, p. 325. Harry F. Guggenheim, The Seven Skies, p. 151.

2. Donald R. Whitnah, Safer Skyways, pp. 97–99, 101–4.

3. Charles H. Colvin to James E. Fechet, Aug. 19, 1921, record group 18, AAF Central Decimal Files, box 909, file 413.6 "A," National Archives.

4. Lindbergh, The Spirit of St. Louis, p. 326.

5. Malcolm W. Cagle, The Naval Aviation Guide, p. 253.

6. Theodore C. Lonnquest, "Instrument Navigation and Fog Flying," and William C. Ocker, "Memorandum," in papers presented at the First National

Aeronautical Safety Conference, Oct. 4–5, 1928, New York City; J. H. Doolittle, "Early Blind Flying: An Historical Review of Early Experiments in Instrument Flying," Third Lester Gardner Lecture, Massachusetts Institute of Technology, April 28, 1961, reprinted in *Aerospace Engineering* 20, no. 10 (Oct. 1961): 14–15, 56–68. See also William C. Ocker and Carl J. Crane, *Blind Flight in Theory and Practice*, pp. 13–14, 16.

7. See Monte Duane Wright, *Most Probable Position*, pp. 123–25; Rexmond C. Cochrane, *Measures for Progress*, p. 295; U.S. Department of Commerce, Aeronautics Branch, "Aircraft Radio Development," *Air Commerce Bulletin* 1, no. 4 (Aug. 15, 1929): 5–6.

8. U.S. Department of Commerce, Aeronautics Branch, "Visual Radio Direction Beacon to be Installed at Bellefonte, Pa., for Practical Service Trials," *Air Commerce Bulletin* 1, no. 22 (May 15, 1930): 3–8, esp. 5; Director of Aeronautics, *Annual Report to the Secretary of Commerce* (Washington, D.C., 1927), p. 13.

9. U.S. Department of Commerce, Aeronautics Branch, "Visual Radio Direction Beacon to be Installed at Bellefonte, Pa., for Practical Service Trials." See also J. H. Dellinger, "Directional Radio as an Aid to Safe Flying."

10. Director of Aeronautics, *Annual Report to the Secretary of Commerce* (Washington, D.C., 1927), pp. 13–14; *Annual Report to the Secretary of Commerce* (Washington, D.C., 1928), p. 29.

11. HFG to directors, DGF, June 2, 1926, Wright Papers, box 21; Minutes, Special Meeting of the Board of Directors, DGF, Oct. 26, 1926, Wright Papers, box 21.

12. DGF, *Solving the Problem of Fog Flying*, pp. 3–4. For early contact between the Guggenheim fund and the Department of Commerce on commercial aviation development, see J. Walter Drake to Cone, July 2, and Drake to HFG, July 10, 1926, record group 40, Records of the Department of Commerce, Office of the Secretary, box 568, National Archives. Concerning Guggenheim research on blind flying and radio aids, Drake wrote, "I believe this investigation promises results of greater importance than may be obtained in any other line in furthering safety in aeronautics."

13. Jerome C. Hunsaker, "A Survey of Air Transport and Its Communication Problems," July 1, 1927, p. 23, Hunsaker Papers, box 10.

14. See H. Cooch, Landing Aircraft in Fog," DGF Papers, box 15. See also DGF, *Solving the Problem of Flying*, pp. 37–38; R. H. Mayo, "The Promotion of Aeronautics: A Review of the Work of the Daniel Guggenheim Fund" (unpublished manuscript, n.d., hereafter referred to as Mayo Manuscript), pp. 176–77, DGF Papers. The localizer, with the addition of marker beacons and the glide slope beam, later formed the basis for the all-weather Instrument Landing System (ILS) in federal service by 1950.

15. Albert F. Hegenberger, "Navigation Instruments and Fog Flying."

16. E. Kaupa, "Report on the Sound of an Aeroplane Motor with Relation to the Echo Altimeter," July 24, 1929; Kaupa, "Acoustical Methods for Measuring the Height of an Airplane Above the Ground in Fog," Sept. 19, 1927; Cone to Von Baumhauer, Oct. 11, 25, Dec. 20, 1927; Baumhauer to DGF, Dec. 3, 1927, April 8, 1929; HFG to Baumhauer, Dec. 19, 1927; George K. Burgess to DGF, Aug. 9, 1929; DGF Papers, box 5.

17. L. P. Delsasso, "A New Acoustic Analyzer: Determination of the Sound Spectra Produced by Aircraft in Flight." Delsasso to Land, Sept. 24, Nov. 5, 1928, Nov. 18, Dec. 20, 1929; Land to Delsasso, Oct. 23, Dec. 6, 21, 1928, May 24, Dec. 27, 1929; Land to Durand, Oct. 23, 1928; Durand to Land, Nov. 22, 1928; Campbell to Land, Jan. 4, 1929; HFG to Campbell, Jan. 11, 1929; Nichols to HFG, Feb. 20, 1929; Delsasso to DGF May 17, 1929; DGF Papers, box 6.

18. W. L. Everitt, "Aeronautical Research Proposed at the Engineering Experiment Station, Ohio State University," n.d.; agreement, DGF and Ohio State University, Sept. 30, 1929; Everitt to Land, July 1, 1929; Brown to Bush, May 29, 1929; Bush to Brown, June 20, 1929; HFG to George W. Rightmire, Oct. 15, 1929; DGF Papers, box 15. See also DGF, *Solving the Problem of Fog Flying*, pp. 29–30.

19. Frank J. Taylor, *High Horizons*, p. 62. DGF, *Solving the Problem of Fog Flying*, pp. 47–50; Merritt to Geer, June 3, 12, 1929; Geer to Land, June 5, 13, Dec. 20, 1929, Jan. 4, 1930; Land to Geer, June 7, 1929; Farrand to Geer, June 12, 1929; Geer to HFG, June 26, 1929; Farrand to HFG, July 20, Sept. 23, 1929; HFG to Farrand, July 23, Sept. 25, 1929; DGF Papers, box 6. William C. Oeker and Carl J. Crane, *Blind Flight in Theory and Practice*, pp. 153–55.

20. Gillmore to HFG, March 16, 1929, DGF Papers, box 5. See also Aldrin to Cone, Dec. 29, 1927; Cone to Aldrin, Jan. 5, 1928; Cone to Harms, Jan. 16, April 5, 1928; Harms to Cone, Jan. 30, April 11, 1928; Cone to Gillmore, April 5, 1928; Gillmore to Cone, May 10, 1928; Cone to Anderson, April 5, 25, 1928; Anderson to Cone, April 12, 1928; Gillmore to HFG, July 5, 1928; telegrams, Anderson to Cone, May 1, 1928, Cone to Anderson, May 1, 1928, HFG to Land, March 9, 1929; Anderson, "Investigation of the Transmission of Light Through Fog," Dec. 1929; DGF Papers, box 5.

21. News release, DGF, June 22, 1928, DGF Papers, box 1.

22. Ibid.

23. Fechet to Gillmore, July 12, 1928, and Gillmore to Fechet, July 16, 1928, DGF Papers, box 5.

24. Herbert Hoover to secretary of war, Jan. 7, 1928, "Aviation: Experimental Flight to South America," Commerce Papers, Hoover Library. Aldrin should not be confused with his son Col. Edwin E. "Buzz" Aldrin, crewman on Apollo 11.

25. News releases, DGF, Aug. 9 and Sept. 25, 1928, DGF Papers, boxes 2 and 1, respectively; Minutes, Annual Meeting of the Board of Directors, DGF, Dec. 1928, Wright Papers, box 21.

26. Letter and enclosures, Robert C. Mikesh to Smithsonian NASM, Feb. 28, 1962, in personal files of Robert C. Mikesh, Smithsonian NASM. Performance characteristics for the O2U-1 Corsair and NY-2 are in Gordon Swanborough and Peter M. Bowers, *United States Navy Aircraft Since 1911*, pp. 71–73, 367–69.

27. Doolittle to Fleet, Jan. 24, 1929, NY-2 file, Smithsonian NASM; Doolittle, "Early Blind Flying."

28. DGF, *Equipment Used in Experiments to Solve the Problem of Fog Flying*, pp. 23–35. DGF, *Solving the Problem of Fog Flying*, pp. 8–9, 21–22, 27, 51–52; U.S. Department of Commerce, Aeronautics Branch, "Fog Landing Beacon," *Air Commerce Bulletin* 1, no. 2 (July 15, 1929): 19, and no. 3 (Aug. 1, 1929): 13; Doolittle, "Early Blind Flying." The Guggenheim fund trustees also hoped to test the Mitchel Field aural beacon system for long-range navigation. In this case, the pilot would navigate on the aural beacon until he approached the airfield, then switch over to the localizer.

29. News release, DGF, Jan. 18, 1929, DGF Papers, box 2; Doolittle, "Early Blind Flying." DGF, *Equipment Used in Experiments to Solve the Problem of Fog Flying*, p. 13.

30. Doolittle, "Early Blind Flying"; Joseph W. Benkert, *Introduction to Aviation Science*, pp. 93–99, 123–26.

31. Doolittle, "Early Blind Flying"; E. O. Kollsman obituary, *New York Herald Tribune*, Aug. 14, 1942; Quentin Reynolds, *The Amazing Mr. Doolittle*, pp. 101–2. DGF, *Equipment Used in Experiments to Solve the Problem of Fog Flying*, pp. 49–52.

32. Thomas Parke Hughes, *Elmer Sperry*, p. 237.
33. It could also indicate pitch angle as well. See Ibid., p. 238; also Doolittle, "Early Blind Flying"; DGF, *Solving the Problem of Fog Flying*, pp. 14–15; DGF, *Equipment Used in Experiments to Solve the Problem of Fog Flying*, pp. 42–47; William C. Ocker and Carl J. Crane, *Blind Flight in Theory and Practice*, pp. 49–54.
34. Doolittle, "Early Blind Flying"; Reynolds, *The Amazing Mr. Doolittle*, p. 105; DGF, *Equipment Used in Experiments to Solve the Problem of Fog Flying*, pp. 47–49; William C. Ocker and Carl J. Crane, *Blind Flight in Theory and Practice*, pp. 54–59.
35. Doolittle, "Early Blind Flying."
36. Ibid.
37. Ibid. Also DGF, *Equipment Used in Experiments to Solve the Problem of Fog Flying*, pp. 35, 37–41.
38. Doolittle, "Early Blind Flying." See also Reichelderfer to Cone, April 12, 1928, DGF Papers, box 8.
39. Doolittle, "Early Blind Flying"; DGF, *Solving the Problem of Fog Flying*, pp. 44–45.
40. Doolittle, "Early Blind Flying."
41. Ibid.; Reynolds, *The Amazing Mr. Doolittle*, pp. 108–9; Lomask, *Seed Money*, p. 101.
42. Doolittle, "Early Blind Flying"; Reynolds, *The Amazing Mr. Doolittle*, pp. 108–9.
43. Telegram, HFG to Wright, Sept. 24, 1929, Wright Papers, box 29.
44. Annotated news release, DGF, Sept. 24, 1929, DGF Papers, box 2.
45. "Colvin Analyzes the Doolittle Flight," *U.S. Air Services* 14, no. 11 (Nov. 1929): 50; see also "Simulated Landings, Take-offs in Fog Made by Lieut. Doolittle," *Aviation* 27, no. 14: 718, 724.
46. "Blind Flying," *The Aeroplane* 37, no. 14 (Oct. 2, 1929): 848.
47. Telegram, Byrd to HFG, Sept. 27, 1929, DGF Papers, box 1.
48. Miller to Barrette, Nov. 25, 1929, and Whitman to Land, Oct. 10, 1929; DGF Papers, box 2. See also Whitman to Doolittle, Oct. 4 1929, and Schnacke to Whitman, Oct. 5, 1929, NY-2 file, Smithsonian NASM. Conversation with James H. Doolittle, December 23, 1974.
49. Foulois to Land, March 13, 1930, DGF Papers, box 3.
50. Release form, DGF to International Railway Company and Riverside Service Corporation, April 25, 1930; Tiffin to Fuhr, May 20, 1930; DGF Papers, box 3.
51. DGF, *The Final Report of the DGF*, 1929, p. 19.
52. William C. Ocker and Carl J. Crane, *Blind Flight in Theory and Practice*, p. 16. Clarke Van Vleet, Lee M. Pearson, and Adrian O. Van Wyen, *United States Naval Aviation, 1910–1970*, p. 77.
53. U.S. Department of Commerce, Aeronautics Branch, "Radio and the Nation's Airways," *Air Commerce Bulletin* 1, no. 10 (Nov. 15, 1929): 1–3; U.S. Department of Commerce, Aeronautics Branch, *Annual Report of the Director of Aeronautics*, pp. 32–33.
54. See Clarence M. Young to R. P. Lamont, Dec. 14, 1929, in record group 40, Records of the Department of Commerce, Office of the Secretary, box 536, National Archives.
55. U.S. Department of Commerce, Aeronautics Branch, "Aeronautical Radio Research, Bureau of Standards," *Air Commerce Bulletin* 1, no. 8 (Oct. 15, 1929): 25; Cochrane, *Measures for Progress*, pp. 295–97; U.S. Department of Commerce, Bureau of Standards, *Annual Report of the Director of the Bureau of Standards*, p. 44.
56. Doolittle, "Early Blind Flying"; Cochrane, *Measures for Progress*, pp. 296–97.

57. Whitnah, *Safer Skyways*, pp. 164–65, 221. A photograph of the instrument panel used during Kinney's flight in the Bellanca is in Whitnah's book, between pp. 212 and 213.

58. Doolittle, "Early Blind Flying"; Eugene M. Emme, *Aeronautics and Astronautics*, p. 29. Doolittle had not sat under the hood on his first flight, and on his second, Kelsey was flying along as safety pilot. See also USAF, *A Chronology of American Aerospace Events*, pp. 31–32.

59. Foulois to Gillmore, Jan. 25, 1930, in record group 18, AAF Central Decimal Files, box 1056, file 452.5 "B," National Archives.

60. Emme, *Aeronautics and Astronautics*, pp. 35, 184. USAF, *A Chronology of American Aerospace Events*, p. 36.

61. DGF, *The Daniel Guggenheim Safe-Aircraft Competition*, p. vi.

CHAPTER 8

1. R. H. Mayo, "The Promotion of Aeronautics: A Review of the Work of the Daniel Guggenheim Fund" (unpublished manuscript, n.d., hereafter referred to as Mayo Manuscript), p. 15, DGF Papers.

2. Report, HFG to DGF directors, May 1, 1926, in "Aviation—Daniel Guggenheim Fund," Commerce Papers, Hoover Library.

3. Minutes, Special Meeting of the Board of Directors, DGF, June 2, 1926, Wright Papers, box 21.

4. "The Guggenheim Aircraft Competition," *Aviation* 20, no. 26 (June 28, 1926): 974; HFG to Orville Wright, Sept. 4, 1926, Wright Papers, box 21.

5. "The Guggenheim Competition," *Aviation* 20, no. 26 (June 28, 1926): 973.

6. DGF, *The Daniel Guggenheim Safe-Aircraft Competition*, p. vii.

7. Draft letter, HFG to various American and foreign aeronautical experts, n.d. Copy in Wright Papers, box 21.

8. Memorandum, Grover Loening to HFG, Aug. 25, 1926; HFG to Loening, March 17, 31, and Loening to HFG, March 29, 1927; Grover Loening Papers, Library of Congress, box 7. See also Grover Loening, *Our Wings Grow Faster*, pp. 186–187.

9. Mayo's reports on German and French opinions are in the Guggenheim Document Collection, Science and Technology Division, NASM, Smithsonian Institution.

10. DGF, *The Daniel Guggenheim Safe-Aircraft Competition*, pp. iv–viii; news release, DGF, April 29, 1927; dinner plan for safe aircraft competition dinner, April 29, 1927; DGF Papers, box 1. HFG to Orville Wright, March 17, 1927, Wright Papers, box 29. Edward Jablonski, *Atlantic Fever*, pp. 90–91.

11. DGF, *The Daniel Guggenheim Safe-Aircraft Competition*, pp. 1–23.

12. DGF, *The Daniel Guggenheim International Safe Aircraft Competition: Final Report*, p. 8 (hereafter cited as *Safe Aircraft Final Report*).

13. Ibid., pp. 51–136; Reginald M. Cleveland, *America Fledges Wings*, p. 75. McDonnell later founded the McDonnell Aircraft Corporation of St. Louis, Missouri, famous for its series of U.S. Navy and Air Force turbojet fighters.

14. *Safe Aircraft Final Report*, pp. 61–66, 91–95.

15. "The Guggenheim Competition," *Aviation* 23, no. 20 (Nov. 14, 1927): 1159.

16. Mayo Manuscript, pp. 190–92, DGF Papers.

17. Ibid., p. 196.

18. Ibid., pp. 195–96; *Safe Aircraft Final Report*, pp. 5, 11.

19. Alexander Klemin, "Notes on the Guggenheim Safety Competition," *Aviation* 24, nos. 5 and 6 (Jan. 30 and Feb. 6, 1928): 246–54, 314–19.

20. Miller and Sawers, *The Technical Development of Modern Aviation*, pp. 80–81; Oliver Stewart, *Aviation*, p. 114.

21. Miller and Sawers, *The Technical Development of Modern Aviation*, p. 80; Stewart, *Aviation*, pp. 115–17.

22. Miller and Sawers, *The Technical Development of Modern Aviation*, p. 82; Stewart, *Aviation*, pp. 117–20. Harald Penrose, *British Aviation*, p. 696; Alexander Klemin, "Notes on the Guggenheim Safety Competition," *Aviation* 24, no. 6 (Feb. 6, 1928): 314–19. In 1921, the U.S. Navy had ordered three experimental Handley Page slot-equipped HPS-1 aircraft, single-engine low-wing monoplanes, extensively flight-testing these planes. See Swanborough and Bowers, *United States Navy Aircraft Since 1911*, p. 461.

23. Information from *Safe Aircraft Final Report*, pp. 121–24. The HP 39, in 1976, was in storage at Hayes, Middlesex, for the Science Museum. Some details are contained in the HP 39 file, no. 1934–313, Science Museum, London. See also M. J. B. Davy, *Handbook of the Collections Illustrating Aeronautics*, vol. 1, *Heavier-than-Air Aircraft*, pp. 108–9.

24. Philip Jarrett, "HP 39 'Gugnunc,'" *Aeroplane Monthly* 2, no. 6 (June 1974): 710–11; conversation with Philip Jarrett, Oct. 10, 1974.

25. Penrose, *British Aviation*, p. 632; Stewart, *Aviation*, p. 122; Donald C. Clayton, *Handley Page*, pp. 58–59. See also E. S. Land to Orville Wright, Nov. 13, 1929, Wright Papers, box 21; and *New York Times*, Aug. 21, Sept. 23, Oct. 4, 1929.

26. Robert R. Osborn, "The 'Tanager' and Some of Its History," *Aviation* 28, no. 6 (Feb. 8, 1930): 242–48; Milton Lomask, *Seed Money*, p. 107; G. Edward Pendray, ed., *The Guggenheim Medalists*, p. 30.

27. Osborn, "The 'Tanager' and Some of Its History," 245–46.

28. Ibid., pp. 246–47. See also T. P. Wright, "The Development of a Safe Airplane, the Curtiss Tanager."

29. *Safe Aircraft Final Report*, pp. 97–99.

30. Osborn, "The 'Tanager' and Some of Its History," p. 248; Wright, "The Development of a Safe Airplane."

31. DGF, *The Daniel Guggenheim Safe-Aircraft Competition*, p. 2.

32. E. S. Land to Orville Wright, Nov. 13, 1929; Wright Papers, box 21.

33. Mayo Manuscript, p. 204, DGF Papers.

34. Land to Wright, Nov. 13, and Wright to Land, Dec. 4, 1929; Wright Papers, box 21. There is a comprehensive collection of letters between Handley Page, the Guggenheim fund, and Curtiss officials in the "Daniel Guggenheim Fund for the Promotion of Aeronautics: folder 2," Wright Papers, box 21.

35. *New York Times*, Dec. 2, 1929; *New York Sun*, Jan. 2, 1930; *New York Herald Tribune*, Jan. 5, 1930.

36. *New York Times*, June 19, 23, July 28, Sept. 19, Oct. 4, 1929; Pendray, *The Guggenheim Medalists*, p. 31.

37. Osborn, "The 'Tanager' and Some of Its History," p. 248; Wright, "The Development of a Safe Airplane"; and conversation with Charles A. Lindbergh, July 22, 1974.

38. *Safe Aircraft Final Report*, pp. 19, 143–44; Mayo Manuscript, 205–7; DGF Papers.

39. *New York Sun*, Nov. 15, Dec. 2, 1929.

40. *Safe Aircraft Final Report*, pp. 19, 143; Osborn, "The 'Tanager' and Some of Its History," p. 248; *New York Times*, Oct. 20, 1929.

41. *Safe Aircraft Final Report*, pp. 19, 143; Penrose, *British Aviation*, p. 696.

42. *Safe Aircraft Final Report*, pp. 15, 19–20.

43. Ibid.

44. *New York Times*, Dec. 25, 26, 1929, Jan. 2, 1930.

45. *Safe Aircraft Final Report*, p. 20. The point totals represented bonuses

based on completion of certain tests, and thus are not unreasonably low or indicative of a general low standard of performance.

46. Warner to Grey, Feb. 4, and Warner to Aldrin, Feb. 10, 1930, Guggenheim biographical file, Smithsonian NASM. See also "Three Thousand Miles from the Facts," *Aviation* 28, no. 6 (Feb. 8, 1930): 233.

47. *Safe Aircraft Final Report*, p. 14; Mayo Manuscript, p. 208, DGF Papers.

48. *New York Times*, Jan. 7, 1930.

49. *Safe Aircraft Final Report*, p. 9.

50. *New York Times*, Jan. 7, 1930.

51. T. P. Wright, *Articles and Addresses of Theodore P. Wright*, vol. I (Buffalo: Cornell Aeronautical Laboratory, 1961), p. 163.

52. *Safe Aircraft Final Report*, p. 9.

53. Ibid., p. 13; news release, DGF, March 1, 1930; DGF Papers, box 3.

54. Conversation with G. Edward Rice, Feb. 27, 1975. Lesley Forden, *The Ford Air Tours*, p. 183.

55. Jarrett, "HP 39 'Gugnunc,' " p. 710.

56. *Safe Aircraft Final Report*, p. 15.

57. Data from William Green, *The War Planes of the Third Reich*, pp. 165–68; and James C. Fahey, *U.S. Army Aircraft (Heavier-Than-Air), 1908–1946*, pp. 31, 53.

58. Conversation with Otto C. Koppen, March 27, 1974; "New Slow-Flying Plane Developed," *Aviation Week* 50, no. 20 (May 16, 1949): 51–52.

59. Koppen conversation; "The Kay-Bee Helioplane," *Pegasus* 14, no. 2 (Aug. 1946): 6–9; Helio Corporation news release, May 15, 1949, "Helio" file, Smithsonian NASM.

CHAPTER 9

1. Lesley Forden, *The Ford Air Tours*, pp. 1–2.

2. Letter and enclosure, HFG to directors, DGF, June 2, 1926, Wright Papers, box 21.

3. Telegram, HFG to Byrd, May 11, 1926, DGF Papers, box 1. On the subject of transatlantic flights, see HFG to Orville Wright, July 19, 1926, Wright Papers, box 29.

4. Richard E. Byrd, *Skyward* (New York: Blue Ribbon Books, 1931), pp. 335–36.

5. R. H. Mayo, "The Promotion of Aeronautics: A Review of the Work of the Daniel Guggenheim Fund" (unpublished manuscript, n.d., hereafter referred to as Mayo Manuscript), pp. 78–79, DGF Papers. See also MacCracken to HFG, October 11, 1926, in record group 40, Records of the Department of Commerce, Office of the Secretary, box 568, National Archives.

6. News release, DGF, n.d., in DGF Papers, box 1.

7. News release, DGF, Oct. 6, 1926, in DGF Papers, box 1; "Report of the Byrd North Pole Plane Tour," n.d., pp. 1–2, DGF Papers, box 20.

8. "Report of the Byrd North Pole Plane Tour," p. 2, DGF Papers, box 20.

9. Ibid., p. 3.

10. Ibid.

11. Walter S. Ross, *The Last Hero*, pp. 130–36. See also John Lardner, "The Lindbergh Legends," in Isabel Leighton, ed., *The Aspirin Age: 1919–1941*, pp. 190–213.

12. Milton Lomask, *Seed Money*, p. 92.

13. A print of this photograph is in William Wagner, *Ryan, the Aviator* (New York: McGraw-Hill, 1971), p. 133.

14. Lomask, *Seed Money*, p. 94; Ross, *The Last Hero*, pp. 139–43; Kenneth S. Davis, *The Hero*, p. 235.

15. Morrow to HFG, July 8, 1927, DGF Papers, box 6; Minutes, Annual Meeting of the Board of Directors, DGF, June 16, 1927, Wright Papers, box 21.

16. HFG to Lindbergh, July 19, 1927, DGF Papers, box 6.

17. Donald E. Keyhoe, *Flying with Lindbergh*, pp. 3–13.

18. News release, DGF, June 28, 1927, DGF Papers, box 1.

19. News release, DGF, Oct. 22, 1927; Harry New to DGF, Oct. 23, 1927; DGF Papers, box 1.

20. News release, DGF, Oct. 23, 1927, DGF Papers, box 1. See also "Lindbergh Tour Great Boost to Commercial Aeronautics," July 13, 1927, in "H. H. Personal—Lindbergh, Charles A." folder, box 52, Hoover Library.

21. Keyhoe, *Flying with Lindbergh*, pp. 31–35.

22. Ibid., pp. 46–55.

23. Mayo Manuscript, pp. 99–101, DGF Papers; Ross, *The Last Hero*, pp. 158–59; Lomask, *Seed Money*, p. 95; news release, DGF, Aug. 16, 1927, DGF Papers, box 1.

24. "Greetings" message, DGF, n.d., DGF Papers, box 1. The full text of this message form is also reprinted in the Mayo Manuscript, pp. 101–2, DGF Papers, and in Reginald M. Cleveland, *America Fledges Wings*, pp. 97–98.

25. Keyhoe, *Flying with Lindbergh*, pp. 241–42.

26. U.S. Department of Commerce, "Air Marking for Cities," information bulletin no. 38, Aug. 15, 1927, in record group 40, Records of the Department of Commerce, Office of the Secretary, box 568, National Archives. See also, for example, Hoover to Governor of Alabama, Aug. 10, 1927, in "Aviation—Painted Names on Highest Buildings," Commerce Papers, Hoover Library.

27. Report of the Aeronautics Committee, Tenth Annual National Convention of the American Legion, Oct. 8–11, 1928, San Antonio, Texas; telegram, Fisher to HFG, Oct. 22, 1928; HFG to Fisher, Oct. 23, 1928; Kusterer to HFG, Aug. 21, 1928; Land to Kusterer, Aug. 31, 1928; Davison to HFG, Sept. 27, 1928; HFG to Warner, MacCracken, and Davison, Oct. 15, 1928; DGF Papers, box 11.

28. News releases, DGF, Oct. 21, 31, 1928, Feb. 15, May 25, 1929, DGF Papers, box 2; memo, HFG to Land and Kusterer, Oct. 2, 1928; HFG to Will Rogers, Oct. 16, 1928; HFG to New, Oct. 16, 1928; HFG to Atterbury, Oct. 17, 1928; DGF Papers, box 11.

29. Reports, Kusterer to HFG, Nov. 7, 15, 22, 1928, Jan. 29, April 16, July 16, 1929, final report, n.d.; DGF Papers, box 11. See also news release, DGF, Jan. 8, 1930, DGF Papers, box 3; and Mitchell V. Charnley to Herbert Hoover, Dec. 31, 1929, "Aeronautics—Correspondence, 1929, October–December," Presidential Papers, Hoover Library.

30. Memorandum, "Landing Room: The Unfilled Need in American Aviation," DGF, Feb. 1929, DGF Papers, box 2. This memo is also reproduced between pp. 212–13 in Cleveland, *America Fledges Wings*.

31. DGF bulletins: no. 1, "Guggenheim Fund Makes Grants to Finance Study and Experiments in Aeronautics," Aug. 14, 1926; no. 2, "Expansion of Air Mail Service Will Promote Commercial Aviation," Oct. 7, 1926; no. 3, "Aerial Services," Jan. 7, 1927; no. 4, "Safety in the Air," Oct. 11, 1927; no. 5, "The Airplane and the British Empire," March 10, 1928; no. 6, "Aviation on the Continent: Germany," May 22, 1928; no. 7, "Fundamental Principles for Flying School Instruction," June 5, 1928; no. 8, "Opportunities for Trained Mechanics and Pilots," June 20, 1928; no. 9, "Celestial Avigation," July 13, 1928; no. 10, "The Hazard of Lightning in Aviation," Sept. 26, 1928; no. 11, "State Aids to Aviation," Feb. 27, 1929; no. 12, "Aeronautic Education and Training," March

16, 1929; no. 13, "The Problems of Air Sickness," Nov. 1, 1929. Copies of all of these bulletins can be found in the DGF Papers, boxes 1, 2, and 6.

32. V. E. Clark, "A Report on Airplane Construction in Europe," n.d.; Brown to Cone, March 29, 1928; Ware to Cone, April 2, 1928; Miller to Clark, Feb. 14, 1928; DGF Papers, box 8.

33. See William E. Gillmore, *Aeronautical Observations on a European Trip*, and DGF, *Safety and Accommodation in European Passenger Planes*. Also various letters in the "European Report on Maintenance, Repair, and Supply, 1928–29" file, DGF Papers, box 8.

34. See Clarence M. Young, *Airport Management and Administration in Europe*. See also various letters in the "European Report: Clarence M. Young, 1929" file, DGF Papers, box 8.

35. U.S. Department of Commerce and the American Engineering Council, Joint Committee on Civil Aviation, *Civil Aviation*, p. 160.

36. Davison to HFG, May 6, 1929, DGF Papers, box 5; Dunn obituary, *Washington Post*, July 29, 1974. Dunn retired as an Air Force brigadier general in 1949, and died, age eighty, on July 27, 1974, at McLean, Virginia.

37. News release, DGF, March 7, 1930, DGF Papers, box 3. See Ray A. Dunn, *Aviation and Life Insurance*. See also various related papers in the "Aviation Insurance Survey: R. A. Dunn" folder, DGF Papers, box 5.

38. Dunn, *Aviation and Life Insurance*, pp. 7–36; Dunn to HFG, Oct. 12, 1929, DGF Papers, box 5.

39. *New York Times*, Sept. 2, 1928; program for the First National Aeronautical Safety Conference, Oct. 1–5, 1928, in the Guggenheim Document Collection, Science and Technology, Smithsonian NASM; news releases, DGF, Sept. 21 and Oct. 4, 1928, DGF Papers, box 1; Land to Fechet, Nov. 15, 1928, and Fechet to Land, Nov. 23, 1928, in record group 18, Office of the Chief of Air Corps, Gen. James Fechet, "Correspondence, 1925–30," box 3, National Archives.

40. The Daniel Guggenheim Medal Fund, Inc., certificate of incorporation (copy), n.d., and other letters and correspondence, in "Guggenheim Medal," DGF Papers, box 11.

41. Alfred D. Flinn to Orville Wright, Dec. 19, 1929, Wright Papers, box 21; news release, DGF, March 3, 1928, DGF Papers, box 3. Durand to Daniel Guggenheim, Jan. 7, 1930, DGF Papers, box 11.

42. Pendray, *The Guggenheim Medalists*, pp. 53–54.

43. Pendray, *The Guggenheim Medalists*, p. 7. The Daniel Guggenheim Medal Board of Award, *Pioneering in Aeronautics*. Listing of medal winners in the aeronautics collections, National Air and Space Museum, Smithsonian Institution.

44. See, for example, speech, HFG before Governors' Conference, New London, Conn., July 17, 1929; speech, HFG over NBC radio network, June 22, 1929; speech, HFG before the Institute of Politics, Williamstown, Mass., Aug. 5, 1929; DGF Papers, box 2. See also HFG, "Commercial Aviation," New York Railroad Club Annual Dinner, Dec. 15, 1927. Copy in Library of Congress.

45. Harry F. Guggenheim, *The Seven Skies*, p. 12.

46. Committee of Experts on Civil Aviation to the Preparatory Commission for the Disarmament Conference, *International Disarmament as Related to the Development of Civil Aviation*, pp. 3–6.

47. Remarks of HFG, Sept. 7, 1927, place unknown; DGF Papers, box 1. See also Lomask, *Seed Money*, p. 96.

48. Quoted in Kendall K. Hoyt, *Ink and Avgas*, p. 8. HFG to various newspaper editors, Nov. 3, 1928, DGF Papers, box 2.

49. Hoyt, *Ink and Avgas*, pp. 5–8.

CHAPTER 10

1. HFG to Orville Wright, Sept. 7, 1929, Wright Papers, box 21.
2. DGF, *Final Report*, p. iv.
3. One other trustee, Maj. Gen. George W. Goethals, had died in 1928.
4. Hoover to Curtis D. Wilbut, May 28, 1928, "General Correspondence 1926–1929," Emory Scott Land Papers, Library of Congress.
5. National Advisory Committee for Aeronautics, *Sixteenth Annual Report, 1930* (Washington, D.C.: G.P.O., 1931), p. 14.
6. Ibid.
7. Grover Loening, *Takeoff Into Greatness*, p. 201.
8. Milton Lehman, *This High Man*, p. 172; Conversation with Charles A. Lindbergh, July 22, 1974.
9. Klemin to Reginald M. Cleveland, Feb. 6, 1940, DGF Papers, box 21.
10. Figures are taken from a chart of Guggenheim fund appropriations and expenditures as of Jan. 27, 1930, in DGF Papers, box 18. The expended amounts were, in some cases, slightly more or less than the appropriated amounts, depending on the purposes and results of initial work on individual grants. Due to prudent investments, the total capital of the fund rose above the $2.8 million figure.
11. Harvey O'Connor, *The Guggenheims*, p. 428. American Society of Mechanical Engineers, "Aeronautical Roll of Honor, 1927–1929," (St. Louis, Mo.: ASME, 1929), p. 5.
12. See Robert H. Goddard, "A Method of Reaching Extreme Altitudes," *Smithsonian Miscellaneous Collections* 71, no. 2 (1919). See also Lehman, *This High Man*, pp. 62–104, 123–27; G. Edward Pendray, *The Coming Age of Rocket Power*, pp. 88–94.
13. Lehman, *This High Man*, pp. 126–31, 139–44; Pendray, *The Coming Age of Rocket Power*, pp. 96–99. See also Goddard diary entry, March 16–17, 1926, in Esther C. Goddard and G. Edward Pendray, eds., *The Papers of Robert H. Goddard*, vol. 2, *1925–1937*, pp. 580–82.
14. Cited in Goddard and Pendray, *Papers*, 1:674. See also Lehman, *This High Man*, pp. 152–156; Milton Lomask, *Seed Money*, pp. 139–41; Pendray, *The Coming Age of Rocket Power*, p. 99.
15. Conversation with Charles A. Lindbergh, July 22, 1974; Lomask, *Seed Money*, p. 141; Lehman, *This High Man*, pp. 173–74. Lindbergh introduction to Michael Collins, *Carrying the Fire*, pp. ix–xiii.
16. Conversation with Charles A. Lindbergh, July 22, 1974; Lomask, *Seed Money*, p. 142.
17. Taylor to Goddard, Nov. 22, 1929; Goddard diary entries, Nov. 23–27, 1929; Goddard to C. G. Abbot, Nov. 29, 1929; in Goddard and Pendray, *Papers*, 1: 711–16.
18. Goddard memo on the Carnegie conference, Dec. 15, 1929; Atwood to Goddard, Nov. 29, Dec. 5, 19, 1929; Abbot to Goddard, Dec. 2, 1929; Merriam to Goddard, Dec. 5, and Goddard to Merriam, Dec. 14, 1929; in Goddard and Pendray, *Papers*, 2: 717–26. See also Lehman, *This High Man*, pp. 148, 166–71.
19. Conversation with Charles A. Lindbergh, July 22, 1974; Lehman, *This High Man*, pp. 172–74. Breckinridge to Atwood, June 9, 1930; Daniel Guggenheim to Atwood, June 12, and Atwood to Daniel Guggenheim, June 13, 1930; in Goddard and Pendray, *Papers*, 2: 744–45.
20. Lehman, *This High Man*, pp. 175–204.
21. Ibid., pp. 204–98. See also "Memorandum by R. H. Goddard on Conference in Washington Regarding Rocket Developments, May 28, 1940," in Goddard and Pendray, eds., *The Papers of Robert H. Goddard*, vol. 3, *1938–1945*, pp. 1310–11, 1664–70.

22. Lomask, *Seed Money*, p. 148.

23. HFG to Goddard, July 27, 1945, in Goddard and Pendray, eds., *Papers*, 3: 1609.

24. Lehman, *This High Man*, pp. 395–99.

25. G. Edward Pendray, *Opinion Survey of Leading Engineers and Scientists on Future Developments in Rockets and Jet Propulsion* (New York: The Daniel & Florence Guggenheim Foundation, 1948), copy in Hunsaker Papers, box 13. See also various letters between HFG and Hunsaker, in Hunsaker Papers, box 13, "Guggenheim Fund" file.

26. The Daniel and Florence Guggenheim Foundation, "Daniel and Florence Guggenheim Jet Propulsion Centers," Dec. 14, 1948, in Hunsaker Papers, box 13.

27. Conversation with Dr. Frank J. Malina, Sept. 30, 1974. See Frank J. Malina, "America's First Long-Range Missile and Space Exploration Programmes." See also R. Cargill Hall, "JPL Facility History," Feb. 1968, p. 3, copy in NASA Historical Office files.

28. Hsue-Shen Tsien, "Instruction and Research at The Daniel and Florence Guggenheim Jet Propulsion Center," *Journal of the American Rocket Society* 20, no. 81 (June 1950): 51–63, esp. 63. For information on Crocco and Princeton, see Luigi Crocco, "Instruction and Research in Jet Propulsion," *Journal of the American Rocket Society* 20, no. 80 (March 1950): 32–43.

29. Malina, "America's First Long-Range Missile and Space Exploration Programmes."

30. Hall, "JPL Facility History."

31. Grover C. Loening, "Notes on Test of Waterman Aeroplane by Arrangement with Department of Commerce," n.d. (presumably 1932–34), in Loening Papers, box 14.

32. C. C. Furnas, address before the Sixth Annual Personal Aircraft Meeting, Wichita, Kansas, April 29, 1949.

33. The Daniel and Florence Guggenheim Foundation, "Information on The Daniel and Florence Guggenheim Aviation Safety Center at Cornell University," (New York, n.d.). See also The Daniel and Florence Guggenheim Foundation, *Report of the President, 1961*, pp. 20–21. Copies are in the Guggenheim Document Collection, NASM archives.

34. Much of the correspondence between center officials and this advisory group can be found in the Hunsaker Papers, "Guggenheim Safety Center, 1950–1959," file, box 9, and "Guggenheim Memorial Foundation," file, box 14.

35. Jerome Lederer and R. M. Woodham, *Safety through Steep Gradient Aircraft*.

36. Ibid.

37. Cornell-Guggenheim Aviation Safety Center, "Surface Controls: Control Column Installation," *Design Notes*, bulletin no. 12, series 52–5 (n.d.), Hunsaker Papers, box 9.

38. There is a useful summary of the Cornell-Guggenheim Aviation Safety Center's activities in Theodore P. Wright, *Articles and Addresses of Theodore P. Wright*, 4 vols. (Buffalo: Cornell Aero Lab, 1970), 4:44–55. See also C. R. Smith, "Safety in Air Transportation over the Years," Eighth Wings Club "Sight" Lecture, The Wings Club, New York City, May 19, 1971.

The Elwood R. Quesada Papers, on deposit at the Dwight D. Eisenhower Library, Abilene, Kansas, contain a small amount of material on the Cornell-Guggenheim Aviation Safety Center and Quesada's participation in its affairs. The collection also holds approximately 750 pages of material relating to aviation safety in general.

39. A good summary of foundation activities can be found in The Daniel and Florence Guggenheim Foundation, *Report of the President, 1974*, and The Daniel and Florence Guggenheim Foundation, "Educational and Research Centers

Sponsored by The Daniel and Florence Guggenheim Foundation," April 1960. Copies of both are in the Guggenheim Document Collection, NASM archives.
40. Harry F. Guggenheim, *The Seven Skies*, p. 142.

APPENDIXES: INTRODUCTION

1. Vannevar Bush, *Modern Arms and Free Men*, p. 26.

APPENDIX 1

1. In the overall scope of its program, Caltech clearly overshadowed the other Guggenheim schools. Progress at the other Guggenheim schools is contained in Appendix 2.

2. Edward Barrett to HFG, Nov. 3, 1926; HFG to Barrett, Nov. 12, 1926; Barrett to HFG, June 24, 1927; Cone to Barrett, June 29, 1927; DGF Papers, box 6.

3. Barrett to Cone, July 27, 1927; HFG to Barrett, Aug. 4, 1927; H. H. G. Nash to HFG, Sept. 1, 1927; HFG to Nash, Sept. 7, 1927; Barrett to HFG, Oct. 12, 1927; HFG to Barrett, Sept. 24, 1927; Barrett to HFG, Dec. 8, 1927; HFG to Barrett, Dec. 13, 1927; Barrett to HFG, Dec. 24, 1927; HFG to Barrett, Dec. 29, 1927; Millikan to HFG, Oct. 5, 1927; HFG to Millikan, Oct. 19, 1927; HFG to Millikan, Nov. 3, 1927, and Dec. 3, 1927; Millikan to HFG, June 10, 1928; HFG to Millikan, June 19 and July 13, 1928; DGF Papers, box 6. Minutes, Special Meeting of the Board of Directors, DGF, June 15, 1928, Wright Papers, box 21.

4. Millikan to HFG, Dec. 6, 1928, DGF Papers, box 6. See also von Kármán with Edson, *The Wind and Beyond*, pp. 141–42.

5. Telegram, HFG to Millikan, Dec. 17, 1928, DGF Papers, box 6.

6. Von Kármán with Edson, *The Wind and Beyond*, p. 141. William F. Durand visited Germany in 1929 in connection with the fund supporting an "aeronautical encyclopedia." HFG later wrote to Millikan that Durand met with von Kármán, who stated that his acceptance or rejection of the Caltech offer was dependent on his mother.

7. Von Kármán with Edson, *The Wind and Beyond*, pp. 142–46. Von Kármán became an American citizen in 1936.

8. California Institute of Technology, *75: An Informal History of the California Institute of Technology*, p. 17.

9. "The Daniel Guggenheim Graduate School of Aeronautics of the California Institute of Technology: A History of the First Ten Years," *Bulletin of the California Institute of Technology* 49, no. 2 (May 1940): 7.

10. Von Kármán with Edson, *The Wind and Beyond*, pp. 162–64; Reginald M. Cleveland, *America Fledges Wings*, p. 139; "History of the Daniel Guggenheim Graduate School of Aeronautics at the California Institute of Technology," n.d. (but 1939), typescript report in DGF Papers, box 21. See also Douglas H. Robinson, *Giants in the Sky*, pp. 235–38.

11. Young interview, Hoover oral history project, Hoover Library; Douglas J. Ingells, *The Plane That Changed the World*, pp. 9–13.

12. Harold Mansfield, *Vision*, pp. 85–106. Ronald Miller and David Sawers, *The Technical Development of Modern Aviation*, pp. 63–64, 67–69; Douglas J. Ingells, *The Plane That Changed the World*, pp. 16–18; Kenneth Munson, *Airliners between the Wars, 1919–39*, pp. 161–62.

13. Ingells, *The Plane That Changed the World*, pp. 16–19. Letter quoted on p. 19.

14. Ibid., pp. 26–35.

15. Miller and Sawers, *The Technical Development of Modern Aviation*, pp. 54–55; von Kármán with Edson, *The Wind and Beyond*, pp. 75–78; Munson, *Airliners between the Wars, 1919–39*, pp. 60–61, 145–47.

16. Douglas Aircraft Co., Engineering Department Technical Data Report SW–157A, "Development of the Douglas Transport" (Santa Monica, Calif., n.d.); Miller and Sawers, *The Technical Development of Modern Aviation*, pp. 63–65; John B. Rae, *Climb to Greatness*, pp. 68–69; H. Guyford Stever and James J. Haggerty, *Flight*, pp. 103–4.

17. Smithsonian NASM, *The California Institute of Technology, Development*, pp. 11–13; "History of the Daniel Guggenheim Graduate School of Aeronautics at the California Institute of Technology," DGF Papers, box 21; Miller and Sawers, *The Technical Development of Modern Aviation*, pp. 64–65; von Kármán with Edson, *The Wind and Beyond*, pp. 171–72; Douglas report SW–157A, "Development of the Douglas Transport."

18. Miller and Sawers, *The Technical Development of Modern Aviation*, pp. 62–63; Langley Research Center, NASA, *Fifty Years of Flight Research* (Hampton, Va.: NASA, 1967), pp. 14–15; George W. Gray, *Frontiers of Flight*, pp. 113–14. Conversation with Fred Weick, Oct. 22, 1976.

19. Ingells, *The Plane That Changed the World*, p. 39.

20. Richard G. Hubler, *Big Eight: The Biography of an Airplane* (New York: Duell, Sloan and Pearce 1960), p. 34.

21. Miller and Sawers, *The Technical Development of Modern Aviation*, pp. 68–69, 98–100.

22. Ingells, *The Plane That Changed the World*, pp. 39–40; von Kármán with Edson, *The Wind and Beyond*, pp. 169–71.

23. Douglas report SW–157A, "Development of the Douglas Transport."

24. Ingells, *The Plane That Changed the World*, 48–50; Robert A. Millikan, *The Autobiography of Robert A. Millikan*, p. 244. Millikan's comments actually apply to the DC–1. By the time of the DC–3, the 247 no longer offered any serious competition.

25. *Washington Post*, Feb. 25, 1934; *Chicago Daily News*, March 7, 1934.

26. There is a comprehensive archive of literature on the 1934 airmail controversy in "Airmail cancellation: Articles, Press releases, & editorials," Presidential Papers, Hoover Library. The most significant are: War Department release, Feb. 15, 1934; speech, Maj. Gen. Benjamin D. Foulois, AAC, Feb. 27, 1934; *Kansas City Star*, March 8, 1934; "Special Air Mail Issue," *The National Aeronautic Magazine*, March 1934.

27. Miller and Sawers, *The Technical Development of Modern Aviation*, p. 100; Munson, *Airliners between the Wars, 1919–39*, pp. 163–64. For a good memoir of flying DC–2's on airline service prior to World War II, see Ernest K. Gann, *Fate Is the Hunter*.

28. Ingells, *The Plane That Changed the World*, pp. 84–85.

29. Ibid., pp. 85–91; Miller and Sawers, *The Technical Development of Modern Aviation*, pp. 100–4; Arthur Pearcy, *The Douglas DC–3 (pre-1942)*, pp. 3–5; John B. Rae, *Climb to Greatness*, pp. 68–71.

30. Rae, *Climb to Greatness*, p. 71.

31. For European aspects of the "airframe revolution" (as Prof. John B. Rae has termed it), see Nicholas J. Hoff, "Thin Shells in Aerospace Structures."

32. Frank J. Malina, "Memoir on the GALCIT Rocket Research Project, 1936–1938," Frank J. Malina, "Origins and First Decade of the Jet Propulsion Laboratory," in Eugene M. Emme, ed., *The History of Rocket Technology*, pp. 46–66; von Kármán with Edson, *The Wind and Beyond*, pp. 234–39. Millikan later became a rocket research advocate.

33. Malina, "Memoir on the GALCIT Research Project;" Malina, "Origins and First Decade of the Jet Propulsion Laboratory," pp. 47–48; von Kármán with Edson, *The Wind and Beyond*, p. 235.

34. Malina, "Origins and First Decade of the Jet Propulsion Laboratory," p. 48.

35. Ibid.; R. Cargill Hall, A Selective Chronology. For Goddard quote, see Goddard to Millikan, Sept. 1, 1936, in Esther C. Goddard and G. Edward Pendray, The Papers of Robert H. Goddard, 2:1012–13. For an account of the Millikan-Malina-Goddard meeting, see Milton Lehman, This High Man, pp. 234–35.

36. Hall, Selective Chronology, GALCIT-JPL; Malina, "Origins and First Decade of the JPL," pp. 49–50. The Malina-Smith sounding rocket study was published as "Flight Analysis of a Sounding Rocket," Journal of the Aeronautical Sciences 5 (1938): 199.

37. Hall, Selective Chronology, GALCIT-JPL; Malina, "Origins and First Decade of the JPL," pp. 49–50; von Kármán and Edson, The Wind and Beyond, p. 309.

38. GALCIT, "Research and Development at the Jet Propulsion Laboratory, GALCIT," June 22, 1946. Copy in Smithsonian NASM files. Hall, Selective Chronology, GALCIT-JPL.

39. Von Kármán and Edson, The Wind and Beyond, pp. 243–44; Theodore von Kármán, review of Calvin M. Bolster's "Assisted Take-off of Aircraft," James Jackson Cabot Fund Lecture, Norwich University, reviewed in Journal of the American Rocket Society, no. 85 (June 1951): 92–93.

40. "Research and Development at the Jet Propulsion Laboratory, GALCIT," NASM files.

41. Ibid.

42. Ibid.; Malina, "Origins and First Decade of the JPL," pp. 54–56; von Kármán and Edson, The Wind and Beyond, pp. 245–46.

43. "Research and Development at the Jet Propulsion Laboratory, GALCIT," NASM files; Malina, "Origins and First Decade of the JPL," pp. 54–56.

44. Von Kármán and Edson, The Wind and Beyond, pp. 249–50.

45. Ibid.

46. Ibid.

47. "Research and Development at the Jet Propulsion Laboratory, GALCIT," NASM files.

48. "Research and Development at the Jet Propulsion Laboratory, GALCIT;" von Kármán and Edson, The Wind and Beyond, pp. 257–67.

49. James Phinney Baxter 3rd, Scientists Against Time, pp. 206–11.

50. Von Kármán and Edson, The Wind and Beyond, pp. 208–10; Don Guy, "A Promise in the Wind," Yankee 38, no. 3 (March 1974): 84–97; letter to L. S. Jacobson, Stanford University, Feb. 3, 1941, (author unknown), in Guggenheim Document Collection, Science and Technology Division, National Air and Space Museum, Smithsonian Institution. See Frank R. Eldridge, Wind Machines: A Report Prepared for the National Science Foundation (Washington: The Mitre Corporation, 1975), pp. 8, 14.

51. Von Kármán and Edson, The Wind and Beyond, pp. 62–65, 211–15; Derrick Beckett, Bridges, pp. 16, 18, 182–84.

APPENDIX 2

1. "Opening of Guggenheim Aeronautics School," Aviation 21, no. 22 (Nov. 29, 1926): 920; Frederick K. Teichmann, Report on the Daniel Guggenheim School of Aeronautics, Covering the Period 1923–1944 (New York, April 1944), pp. 5–10, in Smithsonian NASM archives; letter and transmittal, Alexander Klemin to F. A. Collins, June 29, 1939, DGF Papers, box 21; Daniel Guggenheim School of Aeronautics, New York University, Pioneer Educator in the Air Age, pp. 2–3; Reginald Cleveland, America Fledges Wings, pp. 134–37.

2. Teichmann, *Report on the Daniel Guggenheim School of Aeronautics*, pp. 9–15; NYU, *Pioneer Educator in the Air Age*, pp. 18–26; letter and transmittal, Klemin to Collins, June 29, 1939, DGF Papers, box 21; Cleveland, *America Fledges Wings*, pp. 134–37.

3. NYU, *Pioneer Educator in the Air Age*, pp. 18–26. Klemin died in 1950, at the age of sixty-one. See Klemin biographical file, Smithsonian NASM.

4. NYU, *Pioneer Educator in the Air Age*, pp. 20–21; letter and transmittal, Klemin to Collins, June 29, 1939; Charles Gablehouse, *Helicopters and Autogiros*, pp. 71–79. For army and NACA interest, see H. F. Gregory, *Anything a Horse Can Do*, pp. 39–110. For Sikorsky's development, see Igor I. Sikorsky, *The Story of the Winged-S.*

5. NYU, *Pioneer Educator in the Air Age*, pp. 20–21, 28–30; Gablehouse, *Helicopters and Autogiros*, p. 65; letter and transmittal, Klemin to Collins, June 29, 1939, DGF Papers, box 21.

6. NYU, *Pioneer Educator in the Air Age*, pp. 27–30; letter and transmittal, Klemin to Collins, June 29, 1939, DGF Papers, box 21; Teichmann, *Report on the Daniel Guggenheim School of Aeronautics*, pp. 25–28; Ronald Miller and David Sawers, *The Technical Development of Modern Aviation*, pp. 83–84.

7. Letter and transmittal, Klemin to Collins, June 29, 1939, DGF Papers, box 21; Teichmann, *Report on the Daniel Guggenheim School of Aeronautics*, pp. 12–13, 59–61.

8. See "The Daniel Guggenheim Aeronautic Laboratory," *Concerning Stanford* 4, no. 4 (Jan. 1928): n.p.; "Statement of the Activities of the Daniel Guggenheim Aeronautic Laboratory, Stanford University, California," Dec. 7, 1927, DGF Papers, box 15.

9. *Palo Alto Times*, May 22, 1939.

10. Letter to L. S. Jacobson, Stanford University, author unknown, Feb. 3, 1941, Guggenheim Document Collection, Science and Technology Division, National Air and Space Museum, Smithsonian Institution. For the origins and creation of the Ames Aeronautical Laboratory, see Edwin P. Hartman, *Adventures in Research*, pp. 18–25.

11. Von Kármán and Edson, *The Wind and Beyond*, pp. 122–23.

12. Hunsaker to HFG, Nov. 18, 1926, Hunsaker Papers, box 6, Smithsonian NASM archives.

13. Ibid.

14. Minutes, Special Meeting of the Board of Directors, DGF, Oct. 28, 1927; Wright Papers, box 21.

15. Durand, *Adventures*, p. 116.

16. Ibid.; Durand, "Survey of Project of Aeronautic Encyclopedia," June 12, 1928; Durand to HFG, Feb. 1, 1928, April 3, 1928, June 6, 1928; DGF Papers, box 4. See also Minutes, Annual Meeting of the Board of Directors, DGF, Dec. 4, 1928, Wright Papers, box 21.

17. Durand, *Adventures*, pp. 117–18. Durand to DGF, Sept. 19, 1929; HFG to Durand, Sept. 25, 1929; Miller to Durand, Oct. 9, 1929; Dec. 17, 1929; Durand to Miller, Dec. 24, 1929; Land to Swain, Dec. 30, 1929; Swain to Land, Jan. 10, 1930; W. F. Durand, "Memo re: Encyclopedia Project," n.d.; DGF Papers, box 4. See also Minutes, Special Meeting of the Board of Directors, DGF, Oct. 1, 1929; Minutes, Annual Meeting of the Board of Directors, Jan. 6, 1930, Wright Papers, box 21; R. H. Mayo, "The Promotion of Aeronautics: A Review of the Work of the Daniel Guggenheim Fund" (unpublished manuscript, n.d., hereafter referred to as Mayo Manuscript), pp. 151–53, DGF Papers.

18. Durand, *Adventures*, p. 118.

19. Ibid., pp. 119–20.

20. Robert P. Weeks, *The First Fifty Years*, pp. 16–17; Sadler to HFG, March 10, 1927; Young to HFG, Aug. 20, 1928; HFG to Young, Aug. 21, 1928;

Sadler to HFG, Aug. 20, 1928; HFG to Sadler, Aug. 28, 1928; HFG to Young, Aug. 28, 1928; Sadler to HFG, July 8, 1929; DGF Papers, box 12.

21. Thompson quoted in Robert P. Weeks, *The First Fifty Years*, p. 17.

22. "Stalker, Blaylock, and Michigan U.," *Astronautics & Aeronautics* 12, no. 4 (April 1974): 7; conversation with Harold D. Hoekstra, Nov. 13, 1976.

23. E. A. Stalker, "A Research Proposal," n.d.; agreement between the DGF and the Regents of the University of Michigan, Sept. 1, 1927; Stalker, "Report on Development of an Injector Induction System for Two Stroke Cycle Engines," April 1928; Stalker to DGF, April 5, 1927; Lewis to Cone, May 14, 1927; Stalker to Cone, May 31 and June 7, 1927; Cone to Stalker, June 18, 1927; Stalker to Cone, May 11, 1928; Stalker to HFG, Sept. 6, 1928; Cone to Lewis, May 19, 1928; Lewis to Cone, June 14, 1928; Land to Stalker, Aug. 6, 1928; Stalker to HFG, Sept. 6, 1928; Land to Stalker, May 17 and July 18, 1929; DGF Papers, box 12. Minutes, Special Meeting of the Executive Committee, DGF, July 22, 1929, Wright Papers, box 21.

24. Hobbs to Sadler, March 10, 1926; Hobbs to DGF, Feb. 24, 1926; memorandum re Hobbs expedition, May 17, 1926, by HFG; DGF Papers, box 12.

25. Hobbs to HFG, April 5, 1927, DGF Papers, box 12. For Hobbs's account of his earlier Greenland researches, see William H. Hobbs, "The University of Michigan Greenland Expedition of 1926–1927," *The Geographical Review* 16, no. 2 (April 1926): 256–63; also, William H. Hobbs, "The First Greenland Expedition of the University of Michigan," *The Geographical Review*, 17, no. 1 (Jan. 1927): 1–35.

26. HFG to Warner, April 11, 1927; HFG to Marvin, April 11, 1927; Warner to HFG, April 14, 1927; Marvin to HFG, April 14, 1927; DGF Papers, box 12.

27. Telegram, Hobbs to HFG, May 3, 1927; Cone to Hobbs, May 4, 1927; Rossby to DGF, Dec. 30, 1927; Marvin to Rossby, n.d.; Rossby to director, *Det Norska Meteorologiske Institut*, Feb. 16, 1928; HFG to Hobbs, April 25, 1928; DGF Papers, box 12; Mayo Manuscript, pp. 53–54, DGF Papers. See also "Guggenheim Fund Aids Greenland Weather," *Aviation* 22, no. 25 (June 20, 1927): 1400.

28. Donald R. Whitnah, *A History of the United States Weather Bureau*, pp. 198–99.

29. Hunsaker to HFG, Jan. 28, 1939, DGF Papers, box 21.

30. Ibid. Shatswell Ober, *The Story of Aeronautics at M.I.T.*, p. 22.

31. Ober, *The Story of Aeronautics at M.I.T.*, pp. 34–41. James Phinney Baxter 3rd, *Scientists Against Time*, p. 215. The complete story of wartime research at MIT is found in John Burchard, *Q.E.D.*

32. HFG to Samuel Stratton, June 18, 1928, in DGF Papers, box 11. Later the fellowships at Rossby's suggestion were reduced to two $3,000 grants. See Rossby to HFG, Feb. 5, and HFG to Rossby, Feb. 23, 1929. DGF Papers, box 11.

33. Warner to HFG, Dec. 7, 1927, and Feb. 3, 1928; DGF Papers, box 11.

34. Warner to HFG, Feb. 3 and Oct. 31, 1928; DGF Papers, box 11.

35. HFG to Rossby, Nov. 9 and May 4, 1928; HFG to Warner, Nov. 8, 1928; Warner to HFG, June 23, July 3, Dec. 4, 1928; Frank Locke to HFG, Sept. 8, 1928; J. W. Miller to Rossby, n.d.; Warner to Rossby, April 9, and Rossby to Warner, April 27, 1928; Rossby to HFG, April 17 and Oct. 13, 1928; Stratton to HFG, May 26 and June 21, 1928; HFG to Stratton, July 13, 1928; telegram, Warner to HFG, Aug. 27, 1928; DGF Papers, box 11.

36. Warner to HFG, Dec. 4, and HFG to Warner, Dec. 19, 1928; C. G. Rossby, "First Annual Report of the Meteorological Course of the M.I.T.," Oct. 1929; DGF Papers, box 11.

37. Rossby, "First Annual Report of the Meteorological Course of the M.I.T."

38. Ibid.; Hunsaker to HFG, Jan. 28, 1939; Ober, *The Story of Aeronautics at M.I.T.*, p. 21.

39. "A Retrospect on the Development of the Guggenheim School of Aeronautics at the University of Washington," (author unknown, presumably E. O. Eastwood), Feb. 3, 1939. Copy in the DGF Papers, box 21. See also F. K. Kirsten, Bulletin No. 79, "Cycloidal Propulsion" (University of Washington: Engineering Experiment Station, 1935).

40. Ibid. Conversation with William H. Rae, associate director, Department of Aeronautics and Astronautics, University of Washington, Aug. 13, 1974; Rae to author, Aug. 19, 1974. The University of Washington later dedicated the tunnel as the F. K. Kirsten Memorial Wind Tunnel.

41. "A Retrospect on the Development of the Guggenheim School of Aeronautics at the University at Washington," (author unknown, presumably E. O. Eastwood). Rae conversation and letter. Harold Mansfield, Vision, pp. 109–81.

42. Rae conversation and letter.

43. Annual Reports of the Daniel Guggenheim School of Aeronautics, Georgia School of Technology, for the years 1931–34; Guggenheim Document Collection, Science and Technology Division, Smithsonian NASM.

44. Ibid.

45. Ibid.

46. Montgomery Knight, Daniel Guggenheim School of Aeronautics, Georgia School of Technology, p. 2; DGF Papers, box 21.

47. Georgia Guggenheim School annual reports for 1933–35; Guggenheim Document Collection, Science and Technology Division, Smithsonian NASM.

48. Montgomery Knight, "Report on the Daniel Guggenheim School of Aeronautics, Georgia School of Technology, for the First Five Years," April 3, 1935; Guggenheim Document Collection, Science and Technology Division, Smithsonian NASM.

49. Montgomery Knight, "Helicopter Development, Guggenheim Aeronautics Division of the State Engineering Experiment Station," Sept. 10, 1938; Guggenheim Document Collection, Science and Technology Division, Smithsonian NASM.

50. Ibid.

51. Paul Lambermont and Anthony Pirie, Helicopters and Autogyros of the World, pp. 25, 32–34, 59; Kenneth Munson, Helicopters and Other Rotorcraft Since 1907, pp. 17, 32, 40–41, 97–98, 115–16, 125–27; Gablehouse, Helicopters and Autogiros, pp. 101–4.

52. Von Kármán and Edson, The Wind and Beyond, pp. 159–61; Theodore Troller, "The Daniel Guggenheim Airship Institute," Journal of Applied Physics 9, no. 1 (Jan. 1938): 24–29. Theodore Troller, "The Daniel Guggenheim Airship Institute," Feb. 21, 1939; DGF Papers, box 21.

53. Theodore Troller, "The Daniel Guggenheim Airship Institute," Feb. 21, 1939, DGF Papers, box 21; Theodore Troller, "The New Whirling Arm," Journal of the Aeronautical Sciences 1 (Oct. 1934): 195–97; Theodore Troller, "A Test Stand for the Investigation of Gust Effects," Journal of the Aeronautical Sciences 5 (Jan. 1938): 113–16.

54. Theodore Troller, "The Daniel Guggenheim Airship Institute," Feb. 21, 1939, DGF Papers, box 21; Arnold M. Kuethe, "A Water Tank for Model Tests on the Motion of Airships in Gusts," Journal of the Aeronautical Sciences 5 (April 1938): 243–44.

55. Theodore Troller, "The Daniel Guggenheim Airship Institute," Feb. 21, 1939, DGF Papers, box 21. For conference reports, see Daniel Guggenheim Airship Institute, Publication Nos. 1–3.

56. Several outstanding books exist on dirigible development, notably, Richard K. Smith, The Airships Akron and Macon; Robin D. S. Higham, The British Rigid Airship, 1908–31; Douglas H. Robinson, Giants in the Sky; Nevil Shute Norway, Slide Rule; Gordon Vaeth, Graf Zeppelin.

57. Hugh Allen, The House of Goodyear, p. 308.

Bibliographical Essay

THE research materials for this study came from a number of agencies and organizations. Individuals affiliated with the following institutions provided useful records and information incorporated into this work:

Library of Congress, Washington, D.C.
National Archives, Washington, D.C.
National Air and Space Museum, Smithsonian Institution,
  Washington, D.C.
The Daniel and Florence Guggenheim Foundation,
  New York, New York
Herbert Hoover Presidential Library,
  West Branch, Iowa
Dwight D. Eisenhower Presidential Library,
  Abilene, Kansas
Historical Office, National Aeronautics and Space Administration,
  Washington, D.C.
Historical Monitor, Federal Aviation Administration,
  Washington, D.C.
Historical Archives, Bureau of Standards,
  Gaithersburg, Maryland
Sterling Memorial Library, Yale University,
  New Haven, Connecticut.
Historical Office, Jet Propulsion Laboratory,
  Pasadena, California
Robert A. Millikan Library, California Institute of Technology,
  Pasadena, California
Library, University of California at Los Angeles
Department of Manuscripts and University Archives,
  John M. Olin Library, Cornell University, Ithaca, New York

University of Washington Aeronautical Laboratory,
  Seattle, Washington
University of Akron, Akron, Ohio
Science Museum, South Kensington, London, England

Necessarily, my debt to all who assisted and encouraged me on this project is great. The single most valuable collection of documents relating to the Guggenheims are the Papers of The Daniel Guggenheim Fund for the Promotion of Aeronautics, donated in August 1955 to the Manuscript Division, Library of Congress, by Harry F. Guggenheim. The twenty-one containers include more than six thousand items relating to the Guggenheim fund. The first three containers include general correspondence in six folders and three bound volumes. Containers four through sixteen hold records of the fund filed alphabetically. Containers seventeen through nineteen include financial records, monthly financial statements, and tax records. Containers twenty and twenty-one hold material concerning Maj. R. H. Mayo, the fund's British representative, including his unpublished manuscript, *History of The Daniel Guggenheim Fund*, which served as the basic reference for Reginald M. Cleveland's later work, *America Fledges Wings: The History of The Daniel Guggenheim Fund for the Promotion of Aeronautics*. This record collection is mandatory for any Guggenheim research, and it provides information on the general state of American and European aeronautical education, research, and development in the mid-1920s.

The Manuscript Division possesses other collections that furnish material on Guggenheim activities. The Papers of Orville Wright, a Guggenheim fund trustee, include all of the fund's meeting minutes and various correspondence between Wright and Guggenheim representatives on fund matters. The Papers of Grover Loening, a pioneer American aeronautical engineer and designer, include material indicating his close interest in various Guggenheim projects such as the fund's safe aircraft competition. The Papers of Emory S. Land, vice-president of the Guggenheim fund from 1928 through its closing in 1930, contain some Guggenheim correspondence. The Papers of the American Institute of Aeronautics and Astronautics include the collection of the Institute of Aeronautical Sciences, consisting of over 150 containers holding a large amount of published and pictorial information on aeronautical history, key individuals in the aircraft industry and government, and different aircraft types. Less useful, though providing some information used in this study, were the Papers of Henry C. Breckinridge, who acted as a legal advisor to the Guggenheim fund; the Papers of the Morrow Board; and the Papers of Washington I. Chambers, which provided some information on early aeronautical education at the Massachusetts Institute of Technology.

The Industrial and Social Records Branch, the Modern Military Records Branch, and the Old Military Records Branch at the National Archives contain several record groups that furnished source material for this study. The most useful was Record Group 18, Records of the Army Air Service and Army Air Corps, especially the Central Decimal Files, boxes 908, 909, 911, and 1056, and selected correspondence of Gen. James Fechet, Office of the Chief of the Air Corps. Record Group 40, Records of the Department of Commerce, especially papers from the Office of the Secretary, boxes 536 and 568, proved helpful. Other record groups that contain information relative to American aeronautical research are Record Group 72, Records of the U.S. Navy Bureau of Aeronautics, and Record Group 255, Records of the National Advisory Committee for Aeronautics.

The Herbert Hoover Presidential Library contains the Papers of Herbert Hoover from his pre-Commerce, Commerce, presidential, and postpresidential years. These papers proved quite useful, as did other special collections at the Hoover Library. The library also has limited records from the Bureau of Standards and the Aeronautics Branch of the Department of Commerce, as well as the Papers of William P. MacCracken, Jr., Assistant Secretary of Commerce for Aeronautics. Further, the library contains oral interviews completed with important aviation figures from the Hoover years, including F. Trubee Davison, Assistant Secretary of War for Aeronautics; David S. Ingalls, Assistant Secretary of the Navy for Aeronautics; and Clarence M. Young, director of the Aeronautics Branch of the Department of Commerce. The Dwight D. Eisenhower Presidential Library at Abilene, Kansas, contains the Papers of Elwood R. Quesada, some of which relate to the Cornell-Guggenheim Aviation Safety Center and other Guggenheim matters.

The National Air and Space Museum (NASM) of the Smithsonian Institution possesses extensive reference materials relating to the growth of American aeronautics. Since August 1967, the NASM, first through Alexis Doster III and then through the author, has acquired a collection of documents relating to The Daniel Guggenheim Fund for the Promotion of Aeronautics. These documents are now on file with the Department of Science and Technology, NASM. The NASM Historical Research Center's oral history collection contains a series of taped interviews by Ernest Robischon of various individuals affiliated with the Guggenheim-funded schools. Of special importance are the Papers of Jerome C. Hunsaker, on deposit with the NASM. Hunsaker's papers provide a wealth of information on the Guggenheim Model Air Line and blind flying research, as well as numerous other topics in American aerospace history.

Other Guggenheim-related document collections are on deposit with various universities. The California Institute of Technology holds the Papers of Robert A. Millikan, a Guggenheim fund trustee, and the Papers of Theodore von Kármán, the director of GALCIT. Yale University holds the Papers of Charles A. Lindbergh, another Guggenheim fund trustee. The University of California at Los Angeles has the Papers of Alexander Klemin, long affiliated with the Guggenheim school at New York University. Cornell University holds the Papers of Theodore P. Wright, project manager on the Curtiss Tanager, and chairman of the Cornell-Guggenheim Aviation Safety Center. His papers consist primarily of pamphlets, clippings, and correspondence relating to other aviation matters. The Robert H. Goddard papers, already well edited by Esther Goddard and G. Edward Pendray under the sponsorship of The Daniel and Florence Guggenheim Foundation, are on deposit at Clark University.

Guggenheim activities in aeronautics have been previously treated in two works, Reginald M. Cleveland's *America Fledges Wings*, and Milton Lomask's *Seed Money: The Guggenheim Story*. The former is based primarily on an earlier unpublished manuscript by R. H. Mayo, and the latter covers in brief all of the major Guggenheim family philanthropic efforts, whether they deal with aeronautics or with other areas. Both books are good introductory works for the interested researcher. The following selected bibliography lists books, reports, journals, newspapers, and scholarly papers that were of use in this study.

Selected Bibliography

BOOKS AND REPORTS

Aero Club von Deutschland. *Mitteilungen des von Tschudi-Archiv beim Aero Club von Deutschland gegrundet durch Stiftung des Daniel Guggenheim Fund.* Berlin: German Aero Club, 1929–32.

Aeronautical Chamber of Commerce of America, Inc. *Aircraft Year Book.* New York: Aeronautical Chamber of Commerce, 1923–30.

Allen, Hugh. *The House of Goodyear: Fifty Years of Men and Industry.* Cleveland: Corday & Gross, 1949.

Allen, Richard S. *Revolution in the Sky.* Brattleboro, Vt.: Stephen Green Press, 1964.

Anderton, David A. *Progress in Aircraft Design Since 1903.* Washington, D.C.: NASA, 1974.

Baruch, Bernard M. *Baruch: The Public Years.* New York: Holt, 1960.

Baxter, James Phinney 3rd. *Scientists Against Time.* Cambridge, Mass.: MIT, 1968.

Beckett, Derrick. *Bridges.* London: Paul Hamlyn, 1969.

Billyou, De Forest. *Air Law.* New York: Ad Press, 1964.

Bilstein, Roger. *Prelude to the Air Age: Civil Aviation in the United States, 1919–29.* Ann Arbor: University Microfilms, 1973.

Bonney, Walter T. *The Heritage of Kitty Hawk.* New York: Norton, 1962.

Bowie, Edward Hall. *Weather and the Airplane: A Study of the Model Weather Reporting Service over the California Airway.* New York: Daniel Guggenheim Fund, 1929.

Briddon, Arnold E., Champie, Ellmore A., and Marraine, Peter A. *FAA Historical Fact Book: A Chronology, 1926–71.* Washington, D.C.: FAA, 1974.

Brittain, M. L. *The Story of Georgia Tech.* Chapel Hill, N.C.: University of North Carolina Press, 1948.

Brooks, Peter W. *The Modern Airliner: Its Origins and Development.* London: Putnam, 1961.

Burchard, John. *Q.E.D.: M.I.T. in World War II.* New York: Wiley, 1948.

Bush, Vannevar. *Modern Arms and Free Men: A Discussion of the Role of Science in Preserving Democracy.* Cambridge, Mass.: MIT, 1968.

Cagle, Malcolm W. *The Naval Aviation Guide.* Annapolis: U.S. Naval Institute, 1969.

California Institute of Technology. *Contributions to Applied Mechanics and Related Subjects by the Friends of Theodore von Kármán on His 60th Birthday.* Pasadena: CIT, 1941.

————. *The Daniel Guggenheim Graduate School of Aeronautics of the California Institute of Technology: A History of the First Ten Years.* Pasadena: CIT, 1940.

————. *The Guggenheim Aeronautical Laboratory of the California Institute of Technology: The First 25 Years.* Pasadena: CIT, 1954.

————. *Research and Development at the Jet Propulsion Laboratory, GALCIT.* Pasadena: CIT, 1946.

————. *75: An Informal History of the California Institute of Technology.* Pasadena: CIT, 1966.

Clark, Virginius C. *A Report on Airplane Construction in Europe.* New York: Daniel Guggenheim Fund, 1928.

Clayton, Donald C. *Handley Page: An Aircraft Album.* London: Allan, 1970.

Cleveland, Reginald M. *America Fledges Wings: The History of The Daniel Guggenheim Fund for the Promotion of Aeronautics.* New York: Pitman, 1942.

Cochrane, Rexmond C. *Measures for Progress: A History of the National Bureau of Standards.* Washington, D.C.: NBS, 1966.

Collins, Michael. *Carrying the Fire.* New York: Farrar, Straus and Giroux, 1974.

Cornell Aeronautical Laboratory. *Articles and Addresses of Theodore P. Wright.* 4 vols. Buffalo, N.Y.: CAL, 1961–70.

Courtney, Frank T. *The Eighth Sea.* Garden City: Doubleday, 1972.

The Daniel and Florence Guggenheim Aviation Safety Center. *Air Turbulence: A Bibliography Covering Physical, Meteorological, and Operational Aspects.* New York: Guggenheim Safety Center, 1965.

————. *Commemoration Booklet.* New York: Guggenheim Safety Center, 1968.

————. *The Current State of Aviation Safety.* New York: Guggenheim Safety Center, 1960.

————. *Review of Research and Educational Activities in Aviation Safety.* New York: Guggenheim Safety Center, 1952.

————. *Survey of Recent Projects in the Field of Aviation Safety.* New York: Guggenheim Safety Center, 1951.

The Daniel and Florence Guggenheim Foundation. *The Future of Rocket*

Power: Addresses Delivered by Harry F. Guggenheim and J. H. Doolittle at the Preview Opening of the Robert H. Goddard Rocket Exhibit. New York: Guggenheim Foundation, 1948.

————. *Report of the President, 1961.* New York: Guggenheim Foundation, 1961.

————. *Report of the President, 1974: Golden Anniversary, 1924–74.* New York: Guggenheim Foundation, 1974.

The Daniel Guggenheim Airship Institute. *Publication Nos. 1–3.* Akron, Ohio: Guggenheim Airship Institute, 1933–35.

The Daniel Guggenheim Fund for the Promotion of Aeronautics. *Aviation Notes, Nos. 1–3.* New York: Daniel Guggenheim Fund, 1927.

————. *Books on Aeronautics.* New York: Daniel Guggenheim Fund, 1928.

————. *Bulletins, Nos. 1–13.* New York: Daniel Guggenheim Fund, 1926–29.

————. *The Daniel Guggenheim International Safe Aircraft Competition: Final Report.* New York: Daniel Guggenheim Fund, 1930.

————. *The Daniel Guggenheim Safe-Aircraft Competition.* New York: Daniel Guggenheim Fund, 1927.

————. *Equipment Used in Experiments to Solve the Problem of Fog Flying.* New York: Daniel Guggenheim Fund, 1930.

————. *The Final Report of The Daniel Guggenheim Fund for the Promotion of Aeronautics, 1929.* New York: Daniel Guggenheim Fund, 1930.

————. *Organization.* New York: Daniel Guggenheim Fund, 1926.

————. *Proceedings, National Conference on Aeronautical Education.* New York: Daniel Guggenheim Fund, 1930.

————. *Report of The Daniel Guggenheim Fund for the Promotion of Aeronautics, 1926 and 1927.* New York: Daniel Guggenheim Fund, 1928.

————. *Report: Problems of Aeronautics in the Schools.* New York: Daniel Guggenheim Fund, 1929.

————. *Safety and Accommodation in European Passenger Planes.* New York: Daniel Guggenheim Fund, 1928.

————. *The Second Report of The Daniel Guggenheim Fund for the Promotion of Aeronautics, 1928.* New York: Daniel Guggenheim Fund, 1929.

————. *Solving the Problem of Fog Flying: A Record of the Fund's Full Flight Laboratory to Date.* New York: Daniel Guggenheim Fund, 1929.

————. *Some Present Practices in Secondary Aeronautical Education.* New York: Daniel Guggenheim Fund, 1930.

————. *Tentative Report on Program.* New York: Daniel Guggenheim Fund, 1926.

The Daniel Guggenheim Fund for the Promotion of Aeronautics and the National Safety Council. *Proceedings, Seventeenth Annual Safety Congress, National Safety Council: First National Aeronautical Safety Conference.* New York: National Safety Council, 1928.

The Daniel Guggenheim Medal Board of Award. *Pioneering in Aero-*

nautics: Recipients of The Daniel Guggenheim Medal, 1929–52. New York: Board of Award, 1952.

The Daniel Guggenheim School of Aeronautics, New York University. *Pioneer Educator in the Air Age: 30th Anniversary.* New York: NYU, 1955.

―――. *Technical Notes of The Daniel Guggenheim School of Aeronautics.* New York: NYU, 1931.

Davies, R. E. G. *A History of the World's Airlines.* London: Oxford University Press, 1964.

Davis, Kenneth S. *The Hero: Charles A. Lindbergh and the American Dream.* Garden City: Doubleday, 1959.

Davy, M. J. B. *Handbook of the Collections Illustrating Aeronautics.* Vol. I: *Heavier-Than-Air Aircraft.* London: Sceince Museum, 1935.

Delear, Frank J. *Igor Sikorsky: His Three Careers in Aviation.* New York: Dodd, Mead, 1976.

Donovan, Frank. *The Early Eagles.* New York: Dodd, Mead, 1962.

Dunn, Ray A. *Aviation and Life Insurance: A Study of the Death Rate and the Hazard of Flying in Relation to Policy Underwriting.* New York: Daniel Guggenheim Fund, 1930.

Durand, William F. *Adventures: In the Navy, in Education, Science, Engineering, and in War—A Life Story.* New York: McGraw-Hill, 1953.

―――. *Aeronautic Education: Creating a Background of Understanding for a Fundamental Economic and Social Enterprise.* New York: Daniel Guggenheim Fund, 1928.

Dwiggins, Don. *The Barnstormers.* New York: Grosset & Dunlap, 1968.

Eldridge, Frank R. *Wind Machines: A Report Prepared for the National Science Foundation.* Washington, D.C.: The Mitre Corporation, 1975.

Emme, Eugene M. *Aeronautics and Astronautics: An American Chronology of Science and Technology in the Exploration of Space, 1915–60.* Washington, D.C.: NASA, 1961.

Emme, Eugene M., ed. *The History of Rocket Technology: Essays on Research, Development, and Utility.* Detroit: Wayne State University, 1964.

―――. *The Impact of Air Power: National Security and World Politics.* New York: Van Nostrand, 1959.

Fahey, James C. *U.S. Army Aircraft (Heavier-Than-Air) 1908–46.* Falls Church, Va.: Ships and Planes, 1946.

Fokker, Anthony H. G., and Gould, Bruce. *Flying Dutchman.* New York: Holt, 1931.

Forden, Lesley. *The Ford Air Tours, 1925–31.* Anaheim, Calif.: Nottingham Press, 1973.

Foxworth, Thomas G. *The Speed Seekers.* New York: Doubleday, 1975.

Freudenthal, Elsbeth E. *The Aviation Business: From Kitty Hawk to Wall Street.* New York: Vanguard, 1940.

Gablehouse, Charles. *Helicopters and Autogiros.* Philadelphia: Lippincott, 1969.

Gibbs-Smith, Charles H. *The Aeroplane: An Historical Survey of Its Origins and Development.* London: HMSO, 1960.

———. *Aviation: An Historical Survey from Its Origins to the End of World War II.* London: HMSO, 1970.

Gillmore, William E. *Aeronautical Observations on a European Tour: 1928.* New York: Daniel Guggenheim Fund, 1928.

Glines, Carroll V. *The Compact History of the United States Air Force.* New York: Hawthorn, 1963.

———. *Jimmy Doolittle.* New York: Macmillan, 1972.

Glines, Carroll V., and Moseley, Wendell F. *The DC–3: The Story of a Fabulous Airplane.* Philadelphia: Lippincott, 1966.

Goddard, Esther C., and Pendray, G. Edward, eds. *Rocket Development: Liquid Fuel Rocket Research, 1929–41.* New York: Prentice-Hall, 1948.

———. *The Papers of Robert H. Goddard.* 3 vols. New York: McGraw-Hill, 1970.

Gray, George W. *Frontiers of Flight: The Story of NACA Research.* New York: Knopf, 1948.

Green, William. *The War Planes of the Third Reich.* Garden City: Doubleday, 1970.

Gregory, H. F. *Anything a Horse Can Do: The Story of the Helicopter.* New York: Reynal & Hitchcock, 1944.

Grey, C. G., ed. *Jane's All the World's Aircraft.* London: Sampson Low Marston, 1919 and 1922.

Guggenheim, Harry F. *The Seven Skies.* New York: Putnam, 1930.

———. *The United States and Cuba.* New York: Macmillan, 1934.

Hall, R. Cargill. *A Selective Chronology: GALCIT-JPL Developments, 1926–50.* Pasadena: JPL, 1967.

Hallion, Richard P. *Supersonic Flight: Breaking the Sound Barrier and Beyond.* New York: Macmillan, 1972.

Hartman, Edwin P. *Adventures in Research: A History of Ames Research Center, 1940–65.* Washington, D.C.: NASA, 1970.

Heron, S. D. *History of the Aircraft Piston Engine.* Detroit: Ethyl Corp., 1961.

Higham, Robin D. S. *The British Rigid Airship, 1908–31.* London: Foulis, 1961.

Holland, Maurice, and Smith, Thomas M. *Architects of Aviation.* New York: Duell, Sloan and Pearce, 1951.

Hook, Thom. *Shenandoah Saga: A Narrative of the U.S. Navy's Pioneering Large Rigid Airships.* Annapolis: Air Press, 1973.

Hoover, Herbert. *The Memoirs of Herbert Hoover.* Vol. I: *Years of Adventure, 1874–1920.* Vol. II: *The Cabinet and the Presidency, 1920–33.* New York: Macmillan, 1952.

Hoyt, Edwin P. *The Guggenheims and the American Dream.* New York: Funk & Wagnalls, 1967.

Hoyt, Kendall K. *Ink and Avgas: The First 25 Years of the Aviation/Space*

Writers Association. Jenkintown, Penn.: Aviation/Space Writers Association, 1963.

Hughes, Patrick. *A Century of Weather Service: A History of the Birth and Growth of the National Weather Service.* New York: Gordon and Breach, 1970.

Hughes, Thomas Parke. *Elmer Sperry: Inventor and Engineer.* Baltimore: Johns Hopkins, 1971.

Hunsaker, Jerome C. *Aeronautics at the Mid-Century.* New Haven, Conn.: Yale, 1952.

Ingells, Douglas J. *The Plane That Changed the World: A Biography of the DC–3.* Fallbrook, Calif.: Aero Publishers, 1966.

———. *They Tamed the Sky: The Triumph of American Aviation.* New York: Appleton-Century, 1946.

Jablonski, Edward. *Atlantic Fever.* New York: Macmillan, 1972.

Johnson, S. Paul. *Horizons Unlimited.* New York: Duell, Sloan and Pearce, 1941.

Jones, H. A. *The War in the Air.* Vol. 3. Oxford: Clarendon, 1922.

Josephson, Matthew. *Empire of the Air: Juan Trippe and the Struggle for World Airways.* New York: Harcourt, Brace, 1944.

Keyhoe, Donald E. *Flying With Lindbergh.* New York: Putnam, 1928.

Knowlton, Hugh. *Air Transportation in the United States: Its Growth as a Business.* Chicago: University of Chicago Press, 1941.

La Cierva, Juan de, and Rose, Don. *Wings of Tomorrow: The Story of the Autogiro.* New York: Brewer, Warren, & Putnam, 1931.

Lambermont, Paul, and Pirie, Anthony. *Helicopters and Autogyros of the World.* London: Cassell, 1958.

Lausanne, Edita. *The Romance of Ballooning: The Story of the Early Aeronauts.* New York: Viking, 1971.

Lawson, Alfred. *Lawson: Aircraft Industry Builder.* Detroit: Humanity Publishing Co., 1943.

League of Nations, Committee of Experts on Civil Aviation to the Preparatory Commission for the Disarmament Conference. *International Disarmament as Related to the Development of Civil Aviation.* New York: League of Nations and Daniel Guggenheim Fund, 1927.

Lederer, Jerome, and Woodham, R. M. *Safety through Steep Gradient Aircraft.* New York: Guggenheim Safety Center, 1955.

Lehman, Milton. *This High Man: The Life of Robert H. Goddard.* New York: Farrar, Straus, 1963.

Leighton, Isabel., ed. *The Aspirin Age, 1919–1941.* New York: Simon & Schuster, 1949.

Ley, Willy. *Rockets, Missiles, and Space Travel.* New York: Viking, 1954.

Lindbergh, Anne Morrow. *Bring Me a Unicorn.* New York: Harcourt Brace Jovanovich, 1971.

———. *Hour of Gold, Hour of Lead.* New York: Harcourt Brace Jovanovich, 1973.

Lindbergh, Charles A. *The Spirit of St. Louis.* New York: Scribner's. 1953.
————. *The Wartime Journals of Charles A. Lindbergh.* New York: Harcourt Brace Jovanovich, 1970.
————. *We.* New York: Putnam, 1927.
Litchfield, Paul W. *Industrial Voyage: My Life as an Industrial Lieutenant.* Garden City: Doubleday, 1954.
Livingston, Dorothy Michelson. *The Master of Light: A Biography of Albert A. Michelson.* New York: Scribner's, 1974.
Loening, Grover. *Amphibian: The Story of the Loening Biplane.* New York: New York Graphic Society, 1973.
————. *Our Wings Grow Faster.* Garden City: Doubleday, Doran, 1935.
————. *Takeoff into Greatness: How American Aviation Grew So Big So Fast.* New York: Putnam, 1968.
Lomask, Milton. *Seed Money: The Guggenheim Story.* New York: Farrar, Straus and Giroux, 1964.
Lyons, Eugene. *Herbert Hoover: A Biography.* Garden City: Doubleday, 1964.
McFarland, Marvin W., ed. *The Papers of Wilbur and Orville Wright.* 2 vols. New York: McGraw-Hill, 1953.
Mansfield, Harold. *Vision: A Saga of the Sky.* New York: Duell, Sloan and Pearce, 1956.
Mason, Herbert M. Jr. *Bold Men, Far Horizons.* Philadelphia: Lippincott, 1966.
Mehrens, Harold E. *Aviation in School and Community.* Washington, D.C.: American Council on Education, 1954.
Miller, Ronald, and Sawers, David. *The Technical Development of Modern Aviation.* New York: Praeger, 1970.
Millikan, Robert A. *The Autobiography of Robert A. Millikan.* New York: Prentice-Hall, 1950.
MIT Alumni War Records Committee. *Technology's War Record.* Cambridge, Mass.: Murray Printing Co., 1920.
Morris, Lloyd, and Smith, Kendall. *Ceiling Unlimited: The Story of American Aviation from Kitty Hawk to Supersonics.* New York: Macmillan, 1953.
Mosley, Leonard. *Lindbergh: A Biography.* New York: Doubleday, 1976.
Munson, Kenneth. *Airliners between the Wars, 1919–39.* New York: Macmillan, 1972.
————. *Helicopters and Other Rotorcraft Since 1907.* New York: Macmillan, 1969.
Nicolson, Harold. *Dwight Morrow.* New York: Harcourt, Brace, 1935.
Nielsen, Waldemar A. *The Big Foundations.* New York: Columbia University Press, 1972.
Norway, Nevil Shute. *Slide Rule.* New York: Morrow, 1954.
Ober, Shatswell. *The Story of Aeronautics at M.I.T.: 1895 to 1960.* Cambridge, Mass.: MIT Dept. of Aerospace Engineering, 1965.

Ocker, William C., and Crane, Carl J. *Blind Flight in Theory and Practice.* San Antonio, Texas: Naylor Printing Co., 1932.

O'Connor, Harvey. *The Guggenheims: The Making of an American Dynasty.* New York: Covici, 1937.

Osborn, Michael, and Riggs, Joseph. *"Mr. Mac": William P. MacCracken, Jr., on Aviation—Law—Optometry.* Memphis: Southern College of Optometry, 1970.

Paine, Ralph D. *The First Yale Unit: A Story of Naval Aviation, 1916–19.* 2 vols. Cambridge, Mass.: Riverside Press, 1925.

Pearcy, Arthur. *The Douglas DC–3 (pre-1942).* Profile Publication no. 96. Surrey, Eng.: Profile Publishers, 1966.

Pendray, G. Edward. *The Coming Age of Rocket Power.* New York: Harper, 1945.

Pendray, G. Edward, ed. *The Guggenheim Medalists: Architects of the Age of Flight.* New York: Board of Award, 1964.

Penrose, Harald. *British Aviation: The Adventuring Years, 1920–29.* London: Putnam, 1973.

President's Aircraft Board. *Aircraft in National Defense.* Senate Doc. 18, 69th Cong., 1st sess. Washington, D.C.: U.S. Congress, Senate, 1925.

Rae, John B. *Climb to Greatness: The American Aircraft Industry, 1920–60.* Cambridge, Mass.: MIT, 1968.

Reynolds, Quentin. *The Amazing Mr. Doolittle: A Biography of Lieutenant General James H. Doolittle.* New York: Appleton, 1953.

Robinson, Douglas H. *Giants in the Sky: A History of the Rigid Airship.* Seattle, Wash.: University of Washington Press, 1973.

Ross, Walter S. *The Last Hero: Charles A. Lindbergh.* New York: Harper & Row, 1964.

Royal Aeronautical Society. *The Royal Aeronautical Society, 1866–1966: A Short History.* London: RAS, 1966.

Schlaifer, Robert, and Heron, S. D. *Development of Aircraft Engines and Fuels.* Cambridge, Mass.: Harvard Business School, 1950.

Schmeckebier, Laurence F. *The Aeronautics Branch, Department of Commerce: Its History, Activities, and Organization.* Washington, D.C.: The Brookings Institution, 1930.

Serling, Robert J. *The Only Way to Fly: The Story of Western Airlines, America's Senior Air Carrier.* Garden City: Doubleday, 1976.

Shamburger, Page. *Tracks Across the Sky: The Story of the Pioneers of the U.S. Air Mail.* Philadelphia: Lippincott, 1964.

Shamburger, Page, and Cristy, Joseph. *Command the Horizon.* New York: Castle Books, 1968.

Shrader, Welman A. *Fifty Years of Flight: A Chronicle of the Aviation Industry in America, 1903–53.* Cleveland: Eaton, 1953.

Sikorsky, Igor I. *The Story of the Winged-S.* New York: Dodd, Mead, 1938.

Smith, Dean. *By the Seat of My Pants.* Boston: Little, Brown, 1961.

Smith, Henry Ladd. *Airways: The History of Commercial Aviation in the United States.* New York: Knopf, 1942.

Smith, Richard K. *The Airships Akron and Macon.* Annapolis: U.S. Naval Institute, 1965.

———. *First Across! The U.S. Navy's Transatlantic Flight of 1919.* Annapolis: U.S. Naval Institute, 1973.

Spaulding, Roland. *Dictionary of Aeronautical Terms and Phrases.* New York: Daniel Guggenheim Fund, 1931.

Stever, H. Guyford, and Haggerty, James J. *Flight.* New York: Time, Inc., 1965.

Stewart, Oliver. *Aviation: The Creative Ideas.* New York: Praeger, 1966.

Stout, William B. *So Away I Went.* Indianapolis: Bobbs-Merrill, 1951.

Swanborough, Gordon, and Bowers, Peter M. *United States Navy Aircraft Since 1911.* New York: Funk & Wagnalls, 1968.

Taylor, C. Fayette. *Aircraft Propulsion: A Review of the Evolution of Aircraft Piston Engines.* Washington, D.C.: National Air and Space Museum, 1971.

Taylor, Frank J. *High Horizons.* New York: McGraw-Hill, 1951.

Taylor, John W. R., and Allward, Maurice F. *Westland 50.* London: Allan, 1965.

Taylor, Richard L. *Instrument Flying.* New York: Macmillan, 1972.

Toland, John. *Ships in the Sky.* New York: Holt, 1957.

U.S. Department of the Air Force, Office of Information Services. *A Chronology of American Aerospace Events.* Washington, D.C.: Government Printing Office, July 1, 1959.

U.S. Department of Commerce, Aeronautics Branch. *Annual Report of the Director of Aeronautics.* Washington D.C.: Government Printing Office, 1927–30.

U.S. Department of Commerce, Bureau of Standards. *Annual Report of the Director, Bureau of Standards.* Washington, D.C.: Government Printing Office, 1922–34.

U.S. Department of Commerce, Radio Division. *Annual Report of the Chief, Radio Division.* Washington, D.C.: Government Printing Office, 1929–32.

U.S. Department of Commerce, and the American Engineering Council, Joint Committee on Civil Aviation. *Civil Aviation: A Report.* New York: American Engineering Council, 1926.

U.S. Department of Transportation, Federal Aviation Administration. *Flight: The Story of Electronic Navigation.* Oklahoma City: FAA, 1972.

U.S. National Advisory Committee for Aeronautics. *Annual Report of the National Advisory Committee for Aeronautics.* Washington, D.C.: Government Printing Office, 1920–31.

U.S. Post Office Department. *Annual Report of the Postmaster General.* Washington, D.C.: Government Printing Office, 1929–32.

U.S. Weather Bureau. *Annual Report of the Chief of the Weather Bureau.* Washington, D.C.: Government Printing Office, 1925–31.

Vaeth, Gordon. *Graf Zeppelin: The Adventures of an Aerial Globetrotter.* New York: Harper & Bros., 1958.

Van Vleet, Clarke, Van Wyen, Adrian O., and Pearson, Lee. *U.S. Naval Aviation, 1910–70*. Washington, D.C.: Naval Air Systems Command, 1970.

Von Kármán, Theodore. *Aerodynamics: Selected Topics in Light of Their Historical Development*. New York: McGraw-Hill, 1963.

Von Kármán, Theodore, with Edson, Lee. *The Wind and Beyond: Theodore von Kármán, Pioneer in Aviation and Pathfinder in Space*. Boston: Little, Brown, 1967.

Wagner, William. *Reuben Fleet and the Story of Consolidated Aircraft*. Fallbrook, Calif.: Aero Publishers, 1976.

Weeks, Robert P. *The First Fifty Years: A Fragmentary, Anecdotal History*. Ann Arbor, Mich.: University of Michigan Press, 1964.

Whitnah, Donald R. *A History of the U.S. Weather Bureau*. Urbana, Ill.: University of Illinois Press, 1961.

———. *Safer Skyways: Federal Control of Aviation, 1926–66*. Ames, Iowa: Iowa State University Press, 1966.

Wilbur, Ted, and the NC-4 Fiftieth Anniversary Committee. *The First Flight Across the Atlantic, May, 1919*. Washington, D.C.: NC-4 Committee, 1969.

Wright, Monte D. *Most Probable Position: A History of Aerial Navigation to 1941*. Lawrence, Kansas: University Press of Kansas, 1972.

Young, Clarence M. *Airport Management and Administration in Europe*. New York: Daniel Guggenheim Fund, 1929.

Zahm, Albert F. *Aeronautical Papers, 1920–45*. Vol. II. South Bend, Ind.: Notre Dame, 1950.

JOURNALS AND PERIODICALS

Aerial Age Weekly
Aero Digest
Aeronautical Engineering Review
The Aeroplane
Aeroplane Monthly
Air Commerce Bulletin
Air Corps News Letter
Air International
Air Line Pilot
Air Transport
Astronautics & Aeronautics
Aviation (later *Aviation Week*)
Bulletin of the California Institute of Technology
Concerning Stanford
FAA Aviation News
Flight
Flying

The Geographical Review
Historical Messenger of the Milwaukee County Historical Society
Journal of Applied Physics
Journal of the Aeronautical Sciences
Journal of the American Aviation Historical Society
Journal of the American Rocket Society
Journal of the Royal Aeronautical Society
The Michigan Alumnus
The National Aeronautic Magazine
Northwestern University Bulletin
Pegasus
Standard Oil Bulletin
U.S. Air Services
Western Flying
Yankee

NEWSPAPERS

Boston Evening Transcript
Chicago Daily News
Chicago Tribune
Cleveland Plain Dealer
Kansas City Star
Los Angeles Times
Newark Evening News
New York American
New York Herald Tribune
New York Sun
New York Times
Palo Alto Times
Seattle Interbay Tribune
Seattle Post Intelligencer
Washington Post
Washington Star (later *Washington Star-News*)
Washington Times Herald

PAPERS

Brooks, Robert F. "The Airliner and Its Inventor: Alfred W. Lawson."
    Paper presented at the annual meeting of the American Institute of
    Aeronautics and Astronautics, Anaheim, Calif., Oct. 20, 1969.
Cooch, H. "Landing Aircraft in Fog." Paper presented before the Royal
    Aeronautical Society, London, Feb. 25, 1926.

Crouch, Tom D. "General Aviation: For Pleasure and Profit, from Jennies to the Learjet, 1919–76." Paper presented at the "Two Hundred Years of Flight in America" symposium, National Air and Space Museum, Washington, D.C., Nov. 4, 1976.

Dellinger, J. H. "Directional Radio as an Aid to Safe Flying." Paper presented at the First National Aeronautical Safety Conference, New York, Oct. 4–5, 1928.

Delsasso, L. P. "A New Acoustic Analyzer: Determination of the Sound Spectra Produced by Aircraft in Flight." Paper presented at the second meeting of the Acoustical Society of America, Chicago, Dec. 13–14, 1929.

Doolittle, James H. "Early Blind Flying: An Historical Review of Early Experiments in Instrument Flying." Third Lester Gardner Lecture, presented at the Massachusetts Institute of Technology, April 28, 1961.

Furnas, C. C. Address presented to the Sixth Annual Personal Aircraft Meeting, Wichita, Kansas, April 29, 1949.

Hallion, Richard P. "American Flight Research and Flight Testing: An Overview from the Wright Brothers to the Space Shuttle." Paper presented at the Northeast Aero Historians' symposium, National Air and Space Museum, Washington, D.C., Oct. 9, 1976.

Hallion, Richard P. "Commercial Aviation: From the Benoist Airboat to the SST, 1914–76." Paper presented at the "Two Hundred Years of Flight in America" symposium, National Air and Space Museum, Washington, D.C., Nov. 4, 1976.

Hegenberger, Albert F. "Navigation Instruments and Fog Flying." Paper presented at the First National Aeronautical Safety Conference, New York, Oct. 4–5, 1928.

Hill, G. T. R. "The Tailless Aeroplane." Paper presented before the Royal Aeronautical Society, London, April 22, 1926.

Hoff, Nicholas J. "Thin Shells in Aerospace Structures." Fourth von Kármán Lecture, presented at the Third Annual Meeting of the American Institute of Aeronautics and Astronautics, Boston, Nov. 29, 1966.

Lederer, Jerome. "Safety in the Operation of Air Transportation." James Jackson Cabot Professorship Lecture, presented at Norwich University, Northfield, Vermont, April 20, 1939.

Lonnquest, Theodore C. "Instrument Navigation and Fog Flying." Paper presented at the First National Aeronautical Safety Conference, New York, Oct. 4–5, 1928.

Malina, Frank J. "Memoir on the GALCIT Rocket Research Project, 1936–1938." Papers presented at the First International Symposium on the History of Astronautics, International Academy of Astronautics and International Union of the History and Philosophy of Science, Belgrade, Yugoslavia, Sept. 25–26, 1967.

————. "America's First Long-Range Missile and Space Exploration Programmes." Paper presented at the Fifth International Symposium on the History of Astronautics, International Academy of Astronautics, Brussels, Belgium, Sept. 23, 1971.

Smith, C. R. "Safety in Air Transportation Over the Years." Eighth Wings Club 'Sight' Lecture, presented at the Wings Club, New York City, May 19, 1971.

Wright, Theodore P. "The Development of a Safe Airplane: The Curtiss Tanager." Paper presented at the Detroit Aeronautic Meeting, Society of Automotive Engineers, Detroit, Mich., April 8, 1930.

Index